D1301988

Goldberg, Ray Allan, 1926-
　　Agribusiness management for
developing countries--Latin America
[by] Ray A. Goldberg [and] Leonard M.
Wilson [and others] Cambridge, Mass.,
Ballinger Pub. Co. [1974]
　　xviii, 411 p. illus. 24 cm.

Agribusiness Management for Developing Countries— Latin America

Agribusiness Management for Developing Countries— Latin America

Ray A. Goldberg
Harvard Business School
(Project Director)

Leonard M. Wilson
James E. Austin
August T. Schumacher
Edward L. Felton, Jr.
Paul M. Roberts
J. David Morrissy
Geronimo Collado

Joseph Ganitsky, B.
James G. Wayne, Jr.
Thomas W. Wenstrand
Joan Lanigan McRobbie
Diane P. Hunt
Ernette L. Au
Christina W. O'Bryan

Ballinger Publishing Company • Cambridge, Mass.
A Subsidiary of J. B. Lippincott Company

Contract Between the Fellows of Harvard University and the Agency for International Development Contract No. AID/csd— (HBS Project No. 928).

International Standard Book Number: 0–88410–267–X

Library of Congress Catalog Card Number: 74–9525

Printed in the United States of America

Library of Congress Cataloging in Publication Data

Goldberg, Ray Allan, 1926–
  Agribusiness management for developing countries—
Latin America.

   1. Produce trade—Central America. 2. Agriculture—Economic aspects—
Central America. 3. System analysis—Case studies. I. Title.
HD9014.C462G64   338.1'0972   74–9525
ISBN 0–88410–267–X

Contents

List of Figures

List of Tables

Acknowledgments

The purpose of this study was to indicate the usefulness of an agribusiness commodity systems approach for the educational system of Central America. The selection of the fruit and vegetable system as an example of this approach required the cooperation of various participants in that system in Central America, Mexico, Colombia, and the United States. From Appendix O, one can note the number of people who not only contributed to the study itself, but also participated in brief seminars at various stages in the development of the project. In addition, a number of managers in selected firms responded to confidential questionnaires that provided the basis for estimating a number of future trends. We are also grateful for the cooperation of the educational institutions and agricultural ministries of each country in Central America.

We are most indebted to Dr. John K. Hanes, Chief of the Horticultural and Special Crops Branch, Marketing Economics Division, U. S. Department of Agriculture, for his final review of all of our statistical material and the updating of it with the most recent U. S. Department of Agriculture data. We wish to acknowledge the excellent review and suggestions provided by Professor Noel McGinn of the Graduate School of Education and its Center for Studies in Education and Development at Harvard University. We are grateful for the participation and constructive suggestions of Professor Lee F. Schrader of Purdue University, who has been a visiting member of our faculty this past academic year. We also appreciate the splendid cooperation that we had throughout this project from INCAE. Dr. Ernesto Cruz, Rector of this institution, together with Deans Harry Strachan and David Korten, Professor Gerrit de Vos and Professor Rodolfo Paiz provided us with much detailed information and insight into Central American agribusiness. In addition, four research assistants worked on each of the four case studies: Mr. Jaime Roman, Mr. Billy Joe Ross, Mr. Alberto Sarthou, and Mr. Guillermo Meza. We are also grateful for the review and guidance of Professor Henry B. Arthur, Moffett Professor of Agriculture and Business, Emeritus, of Harvard Business School.

We are indebted to Professor Robert W. Merry, Director of Course Development and Educational Services and member of the educational advisory committee to INCAE, who was an active participant in all of our seminars.

We wish to thank the World Bank for permitting Mr. August Schumacher from that institution to play a leading role in co-authoring this study during his stay at Harvard Business School for the academic year 1971–1972, and for cooperating in providing meaningful data to the study.

We are most grateful to Dean Lawrence E. Fouraker and Senior Associate Dean George F. Lombard for their excellent encouragement and support, and for arranging our other research and teaching assignments in such a way as to permit us to carry out this project. We are also most appreciative of the advice and direction provided by the research division of Harvard Business School under the leadership of Professor Richard E. Walton, Director of the Division of Research, and Professor James P. Baughman, Associate Director.

We are also most grateful to Mr. Jack Koteen, Director of the Office of Development Administration, Technical Assistance Bureau, Agency for International Development, Department of State, and Dr. Gerald Horne, Deputy Director of the same program, for the encouragement and leadership they have given to agribusiness management education in developing countries and for bringing their technical and personal backgrounds to the study.

We are indebted to Mr. Joseph Elder for his editorial assistance, and to Mrs. Diane Hunt, Miss Christina O'Bryan, and Mrs. Ernette Au, who supervised the collating of material in the final draft from the various authors, and to Mrs. Edith Hayes, who was in charge of typing the final manuscript. To Mr. Richard McGinity, Mr. Richard Gartrell, and Mrs. Emily Tipermas who did the final editing, we are grateful as well.

Finally, the project was researched and written at a time when the Agribusiness Program was already overcommitted, therefore much of the time given to this project was taken away from family responsibilities. We are especially grateful to our families for their patience and understanding as we completed this study.

Agribusiness Management for Developing Countries— Latin America

Chapter One

Introduction

The purpose of this study is to provide a conceptual framework, based on an agribusiness commodity systems analysis, that we believe will be useful to educators in Central America as they train future participants in agribusiness in their countries. This approach will enable the leaders of both formal and informal educational institutions to establish programs for improving the effectiveness of commercial agribusiness and subsistence agriculture, in accordance with each country's national priorities.

The study begins with a systems approach to the fruit,[1] vegetable, and floriculture industries. These industries were selected as producing complementary crops to the current coffee, sugar, cotton, and banana export crops that are now grown in most Central American countries, and because of the exciting market opportunities available in the United States. Another consideration was the logistical fit between nontraditional fruit and vegetable production in Central America and changing consumption patterns in the United States. These industries are also consistent with the national economic goals of several of the Central American countries—diversifying exports, increasing foreign exchange, and utilizing underemployed human resources.

The agribusiness system exists for the ultimate purpose of satisfying the food, fiber, and floriculture needs of the consumer, given the political and economic priorities of the government. It has three levels of operation. The first involves the total macroenvironment and public policy. The second involves the special commodity system itself in relation to its macroenvironment; on this level the commodity system is described in great detail—its functions, its participants, and its coordinating arrangements, all of which are related to the ultimate purposes of the system. The third is the level of the firm, in which management operations of individual participants are discussed in terms of specific needs of specific firms, as in our case studies in Chapter 4. In addition to a broad environmental analysis and a description of the system, and of specific functions of firms in it, the approach includes the major linkages that hold the system together, such as transportation, contractual coordination, vertical integration, joint ventures, tripartite marketing arrangements that include producers in one country, marketers in another, and a partner such as the Latin American Agribusiness Development Corporation[2] (LAAD) bringing them together, and a host of financial arrangements.

The systems approach emphasizes the interdependence and interrelated nature of all aspects of agribusiness, from farm supply to the growing, assembling, storing, processing, distribution, and ultimate consumption of the crop. By using the systems approach and applying it to these specific industries, we felt that we would be in a better position to identify the managerial requirements at the various functional levels of the vertical agribusiness structure.

Applied to Central America, the systems approach stresses the need for an interrelated educational network. This project has already led to the formation of a working committee to coordinate the wide variety and range of technical and managerial training that currently exists. This committee, in turn, will help to develop a coordinated program for future use by the institutions providing the training. We hope that an additional activity of this committee will be to develop training programs sponsored and carried out under the auspices of agribusiness leaders and associations in Central America.

In viewing the U. S. and Central American fruit, vegetable, and floriculture systems, we could not help but note that these particular industry systems are in the embryonic stages of coordination. Therefore, both the challenge and the opportunity to create coordinating machinery and profitable business and farmer cooperative entities exist in these industries. We hope that the information contained in this book will prove of immediate benefit to managers operating in this system in Central America and in the United States, to those who may become participants in it, to public policy makers, and to the academic community.

Agribusiness Commodity Systems
Approach

An agribusiness commodity system exists for the purpose of catering to the consumer's nutritional needs, his style of living, and his society's changing value structure. It encompasses all the participants in the production, processing, and marketing of a single farm product, including farm suppliers, farmers, storage operators, processors, wholesalers, and retailers involved in a commodity flow from initial inputs to the final consumer. It also includes all the institutions and arrangements that affect and coordinate the successive stages of a commodity flow, such as the government, markets, futures markets, contractual integration, vertical integration, trade associations, cooperatives, cooperative-corporate joint ventures, financial partners, financial entities, transport groups, and educational organizations.

The agribusiness commodity systems approach to private and public decision making has gained widespread acceptance in the United States in the strategic planning activities of private and public decision makers and in the development of a variety of agribusiness management courses and programs at a number of educational institutions. From the development of the concept at the Harvard Business School in 1957,[3] agribusiness programs or courses have been established in over 80 universities in the United States and at least 10 in other countries.

Conceptually, the discipline is an integrative one, relating the specific decision problem of a manager located in the vertical structure of agribusiness to the interaction of his operation with the system of which he is a part. The uniqueness of an agribusiness commodity system is due to the agronomic features of the system. The combination of seasonal crop production and estrus cycles of livestock with the year-round consumption of food products results almost invariably in serious imbalances between supply and demand. These imbalances are aggravated by unforeseen weather conditions over which the producer has no control. In addition to volume imbalances, the changing nature of habits and styles of consumption and the changing structure of the distribution network result in the need to transpose priorities of product, time, and place up and down the vertical network to develop an appropriate and economically feasible response at each stage of the food structure. Therefore, the development, understanding, and use of unique coordinating institutions and arrangements especially useful for agribusiness are essential elements of the private and public manager's understanding of an agribusiness commodity systems approach to his particular situation.

It is also an interdisciplinary approach, establishing the boundary line of the agribusiness economy and relating it to the general economy. It utilizes the managerial concepts of business and public policy, finance, marketing, production, control, human behavior, and labor analysis, and combines them with the disciplines of agricultural economics, technical agriculture, and developmental economics. The agribusiness statistical base provided by governments and by the Food and Agriculture Organization of the United Nations also facilitates the use of various analytic tools, such as simulation models. In addition, the broad nutritional concerns of agribusiness require a working relation with medical, food science, and population programs.

In summary, the agribusiness commodity systems approach makes use of disciplines that (1) design and analyze the agribusiness environment; (2) set forth the structure and operations of a particular commodity system in the larger environment; and (3) relate the specific operations of a firm or institution to the total vertical commodity system and to the ultimate purpose of that system, namely, to provide food in an efficient, nutritionally acceptable, and socially desirable manner.

The Private Decision Maker's Use
of the Agribusiness Approach

An agribusiness commodity systems approach must be both domestic and international in scope. From this kind of analysis, the manager can derive several advantages:

1. The manager is in a better position to identify the critical variables and trends that affect the system. These variables include social, economic, and political considerations as well as technological changes.
2. The manager is in a better position to evaluate the strengths and weaknesses of his firm in a changing environment.
3. In many agribusiness commodity systems, the individual firm is large enough for its manager to make important changes in the system instead of being a passive reactor to the system. But in making changes, he should give attention to the health of the system; a statesmanlike attitude rather than a special-interest focus is needed.
4. From a detailed, comprehensive, structural analysis, the manager may see new ways of coordinating his firm's activities with those of the system through one or more of the following avenues: futures markets, contractual integration, vertical integration, central markets, cooperatives, joint cooperative-corporate arrangements, special financial arrangements and institutions, unique transportation arrangements, market orders, trade associations, and effective government-business relations.
5. With an understanding of an entire system, the manager is better able to recognize significant trends and the importance of timing. Various industry systems have life cycles all their own, and a realization of when to get into or out of a system may well be as important as what to do in that system.
6. Finally, with a systems approach a manager can more readily discover the kinds of escape hatches that may be available when he is in difficulties and has to change the direction of his operations in a drastic manner.

The Public Policy Maker's Use
of the Agribusiness Approach

1. The public policy maker is in a better position to formulate policies that will be effective for the *total system* if he develops them in terms of the commodity system and if he understands the implications of his policy for all of its parts. A public policy maker cannot make a policy for one segment of agribusiness without affecting the whole structure, which will in turn affect the segment that once was viewed in isolation.
2. With a common understanding of the commodity system of which they are parts (even though priorities may be different), there can be more effective cooperation and interaction between the public and the private policy maker.

3. With an appropriate emphasis on coordinating institutions and arrangements, the government is in a better position to determine which such institutions (cooperatives, for example) to encourage and in what manner.
4. A systems approach enables government policy makers to relate the agribusiness economy's interactions to the total domestic economy and in turn to international factors.
5. A systems approach enables government policy makers to provide new services to the domestic and international agribusinessmen who are constantly reaching back to distant places for sources of supply and further out for new domestic and international markets.
6. A systems approach by the government helps the public policy maker to organize government agencies in such a way as to provide greater interchange between business and government and among a wide variety of government agencies so that all will have a broader perspective of an efficient and workable commodity system.
7. A systems approach by the public policy maker should enable him to help to develop coordinating linkages between subsistence agriculture and a commercial agribusiness commodity system.
8. A systems perspective would naturally lead to periodic studies of the total agribusiness system so that the public policy maker would have a current and projected agribusiness matrix to use in evaluating the potential significance of alternative programs of action.

The Educator's Use of the Agribusiness Commodity Systems Approach

In our discussion of the agribusiness commodity systems approach thus far, we have stressed that corporate, cooperative, and farm managers in the system must be responsive to the ultimate consumer's food and nutritional needs, and must perform their functions in an effective and efficient manner in order to maintain their own viability. In other words, managers must be market oriented. Educators, in turn, are responsive to the needs of developing human resources that can find productive opportunities in the expanding agribusiness commodity systems emerging in various countries. For their training to be relevant, they must understand the managerial and labor requirements of these changing agribusiness commodity systems. So, educators too must be market oriented. This market orientation must serve the public priority system of each country as well as be related to improving the wide variety of functions to be performed in agribusiness.

Our definition of "education," as used in this study, is extremely broad in order to not only encompass the traditional formal educational institutions, but to include a great many informal educational activities, such as on-the-job training and joint ventures with groups like LAAD.[4] LAAD's joint ventures with producers and marketing firms help to coordinate movements of fruit, meat, vegetables, and flowers from Central America to the United States and Europe. In the process of this coordination, LAAD is training its partners in defining marketing goals, establishing product quality controls, and setting up equitable pricing mechanisms.

The commodity systems approach to agribusiness education in Central America is not a substitute for the excellent formal and informal programs that already exist in this important area, but rather an attempt to provide a coordinated perspective of agribusiness in the region that gives special emphasis to fruits and vegetables (and, to a lesser extent, to floriculture). This perspective is provided so that it may be taken into consideration in the future planning of agribusiness education in the area.

This project could not be carried out without the active participation of the educational, private, and public policy makers involved in agribusiness. We are most pleased with the constructive inputs of these leaders from both Central America and the United States. With this type of encouragement and cooperation, and with the development of a common agribusiness perspective, educators should be in a better position to:

1. Determine where their institution, whether formal or informal, fits into the total agribusiness system, what kinds of training are needed at the different functional and coordinating levels of the system, and how these needs are best served by the resources of their respective institutions.
2. Develop joint or cooperative programs in short courses and research for a particular commodity system in which a common perspective would cut across both the technical and conceptual training developed at individual institutions.
3. Encourage banks and private firms to provide technical training on grades and standards, credit, transportation, and marketing in the international markets on a formal basis rather than relying on informal meetings or occasional contractual relations.
4. Develop a common data bank, agribusiness case clearing house, and similar devices for providing more accurate descriptions and evaluations of the changing agribusiness commodity systems.
5. Help to train and utilize the underemployed human resources in subsistence agriculture in emerging agribusiness commodity systems.
6. Develop an informal educational coordinating group to improve the agribusiness education of the region.

Central American Agribusiness

In order to place this project in proper perspective, let us first turn to a brief description of Central American agribusiness. From Figures 1–1 to 1–6 it would appear that the dominant input in Central American agribusiness is labor, with purchased labor accounting for approximately 84 percent of the

Figure 1-1. Central American Agribusiness *(10³ dollars)*.

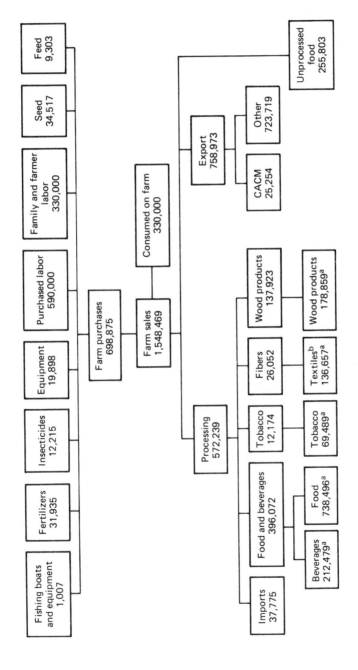

Source: Compiled by the INCAE Agribusiness Program; figures do not reconcile because of variety of sources.

a. To consumer.

b. Includes approximately 10 percent synthetics.

Figure 1–2. Costa Rican Agribusiness (10³ dollars).

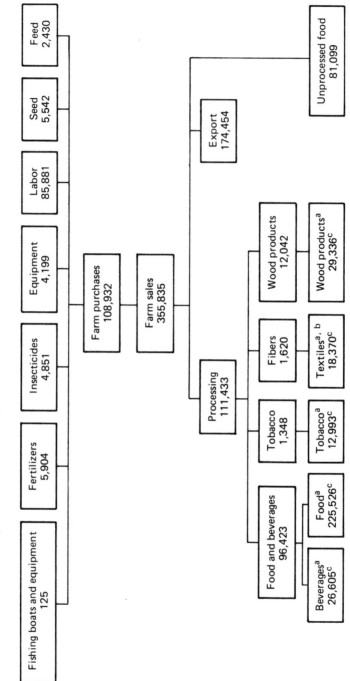

Source: Compiled by the INCAE Agribusiness Program.
a. Dirección General de Estadísticas y Censos, *Anuario Estadístico de Costa Rica* (1970).
b. Includes approximately 10 percent synthetics.
c. To consumer.

Figure 1–3. Guatemalan Agribusiness *(10³ dollars).*

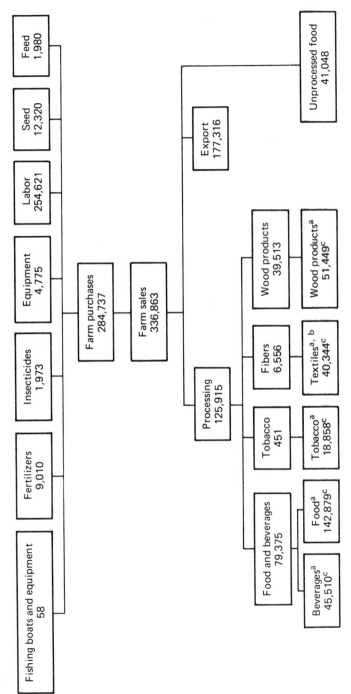

Source: Compiled by the INCAE Agribusiness Program.
Banco de Guatemala, *Estudio Económico y Memoria de Labores* (1970).
a. Includes approximately 10 percent synthetics.
b.
c. To consumer.

Figure 1–4.   Honduran Agribusiness *(10³ dollars)*.

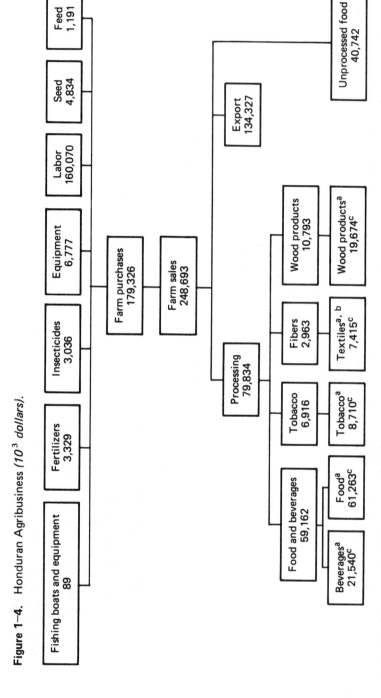

Source: Compiled by the INCAE Agribusiness Program.
a. Banco Central de Honduras, *Memoria* (1969).
b. Includes approximately 10 percent synthetics.
c. To consumer.

Figure 1–5. Nicaraguan Agribusiness *(10³ dollars).*

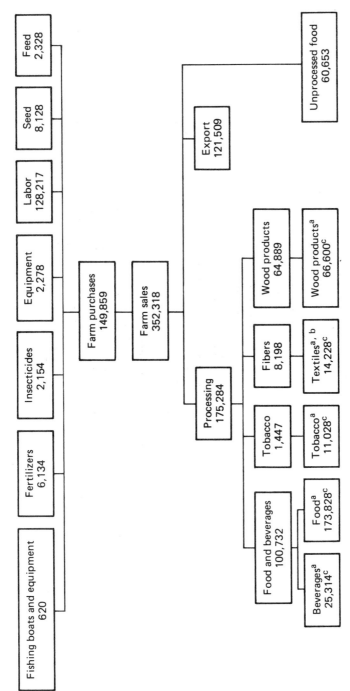

Source: Compiled by the INCAE Agribusiness Program.
a. Banco Central de Nicaragua, *Informe Anual* (1970).
b. Includes approximately 10 percent synthetics.
c. To consumer.

Figure 1–6.   El Salvador Agribusiness *(10³ dollars)*.

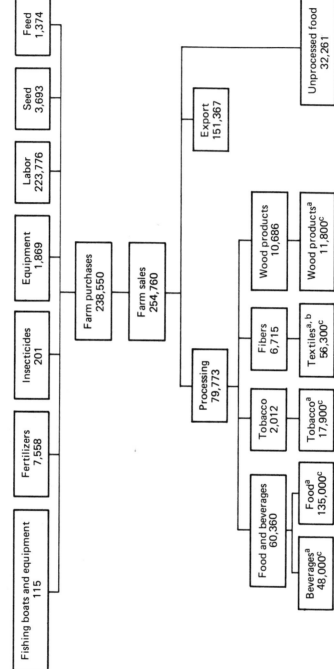

Source: Compiled by the INCAE Agribusiness Program.
Banco Central de Reserva de El Salvador, *Enero* (1972).
a. Includes approximately 10 percent synthetics.
b. To consumer.

farmer's purchased inputs.[5] Also from the flowcharts it is apparent that, of the farm production that is utilized domestically, a significant percentage is consumed on the farm in a subsistence type of agriculture. In fact, the value of family and farm labor is about equal to the value of the food consumed on the farm. Missing from these charts are the coordinating linkages described previously. The training needed for this most important segment of the Central American economy is a combination of broad agribusiness perspective, management discipline, basic and technical agricultural skills, and understanding and utilization of coordinating institutions and arrangements. This understanding includes not only the use of the coordinating or infrastructure entity, but also an identification with it. For example, it is important to be aware of the needs of transportation firms and financial institutions as workable operations, as well as to evaluate their contribution to the well-being of the other participants in the system.

The Fruit and Vegetable System

The fruit and vegetable system of Central America is briefly set forth in Figure 1–7. It is a relatively small agribusiness commodity system—really a combination of a number of specific crop commodity systems—with only 6 percent of total farm sales (see Figures 1–1 and 1–7), but it was selected for this project because of its market potential in the United States, its use of workers in economies that have much unemployment, its ability to use both small and large farms, and the fact that large amounts of capital are not currently necessary for these types of operations. This group of commodity systems was also selected because of the excellent cooperation available to the authors from the Central American and U. S. participants, with the concommitant access to detailed data on specific projects. We also believe that the area is representative in its need for trained managers and workers in the agribusiness economy of Central America, and has applicability to the more mature systems that exist in other commodities in Central America.

The Interface between Agribusiness
Education and the Agribusiness
Commodity Systems Approach
in Central America

In summary, what we are attempting to do is to use the agribusiness commodity systems approach as a means of ascertaining the potential managerial and labor requirements in Central American agribusiness through an analysis of various problems or bottleneck areas in the fruit and vegetable system. An awareness of these training needs of agribusiness should provide incentives for existing formal and informal educational institutions to gear their programs to the training requirements of the participants who will be involved in this system. Therefore the approach provides a conceptual background against which the

Figure 1–7. Central American Fruit and Vegetable System, Simplified[a] *(10⁶ dollars).*

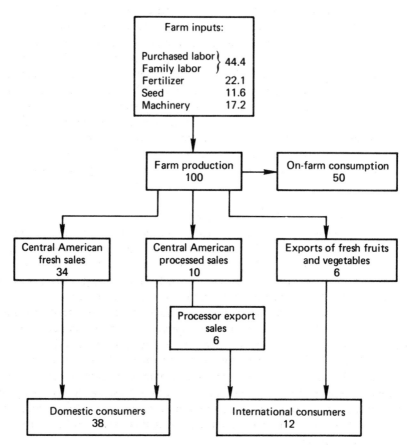

a. Excluding bananas.

educational programs may be planned. We also hope that this approach will develop linkages between subsistence agriculture and commercial agribusiness in Central America as specific procurement programs and training activities bring the subsistence farmer into the market economy.

These interfaces are set forth in a simplified flow relation outlined in Figure 1–8. This chart indicates that the agribusiness education system may desire to coordinate its own teaching and research programs among its participants through an interdisciplinary approach to meet the needs of the changing market structure of the agribusiness commodity systems in Central America. This coordination must take place within the framework of each country's stated policy objectives (a few are suggested as examples in Figure 1–8), which

Figure 1–8. Interface between the Agribusiness Educational System, the Country's Priority System, the Agribusiness Commodity System, and Subsistance Agriculture.

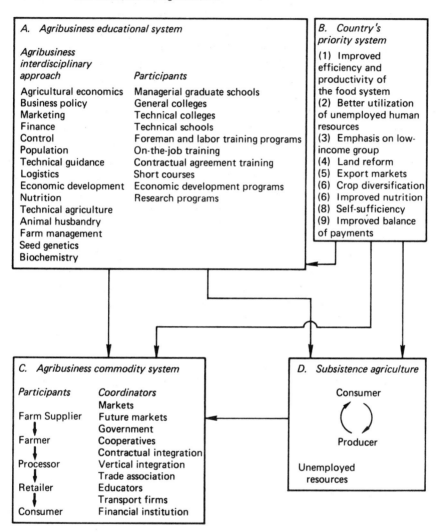

A. Agribusiness educational system

Agribusiness interdisciplinary approach

Agricultural economics
Business policy
Marketing
Finance
Control
Population
Technical guidance
Logistics
Economic development
Nutrition
Technical agriculture
Animal husbandry
Farm management
Seed genetics
Biochemistry

Participants

Managerial graduate schools
General colleges
Technical colleges
Technical schools
Foreman and labor training programs
On-the-job training
Contractual agreement training
Short courses
Economic development programs
Research programs

B. Country's priority system

(1) Improved efficiency and productivity of the food system
(2) Better utilization of unemployed human resources
(3) Emphasis on low-income group
(4) Land reform
(5) Export markets
(6) Crop diversification
(6) Improved nutrition
(8) Self-sufficiency
(9) Improved balance of payments

C. Agribusiness commodity system

Participants

Farm Supplier
↓
Farmer
↓
Processor
↓
Retailer
↓
Consumer

Coordinators

Markets
Future markets
Government
Cooperatives
Contractual integration
Vertical integration
Trade association
Educators
Transport firms
Financial institution

D. Subsistence agriculture

Consumer

Producer

Unemployed resources

in turn affects the manner and speed of change in the transformation of subsistence agriculture into commercially feasible agribusiness commodity systems. If one can expand markets, create new cooperative-corporate joint ventures, and train producers to participate in such programs, the movement of these producers into the market economy can be achieved rapidly.

It would be presumptuous of us to attempt to analyze all the agribusinesses of Central America and all the agribusiness education systems of that area together with the public policies of each nation and the development potential of subsistence agriculture. What we have tried to do is to examine in a general way a group of specific fruit and vegetable commodity systems to see whether we can derive from this limited analysis some generalizations that may be useful for all Central American agribusiness educators. We have set forth this project in a market-oriented fashion. Beginning in Chapter 2, we state the nature of the U. S. fruit and vegetable market and the market potential for Central America. In Chapter 3, we analyze some of the coordinating links between the U. S. market and Central America. In Chapter 4, we look at specific case studies in Central America responding to the U. S. market potential, and in Chapter 5 we try to extract from these specific examples the problem areas and bottlenecks that may be related to the type of training or lack of it that is currently available in Central America. We suggest, with the help of Central American educators, businessmen, and government officials, some directions and actions that may be taken by Central American educational policy makers to improve their own agribusiness educational system. In Chapter 6, we briefly summarize our findings.

The major product of the study is an approach to agribusiness educational development based on a very limited analysis of one embryonic agribusiness commodity system. If the approach has validity, similar studies on other agribusiness commodity systems may be encouraged, and some of the preliminary findings may be put into action. The by-products of the study that may be useful to private and public managers, as well as to educators, include the general descriptive and analytical examination of the U. S. fruit and vegetable system, an abbreviated analysis of the floriculture industry, and a limited but more explicit examination of specific fruit and vegetable projects in Central America. These by-products can be utilized as potential teaching and research tools for educators.

Realizing that we are presenting only a general view of one aggregate of a commodity system as our focus, we caution the reader not to overgeneralize from this limited example. Also, we feel that as other Central American commodity systems, such as meat, sugar, or cotton are examined and analyzed, there will be many activities, operations, coordinating arrangements, and skills in these commodity systems that are transferable to the fruit and vegetable system, and vice versa. None of these systems should be looked upon in isolation from the total agribusiness system or from the total economy of which they are parts.

NOTES TO CHAPTER ONE

1. Because bananas have been such a traditional export crop, we have excluded them from our study and are really examining the nontraditional fruit and vegetable crops. At the same time we recognize bananas as a major crop of the region.

2. Acronyms such as "LAAD" are used frequently in this study. An acronym will first appear in the text with the proper name it represents; thereafter it will usually appear alone. Appendix Q contains a list of acronyms employed in this study and the proper names they represent.

3. John H. Davis and Ray A. Goldberg, *A Concept of Agribusiness* (Division of Research, Harvard Graduate School of Business Administration, Boston, Mass., 1957).

4. This particular institution is singled out in our study because of its unique method of involving producers and marketers in joint ventures to their mutual benefit, and at the same time meeting its own objectives of locating and carrying out agribusiness investment opportunities in Latin America.

5. In all of these figures, the data collected by the Agribusiness Program at INCAE were from such a variety of sources that it is difficult to reconcile specific numbers within each figure and between figures. These charts are presented here only to show broad general relations, and the reader is cautioned not to assume that these numbers are any more accurate than the estimated sources from which they were obtained.

Chapter Two

The Fruit and Vegetable Commodity System in the United States

The market for fruits and vegetables in the United States is very large and relatively stable, but it is growing only moderately.[1] In 1971, Americans consumed fruit and vegetable products, both fresh and processed, with an estimated retail value of $25 billion. This represented 21 percent of consumer expenditures for all foods, next in importance to meat products. The fruit and vegetable share of the retail food dollar has been virtually unchanged throughout the postwar period.

Although the dollar value of retail purchases rose by nearly 60 percent between 1960 and 1971, most of this rise reflected higher prices rather than an increase in the volume consumed. In fact, per capita consumption of fruits and vegetables declined by about 2 percent between 1960 and 1971.

These aggregative trends are highly deceptive, however, because they hide significant changes that are taking place in the markets for individual commodities. The behavior of the overall fruit and vegetable commodity system is the net result of many diverse trends affecting both demand and supply.

The most important of these is the long-term increase in consumption of processed products and the corresponding decline in consumer use of selected fresh fruits and vegetables. This shift reflects basic changes in consumer behavior that have resulted in less time being spent in home-food preparation. It has been facilitated by a steady flow of new canned and frozen products with built-in convenience features, that are available to consumers at costs that make them competitive with home preparation of raw produce.

A related and more recent trend is the increase in consumption of food away from home, in restaurants, other food-service establishments, industrial plants, schools, and institutions. This hotel, restaurant, and institution (HRI) trend reflects the same basic changes in consumer living patterns and new product development that have influenced home consumption of processed convenience-food products. Fruits and vegetables, however, have not benefited from the increase in away-from-home consumption to the same degree as other food products.

There is some evidence that the demand for fresh fruits and vegetables has strengthened in recent years, following a long period of declining consumption. Per capita consumption (except for fresh potatoes) has been relatively stable since 1965, while retail prices of fresh fruits and vegetables have increased more sharply than any other food category. There appears to be renewed interest in "natural" foods arising from such recent sociological trends as consumerism and concern for the environment. This has been reflected particularly in increased consumption of salad vegetables, such as celery, lettuce, and onions. Fresh consumption has also been enhanced by the increased availability of winter produce from Mexico and other foreign sources.

All of these trends appear likely to continue and perhaps even to accelerate during the 1970s, thus suggesting that overall market growth may be somewhat more rapid than in the past and that the growth for certain individual fruit and vegetable products will be quite substantial.

On the supply side, U. S. farm production increased by less than 20 percent during the 1960s, all of the increase going into processing. The increase in output was due primarily to continued gains in yields per acre, since the total acreage devoted to fruit and vegetable crop production showed little change.

The long-term evolutionary trend toward fewer and larger fruit and vegetable farms continued during the 1960s, and major producing areas, especially in California and Florida, accounted for a larger share of total production. The total number of fruit and vegetable farms declined sharply, but this took place almost entirely among farms with gross receipts of less than $10,000 per year. During the late 1960s several large proprietary corporations, including Tenneco, United Brands, and Purex, became direct participants in fruit and vegetable growing in the United States for the first time. More recently, several of these new entrants, such as Purex, have reversed their decisions and left the industry.

These shifts in the structure of fruit and vegetable production reflect efforts by growers to increase productivity and reduce cost through greater utilization of nonlabor inputs. Domestic farm labor has become both relatively scarce and much more costly. Unionization of field workers in grapes, lettuce, and citrus fruits has had a marked impact on farm cost structures. Large-scale growers are becoming increasingly mechanized and are integrating forward into distribution and marketing.

U. S. growers also face increased competition from imports, which rose much more rapidly than domestic production during the 1960s. Although imports still account for less than 10 percent of total U. S. fruit and vegetable supplies, they have made significant inroads in the markets for specific commodities. This has been particularly true in the case of crops that require extensive hand labor and those in which foreign suppliers are able to exploit seasonal gaps in U. S. production. Imported tomatoes and cucumbers, for example, account for about one-fifth of the annual U. S. supply and one-half the supply during the winter and early spring months. Mexico has become by far the leading exporter of fresh produce to the U. S. market, but other sources, including Central America and the Caribbean, are beginning to participate on a limited scale. Imports of processed fruits and vegetables, where mechanization has proceeded more rapidly in the U. S., are also on the increase, though not at the same rate as fresh produce. With developing nations encouraging high-value-added exports, we would expect an increase in processed as well as fresh fruit and vegetable export items.

Government participation in the U. S. fruit and vegetable system is limited in comparison both with other crop and livestock products and with foreign government efforts to promote exports to the United States. Although a large number of marketing orders pertaining to fruits and vegetables are in effect, they are concentrated on relatively few commodities and have proved largely ineffective in influencing either domestic supply or imports. The balance-of-payment problems that affect many countries and the change in regional trading-bloc areas have already indicated a more active interest by governments in these industries. Various export and import trade restrictions, transportation subsidies, and the like are under revision.

Overview of the System

The distribution and marketing system that has evolved to move about 65 million tons of domestic and imported fruits and vegetables from farm to consumer each year is both complex and highly fractionated. Historically, it was composed of a large number of relatively small units at all levels of the system and characterized by widely diffused decision making throughout the system on the basis of highly imperfect market information. One result has been that costs beyond the farm gate account for a relatively large share of the ultimate consumer dollar for both fresh and processed commodities. The retail value of fresh fruits and vegetables is about three times the farm value, and for processed products is five times the farm value.

This fragmented structure is changing in response to changes taking place both in the markets and on the farm. Rising consumer demand for processed convenience products, the cost-price squeeze affecting U. S. growers, and the increasing level of imports have all resulted in needs for greater coordination and increased efficiency throughout the system.

The earliest, and perhaps the most important, impact on this system came from the growth of national retail chains that were able to buy direct from large growers or shippers and even, in some cases, to integrate all the way back into farm production. National and independent chains, controlling over 60,000 individual retail stores, now account for about 70 percent of the retail value of both fresh and processed fruits and vegetables used by American consumers. The balance is divided about evenly between specialty stores and the institutional market.

The national chains supply their stores with fresh produce from chain-owned perishable-food distribution centers, that receive about half of their total supplies directly from shipping-point markets in the major producing areas, and with processed products from chain warehouses supplied directly by food processors. One result of this partial integration has been to push certain operations and their related costs back to earlier stages in the system. In fresh produce, for example, the labor-intensive functions of cutting, trimming, and repacking are steadily moving backward from the individual retail store toward the distribution center and the shipping-point market. In the case of processed fruits and vegetables, the food processor normally bears the cost of inventory handling and storage.

There has also been a trend toward greater concentration at the processor level in response both to the economies of scale inherent in fruit and vegetable canning and freezing and to the growing relative importance of the major producing areas. The number of processing plants has declined, while average plant size has increased sharply. The 50 largest canning firms now account for over two-thirds of the total output, and the 50 largest freezers for more than four-fifths.

Large-scale procurement by food retailers and processors has tended to impose higher and more uniform quality standards on growers, both in the United States and abroad.

Wholesale produce terminal markets reacted to the growth of the integrated retail chain in part through the development of affiliated wholesalers—both cooperatives owned by the retail stores they serve and voluntaries that contract to supply a group of retail outlets, often under a common name. These affiliated wholesalers act in much the same way as the purchasing and warehousing activities of the integrated retailers.

The remaining nonintegrated sector of the wholesale terminal markets has been marked by a tendency to consolidate functions, such as receiving, breaking bulk, repacking, and jobbing, that were traditionally performed by independent firms. There has also been a trend among jobbers toward serving the needs of the growing institutional market. Wholesale terminal markets continue to play an important role in supplying large retailers with both low-volume specialty products and incremental quantities to balance their needs for large-volume commodities. Wholesalers in 1973 still handled 65 percent of all the volume of fruits and vegetables.

Shipping-point markets have become relatively more important, as a result of direct buying by the retail chains and of the increased geographic concentration of fruit and vegetable production. Although the number of firms active in shipping-point markets has declined, the average sizes of both brokers and handlers have increased, while the total volume has remained about constant. Brokers account for about 30 percent of the value of fresh produce moving through shipping-point markets, although their relative importance tends to be greater in the major growing areas, such as Florida and California. Among handlers, integrated grower-shippers have increased in relative importance as shippers have integrated backward into production in order to assure supplies, and large growers have integrated forward into shipping and selling in order to obtain greater influence over the market for their crops.

Nogales, Arizona, became established as the primary shipping-point market for imports of Mexican fruits and vegetables primarily because of its location near available overland transport. The key coordinators in the import system are the distributors located in Nogales who are closely linked with Mexican growers, either through direct investment or through informal communications and trade practices. Buying brokers and direct chain buyers have not become significant direct factors in this import system.

Similarly, Pompano Beach, Florida, is beginning to emerge as the key importing center for Central American and Caribbean fruits and vegetables. Unlike Nogales, which handles about $200 million of Mexican imports annually, the volume imported through Pompano Beach is very small, and the market is composed of only four or five importing brokers, who in turn have only loose ties with growers. Virtually all of the volume is sold on consignment. The grower has access to very little current information on the prices his products bring in the marketplace. There is some evidence that knowledge of qualities and prices will become more available as additional wholesalers and brokers come into this market and new joint ventures are developed.

Because of its diverse nature, it is difficult to summarize the behavior of the U. S. fruit and vegetable commodity system. Historically, it was marked by great diversity and very little effective coordination. This made it very difficult for the distribution system, especially in the case of fresh produce, to respond efficiently to changing consumer needs. The coordinating mechanisms that have evolved are almost entirely private rather than public in nature. The most important forms of coordination have been through common ownership and contractual relations. Not only have retailers integrated backward into distribution and growing, but producers have integrated forward into shipping and marketing. Fruit and vegetable processors obtain about 70 percent of their raw-material requirements through contractual arrangements with growers. These contracts increasingly specify farming methods, quality standards, and timetables to be followed by producers and also usually provide seeds, fertilizers, and financial arrangements.

Both past and prospective future market trends suggest that the processing sector of the fruit and vegetable industry has been more successful in meeting the needs of consumers than the fresh sector. The relatively rapid long-term rise of retail prices of fresh produce has not induced a significant increase in farm production. Prices of processed fruits and vegetables, on the other hand, have risen about in line with the overall cost of living, and food processors have continued to successfully develop and market a steady flow of new canned and frozen products.

More recently, participants in wholesale terminal markets have begun to alter significantly the historical functions they perform and to redefine the markets they can most effectively serve. Competition on the basis of services provided is becoming more important in this new environment. Negotiated and internal transfer prices have eroded the traditional price-making function of the terminal markets.

At the farm level, growers are moving toward coordinated large-scale mechanized operations. The number of growers not only is small relative to those engaged on other farm crops, but is declining. Capital requirements are substantial; they can easily exceed $100,000 for an efficient farm.

The inherently labor-intensive nature of many fruit and vegetable crops, together with climatic advantages and improved transportation, will continue to provide attractive opportunities for foreign suppliers, including Central America, to penetrate the U. S. market. This will require not only adequate sources of capital for expansion, but, more important, much improved coordination between Central American exporters and the needs of the U. S. distribution and marketing system.

Table 2–1 summarizes a projection made by the U. S. Department of Agriculture in October 1972 that indicates that U. S. fruit and vegetable production will expand by some 54,114 billion pounds from 1970 to 2000—an increase of about 45 percent.

DYNAMICS OF THE SYSTEM

Trends in Consumption

Consumer purchases of fruits and vegetables in the United States totaled an estimated $25 billion in 1971. This represented 21 percent of the $117 billion consumers spent for all food products both at home and away.

Table 2–1. Projected U.S. Fruit and Vegetable Production *(10^6 lb.).*

Commodity	Year	
	1970	*2000*
Vegetables and melons	47,457	67,990
Potatoes	32,560	47,500
Citrus fruit	21,285	34,213
Noncitrus fruit	17,725	23,438
Total	119,027	173,141

Source: U.S. Department of Agriculture, Economic Research Service, Economic and Statistical Analysis Division, unpublished projections, October 1972.

Only meat products, with 29 percent of the total, had a greater share of the consumer food dollar. There was little change in the distribution of consumer food expenditures between 1960 and 1971 (Table 2–2).

Fruits and vegetables are relatively more important in home consumption than in the away-from-home institutional market. In 1971, they accounted for 23 percent of the value of consumer purchases for home use, but only 17 percent of away-from-home outlays. This is due in part to the fact that fruits and vegetables are used less frequently at lunch, which is the most important meal eaten away from home. A major challenge facing fruit and vegetable marketers during the 1970s will be to find ways of increasing their penetration of the institutional market, which is growing much more rapidly (6 to 8 percent per year) than home food consumption.

The 1971 spending rate for fruits and vegetables represented an increase of about $10 billion (60 percent) over 1960. Most of this gain, however, reflected higher retail prices for both fresh and processed products rather than an increase in real consumption. Aggregate consumption of all fruits and vegetables increased by only 12 percent, or slightly less than the growth in population.

From 1972 to 1985, the U. S. Department of Agriculture (USDA) expects the civilian disappearance of fruits and vegetables to increase by 21,124 million pounds (see Table 2–3).

Per Capita Consumption. Although total consumption lagged behind population growth during the 1960s as a whole, the long-term decline in per capita consumption appears to have leveled off since about 1966. Up to that time, a continuous decline in consumption of fresh produce more than offset increases in the utilization of processed products. Since then, however, fresh

Table 2–2. U.S. Consumer Expenditures for Domestic Farm Food Products.

Commodity	1960		1971	
	(10⁹ dollars)	*(percent)*	*(10⁹ dollars)*	*(percent)*
Meat products	18.6	27.8	32.5	29.2
Fruits and vegetables	14.7	21.9	23.4	21.0
Dairy products	12.1	18.1	16.8	15.2
Bakery products	6.9	10.3	11.5	10.4
Poultry and eggs	5.2	7.7	8.3	7.5
Grain-mill products	2.6	3.8	3.2	2.9
Miscellaneous	6.9	10.4	15.3	13.8
All farm foods	67.0	100.0	111.0	100.0

Source: Terry L. Crawford, "The Bill for Marketing Farm-Food Products," *Marketing and Transportation Situation* (U.S. Department of Agriculture, Economic Research Service, August 1972).

Table 2–3. Projected Civilian Disappearance of Fruits and Vegetables in the United States $(10^6$ lb.).[a]

Commodity	1972	1980	1985
Fresh vegetables	20,268	20,100	20,331
Melons	4,652	4,686	4,721
Frozen vegetables[b]	4,312	5,441	6,240
Canned vegetables[b]	19,485	22,432	24,538
Subtotal	48,717	52,659	55,830
Potatoes[b]	24,770	28,207	29,680
Citrus fruit[b]	20,248	23,987	25,473
Noncitrus fruit[b]	19,587	22,277	23,463
Total	113,322	127,130	134,446

Source: U.S. Department of Agriculture, Economic Research Service.
a. Series E population projection, 50 states, civilian U.S.: 1980, 222.1 million; 1985, 233.7 million.
b. Fresh weight equivalent basis.

consumption has virtually stabilized, while processed consumption has continued to increase (Table 2–4).

Fresh-fruit per capita consumption declined steadily during 1950–1966, but has shown little change since then. The downward trend in fresh consumption largely reflected reduced use of oranges, apples, and melons—products for which significant processed alternatives were developed relatively early. Per capita consumption of fruits, such as bananas, for which there are no important processed substitutes, has remained relatively stable throughout the entire postwar period.

Per capita consumption of processed fruits, that rose sharply during the early and mid–1950s, actually declined between 1957 and 1963, but this was largely the result of a series of freezes that reduced Florida citrus supplies. Citrus production returned to record levels in recent years, and a renewed uptrend in per capita consumption of processed fruits has taken place since the mid–1960s. This has been due almost entirely to increased consumption of canned, chilled, and frozen citrus juices.

The trend of per capita consumption of fresh vegetables closely paralleled that for fresh fruits, with a continuous decline during 1956–1966 followed by relative stability during 1966–1971. The large decline in per capita consumption of fresh vegetables during the early 1960s was due almost entirely to the rapid switch from fresh to frozen or dehydrated potatoes. Excluding potatoes, fresh-vegetable consumption has actually increased slightly since 1966.

The postwar trend of consumption of processed vegetable products has been stronger than that of fruits, with consistent increases throughout the 20-year period. Frozen-vegetable consumption (including potatoes) increased

Table 2–4. U.S. Per Capita Consumption of Fruits and Vegetables, 1956–1971 *(in pounds, primary distribution weight).*[a]

Commodity	1956	1961	1966	1971
		Fresh		
Fruits	98.9	88.6	81.4	80.1
Melons	27.4	24.8	22.1	22.7
Vegetables	107.0	103.7	95.9	98.6
Potatoes	88.7	84.5	72.4	57.9
Total fresh	322.0	301.6	271.8	259.3
		Processed		
Canned fruit[b]	21.9	23.6	23.4	22.2
Canned fruit juices[b]	14.8	13.4	14.8	20.2
Frozen fruit	4.0	3.6	3.6	3.7
Frozen fruit juices	4.9	5.2	4.5	6.5
Dried fruit	3.7	3.1	3.0	2.6
Canned vegetables	43.9	45.0	49.0	53.1
Frozen vegetables	7.3	9.7	15.8	21.8
Other potato products[c]	10.6	17.4	27.0	30.3
Total processed	111.1	131.0	141.1	160.4
Grand total	433.1	432.6	412.9	419.7

Source: U.S. Department of Agriculture, *Vegetable Situation* (October 1972); *Fruit Situation* (September 1972); *Agricultural Statistics* (1971).
a. Excluding production for home use.
b. Including chilled fruits, citrus sections, and juices.
c. Chips, shoestrings, and dehydrated.

about threefold between 1956 and 1971, but still accounts for less than 25 percent of per capita processed-vegetable consumption. Canned-vegetable per capita consumption increased steadily during the entire postwar period at a rate of about 1.5 percent per year.

Factors Affecting Consumption. Increases in total fruit and vegetable consumption have largely reflected increases in population. In fact, as noted above, until recently fruit and vegetable consumption has not even kept pace with population growth. Although there are some differences among individual fruit and vegetable products, total consumption does not appear to vary significantly either regionally or among age groups within the population.

Food expenditures until 1973 have lagged behind increases in consumer incomes in the United States. Expenditures for food accounted for 22 percent of disposable personal income in 1945, but declined to 20 percent in 1960 and 15.7 percent in 1972 (Table 2–5). Food used in the home declined relative to food consumed away from home, which maintained a constant 3 to 4 percent share of disposable income.

Table 2–5.   U.S. Expenditures for Food in Relation to Disposable Personal Income, 1945–1972.

Year	Total disposable income (10⁹ dollars)	Total expenditure for food (10⁹ dollars)	(Percent of income)
1945	150.2	33.2	22.1
1950	206.9	46.0	22.2
1955	275.3	58.1	21.1
1960	350.0	70.1	20.0
1965	473.2	85.8	18.1
1970	689.5	114.2	16.6
1971	744.4	117.3	15.8
1972	795.1	124.4	15.7

Source: U.S. Department of Agriculture, Economic Research Service, *National Food Situation* (November 1972, and May 1973).

Studies of the demand for individual products indicate that fruits and vegetables tend to be quite income inelastic;[2] that is, a given increase in income will produce a less than proportionate increase in consumption, all other things being equal. Processed fruit and vegetable products tend to be more responsive to income changes than fresh produce, and fruits appear to be more responsive than vegetables. Certain staple products, such as fresh potatoes, may even exhibit negative income elasticity at higher levels of income.

Demand for fruits and vegetables also is relatively unresponsive to price reductions at the retail level.[3] This is partly due to the difficulties of effecting prompt responses of supply to changes in retail prices, particularly for tree fruits, but it also appears to be characteristic of the demand for fruits and vegetables over the long term. Banana prices, for example, not only have lagged behind the increase in other food prices, but are actually lower than a decade ago, yet per capita consumption of bananas has not increased. For fruits and vegetables as a whole, consumer prices of both fresh and processed products have continued to increase during the postwar period, while per capita consumption has not changed appreciably.

The shift in consumption from fresh fruits and vegetables to processed forms reflects both basic changes in consumer behavior patterns and technological innovations by the food-processing industry. Increases in population mobility, numbers of working wives, and leisure time and the unavailability of domestic laborers have all contributed to a marked reduction in the amount of time spent in home-food preparation. With rising incomes, American consumers have clearly demonstrated that they are willing to pay for a wide variety of canned and frozen products offering built-in convenience features. Food manufacturers have responded to this growing demand with an impressive flow of new products designed to minimize in-home preparation, reduce costs, and maintain or improve quality.

Recent studies have indicated that a wide variety of packaged fruits and vegetables are now cost-competitive with purchasing the raw product and preparing it at home. This, in turn, has further stimulated the demand for fruits and vegetables for consumption away from home, both in restaurants and in other institutional outlets, such as hospitals, schools, and industrial plants.

Outlook for the Future. It appears likely that the recent (1966–1971) moderate upward trend in overall per capita consumption of fruits and vegetables will continue during the 1970s. This relatively favorable outlook is based on the probability that there will be some resurgence in the use of fresh fruits and vegetables, continued innovation in processed products, and relatively rapid growth in the institutional markets.

The factors that may cause a more favorable trend in the demand for fresh fruits and vegetables during the 1970s include:

1. Continuation of the recent increases in per capita consumption of salad products (tomatoes, lettuce, cucumbers) for which important processed alternatives have not yet developed;
2. The general concern with ecology and a renewed interest in "natural" foods;
3. Consumer willingness to pay premium prices for consistently high-quality fresh produce, such as greenhouse tomatoes;
4. The greater availability of winter fruits and vegetables from foreign sources, such as Mexico, Central America, and the Caribbean.

The trends in consumer behavior and product innovation mentioned above appear likely to continue during the seventies and to result in further gains in per capita home consumption of processed fruits and vegetables, both canned and frozen. The institutional market will also benefit from the changes in consumer behavior and will receive increased attention from both processors and distributors. The food-service systems of nonmarket institutions, such as hospitals, schools, and the military, have shown little change during the past two decades; but the pressure of rising costs is forcing a reevaluation that may have wide impact on future consumption of processed fruits and vegetables.

Trends in Supply

Total U. S. farm production of fruits and vegetables increased only moderately between 1960 and 1972, but there were significant shifts among individual crops and further concentration of production in the major growing areas, especially California and Florida. Farm productivity, as measured by yields per acre, continued to improve, and accounted for most of the gain in total output. Commercial acreage planted to fruits and vegetables showed little change during the sixties. Imports increased more rapidly than U. S. production, but they still account for less than 10 percent of total available domestic supplies.

Domestic Production. Total production of vegetables and melons, rose from 18.4 million tons in 1960 to 21.6 million tons in 1972, a gain of just 18 percent. (Table 2–6).[4] All of this increase reflected higher yields per acre as total vegetable acreage declined slightly from 3.4 million acres in 1960 to 3.2 million acres in 1972. The long-term rise in vegetable-farm productivity appears to have slowed during the 1960s, however. Average yields per acre increased at a rate of just under 2 percent per year, compared with 2.5 percent per year during the previous decade. All of the increase in vegetable production went into processing, which rose from 40 percent of total output in 1960 to 45 percent in 1970.

Production for the fresh market was virtually unchanged. Fresh cucumbers, lettuce, and onions increased, reflecting in part strong consumer demand for salad vegetables, but the gains were offset by declines in cabbage, snap beans, and asparagus (Table 2–7).

Vegetable production for processing increased 27 percent, from 7.4 million tons in 1960 to 9.3 million tons in 1970. The two most important processed vegetables, corn and tomatoes, accounted for more than 75 percent of the increase in production. Other processed products showing relatively large increases included snap beans, beets, and cucumbers. Processed-vegetable production increased more rapidly than consumption during the early and mid–1960s and reached a peak of more than 12 million tons in 1968. Since 1968, farm output has declined by about one-fifth as processors have attempted to reduce excessive inventory holdings.

Farm production of potatoes, which is excluded from the above figures, increased by about one-fourth during 1960–1970 in sharp contrast to the virtually flat trend of potato production during the previous decade. The increased output during the 1960s reflected strong consumer demand for virtu-

Table 2–6. U.S. Vegetables[a] and Melons: Acreage and Production, 1960–1972.

Year	Total harvested acreage (10^3 acres)	Total production (10^3 tons)	Total production (tons/acre)
1960	3,383.4	18,397.9	5.4
1965	3,286.9	19,263.7	5.9
1966	3,417.3	19,558.5	5.7
1967	3,567.5	21,122.3	5.9
1968	3,637.0	23,395.9	6.4
1969	3,333.0	20,487.2	6.1
1970	3,197.6	20,600.8	6.4
1971	3,159.8	21,273.8	6.7
1972	3,210.0	21,643.8	6.7

Source: U.S. Department of Agriculture, Economic Research Service.
a. Excluding potatoes.

ally all forms of processed potato products, especially frozen products, whose output increased more than fourfold during the period. Production of potato chips and dehydrated potatoes also rose sharply, while use of fresh potatoes declined by about 20 percent.

Farm output of fruits rose 31 percent between 1960 and 1971 (Table 2–8), or about twice as much as the increase in total vegetable production for the same period (Table 2–6). Unlike that of vegetables, total area of fruits

Table 2–7. U.S. Vegetable Production for Fresh Market (10⁵ lb.), Selected Commodities, 1960, 1970, and 1972.

Commodity	1960	1970	1972	Percent change 1960–70	Percent change 1960–72
			Salad vegetables		
Lettuce	38,631	46,328	48,054	+20	+24
Onions[a]	26,457	30,493	27,810	+15	+ 5
Cucumbers	4,401	4,478	4,647	+ 2	+ 6
Peppers[a]	3,633	3,872	4,545	+ 7	+25
Tomatoes	19,006	18,234	19,511	− 4	+ 3
			Other vegetables		
Celery[a]	15,169	15,332	15,497	+ 1	+ 2
Carrots	18,335	18,190	19,305	− 1	+ 5
Cabbage[a]	24,514	23,841	22,472	− 3	− 8
Brussel sprouts	716	587	724	−18	+ 1
Asparagus[a]	3,762	2,755	2,891	−27	−23
Snap beans	4,494	3,109	3,167	−31	−30

Source: U.S. Department of Agriculture, Economic Research Service.
a. Including some production for processing.

Table 2–8. U.S. Fruits and Planted Nuts: Acreage and Production, 1960–1971.

Year	Total acreage (10³ acres)	Total production (10³ tons)	Total production (tons/acre)
1960	2,818.2	17,319	6.1
1965	2,846.9	18,708	6.6
1966	2,889.3	19,198	6.6
1967	2,958.6	20,379	6.9
1968	3,036.1	18,523	6.1
1969	3,107.2	22,602	7.3
1970	3,179.8	21,439	6.7
1971	3,223.9	22,675	7.0

Source: U.S. Department of Agriculture, *Agricultural Statistics* (1972).

increased from 2.8 million acres in 1960 to 3.2 million acres in 1971, representing a gain of about 14 percent. Average yield per hectare also continued to rise, but at a slower rate than earlier in the postwar period. All of the increase in farm output of fruits during the past decade went into processing, accounting for 68 percent of total production in 1970 compared with 60 percent in 1960.

Output of citrus fruits increased much more rapidly than noncitrus production during the 1960s. Citrus production reached 12 million tons in 1970, an increase of more than 60 percent above the 1960 level, most of which went into chilled and frozen juice products. Noncitrus production, on the other hand, increased only 13 percent to a total of 10.1 million tons in 1970.

There has been a gradual trend toward increased concentration of U. S. farm production of fruits and vegetables in the major growing areas. This reflects both increased availability and lower costs of transportation as well as changes in comparative production costs. Large-scale growers, especially in California and Florida, have been able to take advantage of the fact that mechanization has become both technically and economically feasible for an increasing number of fruit and vegetable crops. California is by far the most important producing state; it accounts for 40 percent of vegetable and 45 percent of fruit production in the United States. Some 70 to 75 percent of total production concentrated in only five states (California, Florida, Texas, Arizona, and New York) for vegetables and just two states (California and Florida) for fruits.

Factors Influencing U. S. Supply. Sharply rising costs, combined with relatively moderate increases in farm prices, appear to have resulted in an intensified profit squeeze on U. S. fruit and vegetable growers during the 1960s. Unit prices of virtually all farm inputs rose steadily throughout the decade. Farm wages and real estate costs both increased at rates in excess of 5 percent per year, while machinery costs increased at a rate of about 3.5 percent per year. Among the major inputs, only fertilizer prices failed to rise during the period, reflecting the overcapacity situation that existed in the agricultural chemical industry. Fertilizer use, however, increased sharply as growers attempted to offset rising costs through increased productivity.

Despite greater utilization of nonlabor inputs and relatively heavy capital investment in mechanization equipment, the upward trend of fruit and vegetable farm productivity appears to have slowed down during the 1960s. Between 1960 and 1970, total output per unit of input increased by only half as much as in the preceding 10 years. In any event, gains in productivity were insufficient to offset rising prices of farm inputs, and overall cost per unit of output appears to have risen at a rate of at least 2 to 3 percent per year for the decade as a whole. A Department of Agriculture study[5] of the cost of producing six winter vegetable crops in Florida and Texas indicated that the f.o.b. costs per unit of output (including harvesting, packing, and selling costs) rose by 10 to 25 percent between the 1967–68 and 1970–71 growing seasons (Table 2–9).

Table 2–9. Costs of Producing and Marketing Selected Winter Produce: Florida and Texas

		Cost per unit (dollars)		Percent change
Area and commodity	Units	1967–68	1970–71	
South Florida				
Vine-ripe tomatoes	20-lb.box	2.13	2.39	+12
Mature green tomatoes	40-lb.box	2.61	3.26	+25
Cucumbers	Bushel	2.81	3.37	+20
Peppers	Bushel	2.64	3.12	+18
Eggplant	Bushel	1.95	2.38	+22
Strawberries	12-pt.flat	2.77	3.18	+15
Texas (Rio Grande Valley)				
Cantaloupe	88-lb.crate	4.83	5.33	+10

Source: U.S. Department of Agriculture, *Supplying U.S. Markets with Fresh Winter Produce,* Supplement to Agricultural Economic Report No. 154 (September 1971).

Prices received by farmers for fruits and vegetables increased at a slower rate than unit costs during the 1960s, thus apparently reducing farm profit margins and return on invested capital. At the same time, the total capital required to operate an efficient orchard or vegetable farm has also increased. One result of this situation has been to make fruit and vegetable farming increasingly less attractive as a land-use alternative as compared with both other farm crops and nonfarm uses, especially real estate development in the major growing areas such as California and Florida.

Government assistance programs directed toward fruit and vegetable growers are relatively limited in scope. Direct price supports and subsidy payments are not available to fruit and vegetable producers. Although a large number of federal and state marketing orders pertaining to fruits and vegetables have been adopted at various times, few have been designed primarily to control supply or maintain farm prices. Effective control of supply is difficult to achieve both because of the large number of growers involved in individual crops and because of the perishability of most fruit and vegetable crops. The Florida tomato marketing order, for example, that aimed at limiting Mexican imports through product size classifications, not only proved rather ineffective, but also aroused considerable opposition on the part of consumer groups.

Imports. Although they still represent a small portion of the total supply available to U. S. consumers, imports of fruits and vegetables have grown much more rapidly than domestic farm production during the past two decades. Between 1960 and 1970, for example, imported fruits (excluding bananas) tripled in volume and vegetables about doubled, compared with gains of about one-fourth and one-fifth respectively for domestic output. Bananas, the largest imported commodity, have only increased about evenly with population growth.

Foreign producers are attracted by the large size of the U. S. market for fruits and vegetables relative to the level of production abroad and by strong demand for some commodities. This is particularly true for winter produce, such as tomatoes, cucumbers, melons, peppers, and strawberries, where natural climatic advantages have permitted foreign growers to fill seasonal gaps in the U. S. market while at the same time enjoying lower risks of crop damage due to cold weather.

Lower farm production costs have enabled Mexico and other developing nations to compete effectively in the U. S. market despite higher costs of transportation and distribution. This is particularly true of labor-intensive crops where harvesting and packing constitute a relatively large portion of total farm costs. Production costs per hectare of vine-ripe tomatoes in Mexico, for example, are about one-third of those in Florida. Furthermore, the gap has tended to widen as Mexican growers have become more efficient and yields per hectare, at least for the better growers, have begun to approach those in the United States.

Foreign growers in developing countries have also benefited from government programs to promote exports of nontraditional crops such as fruits and vegetables. The vast vegetable-growing areas of northwest Mexico, for example, were developed as the result of long-term government programs to provide irrigation and highway facilities.

Despite the impressive growth of imported fruits and vegetables, they accounted for only 6 to 7 percent of total U. S. supplies in 1970 compared with about 5 percent a decade earlier. All of the increase was accounted for by commodities other than bananas, which declined from about 60 percent of total imports in 1960 to only 40 percent in 1970. Individual commodities have achieved significantly higher penetration of the U. S. market, especially during the seasons in which they compete (see Appendix A). Tomatoes, eggplants, and cucumbers accounted for over 50 percent of winter and early-spring supplies during the 1970–71 growing season, while peppers represented 40 percent of 1970–71 season supplies.

In the fresh market, Mexico has become by far the dominant supplier. Fresh tomatoes are the leading export crop, accounting for about one-half the total Mexican shipments, followed by strawberries (both fresh and frozen), cantaloupes, cucumbers, and peppers, which together account for an additional 35 to 40 percent of Mexican shipments. In addition, however, Mexico accounts for virtually the entire imported supply of more than 30 individual commodities of lower volume.

Imports of processed fruits and vegetables have not developed as broadly as fresh commodities, but certain specific products have become significant factors in the U. S. market. Taiwan is a major supplier of canned mandarin oranges, pineapples, and mushrooms, all of which have been increasing relatively rapidly. Processed tomato products, although growing less rapidly, have also achieved significant market penetration, with Portugal, Spain, and Italy the leading suppliers. The Dominican Republic is the principal supplier of canned peas.

Other important processed imports include noncitrus juices from Canada, the Philippines, and Europe, concentrated orange juice from Brazil, and dried fruits from Australia and the Middle East.

Except for bananas and plantains, Central America has not yet become a major supplier of fruits and vegetables to the U. S. market. It is interesting to note, however, that for certain commodities, notably cucumbers, melons, okra, and pineapples, significant quantities have begun to be exported in recent years. In total, more than 20 individual fruit and vegetable commodities from Central America were reported in the U. S. import statistics for 1971 and 1972, compared with fewer than 10 in 1964 (Table 2–10).

Trends in Prices

Retail Prices. Retail prices of fresh fruits and vegetables increased more rapidly during the 1960s than any other major category of food consumed at home, reflecting both rising costs throughout the system and some apparent strengthening of consumer demand. Consumer prices of processed fruits and

Table 2–10. U.S. Imports of Fruits and Vegetables[a] from Central America $(10^3$ lb.).

Commodity	1971–72	1970–71	1963–64
	Fresh		
Pineapples	18,543	13,067	3
Cucumbers	13,826	12,869	1,851
Melons	2,559	3,219	412
Okra	991	703	44
Cassava	391	315	487
Limes	266	205	2
Tomatoes	22	113	–
Peppers	772	104	–
Chayotes	463	68	–
Onions	–	56	3
Other[b]	476	71	26
Total	38,309	30,790	2,828
	Frozen		
Okra	1,625	842	–
Cassava	1,201	412	–
Corn	2	103	–
Mamey apples	–	51	–
Total	2.828	1,408	–

Source: U.S. Department of Agriculture, *Foreign Agricultural Trade of the U.S.* (May 1965, September 1971, and September 1972).
a. Excluding bananas and plantains.
b. Including breadfruit, carrots, dasheens, mangoes, mangosteens, papaya, squash, and yams.

vegetables increased about evenly with overall food prices. Prices also rose at the wholesale and farm levels, but at slower rates than consumer prices.

Retail prices of fresh fruits and vegetables rose at a compound rate of 3.3 percent per year between 1960 and 1972, compared with 2.2 percent per year for all food consumed at home. Salad vegetables, peppers, melons, grapes, and grapefruit all rose sharply throughout the period at rates of 3.5 percent per year or more (Table 2–11). Of the fresh items whose prices are reported regularly by the Bureau of Labor Statistics, only bananas, oranges, and strawberries failed to keep pace with the rise in overall food prices. Bananas, in fact, showed a small absolute decline during the 10-year period.

Consumer prices of processed fruits and vegetables rose more slowly than those of fresh produce during the 1960s, reflecting continued product innovation by food processors and strong competition at the retail level between national brands and private labels. For processed fruits and vegetables as a whole, retail prices increased at a rate of 2.1 percent per year, or about the same as all food prices. Prices of processed vegetables increased at a faster rate than the average, whereas those of most canned fruits and juices, as well as frozen citrus concentrate, increased at a slower rate (Table 2–12).

Wholesale and Farm Prices. Wholesale prices of fruits and vegetables, as reported by the Bureau of Labor Statistics, increased less than retail prices from 1960 to 1970. Average prices of fresh commodities rose only 1.1 percent per year compared with 3.3 percent at retail, while processed products increased 1.5 percent per year at wholesale and 2.1 percent per year at retail. The percentage of total fruit and vegetable volume moving through the wholesale terminal markets declined from 74 percent in 1958 to about 65 percent in 1973.[6] Competition for the remaining volume intensified. Furthermore, some

Table 2–11.   Retail Price Index[a] for Selected U.S. Fresh Fruits and Vegetables.

| Commodity | Year | | | Change, 1960–1972, as percentage of 1960 |
	1960	1970	1972	
Grapes	70.4	126.3	163.0	131.5
Watermelon	83.2	124.1	130.0	56.2
Peppers	88.1[b]	140.6	136.9	55.4[c]
Grapefruit	85.4	126.3	144.8	69.6
Lettuce	76.7	108.4	124.7	62.6
Tomatoes	89.4	119.2	132.7	48.4
Onions	66.1	116.9	128.8	94.9
Cucumbers	98.4[b]	116.3	122.1	24.1[c]

Source: U.S. Department of Labor, Bureau of Labor Statistics, *Consumer Price Index.*
a.   1967 = 100.
b.   For 1964.
c.   As a percentage of 1964.

Table 2–12. Retail Price Index[a] for Selected U.S. Processed Fruits and Vegetables.

Commodity	Year			Change, 1960–1972, as percentage of 1960
	1960	*1970*	*1972*	
	Processed vegetables			
Dried beans	84.9	106.3	137.9	62.4
Canned tomatoes	81.0	109.0	116.6	44.0
Canned green peas	81.3	101.8	107.7	32.5
Canned beets	92.1[b]	109.3	122.0	32.5[c]
Frozen broccoli	98.2[b]	113.8	118.5	20.7[c]
	Processed fruits			
Canned fruit cocktail	101.2	108.3	121.7	20.3
Canned pears	106.2[b]	109.1	118.3	11.4[c]
Canned pineapple-grapefruit juice drink	105.3[b]	110.7	115.3	9.5[c]
Frozen concentrate				
Lemonade	108.3	107.8	117.4	8.4
Orange juice	126.9	122.4	136.0	7.2

Source: U.S. Department of Labor, Bureau of Labor Statistics, *Consumer Price Index.*
a. 1967 = 100.
b. For 1964.
c. As a percentage of 1964.

reported wholesale prices may no longer be truly representative of average prices for the total volume of certain fruit and vegetable crops.

Prices received by fruit and vegetable growers increased less than retail prices during the 1960s (Table 2–13). Grower prices for oranges and other citrus fruits actually declined between 1960 and 1970, while noncitrus fruits brought only slightly higher returns. Average fruit prices in the 1960s showed no major net change, although there were sharp year-to-year fluctuations due to short-term supply conditions. In 1971 and 1972, however, price increases have occurred (see Table 2–13). Vegetable prices paid to farmers increased about 2 percent per year on the average.

Farm–Retail Spread. The net result of these conflicting price trends was to maintain the average grower share at about 25 percent of the retail fruit and vegetable dollar in both 1960 and 1970. The farm–retail spread was larger for fruits and vegetables than for any other major category included in the U. S. Department of Agriculture market basket, except bakery and cereal products (Table 2–14). Farm value accounts for about 30 percent of the retail value of fresh fruits and vegetables and less than 20 percent of the value of processed products. During the past decade, the farmers' share of fresh-vegetable retail

Table 2–13.   Indexes[a] of Retail Prices and Prices Received by U. S. Fruit and Vegetable Growers, 1960–1972.

Year	Retail prices	Prices received by growers
1960	88	91
1965	98	97
1966	100	103
1967	100	100
1968	108	117
1969	109	103
1970	113	102
1971	119	112
1972	125	118

Source: U.S. Department of Labor, Bureau of Labor Statistics, *Consumer Price Index,* and U.S. Department of Agriculture, Economic Research Service, *Prices Received and Paid by Farmers.*
a. 1967 = 100.

Table 2–14.   U.S. Market Basket of Farm Foods: Farm Value and Farm-Retail Spread *(percent of retail cost).*

Market basket	Retail cost	Farm value	Farm-retail spread
Market basket	100	40	60
Meats	100	58	42
Dairy products	100	48	52
Poultry	100	49	51
Eggs	100	57	43
Bakery and cereal products	100	17	83
Fresh fruits	100	30	70
Fresh vegetables	100	32	68
Processed fruits and vegetables	100	19	81
Fats and oils	100	28	72
Miscellaneous	100	15	85

Source: Market basket data in U.S. Department of Agriculture, *Marketing and Transportation Situation* (February 1973), p. 188.

prices increased slightly as the result of higher returns for tomatoes, lettuce, and other salad items, while there was a corresponding decline in the case of fruits as the result of lower farm values for fresh oranges.

Government Programs

Direct government involvement in fruit and vegetable production and marketing is minimal compared with major grain commodities or dairy products. Although participants in the fruit and vegetable system are affected by such general projects as school lunch programs and irrigation programs, and by water limitations, soil conservation, market news reporting, federal grading standards, food distribution, and Food and Drug Administration pesticide regulations, the two most immediate areas of government impact upon fruits and vegetables, especially their relation to present or potential future imports, are marketing orders and the structure of import regulations.

Marketing Orders. Marketing orders are devices under both federal and state laws that authorize producers and handlers jointly to regulate the marketing of a commodity in order to enhance the level and stability of grower returns. They attempt to achieve this objective through some combination of provisions manipulating supply, influencing demand, or regulating trade practices. The principal forms of regulation may be summarized as follows:

1. Establishment of minimum standards for grade, size, maturity, or other quality characteristics;
2. Limitation of the amount marketed either in total or by grade, size, or other characteristics during specified time periods;
3. Establishment of specifications for packaging and containers;
4. Specification and prohibition of unfair trading practices;
5. Provision for market research and product promotion.

Generally speaking, federal and state orders are similar in their provisions and their methods of operation. The two principal differences are: (1) processed fruits and vegetables are covered by orders of eight of the states, but are ineligible under federal legislation; and (2) nonbrand advertising on an industry basis is permissible under state orders, whereas the federal legislation permits advertising of only 14 commodities specified in recent amendments to the act. Some services, such as federal and state grading and inspection, are available to producers and handlers with or without a marketing order.

In 1973, over 90 marketing orders and agreements pertaining to fresh fruits and vegetables were in operation, divided about equally between federal orders under the Agricultural Marketing Agreement Act of 1937, as amended, and state orders under enabling legislation in ten producing states. Appendix B lists the commodities covered and the basic provisions contained in the federal and California orders. Marketing orders are most numerous for deciduous-tree fruits, potatoes, other vegetables, and citrus fruits. Provisions most frequently included in fruit and vegetable marketing orders relate to market research and development activities and to quality regulations. In addition, virtually all state orders make provision for nonbrand advertising and promotion, which is not permitted under federal orders.

Few of the marketing orders make provision for any form of supply control through regulation either of total quantities marketed, or of the rate of flow of marketings over some specified time period. Furthermore, with few exceptions such provisions have not generally been invoked, even where they are permissible under the terms of the order. Supply control is difficult at best where there are large numbers of producers spread over several geographic areas, highly perishable products, and reasonably close substitutes for individual fruit and vegetable commodities.

From the point of view of potential exporters of fresh produce to the U. S. market, the grade, size, and maturity regulations contained in most marketing orders are more significant than quantity controls. Such provisions vary widely from order to order and a brief summary is virtually impossible. Generally speaking, however, the regulations are of two types:

1. Minimum standards and grades whereby shipment of commodities falling below the minimum is prohibited;
2. Regulations whereby the entire supply of a certain grade or size is withheld during a particular time period.

Although it is widely felt that uniform quality standards are to the benefit of both producers and handlers and that the product of "lowest" quality should be withheld from the market during periods of oversupply, there are several basic difficulties in the practical application of such standards. In the first place, the standards—often established on the basis of physical characteristics of the product—have little or nothing to do with differences in demand. Furthermore, there is almost always a wide range of administrative discretion in applying quality-standard regulations whether or not a market order is in effect. Unless the quality regulations are supported by uniform inspection and certification requirements, there is substantial opportunity for buyers to discriminate among competing producers of an individual commodity. This is perceived to be a major problem by Central American exporters of fruits and vegetables.

Import Regulations. Appendix C reproduces the currently effective sections of the Tariff Schedule of the United States applying to imports of fruits and vegetables. This Appendix is included for two reasons: to familiarize readers with this type of document which is a basic part of export–import operations, and to facilitate further analyses readers may wish to make of the case studies included in this book.

Virtually all major fresh vegetable crops are subject to tariffs, generally stated as a fixed rate per pound or per hundredweight. For those crops where U. S. production is seasonal, there are corresponding seasonal variations in the import duty designed to protect the American grower. Such seasonal variations are currently in effect for lima beans, cauliflower, celery, cucumbers, eggplant, lettuce, peas, and tomatoes. In the case of potatoes, the duty also varies as between seed and table-stock potatoes and in accordance with the amounts imported.

The Agricultural Marketing Agreement Act of 1937 requires that imports of specific commodities must conform to the grade, size, quality, and maturity requirements applicable to domestic production covered by a marketing order. At present, there are 16 fruits and vegetables subject to this provision. In most cases the standards apply on a seasonal basis, including winter and early spring fresh produce. Inspection by a designated third party is necessary to enforce the quality standards.

The Agricultural Act of 1956 authorizes the United States to enter into agreements with exporting countries to limit shipments of a commodity when economic conditions justify such restrictions. The only important instance in which this authority has been exercised recently is the agreement to restrict Mexican exports of frozen strawberry products during 1972.

Another infrequently utilized restriction is the authority to impose countervailing duties to offset export subsidies granted by foreign governments. This was, however, recently applied to canned tomato products from Italy, France, and Greece.

Fruits and vegetables entering the United States in fresh form are also subject to the requirements of the Agricultural Quarantine Inspection, which is designed to prevent importation of potentially injurious plant pests. A list of admissible fruits and vegetables from each supplying cojntry is maintained and changed periodically as conditions relating to the risk of pest infestation change. In addition to commodities whose entry is prohibited, there are others that can enter only after undergoing treatment, such as fumigation, at the port of entry. Facilities for such treatment are located primarily in the Port of New York. Quarantine restrictions have been applied primarily to tropical fruits and vegetables that are not important U. S. farm crops.

Quarantine restrictions do not apply to processed products, but the Food, Drug, and Cosmetic Act requires that imports meet the same requirements for purity, wholesomeness, and labeling as domestic products.

THE STRUCTURE OF THE SYSTEM

In 1971, U. S. production of fruits and vegetables totaled about 62 million tons, with a farm-gate value of over $5 billion. This was supplemented by imports of 3.5 million tons valued at $700 million. Domestic consumption of all forms of fresh and processed fruits and vegetables totaled about 44 million tons with a retail value of $25 billion, and exports accounted for an additional 2.5 million tons valued at $500 million.[7]

A complex system has evolved for handling the marketing and distribution of this large volume of fresh and processed fruits and vegetables. Figure 2-1 shows, in simplified form, the principal participants in this system and the approximate percentages of the total value flowing through each of the major channels; it also provides estimates of the value added, the number of units, and the number of persons employed at each stage of the system from farmer to retailer.[8] Traditionally, this system has comprised a large number of

Figure 2–1. U.S. Fruit and Vegetable Market System, 1971.
(U. S. Department of Agriculture data; numbers are percentages.)

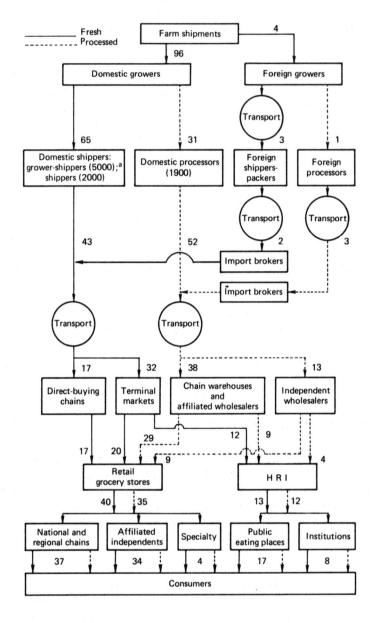

Figure 2–1. (cont.)

VALUE ADDED (U.S. $ BILLION)

FRESH		PROCESSED	
Labor ($0.8)	6%	Labor ($0.2)	2%
Other ($3.8)	23%	Other ($2.0)	17%
Total Farmgate ($3.8)	29%	Total Farmgate ($2.2)	19%
Shipper/packer ($1.8)	14%	Shipper/packer ($4.6)	39%
Transportation ($1.8)	13%	Transportation ($1.2)	10%
Wholesalers and Chain Warehouses ($1.7)	13%	Wholesalers and Chain Warehouses ($1.5)	13%
Retail ($4.1)	31%	Retail ($2.3)	19%
TOTAL ($13.2)	100%	TOTAL ($11.8)	100%

TOTAL VALUE ($25.0)

EMPLOYMENT CONTRIBUTIONS

MAN YEARS		%	TOTAL
80,000 (at supplier level)			
350,000 (at grower level)		51%	630,000
Shipper/ Packer 50,000	Processor 160,000	17%	210,000
Transport 10,000	Transport 6,000	1%	16,000
Wholesaler/ Chain Ware- houses 40,000	Wholesaler/ Brokers 15,000	5%	55,000
Retail 240,000	Retail 75,000	26%	315,000
		100%	1,226,000

individual participants, each performing quite specialized functions, often with only limited knowledge of the activities of the other participants.

The trends in consumption and supply discussed in the preceding section have caused significant changes in the structure of the fruit and vegetable commodity system. These changes may be summarized as follows:

1. A movement toward tighter coordination within the system primarily through common ownership or contracting, especially in processed products;
2. A decrease in the number and an increase in the average size of individual participants at all stages of the system;
3. Greater reliance on negotiated or administered prices rather than market-determined prices, especially for processed products and some large-volume fresh commodities;
4. Increased capital requirements for both individual farms and the farming sector as a whole;
5. Improved over-the-road transportation and storage facilities throughout the system;
6. Increased importance of nonprice competition in both fresh and processed products;
7. The development of new channels of market information.

Retail Distribution. The movement toward tighter coordination began in the 1930s with the entry of national retail chain stores into direct procurement and distribution of fresh produce. During the postwar period this trend has spread to regional and local chains and to affiliated groups of independent retail stores. In 1971, about 70 percent of total retail sales of fruits and vegetables (including processed) was handled by partially integrated firms.

The most common form of retailer participation in fruit and vegetable wholesaling is the chain-owned and chain-operated distribution system. In 1971 major national and regional chains (11 or more stores), with about 35,000 individual retail outlets, operated 150 to 200 warehouses and perishable-commodity distribution centers. These retail chains acquired about one-half their volume direct from shipping-point markets and processors. In both cases, chain buyers increasingly specify the variety, grade, size, and pack of a commodity desired. This contrasts with the historical practice in fresh produce of purchasing a carload or truckload composed of a random mix of varieties, grades, and packs. As terminal-market participants become larger and more sophisticated, they will be better able to meet buyers' demands for quality and consistency.

Smaller regional or local chains, as well as groups of independent retailers (two to ten stores), have responded to the emergence of the partially integrated national chain by creating affiliated wholesaler groups and voluntary merchandising groups. Cooperative wholesalers are owned by the retailers they serve, whereas voluntaries are firms contracting to serve independent stores and chains, often operating under a common name. Sales of retailers associated with such groups have been increasing faster than those of the national chains and by 1971 were nearly equal in total value. Affiliated wholesalers, both cooperatives and voluntaries, operate procurement, warehousing, and distribution systems in much the same way as the partially integrated chains, despite differences in organizational structure.

The remaining 35 percent of retail sales of fruits and vegetables is divided about one-sixth to specialty grocery stores (both independent general groceries and specialized fruit and vegetable stands) and five-sixths to various types of institutional outlets. Although the relative importance of specialty-store sales has declined sharply over the years, there is some basis for believing that this trend may not continue in the future. Renewed consumer interest in fresh produce has created market opportunities for both new commodity varieties and premium-priced quality products.

The food-service sector of the institutional market is growing much more rapidly than retail grocery store sales of fruits and vegetables. Total sales of food-service establishments during the 1960s increased at an annual rate of about 8 percent. In 1969, food-service outlets accounted for 7 percent of total fruit consumption, 20 percent of potatoes, and 11 percent of other vegetables. The food-service industry utilizes processed products to a much greater extent than fresh fruits and vegetables. Frozen potatoes—of which food-service establishments used 40 percent of the total output in 1969—are by far the single most important commodity, followed by processed tomatoes, pickles, and fruit juices; cabbage, lettuce, and onions are the chief fresh products.

The larger food-service organizations are following the pattern established by food retailers and integrating backward into fruit and vegetable wholesaling by means of their own warehouse and distribution systems. This trend appears likely to continue as food-service chains find it economical to make greater use of centralized control techniques, such as menu planning.

One significant result of the backward integration by fruit and vegetable retailers has been the gradual shift of operations formerly performed at the retail-store level to earlier stages of the distribution system. Functions such as cutting, trimming, and packing fresh produce, that are highly labor-intensive, can be performed more cheaply in chain warehouses, packing sheds at the shipping-point markets, or even, in some cases, in the field. Although at present, products prepackaged at the shipping point represent only about 10 percent of total fresh-produce volume, this fraction appears likely to grow substantially as the result of both potential labor savings and the market opportunities it offers to growers and shippers to establish a degree of product differentiation.

Wholesale Terminal Markets. The most immediate impact of the direct-buying retailer was a decline in relative importance of fresh-produce wholesale terminal markets. In 1971, however, terminal markets operated in most of the 41 major metropolitan areas, and in some locations, such as Boston, new facilities have been constructed in recent years. The structure and operating methods of terminal markets have changed significantly.

Produce terminal markets comprise a wide variety of relatively small independent firms. These include carlot receivers, merchant wholesalers, jobbers, purveyors, commission merchants, repackers, and auctioneers. They have traditionally played key roles in receiving, storing, break-bulk handling, and forward distribution of fresh fruits and vegetables. In addition, partly because of their fractionated nature, they have also served as the primary pricing mechanism and source of market information. Wholesalers still handle some two-third of all produce volume, and in certain cities they are increasing their share of the market and are adapting their services to the new market structure that is emerging. Because of their high turnover, their profits on tangible net worth rank them among the top three classes of wholesalers in the United States.[9]

The principal response to competitive pressures by wholesale terminal markets has been to consolidate functions formerly performed separately by independent participants. Full-line service wholesalers who combine receiving, wholesaling, and jobbing have become significant factors in all wholesale terminal markets. These service wholesalers are best equipped to serve both the growing institutional market and the remaining specialized independent retail outlets. They are also better able to meet the needs of retail chains for small-volume specialty commodities and for marginal purchases of large-volume products.

In addition to consolidation, independent terminal-market wholesalers have broadened their product lines in response to the changing needs of institutions and specialty stores by adding processed fruits and vegetables, specialty products, and imports. The more aggressive firms have become leaders in the search for new offshore sources of supply. As a result of these continuing efforts, it seems likely that produce terminal-market firms will continue to play an important, although a different and reduced, role in the fruit and vegetable commodity system of the future.

Shipping-Point Markets. Shipping-point markets have assumed greater relative importance in the fresh-produce distribution system, reflecting both the increase in direct buying by retailers and the concentration of farm production in major growing areas.

Two basic types of firms predominate in shipping-point markets— handlers and brokers. Although the numbers of both types have declined, this has been offset by an increase in the average size of the individual firm. The total annual volume of produce moving through shipping-point markets remained nearly constant between 1960 and 1970. Brokers account for about 30 percent and handlers for about 70 percent of this volume.

Handlers actually take title to the produce and normally assemble, pack, and sell through their own packing houses and sales organizations. They can be organized either as private commercial firms or as marketing cooperatives owned by grower groups. This segment of the market has been characterized by the development of integrated grower-shippers. Large growers with sufficient volume to justify investment in packing and sales facilities ship for both themselves and other growers. At the same time, shippers and packers have begun growing in order to have a greater degree of control over supply. Grower-shippers now account for about 75 percent of the total number of handlers in all fresh-produce shipping-point markets.

Brokers do not take title to the product, but they arrange for shipment, extend credit, and provide market information. Their standard commission of 10 percent to 12 percent may be paid by either buyer or seller. Brokers are able to offer a highly divisible range of marketing services which provides more flexibility than the typical in-house sales organization. They are often used by shippers and grower-shippers to supplement their own sales activities. Brokers have tended to become relatively more important in the larger shipping-point markets located in the principal farm production areas.

Although until recently no individual shipping-point firm has accounted for even as much as 1 percent of the total volume of a single crop, there appears to be a tendency toward increased concentration in the major shipping-point markets. The entry of large nonfarm corporations into the growing and shipping of fruits and vegetables has been one factor of this trend. United Brands, for example, now controls an estimated 5 to 10 percent of total lettuce production. Even without this development, however, shipping-point market structures have been characterized by the existence of a few dominant firms and a much larger number of smaller ones. The large firms have tended to be more stable, with a lower rate of turnover.

Between 1948 and 1971, sales to direct-buying retailers increased from about 10 to nearly 30 percent of total shipping-point sales, while sales to terminal-market wholesalers declined from about 80 to 60 percent of the total. This shift was accompanied by increased demands for quality by retailers and more emphasis on product differentiation. Shippers have begun to compete for customers on the basis of service and quality as well as price. Some of the larger shipping-point firms have entered into stable long-term relations with large buyers.

It appears probable that shipping-point markets will continue to grow in importance. Direct buying by retailers and by institutional outlets appears likely to expand further, while, at the same time, requirements for improved quality and greater reliability of supply will become more demanding. Firms will compete for supplies on the basis of services offered as well as price.

Processing. With consumption of processed fruits and vegetables increasing faster than that of fresh, there has been a corresponding increase in the volume and value of shipments of fruit and vegetable processors. Output of frozen products, that was virtually nonexistent at the end of World War II, has grown much more rapidly than that of canned products. During the 1960s, production of frozen fruits and vegetables increased at the rate of about 6 percent per year, more than double the rate of increase in canned goods. Despite this impressive growth, frozen output still accounts for only about 25 percent of total processed fruit and vegetable production.

Production of processed vegetables is growing more slowly than that of fruits for both canned and frozen products. Canned vegetable output has been about stable since the early 1960s, whereas the rate of growth of frozen vegetables slowed perceptibly during the decade. Both canned and frozen fruit production, on the other hand, has continued to increase steadily. The demand for frozen citrus juices continued to expand, but production showed sharp year-to-year fluctuations as the result of changes in supply. Output of canned vegetable juices has shown little change throughout the entire postwar period.

As the market for processed fruits and vegetables has matured, there has been a marked trend toward greater concentration among both canners and freezers. It began much earlier in the canning segment of the business, where the number of plants declined continuously from over 1750 in 1954 to under 1100 in 1970 (Table 2–15). During this same period, average plant size increased by more than 100 percent, and total capacity increased moderately. The number of frozen-food processing plants, on the other hand, more than doubled between 1954 and 1963, but has declined somewhat since then. Average volume of shipments per plant, that showed little change during the period when the number of plants was expanding rapidly, has increased sharply since 1963.

There are significant economies of large-scale production in canning and freezing. This fact reflects both the high level of capital costs for plant and equipment and the importance of fixed operating costs, particularly for advertising, promotion, and product development. There is evidence to suggest that the increase in average plant size has been the result of expanding output by larger plants, combined with stable or declining output on the part of smaller plants. The decline in the number of canning plants has occurred primarily among the

Table 2–15. Number of Establishments in U.S. Fruit and Vegetable Processing, 1954–1970.

Year	Canning	Freezing
1954	1758	266
1958	1607	426
1963	1430	650
1967	1223	607
1968	1159	567
1969	1120	581
1970	1079	573

Source: U.S. Department of Commerce, Bureau of the Census, *Census of Manufactures* and *Annual Survey of Manufactures.*

smaller units. Both the 20 largest canning establishments (2 percent of the total number) and the 20 largest freezers (3 percent of the plants) account for about 50 percent of total production. The economies of scale inherent in fruit and vegetable processing are also evident in the tendency of larger plants to become multiproduct processors in order to utilize capacity and to extend seasonal operations. The principal constraint on increases in plant size has been the need to locate fruit and vegetable processing operations relatively close to their sources of supply because of perishability of raw products and the high cost of transport. This factor will decline in importance if the trend toward geographic concentration of the principal production areas continues into the future.

As in the case of shipping-point markets, direct sales of fruit and vegetable processors, both to retailers and to institutional outlets, have increased in relative importance. The survey made for the National Commission on Food Marketing[10] showed that in 1964 nearly half the total sales by canners, and about 30 percent of the sales by freezers, were to national, regional, and local chains. The lower percentage for freezers was due primarily to the fact that more than one-fourth of the output of primary processors was sold to other processing plants for use in specialty products such as frozen complete meals, soups, and the like. Only 20 to 25 percent of total output was sold to wholesalers, including voluntaries formed to serve groups of retail stores. The balance was divided among cooperative buying groups, institutions, and other outlets (Table 2–16). Between 60 and 70 percent of processor sales were made through brokers whose commissions typically ranged from 3 to 5 percent depending on the specific services performed.

Trade relations between major food processors and large buyers have

Table 2–16. Distribution *(percent)* **of Types of Buyers of U.S. Processed Fruits and Vegetables, 1964.**

	Process	
Buyer	*Canning*	*Freezing*
Retail chains		
National retail chains	24.8	20.0
Regional retail chains	11.9	5.7
Local retail chains	9.3	4.1
Independent retailers	3.0	0
Cooperatives	9.8	6.1
Wholesalers	25.5	20.8
Institutions	4.5	4.9
Government	4.1	4.9
Food processors	4.7	28.1
Other	2.4	5.4
Total	100.0	100.0

Source: National Commission on Food Marketing, *Organization and Competition in the Fruit and Vegetable Industry* (Technical Study No. 4, 1966), pp. 193, 231.

become quite standardized over time. In the typical case, a contract specifying the annual amount to be supplied is agreed to at the beginning of a pack year and is drawn against during the year in response to buyers' requirements. Prices normally are based on the market at the time of shipment. As a result, the price structure tends to be relatively uniform at any given time, although the level fluctuates in response to changes in inventory holdings and in the rate of product flow. Under arrangements of this type, the processor usually assumes the inventory carrying costs and bears most of the risk of fluctuations in supply and demand. At the beginning of a new pack year, stocks carried over from the previous year are normally utilized before shipments on the current contract are begun.

The importance of private labels has tended to increase relative to national brands for both canned and frozen products. It is estimated that about 50 percent of processor sales in 1970 were under buyer labels, compared with 43 to 44 percent in 1964. Even the major national-brand canning firms have added private-label volume in order to utilize capacity and to make incremental contributions to their high fixed overhead costs. National-brand processors have, however, been able to maintain a 5 to 10 percent price differential in favor of their own labels.

Fruit and vegetable processors exert a greater degree of control in their relation with growers than with large direct-buying organizations. The National Commission on Food Marketing indicated that in 1964, 70 to 75 percent of raw-material supplies were procured under oral and written contracts with growers. The balance was divided between open-market purchases and production from processor-owned or processor-controlled acreage (Table 2–17). Contract purchasing has proved to be an effective device for assuring processors an adequate supply that meets given quality standards without their having to incur the capital costs and higher risks of investment in farm production. As a

Table 2–17. Distribution *(percent)* of Raw Product Sources of Processed U.S. Fruits and Vegetables, 1964.

	Process	
Source	*Canning*	*Freezing*
Owned or rented land	8	9
Written contract	67	69
Oral contract	3	6
Noncontract from farmers	15	12
Grower cooperatives	3	1
Brokers	3	1
Other	1	2
Total	100	100

Source: National Commission on Food Marketing, *Organization and Competition in the Fruit and Vegetable Industry* (Technical Study No. 4, 1966), pp. 185, 225.

result, backward integration into growing by processors has been relatively limited except for certain specific commodities, such as California peaches and Florida citrus.

Appendix D is a typical contract used by a major processor, in this case for the procurement of peas for freezing. This contract specifies the variety to be planted, acreage, quality characteristics, and the timing of both planting and delivery. In return, the processor guarantees the price to be paid to the grower. The National Commission on Food Marketing found this to be the case in about 90 percent of processor-grower contracts. In the typical contract, the processor provides some of the principal farm inputs, such as harvesting machinery. An alternative in common use is for the processor to advance credit to the grower and for the latter to purchase his inputs directly.

A survey by the Farmer Cooperative Service of the U. S. Department of Agriculture[11] indicated that processors organized as cooperatives accounted for 21 percent of the total U. S. fruit and vegetable pack in 1969. Cooperatives are relatively more important in fruits than in vegetables and in the West than in the East. About 40 percent of cooperative sales were to retail chains, 25 percent to wholesalers, and the balance to institutions and others.

Growing. The number of fruit and vegetable growers continued to decline dramatically during the 1960s. The reduction applied to all major crops and growing areas. The number of farmers reporting vegetables harvested for sale in the five leading producing states fell by about one-half, and the number reporting land in fruit orchards in the two primary growing states was down by about one-third during the decade (Table 2–18).

Table 2–18. Number of Farmers Reporting Vegetables Harvested for Sale, and Land in Orchards, Selected States.

	Number		
State	*1959*	*1969*	*Percentage change*
	Reporting vegetables harvested		
California	5,856	3,975	−32
Florida	4,727	2,591	−45
Texas	11,773	5,041	−57
New York	8,010	4,017	−50
Arizona	418	341	−18
Total	30,784	15,965	−48
	Reporting land in orchards		
California	50,372	36,321	−28
Florida	22,015	13,187	−40
Total	72,387	49,508	−32

Source: U.S. Department of Commerce, *1969 Census of Agriculture.*

The continued disappearance of fruit and vegetable farms during the 1960s was concentrated among smaller growers with inadequate financial resources to meet the capital costs of mechanization or to absorb year-to-year fluctuations in crop receipts. Practically all of the decline occurred among farms with cash receipts of less than $10,000 per year. Smaller growers are at a relative disadvantage in bargaining for sale of their crops with both processors and direct buyers of fresh produce. The exodus from fruit and vegetable farming was accentuated by sharp increases in the direct and indirect costs of maintaining land in agricultural uses. In both California and Florida, rising property taxes plus increased land values for development and other nonfarm purposes have made it attractive for marginal growers to leave the business. Florida citrus groves, for example, have been sold to developers for as much as $6000 per acre, whereas gross returns above out-of-pocket operating costs averaged only some $300 per acre per year during the past decade.

The decline in the number of fruit and vegetable farms has been accompanied by an increase in the average size of a farm, the net result being that in the leading producing states, the total acreage of vegetable crops harvested was reduced only moderately during the 1960s, and acreage in fruit orchards actually increased (Table 2–19). Changes in average farm size varied widely among individual crops, with the greatest increases occurring where mechanization has proved economically and technically feasible, as, for example, in the case of tomatoes for processing. Average farm size has tended to show little change for labor-intensive crops, such as fresh tomatoes, cucumbers, eggplant, peppers, squash, and melons. Furthermore, farms devoted to growing

Table 2–19. Acreage of Vegetables Harvested for Sale, and Land in Orchards, Selected States.

State	Acreage (10³ acres)		Percentage change
	1959	1969	
	Reporting vegetables harvested		
California	657.3	675.9	+3
Florida	273.7	273.2	−0.2
Texas	325.9	236.1	−28
Arizona	78.2	88.0	+13
New York	174.6	148.1	−15
Total	1,509.7	1,421.3	− 6
	Reporting land in orchards		
California	1,434.8	1,587.7	+11
Florida	724.1	973.5	+34
Total	2.158.9	2,561.2	+19

Source: U.S. Department of Commerce, *1969 Census of Agriculture.*

these crops tend to be smaller in absolute size, although there is considerable variation among individual farms.

The typical vegetable grower is faced with relatively few alternatives in the sale of his crop, despite the increase in average farm size and concentration of production. Both the timing and the size of his harvest are determined in large part by climatic factors outside his control, while the perishability of his product makes it necessary in most cases to harvest, pack, and sell within a very brief time span. Furthermore, the individual grower has limited flexibility between the processed and fresh markets for his crop. This reflects both the prevalence of contract growing for the processed market and differences in varieties and agricultural practices between the two sectors. Tomatoes grown for processing, for example, have a lower sugar content than tomatoes grown for the fresh market, different taste characteristics, and tougher skins to permit mechanical harvesting.

Grower cooperatives have become the dominant method of marketing certain fruit crops, such as citrus, apples, cranberries, Concord grapes, and cherries. It is estimated that cooperatives handle one-fourth to one-third of the total volume of fresh produce, but only a small fraction of the processed crop.

Except for grower-shipper consolidation in shipping-point markets, there has been relatively little backward integration into fruit and vegetable farming by other participants in the commodity system. The larger canning and freezing companies have traditionally produced a portion of their own raw-material supplies, but this probably represents less than 20 percent of total requirements on a national average basis. In a few cases, such as the acquisition of Pompano Beach Farms by First National Stores, national retail chains have become directly involved in fruit and vegetable production.

Perhaps the most significant recent development in the farming segment of the fruit and vegetable commodity system was the entrance of several large nonfarm corporations during the 1960s. In contrast to processors concerned with their raw-material supply, companies such as United Brands, Purex, and Tenneco have ventured into farming as a potentially profitable diversification strategy in its own right. They have been attracted by potential economies of scale to be achieved through extensive mechanization, by the opportunity to establish differentiated products through consumer advertising, labeling, and quality control, and by the possibility of reducing marketing costs through direct distribution. For some crops, such as iceberg lettuce, individual corporations account for as much as 5 to 10 percent of total production. In total, however, all incorporated farms with more than ten shareholders represent less than 3 percent of farm receipts.

The evidence to date suggests that these large companies are finding it difficult to achieve their objectives in agriculture. Economies of scale in farm operations do not appear to increase in proportion to farm size once a certain efficient size has been achieved. That size tends to be relatively small for labor-intensive fruit and vegetable crops. Furthermore, the size and public nature of the corporate farmers has resulted in some significant diseconomies. These have included the problems of efficient farm management within the framework of corporate planning and control systems, vulnerability to union organizing activities among field and packing-house workers, and susceptibility to retaliatory actions by independent middlemen striving to maintain their role in the commodity system.

Meaningful product differentiation has proved especially difficult, not only because of inability to control the ultimate quality of perishable products, but also because even the largest corporate farming entity accounts for only a small share of the national production of any individual commodity.

Both the Justice Department and the Federal Trade Commission are investigating the activities of large corporate farming organizations for possible violations of the antitrust statutes. A recent ruling by the administrative law judge of the FTC upheld a complaint that the entry of United Brands into lettuce production was in restraint of trade under Section 7 of the Clayton Act. If upheld by the full Commission and the courts, the ruling would require United Brands to divest itself of its growing operations.

Despite these difficulties, however, it seems probable that large, nonfarm corporations will play an expanding role in the fruit and vegetable commodity system of the future. Some of these (such as Purex) have decided to withdraw from the business, but others (like Tenneco) are shifting their emphasis from growing to distribution and marketing, where capital requirements are significantly less and the inefficiencies of the present system seem to offer significant profit opportunities.

Credit requirements for U. S. fruit and vegetable farmers have increased sharply, reflecting both inflationary rises in the cost of farm inputs and the increasingly capital-intensive nature of farm operations. Interest costs for fixed and working capital used in growing Florida vegetable crops were higher during the 1970–71 season than the average for 1966 to 1970 for every one of the 27 crops reported in the annual survey of costs by the University of Florida. Of the $60 billion in new capital estimated to be required by American agriculture between now and 1980, fruits and vegetables may account for as much as $6 billion to $10 billion.

Review of Coordinating Mechanisms. Historically, the fruit and vegetable commodity system has served the purpose of physically moving substantial volumes of farm produce through the various stages of processing and distribution to ultimate consumers. In accomplishing this, however, the system has been characterized by only loose coordination among its component parts. This is almost inevitable because of the perishable nature of crops, which must be harvested and marketed with a minimum of delay. This requirement led to a system composed of many small units at all stages, each acting independently on the basis of localized market information. The net result, however, has been a history of substantial year-to-year fluctuations in both supplies and prices for individual commodities, especially at the farm level. Changes in consumer tastes and requirements have at best induced only sluggish responses on the supply side, particularly in the case of fresh produce.

The coordinating mechanisms that have evolved to cope with this situation are primarily private rather than public. The two most important forms of private coordination in the fruit and vegetable industry are vertical integration through common ownership and contracting.

The trend toward vertical integration developed first among the large retail chains which entered into warehousing of fresh produce. Today, all national and virtually all regional chains operate their own warehouse and distribution systems and procure the bulk of their supplies directly from shipping-point markets. In order to compete, smaller chains and independent retail stores have formed voluntary and cooperative groups that operate in much the same manner as the national chains. These groups grew very rapidly during the 1960s, and now account for about the same percentage (45–50 percent) of total grocery store sales as the national chains.

TOPCO, which was organized in 1948 as a legal cooperative, is a good example of a successful affiliated wholesale group. The 32 members of this cooperative are primarily regional chains, controlling several thousand individual outlets. TOPCO procures both general-line groceries and fruits and vegetables on members' orders. There is no brokerage fee, but TOPCO is paid a flat service charge based on the retail sales volume of each individual store. There is some evidence that the members of TOPCO are increasing their requirements for high-quality, cost-competitive fresh produce as a means of competing with the national chains. TOPCO has begun actively to search for foreign sources to supplement or replace domestically grown supplies.

Although backward integration by retailers has become a dominant factor in fresh-produce wholesale terminal markets, retailers have not integrated back to the shipping-point or grower level to the same extent. Of the retailers responding to a special survey made for this study, only one fifth of the respondents indicated that they obtained fruit and vegetable supplies from company-owned or company-operated farms.

Integration in shipping-point markets has primarily taken the form of grower-shipper consolidation, organized as either private companies or cooperatives. Fresh-produce marketing cooperatives have become important for apples, pears, oranges, cherries, celery, and potatoes. They are more important in fruits than in vegetables, and on the Pacific Coast more important than in other areas of the country. These organizations provide a variety of services to grower members, ranging from assembling and packing to full-line marketing operations and, in some cases, to production services, such as the purchase of farm inputs. Often the marketing organization is a federation of independent cooperatives, such as the Florida Citrus Mutual. Grower members are usually paid for their crops under pooling arrangements in which they receive average prices for specified grades. A major problem faced by marketing cooperatives has been the difficulty of obtaining participation by all, or at least a substantial majority, of the growers of a specific crop.

Backward integration into farm production has also been limited in the case of processed fruits and vegetables. The high capital costs of large-scale farming combined with the uncertainties arising from its agronomic nature have served to discourage extensive investment by publicly held companies. As indicated in the previous section, however, a number of large nonfarm corporations have become direct participants in fruit and vegetable production during the last several years.

Processor cooperatives, which originally were of primary importance for dried fruits, have become significant producers of canned and frozen juices and canned deciduous fruits. Like the marketing cooperatives for fresh produce, they are more important in the West than nationally. Cooperatives accounted for one-fifth of the national pack of canned and frozen products in 1969. California Canners and Growers, Inc. is the largest, with over 1100 members and total sales well in excess of $100 million.

Fruit and vegetable processors have utilized contracts with growers rather than direct ownership as the primary method of assuring adequate quantity and quality of raw materials. As noted previously, over 70 percent of all fruits and vegetables for both canning and freezing are procured in this manner. There has been a steady trend in processor-grower contracts toward increased control by the processor over farm practices, varieties utilized, and farm inputs. Growers, in turn, have increasingly been assured of a guaranteed minimum price for their crops.

Contracting is the dominant method of supply procurement for produce to be processed, but has been utilized to only a limited extent for fresh produce. Virtually none of the retail chains interviewed in the course of this study indicated that they had either written or oral agreements with growers. Chain buyers are still measured by their ability to obtain produce of adequate quality at or below current spot market prices. As fresh-produce quality becomes of greater importance to chain buyers, however, there may be increased utilization of grower contracts in order to obtain more consistent quality over a full season.

Although cooperative bargaining associations represent only a very small portion of total fruit and vegetable production, there is some evidence that they are beginning to assume greater importance as the number of farm producers continues to decline. Such associations have been handicapped in their ability to negotiate specific terms on behalf of growers because they have no effective means of production control. The Capper—Volstead Act, under which the associations are organized, made no provision for supply control. Furthermore, even with supply control, bargaining associations can be effective in helping their farmer members only when they are market-oriented and take account of the needs of the ultimate consumer.

Costs and availability of transportation have been of major importance in shaping the development of the fruit and vegetable commodity system. Losses in transit account for a substantial portion of the total fresh produce "shrink" between farm and consumer, while costs of transporting finished products dictate that processing plants be located close to sources of supply. Complete data on transport costs are not available because truck rates for fresh produce are not regulated, but it is estimated that the total bill in 1971 was nearly $3 billion, or about 12 percent of total retail value (see Figure 2–1).

Motor trucking has replaced railway carriage as the principal means of shipping both fresh and processed fruits and vegetables in the United States. With this shift has come greater flexibility and reliability in scheduling, which, in turn, have tended to reduce both costs and product losses. Transportation is a major problem facing new offshore suppliers and will be discussed in considerable detail below.

The perishability of fruits and vegetables is also a deterrent to the establishment of broadly based government stabilization programs similar to those in food grains, livestock, or dairy products. Although there are a large number of federal and state commissions and agencies that issue regulations and marketing orders applicable to fruits and vegetables, their efforts tend to be fragmented, uncoordinated, and often overlapping. With few exceptions, such as the federal order for Florida celery, marketing orders do not provide for direct control of either supply or entry into the growing of fruits and vegetables. California and Arizona lettuce growers voted down a proposed order that included such provisions in early 1972.

Government programs in the fruit and vegetable commodity system relate primarily to product promotion and research, the establishment of grades and standards, and the provision of information services. In most of these areas, however, similar services are provided in a variety of ways, both public and private.

Federal grades have been established for all fresh produce crops, but the extent to which they are actually utilized varies widely from market to market and commodity to commodity. In some cases, the federal grades are superseded by specifications established by individual buyers or buyer groups. In others, they are modified by the provisions of federal or state marketing orders or by the regulations of various state commissions and agencies. Furthermore, the availability and utilization of inspection services to enforce standard grades also vary widely in actual practice.

The Department of Agriculture estimated that in 1962 a total of some $33 million was spent to promote fruits and vegetables by groups other than private companies. Although this figure has undoubtedly increased substantially since 1962, it is unlikely to exceed 1 percent of the farm value of all fruits and vegetables, and is spread among a large number of separate organizations, including market order bargaining agencies, national trade groups, state commissions and agencies, voluntary producer groups, and cooperatives. Many of these diverse entities by necessity operate with very restricted budgets. A substantial part of the promotional activity is aimed at increasing the market share of individual growing areas or producer brands rather than at improving generic demand for a commodity as a whole.

The Marketing News Service, operated jointly by the U. S. Department of Agriculture and the various state departments of agriculture, has established a comprehensive system of market reporting in both shipping-point and terminal produce markets. The coverage of the information provided by this system may be eroded if common ownership and direct buying increase the relative importance of negotiated and internal transfer prices in fruit and vegetable commodity markets. Despite this, however, federal–state market news services will continue to play a critical role in establishing reference points for price-making throughout the system.

Direct regulation of the behavior of participants in the fruit and vegetable commodity system is also relatively limited in scope. The Perishable Commodities Act specifies at lengthy list of unfair trading practices, such as unwarranted rejection of growers' crops or failure to pay growers promptly, and prohibits their use by brokers and other middlemen. In order to obtain relief under the Act, however, growers or other aggrieved parties must initiate a complaint with the Fruit and Vegetable Division of the Department of Agriculture. This requirement has served to limit the effectiveness of the Act because of both the complexity of the process and fear among growers of retaliation in the sale of their crops.

Education and Training Services. Participants in the U. S. fruit and vegetable commodity system, like those in other agricultural products, have benefited from a long history of publicly supported research and training. Public policy, particularly at the grower level, has traditionally supported programs to improve the effectiveness of agricultural production and marketing.

The major impetus to formal agricultural education is provided by the land-grant college system, which was established under the Morrill Act of 1862. Under this Act, Congress granted over 11 million acres (4.5 million ha.) to the states and territories for the purpose of establishing colleges for the agricultural and mechanical arts. Later amendments provided funds to support the land-grant schools, which have continued to the present time. The original objective of providing formal training for prospective farmers and farm-related workers has been greatly expanded to include comprehensive curricula in all aspects of modern farm management and its relation to the economy as a whole.

There are also more than 50 state agricultural experiment stations in the United States, most of which are located at the land-grant colleges. Although they are state institutions, they are supported by both state and federal funds; the states provide about 75 percent of the total, which approaches $200 million per year. The experiment stations concentrate their efforts primarily in areas directly related to farm production and management. Individual states are concerned with crops and agronomic factors characteristic of their location. The scope of experiment-station research includes basic soil, water, and irrigation requirements, farm inputs, farming methods, equipment, nutrition, plant varieties, and end uses of farm products. The experiment stations have been instrumental in maintaining the long-term rise in fruit and vegetable productivity. The Universities of California, Texas, and Florida, and Michigan State University have been particularly concerned with fruits and vegetables.

At the national level, the Agricultural Research Service (ARS) of the U. S. Department of Agriculture also carries on research activities related to farm production, nutrition, and the utilization of farm products. There are about 20,000 employees of ARS at various locations throughout the United States. Their efforts have led to the development of such new producfs as frozen orange-juice concentrate and instant mashed potatoes.

The Cooperative Agricultural Extension Service is a mechanism for carrying farm training activities beyond formal educational institutions. It is a joint effort of federal, state, and county governments whose purpose is to improve farming methods through on-the-job training, demonstrations, published material, and so forth. A key role is played by local county agricultural extension agents who work closely with individual growers. In total, there are more than 15,000 persons employed in various extension activities.

Summary of Performance. The fruit and vegetable commodity system is not a single system at all; rather, the term is a convenient means of describing the total activities of numerous subsystems relating to individual commodities, both fresh and processed. Because of this, it is difficult to analyze overall system performance in a meaningful way. In this section we have limited ourselves to a brief review of performance from three viewpoints: supply and inventory management, profitability, and consumer satisfaction.

The single factor exerting the most pervasive influence on the production and marketing of fresh produce is the perishability of the product. In the typical case, crops must be harvested, graded, packed, and shipped within a few days or even hours, regardless of prevailing market conditions. This fact alone both introduces a high degree of uncertainty into the system and requires that planning and decision-making be carried out within a very short-run framework.

The result has been a high degree of variability in supplies and prices both within and between seasons. Even though farm production is quite widespread geographically and moves from one growing area to another with the changes in seasons, unfavorable weather conditions have at times virtually wiped out entire crops and have often created significant shortages. A prime example is the Florida orange crop. During the last 10 years, orange production ranged from under 60 million boxes to over 140 million boxes, and the on-tree price to growers from less than $2 to nearly $5 per box. The swings were less drastic at the consumer level, but average annual retail prices of fresh oranges (adjusted for inflation) varied by more than 20 percent during this same period.

Factors that have tended to moderate year-to-year variability in fresh produce markets include the increase of imports, the development of controlled-atmosphere storage, and greenhouse production. As will be discussed in greater detail below, imports of fresh winter produce, primarily from Mexico, have tended to level out the supplies available to the U. S. market. The economic and technical feasibility of controlled-atmosphere storage methods have made it possible to inventory some fresh commodities, such as apples, making it possible to match supplies closer to market requirements. Greenhouse production of tomatoes and other salad vegetables has been begun on a small scale, but costs are still much higher than for field crops. Greenhouse tomatoes, grown primarily in Ohio and Indiana, accounted for an estimated 5 to 10 percent of total supplies in the New York market during the 1971 spring season.

Fruit and vegetable processors typically contract for raw materials directly with growers and market their products to chains and other large buyers under seasonal purchase agreements. In this system, the processor normally bears the costs and risks of inventory fluctuations. The continued rapid expansion in sales of frozen products has, in general, been great enough to prevent excessive stock buildups. For canned products, however, output during the early 1960s increased more rapidly than consumption, and stocks accumulated as processors competed aggressively for shares of a relatively stable market. The problem was accentuated because of the substantial amount of excess processing capacity that apparently existed in fruit and vegetable canning. The carryover of selected major canned goods reached a peak at the end of the 1968–69 and 1969–70 seasons, amounting to about 32 percent of the annual pack (Table 2–20). Production and stocks were reduced sharply during the two succeeding pack years.

Information on the profitability of fruit and vegetable farming is difficult to obtain because most growers are also engaged in growing other crops. Fruits and vegetables accounted for about 10 percent of total cash receipts from farming in 1971. The available data indicate, however, that profits at the farm level are highly variable. In fact, the attitude is common in the industry that profits from good crop years must be sufficient to offset losses during poor years.

The most recent annual survey of costs and returns for Florida vegetable growers[12] presented data on 15 crops during the 1970–71 season (Table 2–21). For seven of these, average net returns per acre were negative

Table 2–20. U.S. Pack (10⁶ cases of 24/303sᵃ) Carryover of Selected Canned Vegetables.

| | Crop Year | | | | | | | |
	1966–67	*1967–68*	*1968–69*	*1969–70*	*1970–71*	*1971–72*	*1972–73*
Pack	233.6	269.4	283.5	239.0	242.5	255.4	245.5
Canners' and distributors' year-ending stock	49.4	70.8	90.8	76.4	66.6	60.3	—
Carryover (percent of pack)	21.2%	26.3%	32.0%	32.0%	27.4%	23.6%	—

Source: U.S. Department of Agriculture, Economic Research Service, Economic and Statistical Analysis Division, unpublished data adapted from National Canners' Association, *Vegetable Situation*, and Department of Commerce.

a. A "303" is a standard can size weighing approximately 15 ounces depending on contents.

Table 2–21.   Net Returns *(dollars per acre)* **to Growers of Florida Vegetable Crops, 1966–1971.**

	1970–71			
Crop[a]	High	Low	Average	Five-year average, 1966–71
Snap beans	$ 52	$ −65	$ 0	$ 8
Pole beans	290	−193	125	102
Cabbage	228	−176	−17	156
	161	−37	60	−2
Celery	−73	−313	−157	150
	−45	−308	−202	171
Sweet corn	75	−182	−27	−11
	128	−102	27	23
	104	−160	−29	10
Cucumbers	261	−433	−109	7
Eggplant	−140	−619	−296	136
Leaf crops	401	−233	77	71
	401	−233	77	71
Green peppers	1233	−1009	−96	−43
	89	−647	−186	186
Irish potatoes	164	- 98	17	107
	215	−131	18	−12
	72	−223	−23	−2
Radishes	152	26	91	−
Squash	181	2	87	93
	203	−246	24	51
	481	−406	68	160
Tomatoes	552	−28	185	35
	1039	−444	14	57
	643	59	81	91
Staked tomatoes	1770	−203	1225	395
	1561	−195	606	−7
	1075	−283	454	225
Watermelons	312	−188	69	−102

Source: D. L. Brooke, *Costs and Returns from Vegetable Crops in Florida*, pp. 1–29.
a. Where more than one figure appears for a crop, data were collected from more than one growing area within the state.

for growers in at least one producing area in the state. The lowest reported net returns were negative for all crops except one (radishes) and in two cases (celery and eggplant) even the highest returns were negative. Furthermore, six of the 14 crops for which average data covering 1966–1970 were shown reported negative net returns per acre in at least one growing area. A companion study of 151 Florida citrus groves for the 1969–1970 season[13] indicated that 36 percent of them earned negative net returns. Over a 10-year period, pretax profits for mature groves averaged only 11 percent on invested capital before any allowance was made for owners' costs of supervision.

Fresh fruit and vegetable wholesalers and terminal markets typically operate on relatively narrow profit margins only about 1 percent of sales; they were from 1963 to 1970 (Table 2–22). Margins on sales consistently lagged

Table 2–22. Profitability of U.S. Fresh Fruit and Vegetable Wholesalers, 1963–1970.

| | | *Profit as percentage of–* | | |
Year	Number reporting	Net sales	Tangible net worth	Net work-ing capital
1963	56	1.12	7.58	15.34
1968	63	1.32	10.17	17.06
1969	64	1.10	10.65	18.10
1970	64	1.14	7.81	14.87

Source: Dun and Bradstreet, *Key Business Ratios* (New York, 1964, 1969, 1970, 1971).

Table 2–23. Profitability of U.S. Fruit, Vegetable, and Seafood Processors, 1963–1970.

| | | *Profit as percentage of–* | | |
Year	Number reporting	Net sales	Tangible net worth	Net work-ing capital
1963	58	2.34	8.35	14.54
1968	68	2.83	9.35	16.19
1969	68	1.93	5.79	13.26
1970	76	2.15	7.73	15.86

Source: Dun and Bradstreet, *Key Business Ratios* (New York, 1964, 1969, 1970, 1971).

behind those for other wholesalers during this period. Measured in terms of return on net worth, however, fruit and vegetable wholesalers ranked much higher because of their relatively low requirements for both fixed and working capital. Between 1963 and 1970, reported after-tax returns on net worth ranged from 8 percent to 11 percent.

Fruit and vegetable processing firms also have below-average margins on sales, but earn lower average returns on capital employed than either all manufacturing firms or all food-processing companies. From 1963 to 1970, after-tax profits for a sample of processing companies averaged 2 to 3 percent of sales and 6 to 9 percent of net worth (Table 2–23). Among five leading food processors (Green Giant, Del Monte, Heinz, Libby; and Stokely–Van Camp), returns on sales were generally above the industry average, but only Del Monte consistently earned in excess of 8 percent on assets employed.

Although the profitability of cooperative fruit and vegetable processors cannot be directly compared with that of publicly held corporations, an analysis of four leading cooperatives (National Grape, Ocean Spray, California Canners and Growers, and Tri-Valley) showed a wide range of variability during the period 1962–1971.

Retail profitability of fruits and vegetables is also difficult to measure because of the problem of allocating store overheads among the various product departments. It is clear, however, that gross margins on fresh produce are higher than those on processed products (Table 2–24). Retail margins are lower for canned than for frozen commodities, reflecting more intense competition among processors. However, private-label sales, which tend to be more profitable for retailers, are more important for canned than for frozen products. Fruits and vegetables account for about one-fifth of total gross profits of retail chain stores.

Until relatively recently, there has been little change in quality, packaging, or end uses of the fresh fruits and vegetables available to the American consumer. The costly and fractionated traditional distribution system acted as an effective deterrent to both innovation and increased efficiency. Marketing and distribution costs beyond the farm gate account for 70 percent of the retail value of fresh fruits and vegetables, a higher ratio than for other nonprocessed-food categories. This is, in part, due to the cost of refrigeration and special handling. Consumer prices of fresh fruits and vegetables have increased more than both the overall cost of living and all food prices since 1960 (Figure 2–2). The rise in fresh fruit and vegetable prices was partially responsible for creating attractive market opportunities for new processed products as well as for imported fresh fruits and vegetables.

The market structure of the fruit and vegetable system is beginning to change as traditional distribution channels are bypassed in favor of direct purchases from growers by large buyers. Growers and retailers have become increasingly concerned with the quality of fresh produce, the former as a means of differentiating his product and the latter as a means of reducing losses on high-margin items. Cost and marketing considerations have led to an increase in prepackaged fresh produce, and this trend can be expected to continue as the technological problems are resolved. Finally, consumer advertising and labeling of fresh produce have increased as a result of efforts to stimulate generic demand and to establish brand preferences among consumers.

The processing sector of the fruit and vegetable industry responded

Table 2–24. Returns from U. S. Canned, Frozen, and Fresh Fruits and Vegetables, 1971 *(percent of margin, sales, and profit).*

Commodity	Percent gross margin	Percent gross profit	Percentage of total store sales
Canned vegetables	20.0	2.3	2.38
Canned fruits	19.1	1.21	1.32
Canned juices	17.6	1.15	1.36
Frozen produce	25.5	5.65	4.61
Fresh produce	31.1	10.60	7.09

Source: Chain Store Age (Supermarket Executive's Edition, July 1972), p. 71.

Figure 2–2. U.S. Consumer and Food Price Indexes, 1960–1972.

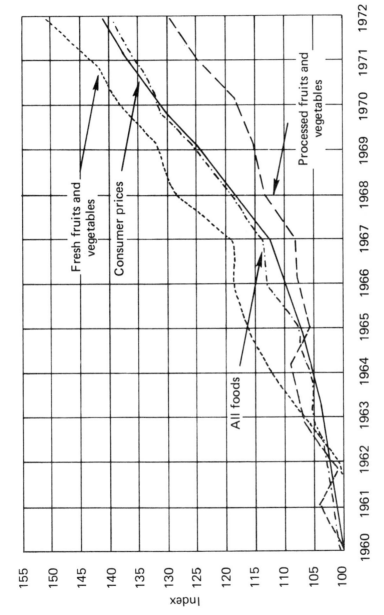

Source: U.S. Department of Labor, Bureau of Labor Statistics.

to changing consumer demands earlier and more effectively than in the case of fresh produce. First canners and then freezers successfully developed and marketed a steady flow of new fruit and vegetable products. Not only have they responded to the growing demand for built-in convenience, but they have done so at costs generally competitive with home preparation of fresh produce. At the outset, these products were primarily new processed forms of fresh commodities, such as various types of canned and frozen vegetables, frozen orange-juice concentrate, instant potatoes, and the like. More recently, the trend has shifted to combination and specialty products, such as frozen casseroles, various ethnic preparations, instant soups, and juice combinations.

Overall, the U. S. fruit and vegetable system, despite built-in weaknesses stemming from high perishability and generally low margins, has been able to supply the U. S. consumer with an ever-increasing variety of quality products at reasonable prices through innovations in grading, processing, and distribution techniques.

The Import System

Introduction. As has been discussed previously, U. S. imports of fruits and vegetables are expanding more rapidly than domestic farm production. Underlying this growth are a number of basic factors characteristic of the exporting countries:

1. Reduced risk of crop loss and extended growing seasons as the result of more favorable climatic conditions;
2. Lower costs of farm production, reflecting the relative abundance of both labor and land;
3. Ability to supply the market during seasonal gaps in U. S. production;
4. Development of cost-competitive processing industries utilizing abundant local raw materials;
5. Ability to supply the market with commodities, such as pineapples and other tropical fruit, that cannot be grown in the United States;
6. Improvements in both the availability and the cost of air and sea transportation;
7. Direct and indirect government support of export-expansion programs.

Although the sources and varieties of fruits and vegetables imported into the United States are numerous, some 80 to 90 percent of the total volume is accounted for by active trade with five major areas:

1. Central and South America (fresh bananas);
2. Mexico (fresh and some frozen produce);

3. The Far East (canned mandarin oranges, pineapples, mushrooms, and other specialty products);
4. Italy, Spain, and Portugal (olives and processed tomato products);
5. Canada (fresh apples, potatoes, and other vegetables).

The growth of these groups of imports has been accompanied by development of an import system responsive to the distinct agronomic characteristics of each area. For the purposes of this research, however, attention has been concentrated on the structure of the system of Mexican fruit and vegetable exports, both because it has grown much more rapidly than the other export systems and because it has direct implications for the future development of fruit and vegetable exports from Central America.

Trends in Mexican Exports. Although there has been production of winter fruits and vegetables for export in western Mexico since the 1930s, this production did not develop on a large scale until the 1950s. The rapid expansion of the last two decades was made possible by large-scale investment by the Mexican government in irrigation projects in the states of Sinaloa and Sonora, which lie directly south of Nogales, Arizona. Railroad service to this region by Pacific Fruit Express also facilitated the export of winter vegetables to the U. S. market. This service was modernized in the early 1950s and, at about the same time, a new interregional highway was constructed on the west coast of Mexico. At the present time, the bulk of the winter vegetable exports move by truck and refrigerated trailer.

The Mexican producing areas enjoy significant climatic advantages compared with Florida, Texas, and Southern California. There is no recorded history of freezing temperatures in the coastal plain of the state of Sinaloa, whereas in south Florida a freeze occurs on the average once every two years. The probability of freezing is even greater in other areas of Florida and in Texas. Winter vegetable production has declined in southern California, partly owing to the high cost of cold-weather protection.

Mexican growers have also benefited to some extent by their ability to take advantage of seasonal gaps in domestic U. S. production. The charts in Appendix I are reproduced from a U. S. Department of Agriculture study[14] and show the pattern of monthly shipments of five winter produce crops during the 1966–67 season. Mexican tomato shipments in that year both began and peaked earlier than shipments from Florida. The same was true for fresh strawberries. Cucumber shipments from Mexico reached their highest level during February and March, corresponding with a decline in Florida output. Florida is not a significant producer of cantaloupes and Mexican shipments reach substantial volumes a good two months before other U. S. producing areas become important.

Mexican fruits and vegetables, including frozen and canned items, have enjoyed a buoyant market growth in the United States during the past decade (Tables 2–25 and 2–26). Fruits and vegetables have replaced cotton as Mexico's leading agricultural export earner. Mexican exports of fruits and vegetables expanded at a very rapid rate through 1970, but leveled off during the following two years. The 9 percent decline in the value of exports in 1971 was due in part to a Mexican policy of internal restrictions on the export of fresh tomatoes and frozen strawberries in order to maintain prices in the U. S. market.

Mexico's share of the U. S. winter and early spring market is now over 50 percent in the case of tomatoes, cucumbers, and eggplant and almost 50 percent for bell peppers (Table 2–27). Annual rates of growth of imports from Mexico since 1960 exceeded 30 percent for cucumbers, eggplant, and fresh strawberries, and 10 percent for tomatoes, bell peppers, and frozen strawberries. Only in the case of cantaloupes, among the fruits and vegetables shown, was the rate of growth of Mexican exports about level with that of the U. S. market as a whole. The tables in Appendix A provide additional details on the growth in Mexico's share of U. S. winter vegetable consumption since 1960.

If the recent rates of growth of imports from Mexico continue, in a relatively short time Mexico will account for almost the entire winter supply of most of these fruits and vegetables. In order to maintain current growth rates, Mexico will have to seek new markets for the fruits and vegetables now being emphasized and to explore the prospects for further expansion of vegetables now not important in export trade, such as broccoli, asparagus, okra, and cauliflower, in both fresh and processed forms.

As regards new export markets, the obvious targets are Europe and Japan. Exploratory work by both the government and private growers is currently under way. Regarding the introduction of new vegetables on the North American market, the easiest opportunities have already been undertaken. Future development will be more difficult, particularly for frozen vegetables, which must compete with domestic vegetables grown under highly mechanized regimes in the summer season. Here the emphasis will not only have to be on supplying acceptable quality but also on competing with relatively low-cost U. S. production.

The USDA study[15] of six winter produce commodities indicates that Mexico had a substantial advantage in production costs per hectare during the 1970–71 growing season, except in the case of cantaloupes grown in the Rio Grande Valley in Texas (Table 2–28). The most important source of Mexico's cost advantage was in its lower labor costs, which are especially important for vine-ripe tomatoes, peppers, and strawberries. Even though Mexican wage rates have increased significantly during the last seven years, the USDA study does not indicate that the gap between Mexico and Florida has narrowed. In fact, for production costs as a whole, Mexico enjoyed a greater advantage during the 1970–71 season than in 1967–68.

Table 2-25. Value of U.S. Imports of Fruits and Vegetables (for consumption) from Mexico Annually, 1960–1972 (10³ dollars).

| | Fruits and preparations (including melons) | | | | | | | | Vegetables and preparations | | | Total fruits and vegetables |
| | Fresh | | | Processed | | | | | | | | |
Year	Fruits	Melons	Total	Fruit juices	Citrus oils	Other	Total	Total	Fresh	Processed	Total[a]	
1960	2,128	6,706	8,834	1,200	906	6,374	8,480	17,314	27,458	534	27,992	45,306
1961	3,004	5,498	8,502	1,346	1,723	6,763	9,832	18,334	17,666	625	18,291	36,625
1962	2,957	5,848	8,805	865	2,659	7,361	10,885	19,690	25,820	1,154	26,974	46,664
1963	6,388	6,056	12,444	1,617	2,933	7,596	12,146	24,590	30,040	751	30,791	55,381
1964	7,308	8,163	15,471	3,961	1,337	10,152	15,450	30,921	35,711	615	36,326	67,247
1965	6,147	8,958	15,105	744	3,789	12,113	16,646	31,751	40,259	1,054	41,313	73,064
1966	6,568	7,436	14,004	271	4,018	20,443	24,732	38,736	66,809	1,948	68,757	107,493
1967	8,503	7,595	16,098	230	5,813	14,572	20,615	36,713	59,962	2,921	62,883	99,596
1968	13,730	6,367	20,097	659	5,682	16,979	23,320	43,417	67,989	1,979	69,968	113,385
1969	12,878	9,048	21,926	302	2,322	19,625	22,249	44,175	100,589	3,265	103,854	148,029
1970	16,119	11,309	27,428	319	3,445	18,835	22,599	50,027	136,861	3,953	140,814	190,841
1971	15,808	12,222	28,030	647	2,841	16,038	19,526	47,556	127,579	4,960	132,539	180,095
Prelim 1972	16,164	12,978	29,122	2,724	4,109	18,175	25,008	54,130	135,619	5,897	141,516	195,646

Source: Fruits and Vegetables, U.S. Imports (for consumption) from Mexico, Foreign Agricultural Service, U.S. Department of Agriculture, March 1971; and the Economic Research Service, June 1973.
a. Excludes dried beans and peas.

Table 2—26. U.S. Imports of Fresh Vegetables, Cantaloupes, and Strawberries *(for consumption)* from Mexico, 1960–1972. *(10³ pounds)*

Year	Beans, green	Cucumbers	Egg-plant	Garlic	Onions	Peas	Peppers
1960	6,747	8,743	1,799	12,544	17,217	4,905	22,183
1961	9,386	10,392	1,899	6,976	29,708	94	12,854
1962	6,376	15,835	2,136	9,059	42,212	4,137	17,282
1963	8,506	21,378	2,671	6,853	35,321	5,298	16,244
1964	7,523	17,226	3,388	6,690	31,964	5,102	13,078
1965	8,255	39,370	4,426	6,968	39,312	4,702	17,672
1966	6,112	48,076	5,686	6,248	50,530	5,767	24,591
1967	7,162	58,412	7,186	9,160	41,407	4,848	27,799
1968	7,841	59,876	10,432	7,997	70,465	3,973	24,429
1969	10,980	109,953	17,769	9,361	51,248	6,164	40,662
1970	12,176	122,160	21,585	8,424	61,809	5,766	63,946
1971	11,493	142,948	23,153	6,790	41,110	5,316	74,319
Prelim 1972	17,668	154,064	28,806	6,861	57,305	5,257	60,948

(10³ dollars)

Year	Beans, green	Cucumbers	Egg-plant	Garlic	Onions	Peas	Peppers
1960	751	735	197	1,383	1,035	375	2,311
1961	1,100	671	187	746	1,409	345	1,304
1962	713	922	198	1,404	2,753	302	1,825
1963	1,266	1,494	182	1,272	1,906	465	2,205
1964	1,128	1,324	307	865	1,705	433	1,951
1965	1,019	2,843	388	962	2,158	642	2,204
1966	951	3,638	481	912	3,097	783	3,702
1967	1,040	4,518	565	1,538	2,776	778	4,293
1968	1,180	4,595	982	1,743	4,597	533	4,068
1969	1,475	10,891	2,008	1,514	3,471	746	7,671
1970	1,669	10,566	2,520	1,390	5,587	1,086	12,222
1971	1,583	12,116	2,581	1,239	3,444	1,013	13,553
Prelim 1972	2,301	13,149	3,319	1,754	4,875	1,002	10,881

Source: Fruits and Vegetables, U.S. Imports (for consumption) from Mexico, Foreign Agricultural Service, U.S. Department of Agriculture, March 1971, and the Economic Research Service, June 1973.

a. Prior to September 1963, classified as "berries, frozen, NES." However, this category is believed to have consisted almost entirely of frozen strawberries.

Table 2–26. (cont.)

Squash	Tomatoes	Other	Total vege-tables	Canta-loupes	Strawberries Fresh	Frozen[a]
850	251,822	1,788	328,598	79,280	562	25,017
1,075	156,070	1,887	230,341	79,551	579	29,817
1,256	233,216	2,846	334,355	97,796	895	32,281
1,823	239,965	3,683	341,742	110,427	3,412	34,550
2,564	246,122	4,583	338,240	130,062	4,092	39,720
5,525	265,459	6,089	397,778	146,532	5,791	51,796
5,057	358,743	13,603	524,413	136,507	11,747	82,825
11,129	362,354	13,329	542,786	117,218	20,499	72,693
9,476	387,401	37,905	619,795	72,146	26,261	68,199
18,944	446,240	29,481	740,802	118,276	44,218	87,962
26,049	641,015	37,763	1,000,693	147,791	48,966	101,519
28,988	570,288	39,902	944,807	178,807	49,248	83,166
36,814	582,289	52,300	1,000,351	152,481	42,074	81,157

Squash	Tomatoes	Other	Total vege-tables	Canta-loupes	Strawberries Fresh	Frozen[a]
61	20,476	134	27,458	4,023	43	3,233
83	11,623	198	17,666	3,964	120	3,715
99	17,364	240	25,820	4,460	142	4,121
172	20,706	372	30,040	4,858	421	4,374
317	27,355	326	35,711	6,686	513	5,679
414	29,425	384	40,259	7,413	845	7,805
546	52,015	684	66,809	5,895	2,048	15,265
1,149	42,607	698	59,962	6,133	3,180	9,991
1,451	46,973	1,867	67,989	4,483	4,425	11,377
2,512	68,018	2,283	100,589	6,750	7,083	14,713
3,387	94,967	3,467	136,861	7,978	8,333	14,458
3,620	84,131	4,299	127,579	9,410	8,206	10,577
4,981	83,150	5,207	135,619	8,882	7,088	12,278

Table 2–27. Mexico's Share in U.S. Market for Winter and Early Spring Fruit and Vegetables.

Commodity	Annual growth since 1960 (percent)		Mexico's share of U.S. market (percent)			
	U.S. consumption	Imports from Mexico	1960–64	1965–69	1970	1971
Tomatoes	1.7	10.1	25.2	37.0	60.2	53.9
Bell peppers	2.8	10.7	11.1	15.0	43.6	44.7
Cucumbers	5.8	33.9	9.1	31.5	48.3	59.2
Eggplant	4.2	30.6	8.6	26.2	56.8	55.2
Fresh strawberries	7.3	62.7	1.2	10.2	16.9	15.5
Frozen strawberries	0.6	17.3	12.3	27.7	36.2	31.6
Cantaloupes	2.3	3.5	21.2	23.3	28.3	31.0

Source: Banco Central de Mexico, Mexico City, Mexico.

Table 2–28. Production Costs *(dollars per acre)* **of Selected Winter Produce, United States and Mexico, 1970–1971.**

Crop	Labor	Equipment	Materials	Overhead	Total
Vine-ripe tomatoes					
Florida	626	116	763	190	1696
Mexico	134	70	234	132	569
Difference	492	46	529	58	1027
Cucumbers					
Florida	67	46	148	87	349
Mexico	40	71	87	81	279
Difference	27	−25	61	6	70
Peppers					
Florida	227	51	277	99	653
Mexico	146	67	179	87	480
Difference	81	−16	98	12	173
Eggplant					
Florida	153	56	310	155	673
Mexico	94	54	165	89	402
Difference	59	2	145	66	271
Cantaloupes					
Texas	68	33	66	86	254
Mexico	100	58	72	117	347
Difference	−32	−25	−6	−31	−93
Strawberries					
Florida	281	98	786	314	1478
Mexico	144	67	411	158	780
Difference	137	31	375	156	698

Source: U.S. Department of Agriculture, *Supplying U.S. Markets with Fresh Winter Produce* (Agricultural Economic Report 154, March 1969; Supplement, September 1971).

When Mexican unit costs f.o.b. the shipping-point market in Nogales are compared with U. S. costs f.o.b. Florida and Texas shipping points, Mexico enjoyed absolute cost advantages only in the case of vine-ripe tomatoes and strawberries during the 1970–71 season (Table 2–29). This was true despite the fact that Mexican growers had substantially lower costs of harvesting and packing for each of the six winter produce commodities included in the USDA study. Lower Mexican production costs per hectare were not in every case translated into correspondingly lower unit costs because of lower yields realized by Mexican growers. These differences in yields are narrowing, however, and the better Mexican growers are now realizing yields comparable to those of the best U. S. farmers. The most important disadvantage faced by Mexico is the cost of transportation, import duties, and sales commissions required to deliver produce to the Nogales market. For the six commodities as a group, these costs averaged about 50 percent of the total f.o.b. cost.

After internal transportation costs in the United States are taken into account, the delivered cost of Mexican produce during the 1970–71 season was generally higher than that for Florida in New York, about competitive in Chicago, and lower on the West Coast (Table 2–30). With the exception of cantaloupes, however, differences in delivered costs between Mexican and U. S. produce changed significantly between 1967–68 and 1970–71 in favor of Mexico.

Structure of the Mexican Export System. Figure 2–3 provides a diagrammatic overview of the structure of the West Mexico—Nogales fruit and vegetable export system. Figure 2–4 is a more detailed diagram of the producing system in West Mexico.

Nogales, Arizona, the major entry point for Mexican produce, has grown rapidly in the past 14 years. Three other entry points are located in Texas; a California entry point, Calexico, is thus far only in the discussion stage. This pattern of shipping into the U. S. market has developed as a function of the locations of the growing regions and the existence of transportation. Nogales enjoys its prime position because Mexican irrigation projects opened up vast tracts of land along the northwest coast, and the best highway as well as rail routes go directly north to Nogales. Crops grown in the northeast and central areas move in an easterly direction into one of the Texas entry points, which is actually closer to the densely populated U. S. market regions of the Midwest and Northeast.

Transportation into and out of Nogales is in two separate loops, since one nation's trucks are permitted only within a five-mile zone of the other's border. According to interviews conducted in the area, for truckers operating south of the border, 65 percent of the fee accrues to trailer owners and 35 percent to tractor owners, whereas north of the border, tractors earn 80 percent of the fee and trailers earn 20 percent. Some truckers have fleets operating in both countries.

Large growers may own fleets of trailers and trucks, which they supplement by hiring from independent truckers or by using piggyback trailers of the Pacific Fruit Express.

Trucks have become predominant on both sides of the border because they offer greater speed, flexibility, and reliability. Railroads may take six to ten days to get to New York, whereas a truck can make it in three days. A truck driven by a responsible driver is generally less subject to continual inspection delays than are untended railroad cars.

The 51 Nogales distributors are the principal coordinating linkages between Mexican growers and U. S. buyers, who normally act as strictly *intra*–U. S. agents rather than importers. This is true even where a chain may have a joint venture with a Mexican grower. Few chains are large enough to have an exclusive on-site buyer, for there are no significant direct economies involved. The chain buyer acts as a broker who, unlike the ordinary broker, does not receive a commission from the distributor. In fact, the chain must bear the costs of his salary and office expenses, but it hopes to recoup these outlays by the shrewdness and diligence of its own buyers' efforts. Most exclusive chain buyers seem to purchase for well over 1200 stores in their chains or cooperatives.

The differences among distributors, brokers, and chain buyers operating in the Nogales market may be summarized as follows:

Distributors

Functions: 1. Provide some inputs and credit, if needed.
              2. Coordinate growers' supplies with market demand.
              3. Warehouse produce in Nogales.
              4. Refrigerate and cure produce as needed, especially important for vine-ripe tomatoes (now 95 percent of Mexican tomatoes).
              5. Promote produce to clients: brokers, chains, terminals.

Payment: Commission of 10 to 12 percent on sales.

Broker

Functions: 1. Inform clients of prices and availability and receive orders.
              2. Put together clients' orders into trucklots by ordering from distributor.
              3. Arrange with trucker or truck broker to have truck pick up lots from distributors and drop off at clients' warehouses.

Payment: Commission (about 3 percent paid by distributor.)

Chain buyer

Functions: Essentially the same as the broker's, except that his clients are each of the chains' divisional perishable-food distribution centers.

Payment: Salary and expenses paid by chain.

Table 2–29. Shipping-Point Costs (dollars per unit) **of Selected Winter Produce, United States and Mexico, 1970–1971.**

Crop	Unit	Producing	Harvesting	Packing and selling	Export and sales commission	Total f.o.b. shipping point
Vine-ripe tomatoes	20 pounds					
Florida		0.94	0.65	0.80	0	2.39
Mexico		.32	.20	.46	1.04	2.02
Difference		0.62	0.45	0.34	−1.04	0.37
Cucumbers	Bushel					
Florida		0.89	1.09	1.39	0	3.37
Mexico		.87	0.41	0.89	2.70	4.87
Difference		0.02	0.68	0.50	−2.70	−1.50
Peppers	Bushel					
Florida		1.01	0.86	1.25	0	3.12
Mexico		0.74	.27	0.95	1.81	3.76
Difference		0.27	0.59	0.30	−1.81	−0.64
Eggplant	Bushel					
Florida		0.80	1.58		0	2.38
Mexico		.33	0.98		1.07	2.38
Difference		0.47	0.60		−1.07	0

Cantaloupes	88 pounds					
Texas		1.69	1.06	2.58	0	5.33
Mexico		3.16	0.52	2.00	4.43	10.11
Difference		-1.47	0.54	0.58	-4.43	-4.78
Strawberries	12 pints					
Florida		1.34	0.04	1.80	0	3.18
Mexico		0.51	.18	0.56	1.51	2.76
Difference		0.83	-0.14	1.24	-1.51	0.42

Source: U.S. Department of Agriculture, *Supplying U.S. Markets with Fresh Winter Produce* (Agricultural Economic Report 154, March 1969; Supplement, September 1971).

Table 2–30.   Delivered Costs *(dollars per unit)* **of Selected Winter Produce, United States and Mexico, 1970–1971.**

Crop	Unit	New York	Chicago	San Francisco
Vine-ripe tomatoes	20 Pounds			
Florida		2.89	2.94	3.19
Mexico		3.15	2.69	2.44
Difference		–0.26	0.25	0.75
Cucumbers	Bushel			
Florida		4.57	4.67	4.78
Mexico		7.37	6.34	5.79
Difference		–2.80	–1.67	–1.01
Peppers	Bushel			
Florida		4.02	4.12	5.02
Mexico		5.89	5.02	4.68
Difference		–1.87	–0.90	0.34
Eggplant	Bushel			
Florida		3.33	3.43	3.78
Mexico		4.57	3.67	3.19
Difference		–1.24	–0.24	0.59
Cantaloupes	88 Pounds			
Texas		8.25	7.21	7.41
Mexico		14.05	12.42	11.56
Difference		–5.80	–5.21	–4.15
Strawberries	12 Pints			
Florida		3.62	3.66	3.88
Mexico		3.44	3.20	3.26
Difference		0.18	0.46	0.62

Source: Department of Agriculture, *Supplying U.S. Markets with Fresh Winter Produce* (Agricultural Economic Report 154, March 1969; and Supplement, September 1971).

Figure 2–3. Mexican Vegetable Marketing System.[a]

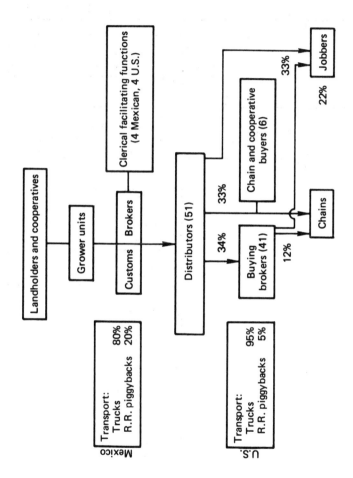

a. Numbers in parenthesis indicate number of entities performing that function.

Figure 2–4. West Mexican Vegetable Production and Marketing System.

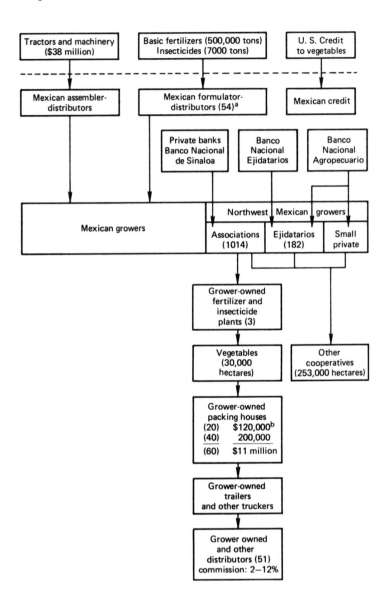

a. Unless otherwise specified, numbers in parentheses represent the number of entities performing that function.

b. Two classes of grower-owned packing houses exist, 20 of them with asset value of approximately $120,000 each, and 40 of them with asset value of approximately $200,000 each.

Distributors and growers are tightly coordinated, either through Mexican growers owning Nogales distributors or through U. S. distributors controlling growers by direct ownership or financing. Growers own some of the packing houses and Nogales distributors own the rest. Where the distributor has no ownership interest, he utilizes verbal or written contracts with growers in order to ensure supplies. Distributors also maintain close day-to-day communications with growers. Over a period of years, this system appears to have developed an attitude of mutual trust and confidence between growers and distributors.

Economies of scale favor distributors dealing with large growing units, which, in accordance with Mexican land-reform laws, may comprise many separate owners related by blood or by commercial ties. In some cases, smaller growers will agglomerate with larger growers to take advantage of the latter's packing facilities and market access. The USDA estimated that hectarage of individual strawberry growers ranged in size up to 2400 hectares, of cantaloupe growers to 600 hectares, and of tomato growers to 400 hectares.[16] Producers of green peppers generally had farms of less than 200 hectares, while eggplant and cucumbers were grown on less than 800 hectares.

Growers have built three formulating plants for insecticides. The first dates back 20 years to cotton-growing times, and normally operated at 100 percent of capacity before other growers united to build their own facilities. Expansion is slow because growers prefer crop terms, that is, until harvest, whereas the insecticide producers adhere to 30-day credit, lest a harvest failure crimp a borrower's ability to repay.

Mexican fruit and vegetable exporters have benefited from medium-term credit granted through official channels. In Culiacán, the center of the Sinaloa producing area, some 25 to 30 percent of the vegetable producer-packers received three to five-year development credit at 12 percent interest to start or expand their operations. Included in many of the credits granted were start-up working-capital expenses for up to 18 months. Combined with the seasonal credit obtained from Nogales distributors, vegetable producers in the Culiacán area have access to a considerable amount of low-cost seasonal and development finance, both types including built-in technical assistance. Nogales distributors provide planting and packing assistance upon request. No medium-term development finance is approved by the FONDO[17] until a complete development plan, including technical and financial statements, is prepared and approved by a local or headquarters FONDO agroindustry specialist. Cash-flow statements typical of those prepared by FONDO are shown in Appendix E for a hypothetical $600,000 (8,130,000 pesos) investment in a Culiacán-area vegetable-packing plant (tomatoes, cucumbers, and bell peppers).

Although Mexican packers now rely on Nogales distributors for seasonal credit, they may, in the future, be able to obtain needed extra working-capital loans in support of expanded operations through official FONDO sources at favorable terms and rates. FONDO appears to be committed to using its development-credit working capital not only to foster exports but also to enable more small producers to participate in employment-creating production and processing of vegetable crops.

The development of the Mexican fruit and vegetable export industry has been marked by the emergence of strong and active grower associations. At the national level, the activities of these associations are directed and coordinated by the National Union of Horticultural Producers. There are affiliated organizations for individual crops at both state and local levels. Unlike counterpart associations in the United States, the Mexican grower groups have legal authority to control both acreage and export quality and quantity. Enforcement of these sanctions is enhanced by the necessity for individual growers to obtain export permits from the state or national government. In addition to coordinating overall export programs, the grower associations are also engaged in gathering information, developing promotional programs, procuring inputs, and providing other services. They are financed by assessing each individual grower a fee based on the volume of his shipments.

The best-known and most active of these associations is CAADES (Confederation of Agricultural Associations of the State of Sinaloa). This association has pioneered in the development of detailed econometric analyses to determine acreage requirements and to establish individual source quotas. The role of CAADES as a coordinator in the export of fresh vine-ripe tomatoes is described in Appendix F.

Although the great growth in Mexican fruit and vegetable exports to the United States has been concentrated in fresh produce for the winter market, exports of processed products have also been increasing. In 1972, they were valued at about $31 million, or about 16 percent of total Mexican fruit and vegetable exports (see Table 2–25). By far the most important processed export commodity is frozen strawberries, which grew from 25 million pounds, valued at $3.2 million in 1960, to over 100 million pounds, with a value of nearly $15 million in 1970, before declining rather sharply in the face of an oversupply in the U. S. market during 1971 and 1972. Mexican strawberry processors have been able to combine the previously noted cost advantages in producing strawberries with efficient freezing operations to permit them to be cost competitive in both the U. S. and Western European markets. Similar efficiencies have not yet been achieved, however, for other canned and frozen commodities.

An export-import system for processed fruits and vegetables similar to that for fresh produce has not yet evolved. Most of the export activity, to date, represents the efforts of individual private companies to establish relations with foreign buyers, either directly or through import brokers. It was only in 1970 that a National Strawberry Board was established as the result of the oversupply situation that existed at that time. This board was charged with establishing export quotas and encouraging market and product diversification. A detailed examination of the experience of one company, Fresas Congeladas, in attempting to develop overseas markets for frozen strawberry products is provided in Appendix G.

Implications of the Mexican System for Central America. The Mexican experience has important implications for the embryonic Central American fruit and vegetable industry. Although it may be argued that the proximity of Mexican land to the United States makes such comparisons partially invalid, a number of important nontransportation lessons for the Central American exporter can be drawn on (1) contract growing with small farmers; (2) close financial, technical, and brokering ties with importing distributors; (3) the type of product to grow; (4) the key role of rapid communications; (5) the need to develop diversified markets from the outset; and (6) the importance of good grading and packaging. These implications are detailed below.

Infrastructure. Development of exports takes time. Mexico was a substantial exporter (50 million lbs. of fresh fruits and vegetables) to the United States in the 1930s, but steady growth did not take place until the late 1950s. Since then, export growth has been exponential, reaching well over one billion pounds in 1972. This growth would have been unlikely, if not impossible, except for the large-scale investment in social overhead capital by the Mexican government. Mexico brought large areas of land into cultivation through massive irrigation projects and then tied them to potential markets in the United States by a network of overland rail and road transportation. Although most of the vegetable production is on the west coast of Mexico, Central American countries will soon face direct competition from lands on the Mexican east coast between Vera Cruz and Tampico, which are to be opened to irrigated cultivation, and from small growers around Mérida on the Yucatán Peninsula.

Official credit banks in Mexico have offered growers and packers medium-term credits (two to five years) for both on-farm development and packing-house construction. Central American banks currently appear not as eager as Mexican banks to participate in this type of financing, and where they are eager, they often neglect key working-capital needs of the grower or packer and place ceilings on the size of loan to any one borrower.

Selection of "Commodity" vs. "Specialty" Products for Export. Several U. S. supermarket buyers who were surveyed as a part of this research stressed the point that developing countries should concentrate on achieving high-volume exports of "commodity" produce of competitive quality and cost instead of low-volume "specialty" goods. This thesis seems to be borne out by the Mexican experience, where tomatoes still represent about 65 percent of total vegetable export volume. Commodities produced in direct competition with U. S. growers account for over 90 percent of vegetable exports.

Mexican success came first in commodities for which either a seasonal shortage existed in the United States or Mexican costs were so much lower that Mexico could compete favorably with domestically grown commodities. The Mexicans concentrated on key commodity items (tomatoes, peppers, melons, and cucumbers) and used well-known varieties, packaged according to U. S. specifications. They did not try to introduce on a large scale specialty products—avocados, mangos, nectarines, papayas, guavas—that have only a limited or ethnic seasonal demand, yet are popular and easy to grow in Mexico.

U. S. brokers generally confirm the basic soundness of the Mexican strategy of production specialization. Although there may be strong arguments for diversifying to spread production risks, brokers emphasize that producers should remember that they are not growing vegetable gardens. Each vegetable has unique growing characteristics, and a grower should specialize if he wants to produce quality at high yield levels. Since the cost and availability of labor are the major sources of production-cost advantages, priority should be given to crops with relatively simple production technology and high labor-input requirements. These would include such items as tomatoes, cucumbers, eggplant, okra, squash, peppers, and melons.

Procurement from Small Farmers.   Processors and packers procuring by contract from small farmers may have greater long-run potential than completely integrated operations, especially in areas where there is significant land pressure. Despite the economies of scale that have resulted in the emergence of large growers in Sinaloa and Sonora, the experience of Mexico suggests that contractual arrangements with small farmers may be preferable for the longer run. As increasing concern is expressed at political levels in Mexico regarding rural-income distribution problems, government credit and infrastructure may be heavily weighted toward such procurement practices. Unlike the Culiacán experience, the trend in other parts of Mexico (Bajio for strawberries and asparagus and, in future, Yucatán, as outlined below) is toward production by small farmers under some type of contractual relation with cooperatives, private packers, or processors.[18]

Potential Yucatán Competition.   Central American producers currently have a potential advantage of $0.01 to $0.04 per pound over West Mexican suppliers to U. S. East Coast markets for fresh vegetables. These producers also may enjoy significant labor, land, and climatic advantages; the last enables them to harvest and ship winter produce from three to six weeks earlier than West Mexican growers. However, the state government in Yucatán is making strenuous efforts to encourage fresh-fruit and vegetable production in this region, an area geographically and ecologically similar to Central America. The official agricultural banks, particularly the Banco Ejido (Bank for Small Farmers), have encouraged export vegetable schemes in this area which, to date, have failed because of the same problems, especially transportation, encountered by the

Central American producers. "Tomatoes, cucumbers, eggplant, and other vegetables are being grown successfully, but lack of financing and efficient transportation keeps the industry from taking any great strides."[19]

Generation of Local Market Demand. Development of domestic demand increases the marketing efficiency of a grower whose cullage increases in relation to his distance from the final marketplace. For example, West Mexican tomato growers are able to pack up to 40 percent of their crop for local markets in Mexico City, Guadalajara, Torreón, and Monterrey. "These tomatoes, equivalent to U. S. No. 2 and No. 3, are packed in 80-pound crates and return about 35 pesos ($2.80) per box. There is a ready domestic market at this price, but local markets will not pay higher prices, and growers cannot grow tomatoes profitably at these prices for the domestic markets. The export flat of 80 percent U. S. No. 1 or better quality is too expensive (U. S. $3.50) for local consumption."[20]

By contrast, in none of the Central American case studies in Chapter 4 of this book could local markets absorb as much as 10 percent of production. Since Central American producers have been realizing only about 35 percent production of export quality at best, the remaining 65 percent must be literally dumped or, where feasible, used as animal feed.

Early Market Diversification. Throughout its history, the Mexican produce export industry has been almost entirely dependent on the U. S. market. Only now, in the early 1970s, is Mexico making serious efforts to broaden its export markets to include Europe and Japan. For a decade, Mexico even neglected Canada, and is only now finding it an attractive market for a variety of fresh and processed vegetables during the winter months. Central America may have a small transportation advantage over Mexico to some European markets. The case of an El Salvador honeydew-melon grower exporting significant quantities to England, Germany, Sweden, and the Netherlands as well as to New York virtually from the beginning of his operations illustrates the benefits of this policy of early market diversification.

Supply Control. In the cases of Mexican exports of both fresh tomatoes and frozen strawberries to the United States, oversupply problems resulted. To rectify them, producer-packers, backed by the American government, were organized to set and allocate quotas. Although Central American exports are unlikely to saturate any particular country, for products competitive with Mexican exports (cucumbers, melons, peppers) a strong market-intelligence system is required—a system geared into a modern and fast telecommunications network.

Cost Accounting. In contrast to the poor records kept in a number of the Central American operations, "Mexican growers are very cost conscious and maintain cost records for every operation and expense connected with growing and handling of tomatoes. These costs are usually figured in unit costs per package."[21]

Distributor Relations. An important lesson from West Mexican operations is their joint-venture arrangements with Nogales distributors. One man interviewed in Culiacán believes that 70 percent of the volume of West Mexican production goes through distributors with significant Mexican ownership. They are the major source of seasonal credit and also provide significant technical assistance on the production side to the West Mexican producers.

The Role of Central America

Emerging Patterns. Historically, Central American exports of fruits and vegetables to the United States have been limited almost entirely to bananas and plantains, for which the area is the leading source of world supply. In 1971, bananas from Central America accounted for nearly 81 percent of U. S. imports, 37 percent of Western European imports, and 8 percent of Japanese imports.[22] Bananas are the leading export commodity from both Honduras and Panama and are second to coffee in Costa Rica. They account for about 50 percent of total export receipts in Honduras, 40 percent in Panama, and significant, though smaller, percentages in both Costa Rica and Guatemala.

The export-import system that moves Central American bananas to world markets is marked by a high degree of centralized control of production, shipping, and distribution by a few large international companies. Tight coordination of the system is necessitated by the high agronomic uncertainties, large capital requirements for both plantation-scale agriculture and shipping, and the need to coordinate trade flows of a highly perishable product. This control originally took the form of common ownership of farms, ships, and sometimes distribution facilities. More recently, contractual arrangements with independent growers and ship operators have assumed greater importance.

The future outlook for the expansion of the Central American banana trade is not promising. World markets (excluding the communist countries) are growing very slowly, competitive producing areas are expanding, costs of production and distribution are rising, and consumer prices are, at best, holding steady. A study by the FAO[23] (United Nations Food and Agriculture Organization) estimated that it would require a decline of about 30 percent in real prices in order for world markets to absorb the production already planned or being planned in the developing countries.

It has only been in very recent years that exports of nontraditional fruits and vegetables have begun to develop in Central America, though still on an experimental basis. In the fiscal year 1964, U. S. import statistics reported only 3 million pounds from Central America, all in fresh form. By fiscal 1972, the reported volume had risen to about 41 million pounds, including cassava and frozen okra (see Table 2–10).

Central America has not yet become a significant factor in the U. S. market for any individual fresh produce commodity. During 1970–71, cucumbers were the only import from Central America for which weekly shipment data were reported separately in the Federal–State Market News Service Summary[24] of the Florida marketing season (Figure 2–5). Central American shipments, although second to those from Mexico among U. S. imports, accounted for only 2 percent of total supplies during the September–June season. They arrived on a fairly consistent basis from mid–December to mid–April with a peak in January, a period in which Mexico dominated the market.

Figures 2–6 through 2–8 indicate that very similar patterns also occurred for tomatoes, peppers, and eggplant, peak shipments from Mexico coinciding with the period between Florida's fall and spring crops. Florida tomato shipments were reduced because of weather damage during February and March, but, even if normal conditions had prevailed, Mexico would have been the leading supplier during these months by a wide margin.

One result of this marketing pattern has been a tendency to reduce the amount of variability in shipping-point prices for these commodities, both from season to season and within a given season. Florida growers are less likely to be able to offset volume losses due to weather damage through higher prices during poor crop years. This also implies that prices for produce from new sources, including Central America, will be determined to a greater extent by relative quality and short-term market conditions than by the ability of these sources to fill seasonal gaps.

An exception to this implication may be cantaloupes, of which Florida is only a minor supplier and Mexican shipments do not achieve significant volume until about mid–March. There is virtually a complete void in the U. S. market during December, January, and February, a period in which Central America might be able to move substantial quantities. Mexico has been able to accomplish this in the case of fresh strawberries. December, January, and February are the only months of the year when California production does not dominate the strawberry market. Until very recently, Florida and Louisiana were the major sources of supply during this period, but shipments from these two states have now declined to less than 10 percent of the total winter supply and have been replaced by imports from Mexico.[25]

Central American countries have made a start in entering the U. S. market. Since they are closer to the U. S. East Coast, they have made their entrance through existing Florida channels rather than trying to tie into the West Mexican channels. No steady pattern of supplies has yet emerged as Central American suppliers, through trial and error, seek the best method of fitting into the U. S. fruit and vegetable systems. The established system for moving bananas

Figure 2–5. U. S. Cucumber Shipments from Selected Producing Areas, 1970–1971.

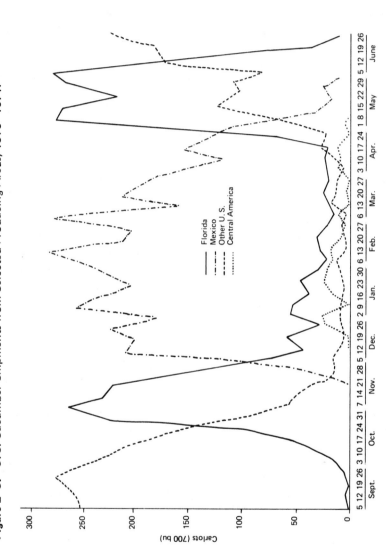

Source: Derived from U.S. Department of Agriculture, Federal–State Market News Service, *Marketing Florida Vegetables: Summary of 1970–71 Season* (November 1971).

Figure 2–6. U. S. Tomato Shipments from Selected Producing Areas, 1970–1971.

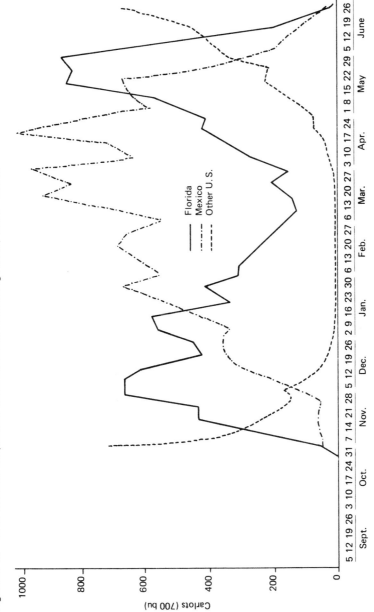

Source: Derived from U. S. Department of Agriculture, Federal–State Market News Service, *Marketing Florida Vegetables: Summary of 1970–71 Season* (November 1971).

Figure 2-7. U.S. Green Pepper Shipments from Selected Producing Areas, 1970–1971.

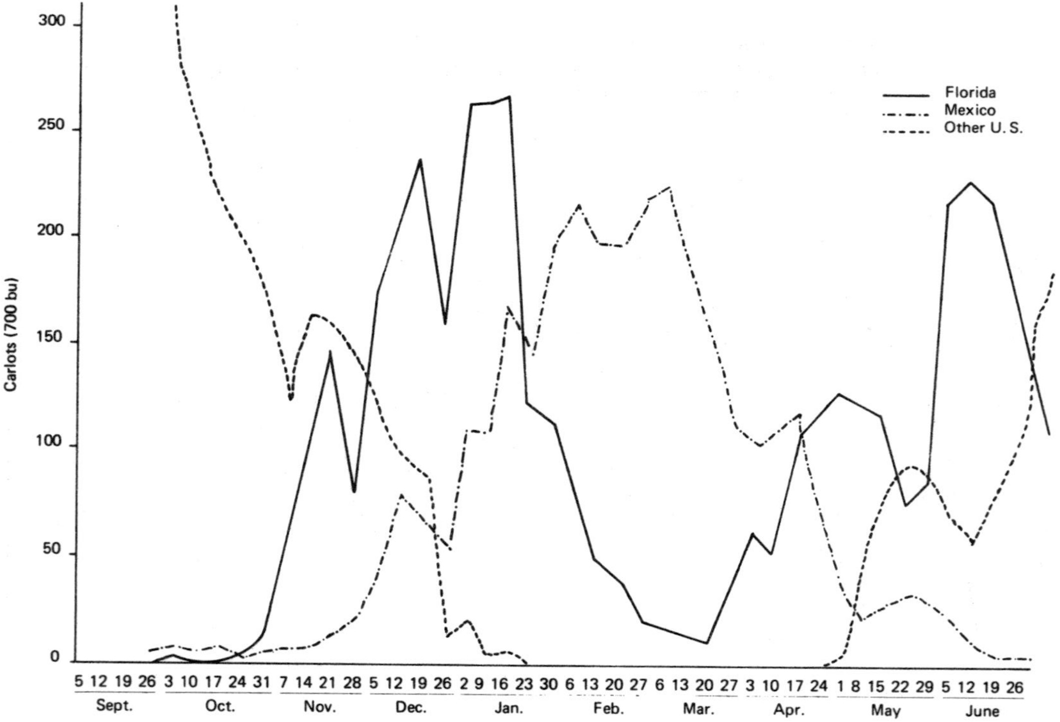

Source: Derived from U.S. Department of Agriculture, Federal–State Market News Service, *Marketing Florida Vegetables: Summary of 1970–71 Season* (November 1971).

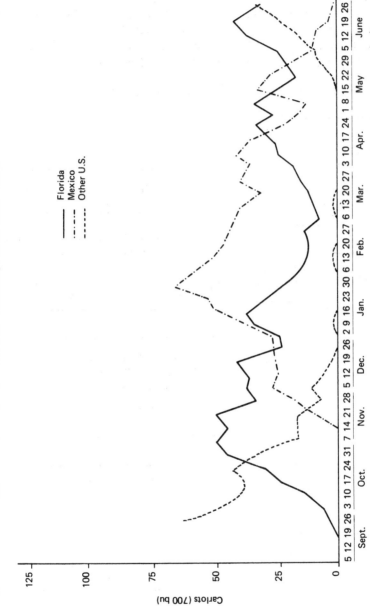

Figure 2–8. U.S. Eggplant Shipments from Selected Producing Areas, 1970–1971.

Florida
Mexico
Other U.S.

Carlots (700 bu)

125

100

75

50

25

0

Sept. | Oct. | Nov. | Dec. | Jan. | Feb. | Mar. | Apr. | May | June

5 12 19 26 | 3 10 17 24 31 | 7 14 21 28 | 5 12 19 26 | 2 9 16 23 30 | 6 13 20 27 | 6 13 20 27 | 3 10 17 24 | 1 8 15 22 29 | 5 12 19 26

Source: Derived from U.S. Department of Agriculture, Federal–State Market News Service, *Marketing Florida Vegetables: Summary of 1970–71 Season* (November 1971).

into world trade is clearly inappropriate for newly established, labor-intensive crops that must compete with both domestic production in the United States and export production in Mexico and elsewhere.

Central American shipments entering through Florida utilize the coordinating role of the Pompano Beach market. Figure 2–9 is a flowchart showing Pompano Beach and other Florida shipping-point markets that handle fresh winter produce. Central American growers have relied almost entirely on

Figure 2–9. Florida Winter-Vegetable Market System *(1973 estimates).*

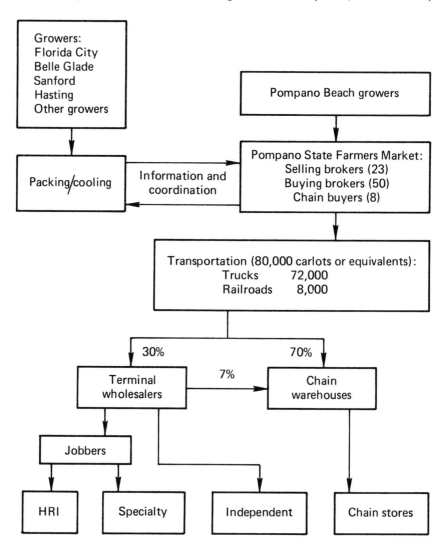

importers who act as selling brokers within the United States. Of the 23 selling brokers in Pompano, however, only four or five actually handle Central American imports. There is thus relatively limited competition among them in meeting the needs of the Central American producer.

Although the Pompano Beach area is not Florida's largest shipping area (Belle Glade ships nearly 30 million packages, to Pompano's 4.5 million), and is not open all year round, it nevertheless remains one of the nerve centers of the winter vegetable market in the eastern United States for two reasons. First, the state runs a marketplace for selling brokers who represent all sizes of growers in the area, which in turn attracts buying brokers and chain buyers, who represent wholesaling and retailing operations in the eastern United States. Second, it once channeled the extensive supply of Cuban winter vegetables into the U. S. market and still handles a supply, though a vastly diminished one, from Caribbean and Central American countries. For these two reasons, Pompano remains the coordinating center for shipments of winter vegetables. Buyers in Pompano contact selling brokers, then arrange with truckers to pick up an initial load at Pompano or Florida City, and then make additional pickups as they travel northward through Florida en route to terminals, chain distribution centers, or other drop-off spots.

The physical facilities at Pompano are limited. A large raised shed with a corrugated roof and open sides, about 365-meters long and 36-meters wide, (1200 ft. by 120 ft.) offers shelter to 23 selling brokers, each of whom has one or a few bays in the shed where he receives, sells, and oversees shipment of local produce. The selling brokers must be bonded, licensed by the state, and fairly well capitalized, for they must pay the grower within a day and wait a week for some large buyers to remit payment. (In contrast to local growers, Central American producers who sell on consignment are often not compensated for many weeks.) It is not uncommon for selling brokers to have accounts receivable of $200,000. In return for his selling services, the broker receives a commission of 15 cents per unit.

The selling broker's counterpart is the buying broker, whose role has undergone some changes as the result of chain-store direct purchasing. The buying broker may buy on a strict brokerage basis, not taking possession but merely servicing the transaction, for which he receives a commission of $0.15 to $0.18 per unit. On the other hand, he may act speculatively, buying a commodity and then seeking a buyer with whom he can turn a profit; less often he may act in joint-account buying in participation with the ultimate purchaser. The latter two variations are much less common today. Small chain stores will use the services of the buying broker at the market shed to inform them of available supplies and quality levels.

The largest chains operate somewhat differently. They have their own buyer at the market, who receives a salary, not a commission, and who coordinates the trucking of various commodities purchased from several of the

Florida vegetable markets to the chains, perishable distribution centers. The chain buyer may, as an alternative to buying at the market, contact, or receive offers from, a large grower to purchase a shipment directly from the grower's packing shed. This reduces costs by sourcing an entire order at once and tends to ensure uniform quality. It might also offer economies on commission payments, especially if the market is sluggish. As a result, many fruits and vegetables are bypassing the terminal market and moving directly from the grower to the warehouses of the large outlets. However, the terminal market still is a very important element in the system. It is the place where many retailers, small wholesalers, and HRI marketers secure the produce they need for their own operations. The terminal market also plays an important role in supplying out-of-stock requirements to chains.

A special survey was conducted for this research, designed to determine more precisely the nature of the involvement of selected U. S. retailers, terminal receivers, brokers, and processors in the import of fruits and vegetables from Central America. In general, the results obtained confirmed the belief that such involvement (except for bananas) is still very limited and fragmentary. In fact, although replies were received from a substantial percentage of those to whom questionnaires were mailed, no statistical summary of the results is justified because of the limited nature of the activities reported.

Respondents at all levels of the system did report widespread interest in developing alternative sources of supply, including Central America. The most frequently mentioned reasons for this interest were lower costs, reduced risk because of better climate, expanded year-round availability, less dependence on either Mexico or Florida, and the ability to supply specialty items, such as tropical fruits. A few respondents indicated interest in backward integration into production in areas not as vulnerable to the same cost-price pressures that appear to be limiting the profitability of U. S. growers.

Both shipping-point brokers and terminal-market receivers indicated considerable dissatisfaction with current supplies from Central America. Their complaints centered on poor (or, at best, erratic) quality, the need to repack and the high degree of product loss involved, lack of continuity in available supplies, and inability to communicate market needs to growers. Potential U. S. importers appear to lack sources of reliable information regarding virtually all aspects of the Central American supply situation. As a result, mistrust and lack of confidence are quite common. Only in a few isolated instances has this communication gap been partially bridged when U. S. importers have become actively involved in production either through financial investment or through the provision of technical assistance.

Although several retail chain organizations reported that they had made survey trips to Central American growing areas, in all but one instance those who had actually purchased Central American produce did so through importing brokers. The one exception was an experimental direct purchase from a Central American grower-shipper. Similarly, U. S. food-processing companies exhibited interest in new sources of fresh-produce supplies for freezing and canning, but the survey disclosed no instance where a contract had been entered into with a local Central American grower.

The Outlook for Central America. There appears to be a favorable opportunity for Central America to sharply increase its shipments of nontraditional fruits and vegetables to east-coast U. S. markets between now and 1980. This opportunity is based in large part on favorable climatic conditions—providing an extended growing season and reduced risks of crop loss—as well as on the availability of low-cost land and labor. In addition, the georgraphic location of Central America offers a transportation-cost advantage, if the present inefficient system can be improved, in serving the eastern portion of the United States.

In order to capitalize on the export opportunity in fresh fruits and vegetables, it will be necessary for Central American growers and shippers to learn to compete effectively with U. S. and Mexican suppliers, and for the new industry to be given strong support by public policy makers. Mexico attained its dominant position only over a long period of time and with the help of substantial government assistance, primarily in the form of infrastructure development and intermediate-term financing. Although the Central American governments all accord relatively high priorities to developing new sources of export earnings, including fruits and vegetables, this has not yet been matched with programs geared to the needs of exporters.

During 1971–72, 95 percent of the volume of Central American fruit and vegetable shipments to the United States (excluding bananas) was accounted for by six commodities: fresh pineapples, fresh cucumbers, cantaloupes, other melons, okra, and cassava (see Table 2–31). The last two were shipped in both fresh and frozen forms. In the aggregate, Central America accounted for about 1 percent of total U. S. supplies of these products. Pineapples, with a 10 percent market share, and cucumbers, with 2 percent, were the most important products. These six, together with green peppers, are the crops in which some export-market experience has been accumulated; these are the primary basis for developing future opportunities.

The nature of the future market opportunity varies widely from commodity to commodity. It depends in part on the strength of U. S. demand, in part on the ability of Central America to become a competitive source of supply, and in part on the opportunity to supply specialty products that do not compete directly with domestic production. Table 2–31 summarizes the present supply-and-demand situation for each of the leading current export crops, plus others that may have potential for the future, but have not yet developed significant export quantities.

The long-run outlook for Central America seems most favorable for

Table 2-31.   U. S. Market Opportunities for Mexican and Central American Fruits and Vegetables

Exports	Increase in U.S. consumption 1960-1971 (percent)	U.S.	Imports Total	Imports Mexico	Imports Cent. Am.	Total
Major						
Pineapples, fresh	15	72	53		13.1	125
canned	15-20	667	8			675
juice	0	500	80			580
Cucumbers, fresh	20-25	428	143	122	12.9	571
pickles	90-100	1126				1126
Cantaloupes, fresh	10-15	1245	148	147	1.4	1393
Honeydews, fresh	40	196	38		1.8	234
Okra, fresh or frozen	–	–	6		1.5	
Minor						
Limes, fresh	70	88	10		0.2	98
Tomatoes, fresh	0	1771	647	641	.1	2418
Peppers, fresh	25	412	70	64	.1	482
Corn, frozen	160	1012	1		.1	1013
Onions, fresh	15-20	2985	82	62	.1	3067
Carrots, fresh	10	1856	56			1912
Squash, fresh	–	–	26	26		
processed	10-15	130				130
Tropical						
Bananas, fresh	0		3978			3978
Plantains, fresh	–		92			92
Bananas and plantains processed	–		15			
Cassava, fresh or frozen	–				0.7	
Chayotes, fresh	–				.1	
Mamey apples, frozen	–				.1	
Breadfruit, fresh	–					
Dasheens, fresh	–		15			
Mangoes, fresh	–		6			
Mangosteens, fresh	–					
Papaya, fresh	15					20
Yams, fresh	–					
Potential						
Strawberries, fresh	60	518	53	49		681
frozen	25		110	102		
Artichokes, fresh	c. 200	79	9			88
Avocados, fresh	40	94	1			95
Eggplant, fresh	40	48	22	22		70
Garlic, fresh	-15	52	19	8		71

Source: Adapted from U.S. Department of Agriculture, Economic Research Service, *Vegetable Situation, Fruit Situation, National Food Situation;* FAS, *Fruits and Vegetables, U.S. Imports (for Consumption) from Mexico;* and study estimates.

Note: Dashed line indicates not available.

Table 2–31. (cont.)

Market share, 1971 (percent)			Comments on future potential for Central America
U.S.	*Imports*	*Cent. Am.*	
58	42	10	High-risk variety trials; plantation
99	1		agriculture
86	14		Growth depends on processed produce
75	25	2	Must compete on costs and quality
100			Strong market, potential new export
89	11		Dec.–Feb. seasonal gap in market
84	16	1	Must compete with Chile
			Could dominate small market
90	10		Large-scale agriculture
73	27		Mexico dominates; probable oversupply
85	15		Must compete on costs and quality
100			Low-cost U.S. processing
97	3		Potential future growth
97	3		Canada supplies almost all imports
			Must compete with Mexico
100			
			No growth; large-scale operations
			Limited ethnic market
			Banana by-products only
			Very small markets; require investment in market development and promotion
84	16		Could compete with Mexico in eastern markets
90	10		Growth market in U.S.
99	1		Difficult to transport
69	31		Must compete with Mexico
73	27		Could displace Peru, Italy

cucumbers and cantaloupes. In both cases, the U. S. market is relatively large and consumption is rising about in line with population. Mexico has increased its share of these markets sharply in recent years and, in fact, has become the leading source of winter and early-spring cucumbers. In order for the Central American countries to capture a significant share of the future growth of these markets, they must become competitive in cost and quality with Mexico. There is some evidence that this is happening in cucumbers, for which Central America has become the second leading source of imports. In the case of cantaloupes, Central America will enjoy a competitive advantage if it is able to ship during the months of December, January, and February before Mexican supplies become available in significant quantities; it now supplies about 1 percent of total imports. It seems reasonable to assume that Central America could supply 10 percent of the *growth* in U. S. consumption of those commodities to 1980. This alone would double the 1970–71 level of fruit and vegetable exports.

Honeydew melons account for only 5 percent of the U. S. melon market, but per capita consumption has been increasing at the expense of watermelons. Central America may have an attractive opportunity in this market if it is able to compete effectively with Chile, the primary source of honeydew imports to date.

U. S. consumption of fresh pineapples, the leading Central American export in 1970–71, has not kept pace with the growth in processed products, both canned and juices. The outlook appears to be for the fresh market to stabilize at 120–150 million pounds. Any future opportunity for Central America depends on its ability to compete with U. S. production, mainly from Hawaii. This is a relatively high-risk alternative, however, because of the need to develop varieties that can be grown successfully in Central America, and because of the capital-intensive nature of pineapple production that necessitates plantation-scale agriculture. Expansion of Central American pineapple production probably depends on the development of a processing industry for both domestic and export markets.

U. S. production of okra is very small and imports account for a substantial portion of the total supply. During 1970–71, Central America provided about one-fourth of the imported volume. Continued growth depends almost entirely on the ability to compete in both cost and quality.

The potential for cassava depends on whether or not a significant market can be developed as well as on Central America's ability to grow and export efficiently.

Among those commodities for which Central America is presently only a very minor supplier, the U. S. market outlook is relatively favorable for tomatoes and peppers. In both of these cases, however, Mexico has become the dominant supplier during the winter season and appears to have the capacity to supply the entire market. In fact, as described in Appendix F, Mexican tomato growers are looking to Europe and other markets and to processing to absorb their expanded production potential. On the basis of present yields and costs, the opportunity for Central American growers to compete in eastern U. S. markets appears better for peppers than for tomatoes.

A systematic and integrated program to expand Central American exports of cucumbers, peppers, cantaloupes, and honeydews could, if successful, provide the basis for increasing total exports to well over 100 million lbs. per year by 1980, compared with 32 million lbs. in 1971−72. These are all commodities that could be produced in substantial quantities, utilizing Central America's inherent labor-cost and climatic advantages. Other basic commodity crops that may have potential for the future, but in which Central America has little or no export experience to date, might include eggplant, garlic, and squash. Imports, primarily from Mexico, now account for significant portions of U. S. supplies of each of these crops.

It is impossible to estimate the export potential for tropical fruits and vegetables, such as mangoes, papayas, and cassavas, for which no real market yet exists in the United States. These products are best viewed as "add-on" market opportunities, incremental to an export trade based on the standard, larger-volume commodities.

The potential for development of Central American exports of processed fruits and vegetables also appears favorable, although it will probably take longer than for fresh produce. The two commodities with significant quantities now (okra and cassavas) have limited markets in the United States. Even though the existing capacity for canning and freezing fruits and vegetables in Central America appears to be in excess of domestic market requirements, processors of these products face formidable problems in entering the export market.

1. Local growers are unable to supply the quantity and quality of raw materials required for processing for export. For most vegetables, different varieties must be developed and grown for the fresh market and for processing. The processing varieties must achieve a high degree of uniformity and quality, even at the cost of some loss in flavor.
2. Canning and freezing plants must be operated on as close to a year-round basis as possible. This requires that a wide variety of commodities be grown throughout the year and makes it difficult for producers to achieve economies of crop specialization.
3. There are substantial economies of scale, even in technologically simple canning operations, that are difficult to realize because of the limited size of domestic markets in Central America.
4. The need to locate processing plants close to sources of raw material increases transportation and handling difficulties in reaching both urban domestic markets and export markets.
5. Small-scale processors cannot afford the high fixed costs required to establish foreign distribution channels and to develop export marketing programs.

Despite these difficulties, however, there is a growing world market opportunity. Rising costs are forcing U. S. processors to search for new supply sources and processing locations in Central America as well as elsewhere. Our survey of the procurement practices of U. S. canners and freezers suggested that imports of fresh produce for processing in the United States may develop more rapidly than imports of processed products themselves. If this proves correct, the experience and training developed in Central America to establish a viable fresh-produce export industry may well serve as a basis for expanding into exports for processing.

Critical Factors for Export Development. In order to penetrate U. S. markets for fresh winter produce, a Central American export system must be developed that copes adequately with the critical factors affecting this industry.

1. Product Perishability. The perishability of fresh produce virtu-ally dictates that operating decisions be made on a day-to-day basis. This requires close coordination among all participants in the system and the availa-bility of reliable market and supply information on a current basis. The prob-lems of coordination increase more than proportionately with increases in the distance between supplying area and market.

2. Market Orientation. The requirements of the U. S. marketplace must be the starting point in planning Central American export production of fresh fruits and vegetables. These include not only quantities demanded and seasonal patterns of consumption and production in the United States, but also an understanding of the factors influencing the demand for these commodities. Consumer purchases of fresh produce are made largely on impulse and depend heavily on the appearance of the product in the retail store. It is essential, therefore, that export production be geared to meet the grade and quality standards used in the U. S. fresh-produce distribution system. No other single factor is as critical to successful entry as the ability to satisfy quality require-ments consistently with an acceptable level of loss and waste of product.

3. Grower-Importer Coordination. Because of the short lead times for decision making in the produce industry, much of the required coordination between growers and importers must be verbal and informal. Its success will depend on the development of attitudes of mutual trust and confidence between suppliers and purchasers. As the Mexican experience clearly indicates, brokers and distributors in the shipping-point market are a primary source of technical assistance, market information, and short-term working capital for growers. Similar relations do not exist at the present time between Central American growers and Pompano Beach importers. Settlement of accounts with Central

American suppliers, for example, is often delayed over a much longer period of time than with domestic growers.

4. Transportation. Mexico has a competitive advantage over Central America because it can utilize overland transportation to Nogales. As a result, Mexican shipments more nearly approximate a continuous flow, in contrast to periodic shiploads from Central America that run a high risk of glutting the Pompano Beach market on arrival. There is a great need for increased reliability, greater availability, and lower costs for Central American transport, which presently suffers from both lack of competition among alternative carriers and inadequate knowledge of the requirements for handling fresh produce. Much will depend on whether the rate of development of fruit and vegetable exports will provide an attractive profit opportunity for suppliers of transport. This will require careful analysis of the requirements of the total transportation system between Central America and the United States and the place of fruits and vegetables in that system. Assuming the availability of efficient transport, Central American shipping costs to the U. S. East Coast should be about 2 cents per pound below those from Mexico.

5. Farm Production. Successful production for export depends on the ability to combine specialization in one or two basic crops with farming methods that capitalize on the relative availability of low-cost land and labor in Central America. Priority should be given to commodities that do not readily lend themselves to mechanization by U. S. growers. One major need is for centralized control and coordination of each step in the farming process, from the procurement of inputs through planting, growing, harvesting, selecting, packing, cooling, and shipping to the port.

New capital, amounting to approximately $2 million, must be infused in the fruit and vegetable production sector in order to expand Central American exports to over 100 million pounds by 1980. A critical need is for intermediate-term financing running beyond a single growing season, on terms similar to those available to Mexican growers.

6. Domestic Market Development. No matter how efficient export production of fresh produce becomes, a substantial percentage of local production will not meet export-quality standards. Increased attention must be devoted to developing domestic markets, which are limited by low income levels and by the unequal distribution of income as well as by competition from home-grown produce. Unlike Mexico, where some 40 percent of fresh tomato output can be sold locally at prices above out-of-pocket costs, Central America now has no similar market mechanisms. In fact, attempts to sell rejects locally can have a serious impact on trade between countries, as is currently the case with El Salvador and Guatemala. Efforts to develop local markets may require a regional approach. In any event, solutions to the problem will require assistance from the public sector as well as from private enterprise.

7. Coordinating Mechanisms. One of the prime lessons to be learned from the Mexican experience relates to the critical role played by both the government and the various growers' associations in supporting the expansion of the fresh-produce export industry. Government investment in irrigation and highway facilities made the rapid expansion of exports possible. In addition, the Mexican government has played an active role in making seasonal and long-term credit available to export growers of fruits and vegetables. The state and local growers' associations have taken the lead in establishing effective controls of export quantities and quality, and in promoting the sale of Mexican produce in U. S. markets. The government has given the growers' associations the necessary legal sanctions and authority to permit them to operate effectively.

8. Training Requirements. Since Central American fresh fruit and fresh vegetable export operations represent a new industry for the area, there is a lack of personnel with specific industry training at all levels of the system. This applies to technical skills required at each stage in the system, as well as to an overall understanding of the way in which the components of the system interact with one another. One result is that Central America's potential competitive advantages are being eroded by inefficiencies in the system. Low wage rates, for example, are not translated into correspondingly lower labor costs per unit of output, because neither supervisors nor workers have the required knowledge of input costs and availabilities, farm methods, and so on. The small scale of present operations not only leads to higher costs, but also limits the market power of Central American suppliers in dealing with potential U. S. importers.

In spite of these and other inefficiencies, Central American exports of nontraditional fruits and vegetables are increasing at a rapid rate in response to both market opportunities in the United States and the initiative of a few individual entrepreneurs. Unless corrective action is taken, a shortage of qualified operating personnel could become the major bottleneck to continued expansion. A rough estimate suggests that in order for the volume of exports to triple by 1980 (to around 100 million lbs. per year), the number of personnel required must increase four to five times in order to provide the necessary technical and coordinating services. This, in turn, suggests the need to train more than 15,000 additional persons at all levels, from top manager to field worker, in fresh fruits and vegetables alone.

9. Educational Priorities. Just as there is a need to coordinate the operational aspects of the system, there is a corresponding need to coordinate the training and educational aspects. Only limited resources of both time and money are at the disposal of either the existing institutions capable of providing the necessary training or the potential participants in need of the training. It is essential, therefore, that priorities be established that are in accord with the realities of the fresh fruit and vegetable export commodity system. On the basis of our analysis of the rapidly changing U. S. marketing and distribution system, we see critical needs for:

a. Public officials capable of relating the requirements of the fruit and vege-
    table system to national and regional development priorities;
b. Managers capable of developing and implementing production and distribu-
    tion plans on the basis of a solid understanding of the requirements of the
    U. S. (and world) market;
c. Technicians with specialized knowledge of fruits and vegetables, especially in
    the areas of agronomy, quality control, and refrigerated transport;
d. Supervisors capable of coordinating harvesting, packing, and shipping
    operations on a day-to-day basis;
e. Effective on-the-job training methods for field and packing-shed workers.

Given these priorities, the major need is to build the capability for delivering them into the present agribusiness education system. Because of the need for new training methods and materials at all levels of fruit and vegetable operations, this will require a high degree of coordination among the various providers of educational services. The embryonic nature of the industry will make it necessary to reach outside the confines of current training programs and outside Central America for new educational resources as well as for operational knowledge and skills. This is particularly important in order to provide partici-pants in the fruit and vegetable export system with an understanding of the requirements of the U. S. and world markets.

NOTES TO CHAPTER TWO

1. One system that is growing more rapidly and holds promise for Central
    America is floriculture. In 1973, the Latin American Agribusiness
    Development Corporation had already brought together several
    Central American growers and U. S. brokers in a joint venture serv-
    ing the U. S. market. Appendix J gives a brief description of the U. S.
    floriculture system and its potential for Central American producers.
2. G. E. Brandon, *Price and Income Elasticities of Food Products* (Bulle-
    tin 680, State of Pennsylvania Agricultural Experiment Station,
    August 1961).
3. Ibid.
4. Throughout this study, pounds and short tons are used as the basic units of
    weight, as they are the units used in the United States which is the
    area of market opportunity in this study. The units of area em-

ployed are acres in the United States and hectares or manzanas in Central America as they are the units commonly used there. Appendix R contains a table of conversion factors for English and metric weights and measures.

5. U. S. Department of Agriculture, *Supplying U. S. Markets with Fresh Winter Produce* (Agricultural Economic Report 154, March 1969; and Supplement, September 1971).

6. *The Structure of Wholesale Produce Markets* (Agricultural Economic Report 45, Economic Research Service, U. S. Department of Agriculture, April 1964); *Market Structure of the Food Industries* (Marketing Research Report 971, Economic Research Service, U. S. Department of Agriculture, September 1972); and Clay J. Ritter, Chief, Market News Service, June 1973.

7. The difference between the volume produced and that consumed represents reductions in weight in processing, plus handling and spoilage losses. There was relatively little change during 1971 in the overall level of canned or frozen inventories.

8. The sources used to develop Figure 2–1 are detailed in Appendix H.

9. *Market Structure of the Food Industries* (Marketing Research Report 971, Economic Research Service, U. S. Department of Agriculture, 1972), p. 74.

10. National Commission on Food Marketing, *Organization and Competition in the Fruit and Vegetable Industry* (Technical Study No. 4, June 1966).

11. G. W. Biggs and J. K. Samuels, *Cooperative Fruit and Vegetable Processors in the United States* (U. S. Department of Agriculture, Farmer Cooperative Service, Report 123, May 1971).

12. D. L. Brooke, *Costs and Returns from Vegetable Crops in Florida Season 1970–71 with Comparisons* (Agricultural Economic Report 123, University of Florida, February 1972).

13. D. L. Brooke, *Citrus Production Costs and Returns in Florida Season 1969–70 with Comparisons* (Agricultural Economic Report 29, University of Florida, September 1971).

14. U. S. Department of Agriculture, *Supplying U. S. Markets with Fresh Winter Produce* (Agricultural Economic Report 154, March 1969; and Supplement, September 1971).

15. Ibid.

16. Ibid.

17. Agricultural Development Fund, a legal subsidiary of the Central Bank charged with ensuring adequate and sound development loans to Mexican agriculture, the FONDO, organized by the Central Bank in 1964, has had an outstanding record in meeting this objective. It mobilizes funds from (1) compulsory reserve requirements established for Mexican city banks (30 percent of liabilities); (2) government and Central Bank equity (20 percent); and (3) AID, World Bank, and Inter-American Development Bank long-term loans (50 percent). Its assets in mid-1972 totaled over $400 million. It carries

out its lending as a "second-floor" operation, discounting an average
of 82 percent of approved agricultural-development paper submitted
by 122 eligible private and public banks, on very favorable terms to
these banks. These discounts, however, are nonrecourse and, in
addition, the "first-floor" bank must have its own approved agricultural technician or one of the regional FONDO technicians (who
currently number over 225 people) prepare a complete integrated
development plan for the investment being supported. Without this
technical-assistance approval, the FONDO head office will not
discount the loan.

18. The success of the small-farmer approach to developing a new area remains
to be proved. A persuasive case can be made that the current
procurement programs in West Mexico were made possible only
because the original risks of development were assumed by large
commercial producing units.

19. William J. Higgins, *Mexico's Production of Horticultural Products for
Export* (U. S. Department of Agriculture, Foreign Agricultural
Service, 1968).

20. Ibid.

21. Ibid.

22. Food and Agriculture Organization of the United Nations, Intergovern-
mental Group on Bananas, Sub-Group on Statistics, *Banana Statistics* (August 1972), p. 9.

23. Ibid.

24. U. S. Department of Agriculture, Federal–State Market News Service,
Marketing Florida Vegetables: Summary of 1970–71 Season (November 1971).

25. Ibid.

Chapter Three

Coordination between Central American Exporters and the U.S. Market for Fruits and Vegetables

In the preceding chapter we described the long-term trends in the U. S. market for both fresh and processed fruits and vegetables. Changes in the structure of the production and distribution system that are taking place in response to these trends were also analyzed. Our emphasis now shifts to the viewpoint of the potential Central American grower or exporter who is attempting to become a participant in the U. S. fruit and vegetable commodity system. In this chapter, we shall look first at the overall problem of developing effective coordinating linkages between Central American exporters of fresh and processed fruits and vegetables and the U. S. market, and then examine in greater detail the transportation situation, which is at once a major current problem and a significant future opportunity.

Export of Fresh Fruits and Vegetables

Figure 3–1 shows in simplified form the connecting linkages between a Central American fresh-produce grower and the U. S. market system, and compares this connection with the situation faced by growers in West Mexico and the United States. The Central American producer is separated from the U. S. consumer by a long and fragmented chain, in which most of the ultimate retail value of his product is added after it leaves his control. The changes that are taking place in this system, such as various forms of vertical integration, have not yet included the Central American grower. Even a significant comparative cost advantage in farm production will not be sufficient to assure successful entry. Central America must find ways of linking itself directly to the changing demands of U. S. consumers.

Overall consumption of fresh produce in the United States is relatively static, but shifts in consumer preferences continually create market opportunities for individual commodities, such as the growth in demand for salad vegetables. More important, however, is the clear trend toward higher and

Figure 3–1. U.S. Fresh Fruit and Vegetable System.

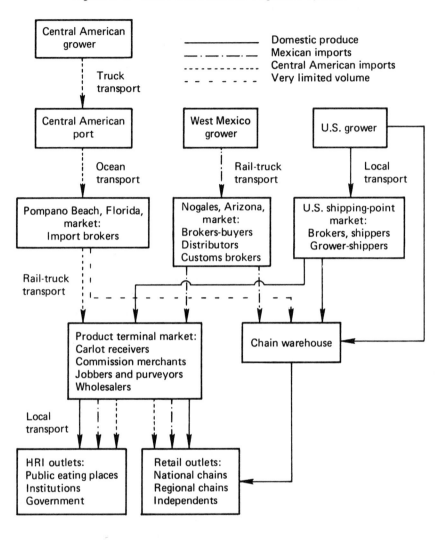

more uniform quality requirements for all types of fresh produce. Only about 10 percent of total fresh fruit and vegetable volume is now prepackaged at the source, but this fraction appears likely to increase rapidly. The recent announcement by Heggblade–Marguleas–Tenneco that they plan to market a broad line of prepackaged fresh fruits and vegetables under a single national brand is an example of this trend. If they are successful, such large-scale produce-marketing organizations will create significant opportunities for new suppliers capable of meeting stringent requirements for product quality and availability.

The changes taking place in the U. S. fresh fruit and vegetable commodity system reflect, in large part, the continuing cost-price squeeze affecting participants throughout the system. This squeeze has taken place even though retail prices of fresh produce have increased more rapidly than those of any other major food category since 1960 and have been a significant factor in the sharp increase in overall food prices since 1971. The marketing bill, that is, the sum of all costs incurred beyond the farm gate, accounts for about 70 percent of the retail value of fresh fruits and vegetables, a relatively high proportion compared to other food categories despite the fact that no value is added through processing. These high marketing costs result from three primary causes: (1) the perishability of fresh fruits and vegetables results in significant product loss and increases handling costs at all stages; (2) fresh produce distribution and marketing is labor-intensive, and increases in productivity have not been sufficient to offset rising wage rates; (3) transportation accounts for at least 10 percent of retail value and, in the case of trucks, rates are not subject to government regulation.

Retail chain stores have responded to these pressures by increasingly bypassing traditional produce terminal markets located in major metropolitan areas, and purchasing from shipping-point markets or, in some cases, directly from large growers. In order to supply individual outlets, retail chains have established their own warehouses and produce distribution centers that now handle an estimated two-thirds of the retail value of fresh fruits and vegetables. To date, however, backward integration has not extended to large-scale chain ownership of shipping-point distribution or farm production facilities. Within the retail chain organizations themselves, a new management position is emerging with responsibility for overall profitability of produce operations and for coordinating the activities of both buyers and merchandisers. This development reflects not only concern with cost-price pressures but also renewed recognition of the potential contribution of fresh produce to overall store profitability. It appears highly probable that managers with these responsibilities will become key decision makers in the fruit and vegetable commodity system of the future. In the long run, Central American exporters must be able to establish effective direct working relations at the retail-chain level.

More immediately, however, Central America is at a disadvantage vis-à-vis both the United States and West Mexico in terms of effective coordination betweeɪ growers and shipping-point markets. Typically, in the United States, the shipping-point market is located in or close to the growing area, and there is considerable overlap among individuals participating in the two functions. In fact, the predominant trend in domestic shipping-point markets has been the emergence of large grower-shippers, organized either as cooperatives or as private businesses. The net result has been a substantial increase in the extent of direct interface between fruit and vegetable producers and both chain buyers and full-line service wholesalers in terminal markets. These links will become increasingly important as both production and shipping-point markets gradually become more concentrated in the major growing areas.

In the case of West Mexico, the shipping-point market is located not in the Culiacán growing area, but some 600 miles north at Nogales, Arizona, on the U. S. border. This lack of proximity has been compensated for, however, by effective coordinating methods that have evolved over time. The key figures in this coordination are approximately 50 distributors located in Nogales, who handle virtually all of the winter-produce volume from Mexico. Typically, these distributors have direct financial interests in the growing operations and are the prime source of short-term working capital for producers. The Nogales distributors have established close daily (or even hourly) communication with Mexican producers, which makes possible efficient handling of individual arrivals. Some 15 to 20 customs brokers located on the Mexican side of the border play critical roles in maintaining the flow of traffic, which reached a peak of about 350 trucks per day during the 1971−72 season. On the selling side, distributors maintain continuous contact with 40 to 50 buying brokers and a small number (less than 10) of chain buyers who are resident in Nogales during the season. Despite the fact that transport costs, customs duties, brokers fees, and so on amount to about 50 percent of total cost f.o.b. Nogales, produce from Mexico is effectively competitive with U. S. production.

By contrast, the principal U. S. shipping-point market for Central American produce, located at Pompano Beach, Florida, has yet to develop effective methods of grower-shipper coordination. There are only four or five importers handling supplies from Central America, and these typically also act as selling brokers to produce-terminal markets or, though less likely, to retail chains. With one exception, the Pompano Beach brokers interviewed in the course of this research had no financial commitment to growers, and generally maintained only irregular contact. Sales are made on a consignment basis and settlement is often long delayed to permit final accounting for product losses. The climate of mutual trust and confidence necessary for effective day-to-day fresh-produce operations has not yet developed in the Pompano Beach market.

Central American shippers are also at a competitive disadvantage at the present time because of the lack of availability and high cost of transport from growing areas to shipping-point markets. This cost is minimal for U. S. producers because of close geographic proximity. Freight from West Mexico to Nogales is a significant cost element, but the impact has been minimized by an efficient overland transportation system developed during the last two decades. Trucks have virtually replaced rail cars in this service, with the result that deliveries approximate a continuous flow during the Mexican winter season. This, in turn, tends to decrease fluctuations in the Nogales price by eliminating the large discrete arrivals that can depress the market substantially on any given day.

Central America faces two rather obvious disadvantages in competing with this system. In the first place, U. S. shipments are almost entirely ocean borne (air transport is still uneconomical for most fruits and vegetables), and thus partly dependent on schedules established for reasons other than the requirements of the fruit and vegetable trade. This by necessity results in irregular arrivals of shipments that tend to be relatively large in relation to market requirements. Second, most Central American growing areas are located at some distance from export ports, which necessitates the use of high-cost domestic truck transport over highway systems that in many cases are ill-suited to the purpose. Both the problem of internal transport within Central America and that of transport to the United States must be approached as matters of national or regional development policy, because the factors involved go far beyond the economics of nontraditional fruit and vegetable exports alone.

Mexican fresh fruit and vegetable exports have benefited greatly from sustained government programs of highway and irrigation development. In addition, the government has made it possible for growers to obtain intermediate-term financing at reasonable costs, and has enacted legislation in support of strong growers' associations. These associations, in turn, have played leading roles in establishing quality standards and developing programs of supply management relating export quantities to market conditions in the United States. This management of supply has been facilitated by the existence of a commercial domestic market for fresh produce in Mexico capable of absorbing nonexportable surpluses.

Conflicting political pressures have developed within the United States against and for the importation of fresh fruits and vegetables. U. S. growers, particularly in Florida, have periodically attempted to limit imports to counteract the steady increases in Mexico's shipments and share of the market. California and Texas have declined in importance as suppliers of fresh vegetables during the winter season. On the other hand, rising retail prices and the spread of consumerism generally have resulted in a growing concern on the part of consumer groups about the cost and quality of U. S. fresh fruit and vegetable supplies. The net result may be greater awareness on the part of both Mexican and U. S. producers of the need to coordinate their efforts to stabilize the winter produce market.[1]

Export of Processed Fruits and Vegetables

Figure 3–2 is a simplified flowchart of the U. S. commodity system for processed fruits and vegetables as it relates to both domestic and foreign processors, including Central America. In contrast to the situation that exists in fresh fruit and vegetable imports, the import system from Mexico is not shown separately because it is still in the early stages of development. Mexican shipments of processed fruits and vegetables to the United States have reached a total of about $20 million per year, but about 75 percent of this volume is a single product, frozen strawberries. More important, no counterpart of the

Figure 3-2. U.S. Processed Fruit and Vegetable System.

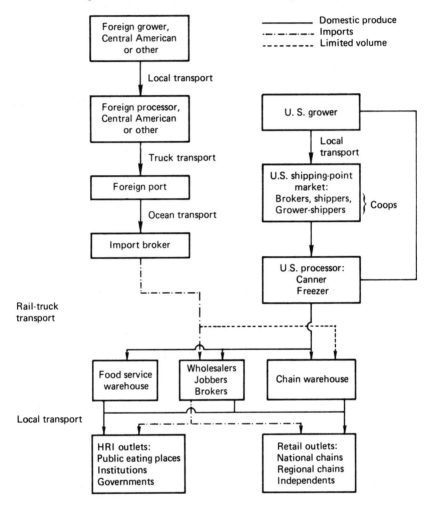

Nogales market for fresh produce has yet been developed. The great majority of Mexican sales in the United States are made through import brokers (see Appendix G).

The U. S. market for processed fruits and vegetables is growing more rapidly than demand for fresh produce. Most of this growth is concentrated in convenience and specialty items, especially frozen products, many of which are designed to be consumed as part of packaged meals. Use in public eating places and institutions is growing faster than retail consumer demand.

Despite the expansion of demand, the processed commodity system faces many of the same cost-price pressures as the fresh system. Competition for retail shelf space is especially keen. Consumer prices have not risen as much for fresh produce and, in fact, some national retail chains have recently adopted widespread policies of price discounting. The chains have also gradually increased the share of their private-label brands at the expense of national-brand processors.

Direct purchases from processors and distribution through chain-owned warehouses account for about 12 percent of the total retail value of processed fruit and vegetable sales. There has been relatively little backward integration into ownership of processing plants by the retail chains. The normal procedure is for a chain to contract for its estimated requirements with a processor at the start of a pack year. Deliveries are made against the contracted volume, with the price usually dependent on the market at the time of delivery. Under these conditions, the processor usually assumes the inventory holding costs. Contractual relations between retail chains and the larger U. S. processors have developed over a long period of time and tend to be relatively stable.

In recent years, some of the larger institutional and industrial food-service systems have followed the lead of the retail chains in establishing their own warehouse and distribution systems and in contracting to purchase directly from processors. In a few cases retail chains themselves have contracted to supply individual food-service outlets through their own warehouses.

Direct procurement by either retail chains or food-service operators from foreign processors of fruits and vegetables has been limited so far, mainly to specialty items not readily obtainable domestically, such as canned mandarin oranges from the Far East or stuffed olives from the Mediterranean. Retailers surveyed in the course of this study, however, indicated widespread interest in developing alternative sources of supply but little knowledge of how to go about it.

The average profitability of U. S. fruit and vegetable processing is, in general, somewhat below that of manufacturing industries. There are, however, significant economies of scale resulting from heavy capital advertising, promotion, and product-development expense. As a result, there has been a long-run tendency toward greater industry concentration and larger plant size among both canners and freezers. As few as 50 plants probably account for as much as 75 percent of total production.

U. S. fruit and vegetable processors have been quite successful in responding to consumer demands for convenience food products. Continued innovations in new product development have produced for consumers a wide variety of items with built-in convenience features at costs that are competitive with home preparation.

On the procurement side, U. S. processors have relied largely on contractual arrangements with grower-shippers to assure themselves of adequate raw-material supplies. Verbal or written contracts, usually providing for a significant degree of processor control over growing operations, account for two-thirds to three-fourths of total fruit and vegetable purchases by U. S. processors. Farms owned or operated by processors account for about 10 percent, and various forms of corporate-cooperative joint ventures account for an additional 15 percent. Fresh-produce distributorships and processing operations owned by farm cooperatives account for 30 percent of the total market sales of fruits and vegetables directly from the farm. The balance is purchased on the open market. There is some interest on the part of U. S. processors in developing foreign sources of new materials or of frozen products for reprocessing.

The major obstacles faced by Central American fruit and vegetable processors in penetrating the U. S. market are their small size, their lack of familiarity with the U. S. market, their limited utilization of the options open to them with respect to contractual integration and transportation arrangements, their lack of adequate financing, and the unavailability of local raw materials meeting quality requirements for export. The processing operations are on a small scale because the domestic markets are undeveloped and therefore are not capable of supporting plants of efficient size.

Even more important, however, is the lack of knowledge of either industry or Food and Drug Administration quality standards in the United States, and the lack of market and transportation information in general. For some relatively low-volume processed commodities, such as frozen okra, Central America could become a significant supplier if the information gap could be reduced or eliminated. This will eventually require the development of either direct sales to U. S. processors or marketing partnerships. Ultimately, exporters may sell directly to the retail chains and food-service establishments rather than continue to rely exclusively on import brokers, whose traditional outlets have been buying brokers or wholesalers. The processed fruit and vegetable commodity system in the United States is much simpler and less fragmented than that for fresh produce. This, in turn, will make it easier for Central American processors to become successful participants if they are able to overcome internal cost and quality problems.

The Transportation System

Perhaps the single most important coordination problem to be overcome in developing an effective export-import system for Central American produce is the development of efficient cost-competitive transportation. As previously noted, the construction in the mid–1950s of a paved highway serving the west coast of Mexico permitted the expansion of fruit and vegetable exports and led to the establishment of Nogales, Arizona, as the primary point of import to the United States.

Although a variety of transport services is available to serve Central America, only one carrier offers integrated, containerized, land-sea services from the entire Central American area to Miami. This is Coordinated Caribbean

Transport, Inc. (CCT), which has been operating from Puerto Cortés in Honduras and Santo Tomás de Castilla in Guatemala to Miami since 1961. Although CCT offers some service to the east coast of Nicaragua and Costa Rica, these areas have not developed to the point that they are of commercial importance. The CCT roll-on roll-off operation is currently one of several practical and economical methods for carrying fresh fruits and vegetables from Central America to U. S. winter markets. Others include that of Sea-Land, which covers Costa Rica through Panama as of October, 1972 and Nicaragua since December 26, 1972. In June, 1973, a new service was initiated by Chester, Blackburn & Roder, who are agents for Flomerca Trailers Service (see Appendix K), based on an agreement of Flomerca in Guatemala and the Pan American Mail Line, Inc. In addition, Sea-Land will initiate service to El Salvador, Honduras, and Guatemala if the Minister of Economy of Guatemala approves their use of the port of Santo Tomás. A new transport agency has also been developed that ships to Miami from Honduras as of June 1973.

Scheduled liner service is also offered by Astra Lines from Santo Tomás, but the high cost of unloading the produce from a truck, storing it in refrigerated warehouses, and transferring it to the ship has made this form of transportation unattractive. Liner service from the west coast is available, and there are occasional tramp ships calling at the west-coast ports.

Overland transport using Mexican roads is possible, but it is both extremely difficult and expensive. It would also require a change of equipment at each of the international boundaries, since the trucks from one country are not currently allowed to haul produce in another, except within the Central American Common Market.

A variety of air services also exists between the Central American countries and the United States. Los Angeles, New Orleans, and Miami are the cities with the most frequent service. The relative positions of the various producing areas, export ports, import markets, and typical final consumption centers in the north and east of the United States are shown in Figure 3—3.

For approximately a year (until April, 1972), CCT offered two sailings per week from the port of Santo Tomás, scheduled so that they could meet the twice-weekly vegetable market in Pompano Beach, Florida. This was offered with two roll-on roll-off ships, the *Mar Caribe,* with a capacity of 55 trailers, and the *Enterprise,* a short-term leased ship with a capacity of 49 trailers.

In early April, 1972, the *Enterprise* was withdrawn from service, the *Mar Caribe* was transferred to Panama, and both were replaced with a new ship, the *Caribbean Progress,* with a capacity of 85 trailers. Service reverted to once-a-week sailings. From the point of view of the shipper, this was a significant reduction in service. If continued, once-a-week sailings will force producers to construct refrigerated warehouses in which to store produce between sailings, unless competitive lines are permitted to use the port of Santo Tomás.

Figure 3-3.   Relative Positions of Producing Areas, Export Ports, Import Markets, and Consumption Centers.

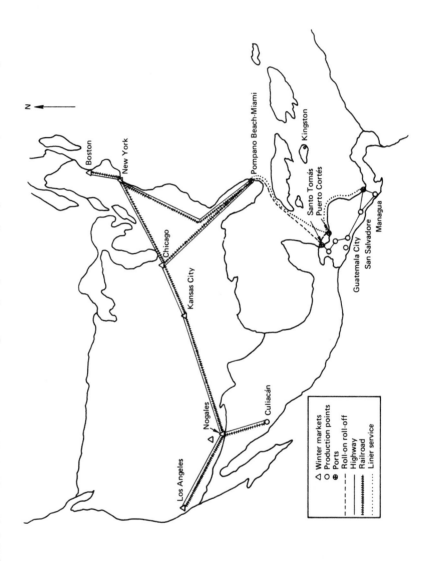

The CCT service includes local delivery to the packing sheds of an empty van that CCT contracts from locally leased truckers using their own trailers. The trailers are 12 meters (40 ft.) in length and capable of hauling 40,000 pounds with approximately 53 to 56 cubic meters (1900 to 2000 cu. ft.) of chilled storage space. This is a designed density of 707 pounds/cubic meters (20 lbs./ft.^{3}). Goods that weigh less than this tend to "cube-out" before they reach the weight limitation.[2]

The shipping characteristics of various kinds of fresh fruits and vegetables are shown in Table 3–1. The produce shown in the table is typical of current production in Central America and Mexico. Where it is possible to distinguish between the particular characteristics of the various commodities, the shipping densities all favor the use of trucks. Optimum storage temperature and maximum storage time give some indication of the degree of flexibility in the transport schedule. It can be seen from this table that ripe tomatoes, peppers, cantaloupes, and strawberries are all quite perishable.

Trailer refrigerator units are started as the trailer is loaded. They run continuously while the trailer is carried to the port, loaded aboard the roll-on roll-off ship, ferried to Miami, disembarked, and hauled without unloading to Pompano Beach. As the result of contract agreements with the International Longshoreman's Association a load-unload fee of $2 per ton is paid, although it is not necessary to physically unload the unit until it arrives at the winter vegetable market in Pompano Beach. Here the load is stored in a refrigerated warehouse until it is sold. Transportation to the final destination is arranged through a truck broker.

Ocean-Transport Cost Analysis

The tariff for the passage, including pick-up and delivery on both ends, was $1250 per refrigerated trailer from production points in eastern Guatemala to the Pompano Beach market during the 1971–72 winter season. With wharfage and other charges, total transportation costs were almost $1400.

The reasonableness of these transport costs from Central America to

Table 3–1. Commodity Shipping Characteristics.

Commodity	Weight per 1-1/9 bu. crate (lb.)	Shipping lbs./cu. ft.	Maximum storage time (days)	Optimum storage temperature (°F)
Cucumbers	55	36.7	14–21	45–50
Tomatoes	59	39.3	Ripe, 8–12	50
			Green, 14–45	55–60
Eggplant	35	23.4	10	45–50
Okra	33	22.0	14	50
Peppers	30	20.0	8–10	45–50
Cantaloupes	50	33.4	7–14	40–50
Strawberries	59	39.3	5–10	31–32

the United States can be evaluated by comparing them with transport costs for other commodities moving from Guatemala to Miami by CCT service. Shrimp, moving by refrigerated trailer, travels from Guatemala through Santo Tomás for $1350 per trailer. Flowers from Guatemala City move for $800 per trailer. Coffee moving in an unrefrigerated trailer on a when-space-is-available basis moves for $560 out of Santo Tomás. Thus there is a wide range of prices, and cucumbers are toward the high end of the range.

The higher prices for shipping cucumbers can be ascribed in part to the lack of alternative shipping modes or times. Flowers, for instance, can be shipped by air at competitive rates. Therefore, ocean shippers must charge lower rates for flowers if they are to attract them as cargo. Coffee, on the other hand, can conveniently be shipped at alternative times since it is dry, does not need refrigeration, and can be shipped on a stand-by basis. Cucumbers, however, since they are too heavy for air shipment and too perishable for stand-by status, must be transported by ship on a priority basis.

Since a large part of a carrier's costs are fixed, it is difficult for him to allocate them. Typically, a carrier faced with this situation will discriminate, charging a higher price where the traffic will bear it. It appears that the fully allocated cost of transport by roll-on roll-off ship is lower than the tariff that is currently being charged for cucumbers. There may be some hope over the long run for reducing these tariffs. However, the nature of the present system suggests that this will not happen until competition increases, or until the shippers convince the carrier that they cannot sustain these costs and continue to ship.

Recent experience is not promising, since in 1972 the charge was $1250 per trailer, compared with $950 in 1971. However, there was a difference in scheduled service, since in 1971 the service was only one sailing per week as contracted with twice-a-week service in 1972, and the cost for this higher level of service is reflected in the higher rate.

The sailing time from Guatemala to Miami is approximately two and one-half days. Adding a stop in Puerto Cortés in Honduras produces a total round-trip time of approximately six days. Since it would be impossible to get more than one round trip per week from a single ship, twice-a-week service requires two ships. When a second ship was leased to provide this service, CCT faced the question of how much to charge shippers for the additional capacity. The leased cost of the ship was $2800 per day plus fuel. Fuel cost per week was approximately $1000.

With the addition of the second ship, it was also necessary to lease additional refrigerated trailers. A short-term lease was negotiated by CCT with Rock Island Lines for 120 refrigerated trailers at a total cost of $65,000. The use of 120 trailers gives CCT the ability to carry 40 trailers at each sailing and to leave them in place for three and one-half days on the average. This is probably more trailers than are needed, but certainly fewer than the capacity of the vessel.

From these basic data, it can be shown that it takes well over 20 trailers per week to break even with that type of service. During the planning stage, approximately 40 trailers of vegetables per week were anticipated.

The overall capacity of the service was clearly increased by the addition of the leased ship, and some growth in traffic probably occurred as a result of the improved service. However, it is clear that the transportation company did not make a profit from the additional service. Unless other traffic increased rather substantially, a loss was incurred in offering this additional service just for the fresh fruit and vegetable trade. Yet if normal traffic growth had placed the company in the position where they needed an additional ship in any event, then twice-a-week service appears to be a reasonable, though high-cost, way to offer this capacity.

The low-cost method of providing this service is with a single larger ship. This is the long-term strategy apparently favored by CCT. Transportation service offered by CCT reverted to once-a-week sailings in April, 1972. Clearly the economics of transporting more trailers on a larger ship favors the use of a single sailing per week over two sailings per week.

This leaves in question the probable situation for the 1973–74 season. If the government and the shippers are not able to persuade CCT that twice-a-week service is necessary or they do not permit Sea-Land to participate, they will have to provide refrigeration within the packing facilities to hold the produce until the next shipment, since picking must be accomplished once every two days as the fruit reaches its optimum harvesting point.

Delivered-Cost Analysis

Transport in the United States from the winter vegetable shipping-point market to the area of final consumption is primarily by refrigerated truck. Some goods are handled by piggyback or by refrigerated rail car.

Fresh fruits and vegetables are agriculturally exempt commodities, and their transportation is not regulated by the Interstate Commerce Commission. Prices for this transportation are neither fixed by rates nor offered in a price schedule, but are negotiated and fluctuate in response to the availability of trucks and the amount of goods to be carried.

The refrigerated truck is the prime mode of transport for winter vegetables and fruits from shipping point to final consumption area. When the demand for the carriage of goods is high and the number of truckers is small, freight rates increase. When it is impossible to secure the services of a trucker, it may be necessary to ship piggyback or by refrigerated rail car. Truck rates vary between $1500 and $2000 per trailer from Nogales to New York, in contrast with a piggyback rate of approximately $1100. Although piggyback service is cheaper than direct trucking, it is also much more time-consuming, requiring between six and ten days from Nogales to New York, for example, as opposed to fourth-morning delivery by truck.

The break-even cost for operating a refrigerated truck is approximately 50 cents per vehicle-mile. Thus, for the 2200-mile haul from Nogales to New York, the truck cost is equal to the rail rate. Rail service does not include pickup and delivery of the refrigerated van, and long travel times tend to result in higher spoilage. A set of very fast, expedited, refrigerated-express, piggyback trains to major eastern cities from Nogales could conceivably compete in this market. However, the railroads are reducing service rather than increasing it. Railroad service between Miami and New York is similar.

Trucking arrangements are handled by a truck broker who arranges for loads for the independent truckers to pick up, and he charges 7 to 8 percent of the total trucking tariff as his fee.

A summary of the costs and time considerations involved in transporting fresh fruits and vegetables from producing areas to importing points and to large eastern and central markets is shown in Table 3–2. Central American growers shipping through Pompano Beach can land goods in New York for transport costs of between 7 and 8 cents per pound. In Chicago and Kansas City, the figure ranges slightly over 7 cents. For Mexican production points, traveling through Nogales, the total cost of transportation to New York is approximately the same as that from Central America via Miami. However, for Kansas City and Chicago there is an advantage held by the Mexican producer, since transport costs amount to only about 6 cents per pound to these two points.

Long-Run Transport Situation

The long-run economics of roll-on roll-off operations depend on the length of haul, the size of the vessel, the balance of flows in the two directions, and their impact on the percentage of back-haul in the direction of imbalance. In general, the larger the ship and the longer the haul, the lower the costs per ton mile. To some extent, seasonality also influences the economics of the operation. The fresh fruit and vegetable industry is very seasonal, with relatively high volume, and this tends to have a detrimental rather than a beneficial impact on costs. There are very few roll-on roll-off ships in operation that carry as few as 50 trailers. Most carry considerably more than this.

A rough comparison can be made with a study of a container ferry for the Boston–New York interchange of containers, that has developed container-mile costs for roll-on roll-off and conventional container designs. The containers being considered are 20-foot boxes rather than the standard 40-foot trailers used in the Guatemala operation. For roll-on roll-off operation they are loaded with wheels attached, 150 per ship. For an 1100-mile trip, at 24 cents per container mile, the cost is $264 per container. For container-ship operations they are loaded without wheels and are placed on chassis for final delivery by truck. At 17 cents per mile the cost is $187. When these figures are adjusted both for container length and for the fact that 40 percent of the empties were assumed to be returned by other means than by ship, the figures come to approximately $550 per container by roll-on roll-off ship, and $400 per container by cellular ship.

Table 3–2. Costs and Times in Transporting Fruits and Vegetables from Producing Areas to Marketing Points

Producing area	Marketing point	Distance (miles)	Times transported per week	Cost of trailer transport (dollars)	Days en route	Transportation cost (dollars/lb.)
Culiacán	Nogales	550	Once daily	$225	1	$.04–.05/lb. (incl. customs and handling)
Santo Tomás	Pompano Beach	1,100	2	1,250	2	.031/lb.
Los Angeles	Los Angeles		Daily market		½ day to unload; ½ day to reprocess	.02625/lb. (incl. customs and handling)
Pompano Beach	Pompano Beach		Daily market		½ day to unload; ½ day to reprocess	.02775/lb. (incl. customs and handling)
Nogales	Chicago	2,000	Once daily	900–1,250	3	.025–.404/lb.
Nogales	New York	2,200	Once daily	1,500–2,000	4	.045–.070/lb.
Nogales	Kansas City	900	Once daily	800–1,100	2	.02–.035/lb.
Pompano Beach	Kansas City	1,470	2	1,015	3	.025/lb.
Pompano Beach	New York	1,200	2	100–1,000	2	.017–.025/lb.

In general, then, roll-on roll-off appears to be approximately 38 percent more costly than cellular ships of the same capacity. However, there is a saving in load-unload time in port, so the productivity of a roll-on roll-off vessel is slightly higher. Also, the handling equipment for containers is expensive and can be avoided entirely with roll-on roll-off. For large volumes, container ships will definitely be cheaper. However, they will be slower and less suited to the carriage of fresh produce.

One might conclude from these figures that there is some room for reduction in rates as the volume of trade builds in this market. But there will always be a problem with seasonality. The fruit and vegetable import season runs from approximately December through May—only six months—with peak volumes for only about three months. The problem is what to do with the unused capacity during the remaining six months of the year. If *counter*cyclical trade could be developed, the cost could be reduced substantially, since a great many of the costs involved are fixed. There will probably be no real reduction in rates until some change in the competitive structure of the transportation market takes place.

Competition in Transportation

For a number of years, Sea-Land, the large container-shipping organization based in New York and operating both Atlantic and Latin American trade routes, has appeared ready to begin service to Central American ports. Service to Panama was instituted in October, 1972, but approval to commence operations from Santo Tomás in Guatemala had not, by mid–1973, been obtained.

The Central American Bank for Economic Integration (CABEI) has recently completed a loan of $1.8 million to a U. S. company, Eagle Lines, to establish a container-ship operation between Puerto Cortés, Honduras, and Miami. The $1.8-million loan of CABEI is only one-half of the investment required to establish the operation and to begin the purchase of the first of two ships that would carry 40 trailers each.

There is some question whether this is adequate financing to purchase a ship and to get the operation under way. It is clear, however, that the CABEI loan will not be lost through bankruptcy, since it will go principally to the purchase of a ship and operating equipment. It seems likely, therefore, that even if this company fails, another will step in to take its place, perhaps with a great deal more expertise.

Another possibility is chartering refrigerated ships for the six-month period of the harvest. In order to get twice-a-week service, two vessels would have to be chartered, at a cost of $25,000 each per month. An initial deposit for the first and last month's charter, payable in advance, amounts to a total of $100,000 for two vessels. This alone is too high to make the operation attractive. Furthermore, a chartered ship with refrigerator facilities does not give comparable service to that offered by a roll-on roll-off ship, since a great deal of transloading would have to be performed to use the charter-ship operation.

Another potential competitor is air freight by scheduled carrier. At the moment the direction of principal haul is from Miami to Central America. Regularly scheduled airlines charge 17 cents per pound for this "fore haul" trip. On the "back haul," space is offered at between 5 and 6 cents per pound from Guatemala City and other Central American capitals to Miami. This price looks interesting for the movement of some commodities. For cucumbers, with a shipping density of 36.7 pounds per cubic foot on the average, the cost of 3.5 cents per pound by roll-on roll-off refrigerated trailer is very difficult to challenge by air; but for peppers, with a density of 20 pounds per cubic foot, the unit cost rises to 4.5 to 6.5 cents per pound, depending on the tightness of packing within the trailer. With air-circulation space allowed, the cost per pound approaches the air-freight back-haul rate from Central America to Miami.

The major problem with scheduled air freight is that there is very little capacity for larger bulk haulage. It would not take many truckloads of peppers to completely fill all the scheduled air-cargo space from Central America to Miami. A Boeing 707 air freighter has about 70,000 pounds of capacity. This is less than two trailerloads.

One way in which this capacity limitation can be overcome is the use of air charter. Pan American, Aviateca (Guatemala), and Tan (Honduras) all offer air charter services. Different types of airplanes have different air charter prices. Other carriers are available, but the Civil Aeronautics Board (CAB) regulations state that a carrier operating more than one air charter per week to and from a specific destination must be certificated. This appears to limit the number of operations that an uncertificated carrier can offer, although there are probably ways in which this regulation could be circumvented if it stood in the way of a profitable operation. The comparative figures for air transportation shown in Table 3–3 include the charter price, the direct and indirect cost, and

Table 3–3. Comparative Figures for Air Transportation, Central America to Miami.

Equipment	Cargo weight (lb.)	Charter price (dollars)	Direct and indirect costs (dollars per available ton mile)	Cost (dollars/lb.)
DC–6	25,000 lbs.	$3240	–	$0.13
DC–7	40,000	–	$0.101	.17
Constellation	35,000	2600		.075
707	66,000 (belly)	6000	0.11	.15
DC–8	92,000	–	.072–.092	–
747	214,000	–	.06 –.07	–
Truck	40,000	1400	.036–.056	–

Note: Air backhaul rates are $.05–.07/ton mile; backhaul rates for charter are $.03–.04/ton mile.

Table 3–4.   Basic Transportation Data.[a]

Country	Mid–1969 population (million)	Area (km.²)	GNP per cap. (U. S. dollars)	Paved	Gravel and earth	Total
Central America and Caribbean						
Costa Rica	1.7	50,695	506	1,300	17,300	18,600
Dominican Republic	4.0	48,730	276	5,100	4,900	10,000
El Salvador	3.4	21,392	294	1,200	7,300	8,500
Guatemala	5.0	108,880	353	1,851	8,533	10,384
Guyana	0.7	214,953	340	592	1,932	2,524
Honduras	2.5	112,079	258	900	3,026	3,926
Jamaica	2.0	11,424	548	3,050	1,300	4,350
Mexico	48.9	1,963,739	586	40,333	29,094	69,427
Nicaragua	1.9	139,689	380	1,200	8,800	10,000
Panama	1.4	75,643	662	1,801	4,981	6,782
Trinidad and Tobago	1.0	5,125	885	4,025	2,737	6,762
Venezuela	10.0	911,993	1,003	18,000	21,600	39,600
Selected capital–exporting countries						
France	50.3	551,458	2,460	629,593	853,146	1,482,739
Germany	60.8	248,477	2,190	290,271	124,402	414,673
Japan	102.3	369,660	1,430	127,188	878,243	1,005,431
United States	203.2	9,374,826	4,241	2,533,374	3,395,420	5,928,794

The column heading "Road network length (km.)" spans the *Paved*, *Gravel and earth*, and *Total* columns.

Source: International Bank for Reconstruction and Development, *World Bank Operations: Sectoral Programs and Policies* (Baltimore: Johns Hopkins University Press, 1972), pp. 182–183.

a. All data are for 1969. They are based on various standard publications, revised according to information available in the Bank. However, many of these figures are inaccurate and should be considered only as orders of magnitude. The weakest information concerns the length of gravel and earth road networks where the distinction between an earth road and a track is an extremely difficult one to make and may vary from country to country. GNP per capita figures are derived from data employed for the world Bank *Atlas;* the fact that they are not rounded, as in the *Atlas,* should not be taken as an indication of greater precision.

b. Road or railway length (km.) divided by area of country (km.²).

the computed cost per pound for charter operations based on operations from Central America to Miami. The costs per ton-mile that are possible for the Boeing 747 seem to indicate that it also will have unacceptably high operating costs in competition with surface roll-on roll-off truck rates.

For floricultural products, however, and for more perishable fruits, such as strawberries, there definitely are air-carrier possibilities. If, in the long run, direct contacts are developed between growers and chain outlets in the United States, direct air shipment from Central America to the point of final consumption appears to be possible for these products.

Table 3–4. (cont.)

Railway route length (km.)	Number of vehicles available			Road density[b] (km.)	Railway density[b] (km.)	Vehicles per 1,000 population
	Light	*Heavy*	*Total*			
548	36,000	20,000	56,000	0.367	0.011	32.9
600	41,734	23,452	65,186	.205	.012	15.5
620	31,300	15,900	47,200	.397	.029	13.9
1,019	33,000	20,500	53,500	.095	.009	10.7
205	14,196	7,924	22,120	.012	.001	31.6
649	14,200	16,600	30,800	.035	.006	12.3
394	60,000	20,000	80,000	.381	.035	40.0
20,207	112,100	524,600	1,636,700	.035	.010	33.5
4,981	14,000	22,000	36,000	.072	.036	18.9
700	41,335	13,785	55,120	.090	.009	39.4
–	67,600	18,800	86,400	1.319	–	86.4
471	498,000	200,000	698,000	0.043	.001	69.8
39,660	11,155,000	2,065,000	13,220,000	2.689	0.072	262.8
33,660	11,682,556	1,045,297	12,727,853	1.669	.136	209.3
24,140	5,209,319	7,027,538	12,236,857	2.720	.065	119.6
356,619	82,821,000	17,137,000	99,958,000	0.632	.038	491.9

Internal Transportation Networks

As explained earlier in this chapter, the infrastructure in the various countries of Central America is also extremely important in the development of coordinating linkages. The basic transport data for Central America shown in Table 3–4 indicates the lack of adequate transportation facilities, especially of rural roads in these areas, compared with selected capital–exporting countries that usually import items from Central America. It is true that these statistics vary from country to country in Central America, but nevertheless, transportation remains a high priority in each country. Table 3–5 details a number of loans to Central American countries made by the World Bank for transportation improvements. Distances between Santo Tomás, the main port, and principal cities are as follows: Guatemala City, 187 miles (301 km.); San Salvador, 333 miles (536 km.); Tegucigalpa, 556 miles (895 km.); Managua, 760 miles (1220 km.); and San José, 982 miles (1580 km.).

Future Transportation Potential

The future of containerized water transport from and to Central America is perhaps much brighter than has been suggested thus far in our analysis. U. S. Bureau of the Census data indicate that in 1970 about 35 trailer

Table 3–5.   World Bank and IDA Loans to Central American and Caribbean Countries for Transport (*10⁶ dollars*), Fiscal Years 1963–1971.

Country	Through 1963	1964	1965	1966	1967	1968	1969	1970	1971	Total, 1964–68	Total, 1967–71
Costa Rica	11.0	—	—	—	—	—	—	15.7	—	—	15.7
Dominican Republic	—	—	—	—	—	—	—	—	—	—	—
El Salvador	24.1	—	—	—	—	2.8	—	—	—	2.8	2.8
Guatemala	18.2	—	—	—	—	—	—	—	—	—	—
Guyana	—	—	—	—	—	—	—	—	—	—	—
Haiti	2.95	—	—	—	—	—	—	—	—	—	—
Honduras	18.7	—	9.5	—	13.4	—	—	—	6.0	22.9	19.4
Jamaica	—	—	5.5	—	—	—	—	—	—	5.5	—
Mexico	116.5	40.0	32.0	—	—	27.5	—	21.8	—	99.5	49.3
Nicaragua	10.2	—	—	—	—	—	—	—	—	—	—
Panama	13.1	—	—	—	—	—	—	—	—	—	—
Trinidad and Tobago	—	—	—	—	8.6	—	—	—	—	8.6	8.6
Venezuela	45.0	—	30.0	—	—	—	20.0	—	—	30.0	20.0
Total bank	236.90	40.0	73.5	—	22.0	30.3	20.0	37.5	6.0	165.8	115.8
IDA	22.85	—	3.5	—	—	—	—	—	—	3.5	—
Total	259.75	40.0	77.0	—	22.0	30.3	20.0	37.5	6.0	169.3	115.8
No. of operations	*19*	*1*	*4*	—	*3*	*2*	*1*	*2*	*1*	*10*	*9*

Source: International Bank for Reconstruction and Development, *World Bank Operations: Sectoral Programs and Policies* (Baltimore: Johns Hopkins University Press, 1972), pp. 188–189.

loads per week of "containerized" products traveled from Santo Tomás to Miami (Table 3–6). Similarly, 1970 tonnage from Miami to Santo Tomás, Guatemala totaled 36,930 tons, or about 67 trailer loads per week (Table 3–7). Shipments from Miami to other Central American ports came to 22 loads per week in 1970. Other Florida cities, such as Tampa and Jacksonville, also ship to Central America an average of 18 trailer loads weekly. New York also shipped about 57 trailer-containerized loads per week to the east coast of Central America in 1970. In addition, shipments to Central America from all U. S. east coast ports, except New York and Miami, averaged about 62 trailer loads per week. Table 3–8 indicates the kinds of materials exported. Using this data for guidance, industry consultants have estimated for 1973 the weekly potential number of trailer loads of principally containerized shipments as follows: from Central America to Miami, 37; to New York, 90; and to Europe, 100; to Central America from Miami, 40; from New York, 90; and from Europe, 180.

As indicated previously, it takes about 33 trailer loads per week into and out of Central America to induce a transportation firm to get involved in the growing potential of the containerized transportation market of Central America and to provide the services so vital for the growth of the fruit and vegetable export markets of Central America. Various trade sources indicate that, on a very limited budget, the original investment for a limited service would be over

Table 3–6. Imports into Miami from Guatemala (Caribbean Ports, including Santo Tomás), Liner Cargo Only, Full Year, 1970.

Selected key commodities[a]	*Trailer loads*[b]		
Commodity description	*Number*	*Weight*[c]	*Total tons*
Beef and veal, exc. offal, fresh, frozen	1,038	20	20,761
Shellfish, exc. prepared, canned	404	12	4,846
Fresh bananas and plantains	180	14	2,518
Coffee, cof. substitutes	30	20	602
Special transactions	29	14	400
Fruit, jams, jellies, etc.	23	17	399
Vegetables, not elsewhere specified–fresh, chill, frozen, dry	17	21	347
Fruits, not elsewhere specified–fresh or in brine	18	18	325
Coffee extracts and concentrates	16	14	222
Canned fish	9	19	117
Fruits and nuts, prepared or preserved	5	21	113
Totals, all commodities	1,804		31,360

Source: U. S. Department of Commerce, Bureau of the Census.
a. The above commodities represent 98 percent of the total tonnage moving from all Guatemala Caribbean ports into Miami for the full year, 1970.
b. Thirty-five trailer loads per week.
c. All weights in short tons–minimum weight equals 50,000 lbs.

Table 3–7.   U. S. Exports from Miami to Guatemala (Caribbean Ports, including Santo Tomás), Full Year, 1970.

| Key loading products[a] | Trailer loads[b] | | |
	Number	Weight	Total tons
Animal fats (tallow)	542	20	10,837
Road vehicles	1,309	3	3,928
Yarns, nylon, etc.	145	16	2,316
Motor vehicle parts, accs.	137	15	2,048
Mchy.–text–and landry	90	16	1,445
H.H. appl.–elec.	110	10	1,101
Industrial tractors (not round)	147	7	1,031
Heating-cooling equip.	57	14	797
Newspapers–periodicals	36	19	680
Mchy.–mining and const.	43	15	641
Finished struct. pts. I and S	27	20	532
Trailers and parts	97	5	484
Mech., mchy. and appl. pts.	28	14	396
Apples, fresh	38	10	379
Pumps, centr. and parts	24	15	353
Base metal articles	18	14	332
Glass bottles and caps	23	10	316
Tires, vehicles and aircraft	32	15	315
Mech. handling equip.	20		303
Totals, key loading products	2,923		28,234
Totals, all products	3,513		36,930

Source: U. S. Department of Commerce, Bureau of the Census.
a. Above products represent 76 percent of the total.
b. Sixty-seven trailer loads per week.

$2.25 million. For the first six months of operation, the company would have to be prepared to lose $250,000 in start-up costs. But, if successful, the eventual cash flow would show a breakeven at the end of one year and a positive potential cash flow of 30 percent on the original investment, *if* all estimates were correct. A typical cash-flow projection is presented in Table 3–9; it does not reflect the actual operating experience of any specific company. From these market potentials and excellent back-haul opportunities, it would seem possible for the future containerized transportation system to develop rapidly in Central America. Such development still requires an unusual amount of cooperation among the individual governmental agencies of each Central American country, the transportation firms, and the various agribusiness participants, and the availability of competent managers and workers to implement the excellent potential transportation plans for this region. With such cooperation, the fruit and vegetable exports of Central America should be stimulated to expand at a much faster rate.

Table 3–8. Annual Exports to Central America from all East Coast Ports except New York and Miami.

Country	Exports (tons)	Annual trailer loads[a]
Guatemala	24,305	1,312
Nicaragua	4,921	202
El Salvador	19,021	165
Costa Rica	27,064	1,549
Totals	75,311	3,228

Selected Exports

Commodity	Annual short tons	Annual trailer loads
Meal and flour	986	44
Vegetables, dried	530	27
Timber, poles, etc.	970	65
Wood pulp, sulfate	8,806	441
Wood pulp, sulfate	2,768	133
Sand, industrial	375	17
Clay	224	11
Mica, feldspar, quartz	424	19
Manganese, ore	475	22
Lubricating oil and greases	1,866	99
Petroleum jelly and waxes	786	37
Animal fats	859	43
Organic chemicals	158	8
Oxides, metallic	246	12
Compounds, aluminum	1,503	84
Fertilizer, nitrogen	4,568	224
Fertilizer, NEC	2,275	104
Plastics	690	46
Insecticides, fungicides	219	11
Printing or writing paper	162	8
Kraft paper and board, uncut	26,000	1,452
Paper and paperboard	432	20
Articles of paper and paperboard	424	43
Bricks and refractories	1,103	52
Iron and steel blooms, slabs	554	28
Tin plate	193	9
Iron and steel rails	256	12
Iron and steel wire	215	10
Heating and cooling equipment	168	12
Totals	58,235	3,093

Source: U.S. Department of Commerce, Bureau of the Census.
a. Sixty-two trailer loads per week.

Table 3–9. Cash-Flow Projection of Central American Service for First Five Quarters on Weekly Voyage Basis.

	Quarter, 1972	Quarter, 1973			
	Fourth	First	Second	Third	Fourth
Number of trailerloads into Central America	6	9	12	15	16
Number of LTL into Central America	6	9	12	15	17
Total loads: into Central America	12	18	24	30	33
from Central America	15	25	30	30	33
Net revenue after trucking and brokerage (dollars): into Central America	8,892	13,338	17,784	22,230	24,196
from Central America	11,250	18,750	22,500	22,500	24,753
Total	20,142	32,088	40,284	44,730	48,949
Expenses (dollars)					
Vessel	8,750	8,750	8,750	8,750	8,750
Port call: Santo Tomás	2,360	2,360	2,360	2,360	2,360
Miami	3,627	4,052	4,302	4,377	4,407
Maintenance	5,364	5,364	5,364	5,364	5,364
LTL handling, Miami	1,800	1,800	1,800	2,250	2,550
Warehouse handling, Central America	360	480	720	900	990
Agency, Central America, at 6 percent	2,000	2,000	2,460	2,730	2,990
Miscellaneous agency expense	1,000	1,000	1,000	1,000	1,000
XYZ manager, Central America	800	800	800	800	800
Container yards, Central America	500	500	500	500	500
Administrative and general @ 6%	1,208	1,931	2,460	2,730	2,990
Miami staff and office	1,050	1,050	1,050	1,050	1,050
Sales and traffic in United States	2,500	2,500	2,500	2,500	2,500
Total	31,319	32,587	34,066	35,311	36,251

Cash flow assuming normal backhaul conditions (dollars)	(11,177)	(499)	6,218	9,419	12,698
Percentage of net revenue		—	15	21	26
Actual cash flow assuming optimal backhaul conditions	(195,301)[a]	(6,487)	80,834	122,447	165,074

Average revenue per load after trucking and brokerage: into Central America, 741; from Central America, 750

Annual cash flow after 1 year, 660,296

Source: Consultant estimates.

a. Includes $50,000 for start-up contingency expense.

Figure 3-4. Costa Rican Processed Fruit and Vegetable Industry *(dollars; metric tons).*

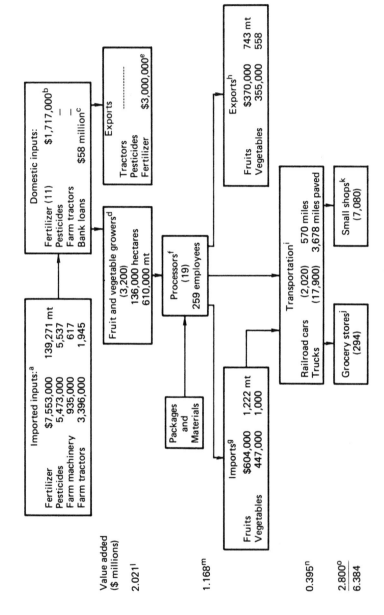

a. *Comercio Exterior de Costa Rica, 1970: Importacion* (Republica de Costa Rica: Direccion General de Estadistico y Censos, 1971): fertilizer, p. 77; pesticides, p. 82; farm machinery, p. 178; farm tractors, p. 180.

b. *Tercero Censo de Industrias Manufacturas 1964* (Republica de Costa Rica: Ministerio de Industria y Comercio, 1967).

c. See Table 2–5, above.

d. Computed from *Projections of Supply and Demand for Selected Agricultural Products in Central America through 1980* (U.S. Department of Agriculture and Battelle Memorial Institute, 1969). Since the number of commercial growers of fruit and vegetables is not available from official statistics, this estimate includes all growers of fruit and vegetables, including subsistence farmers. No distinction is made between growers of crops for the fresh market and those growing for processors. The value of production of fruit and vegetables grown for processors is derived from value-added statistics of processors where the latter are obtainable. The number of growers is estimated to comprise the same proportion of all growers as the number of hectares devoted to agriculture bears to the total number of hectares devoted to cultivation of all crops.

e. *Comercio Exterior: Exportacion.*

f. *Tercero Censo de Industrias Manufacturas 1964,* pp. 5, 12, 13.

g. *Comercio Exterior,* pp. 14, 17.

h. Ibid.

i. *America en Cifras 1970* (Organizacion de los Estados Americanos, Washington, D.C., 1970), Tables 333–01, 333–02, 333–11, 333–12.

j. *Tercero Censo de Comercio* (Republica de Costa Rica: Ministerio de Industria y Comercio, 1967), pp. 11, 19.

k. Ibid., pp. 1, 2, 19.

l. *Anuario Estadistico de Costa Rica 1968* (Republica de Costa Rica: Direccion General de Estadistica y Censos, 1970), p. 183.

m. Ibid., pp. 184, 185.

n. Transportation costs are assumed to be 5 percent of retail price. For estimates of U.S. costs, see Gary Marple and Harry Wissman, *Grocery Manufacturing in the United States* (New York: Praeger, 1968), pp. 243, 244.

o. Wholesale and retail costs are assumed to be 40 percent of retail price.

Source: J. David Morrissy, *Agricultural Modernization through Production Contracting* (New York: Praeger Publishers, Inc., 1974).

Figure 3–5. El Salvadorean Processed Fruit and Vegetable Industry *(dollars; metric tons).*

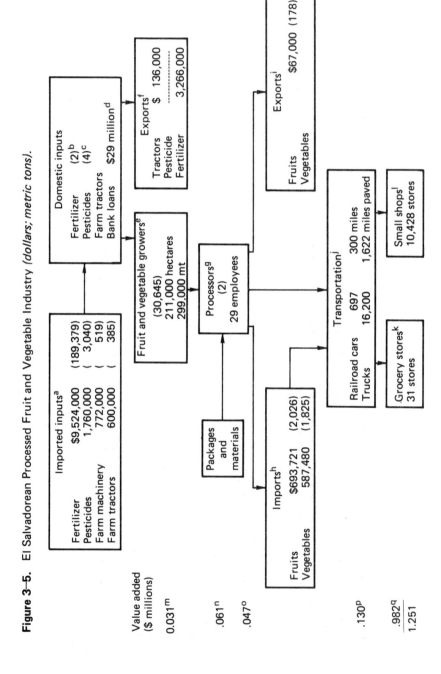

a. *Anuario Estadistico 1969, Comercio Exterior: Importacion* (Republica de El Salvador: Direccion General de Estadistica y Censos, 1970): fertilizer, p. 76; pesticides, p. 79; farm machinery, p. 162; farm tractors, p. 164.

b. *Boletin Estadistico* (Republica de El Salvador: Direccion General de Estadistica y Censos, No. 88, 1971), pp. 23 ff.

c. Ibid.

d. See Table 2–5, above.

e. See Figure 3–4, note d.

f. *Anuario Estadistico 1969, Comercio Exterior: Exportacion:* fertilizer, p. 47; farm machinery, p. 89, farm tractors, p. 90.

g. *Boletin,* pp. 23, 24.

h. *Anuario: Importacion,* pp. 21, 24.

i. *Anuario: Exportacion,* pp. 19, 21.

j. See Figure 3–4, note i.

k. *Tercero Censo de Comercio y Servicios 1961* (Republica de El Salvador: Direccion General de Estadistica y Censos, 1966).

l. Ibid.

m. *Boletin,* pp. 23, 24, 74, 75.

n. Ibid.

o. Ibid.

p. Transportation costs are assumed to be 5 percent of retail price. See Figure 3–4, note n.

q. Wholesale and retail costs are assumed to be 40 percent of retail price.

Source: J. David Morrissy, *Agricultural Modernization through Production Contracting* (New York: Praeger Publishers, Inc., 1974).

Figure 3–6.   Guatemalan Processed Fruit and Vegetable Industry *(dollars; metric tons).*

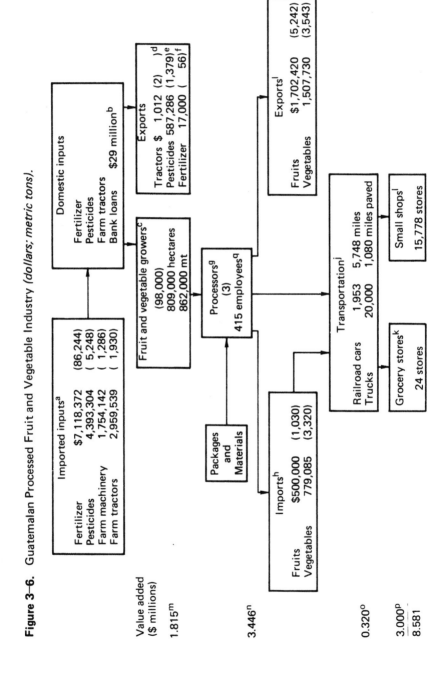

a. *Anuario Comercio Exterior 1969: Importacion* (Republica de Guatemala: Direccion General de Estadistics, 1970): fertilizer, p. 149; pesticides, p. 152; farm machinery, p. 219; farm tractors, p. 221.

b. See Table 2–5, above.

c. See Figure 3–4, note d.

d. *Anuario Comercio Exterior 1969:* p. 65.

e. Ibid., p. 35.

f. Ibid., p. 34.

g. Respondents to questionnaire indicate an additional firm in operation since the last official count in *Trimestre Estadistico* (Republica de Guatemala: Direccion General de Estadistica, 1964), p. 4.

h. *Anuario, Importacion,* p. 103, 105.

i. *Anuario, Exportacion,* p. 8, 10.

j. See Figure 3–4, note i.

k. *Censos Economicos 1965* (Republica de Guatemala: 1968), Tomo II, p. 277.

l. Ibid.

m. Private correspondence with author from Embassy of Guatemala, January 1973. See also *Cuentas Nacionales de Guatemala* (Banco de Guatemala, 1968), p. 39, 43. This figure for purchases from growers by processors includes purchase of other materials since it is the difference between gross-value of production and value added.

n. Ibid.

o. Transportation costs are assumed to be 5 percent of retail price. See Figure 3–4, note n.

p. Wholesaling-retailing costs are assumed to be 40 percent of retail price.

Source: J. David Morrisy, *Agricultural Modernization through Production Contracting* (New York: Praeger Publishers, Inc., 1974).

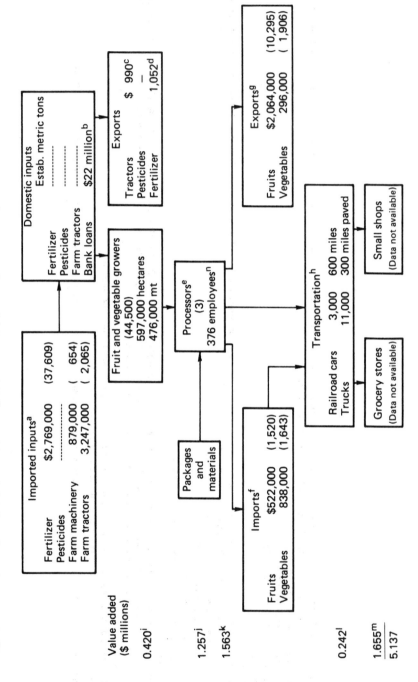
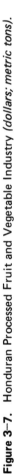

Figure 3-7. Honduran Processed Fruit and Vegetable Industry *(dollars; metric tons).*

a. *Comercio Exterior de Honduras 1968: Importación* (Republica de Honduras: De Estadística y Censos, 1969). Fertilizer, p. 123; farm machinery, p. 276; farm tractors, p. 279.

b. See above, Table 2–5.

c. *Comercio, Exportación, op. cit.* Fertilizer, p. 51; farm machinery, p. 74.

d. See Figure 3–4, note d.

e. Private correspondence with author from the Ministry of Economics of the Republic of Honduras, December, 1972.

f. *Comercio, Importación,* p. 24, 30.

g. *Comercio, Exportación,* p. 40.

h. See Figure 3–4, note i.

i. Private correspondence with author from the Ministry of Economics of the Republic of Honduras, December, 1972.

j. Ibid.

k. Ibid.

l. Transportation costs are assumed to be 5 percent of retail price. See Figure 3–4, note n.

m. Wholesaling-retailing costs are assumed to be 40 percent of retail price.

Source: J. David Morrissy, *Agricultural Modernization through Production Contracting* (New York: Praeger Publishers, Inc., 1974).

Figure 3–8. Nicaraguan Processed Fruit and Vegetable Industry *(dollars; metric tons).*

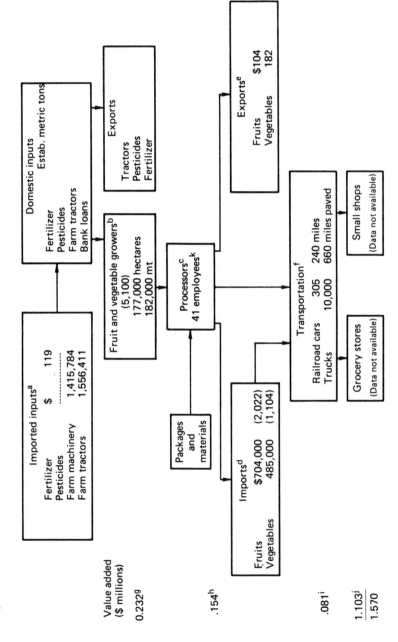

a. *Comercio Exterior de Nicaragua por Productos* (Republica de Nicaragua: Direccion General de Estadistica y Censos, 1969). Fertilizer, p. 25; farm machinery, p. 123; farm tractors, p. 124.

b. See Table 2–5 above.

c. Private correspondence with the author from the Ministry of Economics of the Republic of Nicaragua, December, 1972.

d. *Comercio*, pp. 10, 13.

e. Ibid.

f. See Figure 3–4, note i.

g. Private correspondence with the author from the Ministry of Economics of the Republic of Nicaragua, December, 1972.

h. Ibid.

i. Transportation costs are assumed to be 5 percent of retail price. See Figure 3–4, note n.

j. Wholesaling-retailing costs are assumed to be 40 percent of retail price.

k. Private correspondence with the author from the Ministry of Economics of the Republic of Nicaragua, December, 1972.

Source: J. David Morrissy, *Agricultural Modernization through Production Contracting* (New York: Praeger Publishers, Inc., 1974).

Capital Coordination

In addition to the above coordinating mechanisms, the role of the World Bank, the local development banks, the Atlantic Community Development Group for Latin America (ADELA), LAAD, the Inter-American Development Bank (IABD), the International Basic Economy Corporation (IBEC), CABEI, and the Central American Common Market Export Promotion Agency (PROMECA) are all important elements in linking the U. S. market to the productivity potentials of Central America in fruits, vegetables, and floricultural products, as well as in many other products, such as meat. These institutions are supplying not only credit, but also both market information and, in the case of ADELA and LAAD, direct market involvement. These coordinating activities are part of the formal and informal educational activities being developed in Central America, as we shall note in Chapter 5. In addition, these institutions are working together to provide capital and financial coordination as well as marketing coordination.

Contractual Coordination

The contractual arrangements developed by U. S. food processors and food brokers with Central American producers and processors is another method of linking the market opportunities in the United States with the production and processing capabilities of Central America. The purchasers provide a guaranteed market, some price stability, market and grading information, capital, seed, and some transportation inputs in exchange for a new economical and reliable source for their raw or finished food materials, usually at the best seasonal times for the U. S. market. Contracting for fruit and vegetable processing within the Central American fruit and vegetable system also provides the coordinating links that help to improve the functional operations at the farm level. By having a specific market for which to produce, and by obtaining inputs from processors, the small and large producers alike are in a better position to improve their operations. In many cases, the local processors and the U. S. processors and fresh-fruit handlers also help to train some of the personnel in the farming operations.

The flowcharts in Figures 3–4 through 3–8 for selected countries indicate the organization of the fruit and vegetable processing industry and provide a backdrop against which we can examine in greater depth a few case studies of fruit and vegetable production in Central America. From these studies and the description of the Central American—U. S. fruit and vegetable system, we shall turn to the educational network that is currently training the managerial and labor force needed to improve this embryonic but expanding agribusiness system.

NOTES TO CHAPTER THREE

1. See, for example, the interview with Sr. Manuel Clothile, Jr., president of Mexico's Unión Nacional de Productores de Hortalizas, reported in *The Packer* (January 20, 1973).
2. Actually, the overall limitation on weight is set by the Florida restriction on gross combination weights of vehicles to less than 72,200 pounds. Therefore, a trailer can be loaded to slightly more than 40,000 pounds (18,000 kg.) without too much difficulty.

Chapter Four

Central American Fruit
and Vegetable Production
for Export

The Central American Fruit
and Vegetable System

In 1970, Central America produced an estimated 834,000 tons of vegetables and 610,300 tons of fruit (excluding 2.1 million tons of bananas, of which 11 percent was consumed domestically and the remainder exported). Table 4–1 provides production statistics by type of produce. These output data may understate actual production by a considerable but unknown margin, owing to the failure to fully include production from family plots that does not enter commercial channels. Fruit and vegetable plantings in 1969 covered an estimated 749,000 hectares, representing 19 percent of the total crop area for all of Central America. The 1969 fruit and vegetable output, including bananas, accounted for 25 percent of the total tonnage production of all produce in Central America; the share drops to 18 percent if export banana production is excluded.

Consumption of fruits and vegetables has been increasing because of increases in population and real incomes in Central America. The area cultivated in fruits and vegetables (excluding export bananas) rose from 579,900 hectares in 1960 to 705,100 hectares in 1969, and output expanded from 1,920,300 tons to 2,944,800 tons (Table 4–2). Fruit and vegetable production's share of Central America's total produce output remained approximately the same during the decade of the 60's. This trend does not reflect the potentially large expansion that has begun to occur in the production of nontraditional fruits and vegetables for export. Projected per capita consumption rates vary considerably among the different countries (Table 4–3). Honduras has the lowest projected per capita annual intake of vegetables (5.2 kg.) and fruits (15.7 kg.); Costa Rica ranks highest in projected fruit consumption (57.2 kg.) and Guatemala highest in vegetables (42.0 kg.). The FAO projections in Tables 4–3 and 4–4 indicate that Central American demand for fresh fruits and vegetables, including pulses and starchy roots, will reach 1,699,555 tons per year in 1975 and 2,293,705 tons in 1985.

Table 4–1. Central American Fruit and Vegetable Production, 1969, 1970 (100 tons).[a]

Commodity	Guatemala 1969	Guatemala 1970	El Salvador 1969	El Salvador 1970	Honduras 1969	Honduras 1970	Nicaragua 1969	Nicaragua 1970	Costa Rica 1969	Costa Rica 1970	Total 1969	Total 1970
Vegetables												
Onions	151	161	79	86	20	21	52	49	90	88	392	405
Tomatoes	762	811	204	189	106	108	101	108	134	140	1,307	1,355
Cabbage	146	155	26	26	54	55	87	89	66	68	379	394
Other	883	932	572	613	423	429	40	40	231	214	2,149	2,227
Total	1,942	2,059	881	914	603	613	279	286	521	509	4,227	4,381
Fruit												
Orange	—	—	—	—	518	528	—	—	627	650	1,145	1,178
Other citrus	575	564	418	455	76	26	470	494	—	—	1,539	1,539
Pineapple	181	187	340	364	66	48	269	278	56	59	913	937
Avocados	187	195	264	265	62	62	—	—	172	179	684	700
Other	415	415	683	761	340	337	76	105	184	130	1,697	1,747
Total	1,358	1,361	1,705	1,845	1,061	1,001	815	877	1,039	1,018	5,978	6,101
Bananas												
National	706	744	—	—	2,695	1,971	392	621	1,918	2,079	5,711	5,414
Export	1,415	1,497	—	—	8,722	5,756	301	73	7,259	8,391	17,697	15,717
Total	2,121	2,241	—	—	11,417	7,727	693	694	9,177	10,470	23,408	21,131

Source: Secretaría de Integración Económica de Centro América, Estadísticas sobre la Alimentación y Agricultura en Centro América (1972).
a. In certain instances, totals vary from sums due to rounding of individual figures.

Table 4–2. Central American Fruit and Vegetable Production, 1960, 1970.

Commodity	Area cultivated (100 hectares)		Output (100 tons)	
	1960	1969	1960	1970
Potatoes	78	108	426	671
Cassava	113	514	174	914
Frijoles	2,471	3,068	1,476	2,271
Onions	39	60	253	405
Tomatoes	113	200	700	1,355
Cabbage	48	76	239	394
Other vegetables	318[a]	370[a]	1,462	2,228
Oranges	135	194	802	1,178
Other citrus	161	243	763	1,540
Pineapples	40	55	625	937
Avocados	50	77	452	700
Other fruit	193[a]	290[a]	889	1,747
Plantains	237	258	1,862	2,606
Guineos	1,579[a]	1,175	7,262	7,088
Bananas	224	363	1,818	5,414
Bananas, export	474	439	9,646	15,717
Totals	6,273	7,490	28,849	45,165

a. Estimated.

Table 4–3. Projected Central American Fruit and Vegetable Per Capita Consumption *(kg./yr.).*[a]

Country	Produce	1975	1985
Costa Rica	Vegetables	12.7	13.5
	Fruit	57.2	60.9
El Salvador	Vegetables	6.0	6.1
	Fruit	20.2	22.4
Guatemala	Vegetables	42.0	48.0
	Fruit	37.0	38.4
Honduras	Vegetables	5.0	5.4
	Fruit	15.5	16.4
Nicaragua	Vegetables	12.5	13.3
	Fruit	25.7	28.0

Source: FAO, *Agricultural Commodity Projections for 1975 and 1985* (1967), Vol. II.
a. Excluding bananas, starchy roots, and pulses.

Table 4-4. Projected Central American Fruit and Vegetable Total Consumption *(tons/year).* [a]

Country	Produce	1975	1985
Costa Rica	Vegetables	28,918	40,243
	Fruits	130,244	181,543
El Salvador	Vegetables	26,433	37,353
	Fruits	88,991	126,773
Guatemala	Vegetables	277,200	369,880
	Fruits	244,200	326,515
Honduras	Vegetables	17,446	23,968
	Fruits	52,674	72,791
Nicaragua	Vegetables	31,849	45,207
	Fruits	66,010	95,172
	Total		
	Vegetables	381,846	516,651
	Fruits	582,119	802,794
	Pulses	211,266	287,282
	Starchy roots	524,324	686,977
Total		1,699,555	2,293,704

Source: FAO, *Agricultural Commodity Projections for 1975 and 1985* (1967), Vol. II.
a. Excluding bananas.

The channels through which this fresh produce flows from the farm to the marketplace vary somewhat from country to country in Central America, but the differences are not marked. Figure 4-1 presents a general flow diagram of the Central American fruit and vegetable system. The system is still almost entirely oriented toward the internal markets (except for bananas). To the extent that exports have been generated, they have been confined largely to intraregional trade. El Salvador and Nicaragua have tended to be net importers from the other three Common Market countries. Panama also imports significant quantities of fruits and vegetables.

Although export diversification, including fruits and vegetables for the world markets has been placed high on the development priority list, nontraditional produce exports still remain a relatively small portion of total food and fiber exports. Coffee, cotton, and sugar, the three major traditional exports, accounted for 29 percent of the 1969 crop land and 60 percent of the tonnage output for all of Central America. Nonetheless, the rate of growth of the nontraditional fruits and vegetables has been impressive. As was indicated in Table 2-10, exports of fresh fruits and vegetables to the United States from Central America in 1970-71 were fifteen times those in 1963-64. Central

Figure 4–1. Central American Fruit and Vegetable System.

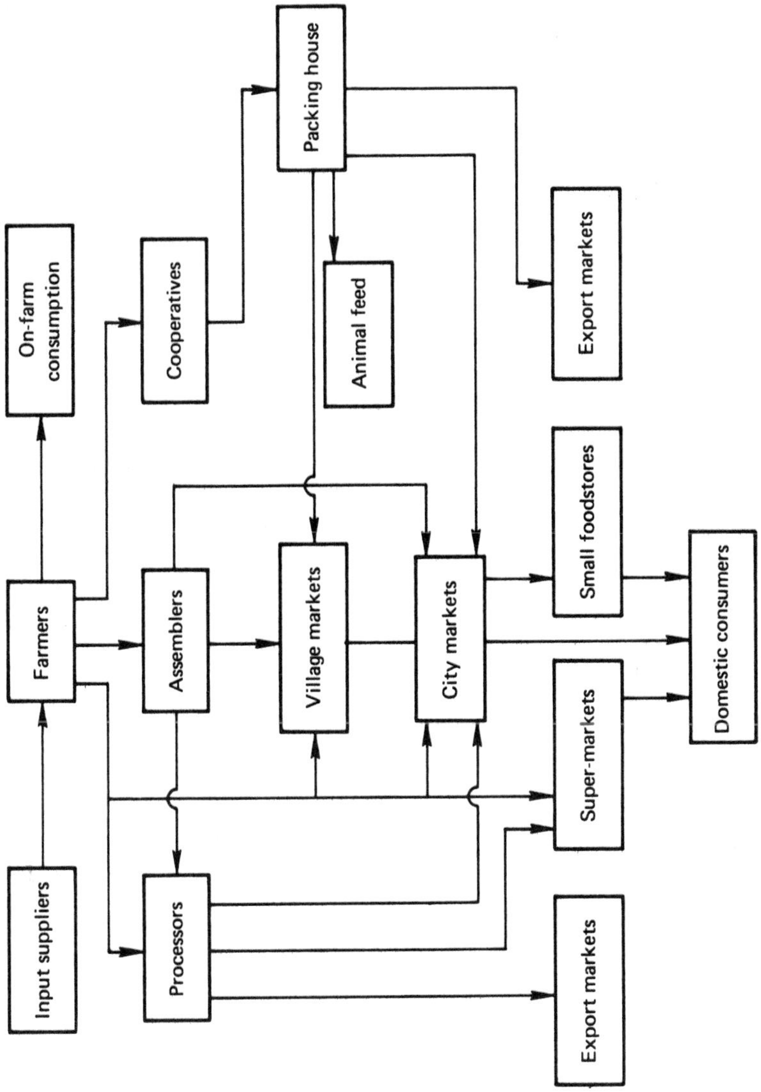

America has become the second largest supplier of cucumbers to the U. S. winter market and has captured 10 percent of the total U. S. pineapple market. Despite this rapid growth, the 30 million pounds of exports still represent only a 1 percent U. S. market share for the six major crops exported and less than 1 percent of the total Central American fruit and vegetable production (excluding export bananas).

The Central American fruit and vegetable export industry is still in its infancy, and its early attempts to penetrate the U. S. market have been fraught with problems. This chapter extends the commodity systems analysis employed in the previous chapters to the Central American fruit and vegetable export system. The purpose is to identify more clearly the problems confronting the system. Chapters 2 and 3 indicated critical requirements that the Central American exporters must meet if they are to successfully enter the U. S. fruit and vegetable system. These success determinants included a market orientation, accurate and timely information channels, close coordination with importers and transporters, tight quality control, high agricultural productivity, close cooperation between government and private sectors, and adequately trained personnel at the managerial, technical, and laborer levels.

This chapter examines in detail the actual experiences of selected nontraditional fruit and vegetable export operations in four Central American countries. These export project analyses provide a basis for determining the extent to which a gap exists between the above-mentioned requirements for success and the actual performance and capabilities of the industry. By delineating the problem-success gap, we are better able to provide a realistic basis for determining the educational needs of participants in the fruit and vegetable export system. Chapter 5 will discuss how these training needs can best be met and the educational implications for the broader agribusiness community in Central America.

The remainder of this chapter is organized into four parts: the first discusses the apparent forces leading to the emergence of nontraditional export projects in Central America; the second briefly describes the export operations selected for analysis; the third provides an overview of the problems identified in the project analyses; and the fourth presents the detailed analyses of export projects in the four countries.

Factors Motivating Export Attempts

The various fruit and vegetable export operations in Central America generally did not emerge as the end result of a systematic analysis of the market opportunities by producers or a correspondingly careful evaluation of the production, processing, and transportation resources. Rather, it appears that the variety of stimuli external to the farms provided the incentives and pressures for organizing these projects. The key initiating forces differ somewhat from country to country, but there seem to be two main factors.

1. Exposure to Market Opportunities. A seminar on the possibilities of exporting nontraditional produce by air made several producers aware of this potential and motivated them to enter into melon production. A U. S. AID study on the potential for nontraditional exports proved to be the primary stimulant. An entrepreneur, during a trip to the United States, observed the high prices of fresh vegetables in the winter season. A U. S. importer sought new fresh-vegetable sources and encouraged local exporters and producers to plant and export nontraditional crops.

2. Pressures on the Production Side. In one country a decline in the production of a major crop—cotton—in a principal agricultural zone led to large rural unemployment and motivated the government to encourage the production of alternative crops; fruits and vegetables for export could be grown there and, consequently, were promoted by the government organizations. In another country a large producer decided to stop growing bananas because of losses, and therefore sought another crop that could be profitable and would enable him to retain his workers. In a third country a farmers' cooperative suddenly lost its market for its members' tomatoes when the processing plants decided not to buy because of excessive unsold inventories. Consequently, the farmers had to seek an alternative use for their land.

From these examples it can be seen that the emergence of the export projects involved many different groups: individual farmers, cooperatives, importers, transportation companies, ministries of agriculture, agrarian reform agencies, and international development organizations. The Central American exporters were generally reacting to external pressures or to information rather than systematically and agressively seeking out new opportunities.

Description of Export Projects Studied

Limitations of resources and time prevented an analysis of all the nontraditional produce export operations in Central America. Nonetheless, the projects studied account for about 20 percent of total Central American exports of nontraditional fruits and vegetables, or about 40 percent, if pineapples are excluded. These export operations ship out an estimated 30 percent of the cucumbers, 64 percent of the melons, and 50 percent of the okra. In order to attain greater geographical representation, we examined projects in Guatemala, El Salvador, Honduras, and Nicaragua. The projects varied in degree of government support and involvement (ranging from intensive to negligible); scale of farming unit (small, medium, large); type of produce (fresh and frozen); organizational form (cooperatives and single grower-shippers); and marketing arrangements (consignment and outright sales). The diversity encompassed in the export projects selected for analysis has allowed a fairly representative coverage of the spectrum of fruit and vegetable export projects in Central America. Figure 4–2 is a map of Central America indicating the location of the producing areas of the export operations studied.

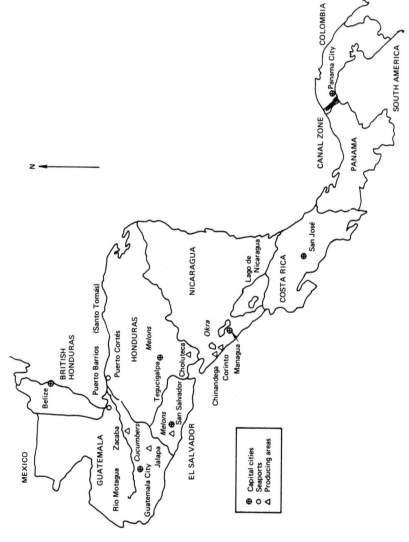

Figure 4–2. Map of Central America

Guatemala. Two export operations primarily exporting cucumbers were studied. The first involved a 200-member farmers' cooperative (CARSVO) that sold its output to a packer-shipper (ELCO, S.A.). The manager of this export company had considerable experience shipping fresh produce from Cuba to the U. S. market. He used a Miami broker with whom he had worked previously. CARSVO planted 257 manzanas[1] (180 ha.), with the average planting size being two manzanas. The cooperative had also planted for export the previous two seasons. During the 1971–72 season, ELCO exported about 700 tons of cucumbers and about 300 tons of chiles; others shipped out smaller amounts of melons, eggplants, and peppers.

The second export operation was conducted by a 26-member farmers' cooperative (La Fragua) in the same region. This cooperative did its own preselection and packaging and shipped to a Pompano Beach broker who would complete the selection, repack, and sell the product on a consignment basis. The 1971–72 season was the first time this cooperative had exported. It planted 213 hectares and shipped out about 1150 tons of cucumbers. The average planting area was 8.3 hectares, which was considerably larger than the CARSVO plots.

The Guatemalan government provided support to both of these projects in the form of irrigation and road infrastructure, production financing, and technical assistance. Several regional and international organizations were also involved. The Central American Bank for Economic Integration (CABEI) had financed the building of the packing house facilities in 1970–71. The Central American Institute for Technological Investigation (ICAITI), in conjunction with U. S. AID's Regional Office for Central America and Panama (ROCAP), provided technical assistance.

El Salvador. The main operation studied was that of the country's major melon grower-shipper, Sr. X. He began exporting honeydew melons to the United States and Europe in 1969. In the United States, he sells on an exclusive consignment basis to one broker, and in Europe he distributes on consignment through four brokers. In 1971–72, he planted 112 hectares in two farms and shipped out 478 tons, of which 68 percent went to the United States and 32 percent to Europe. Sr. X reportedly has not received any major direct help from the government.

A second melon export operation that was examined involved a producer, Sr. A, who began exporting melons in 1969 as part of an 18-member cooperative (COPEX). The cooperative disbanded after two successive years of losses, and Sr. A remained as the surviving exporter. In 1971–72, he planted 140 hectares and packed and exported on consignment 390 tons to the United States. He switched brokers in midseason due to dissatisfaction with the services of the first importer. The government had provided financial and technical assistance to COPEX, but in 1971–72, Sr. A was not receiving any such support.

Honduras. Eighteen cooperatives, that are part of the country's agrarian reform program, and four independent farms cultivated and exported melons to the United States in 1971–72. The cooperatives planted 143 hectares and the four farms 87.5 hectares, and the combined export volume was about 700 tons. The two groups jointly operated a single packing unit. In prior years they had separate packing sheds. They exported on consignment to the same Pompano Beach broker as the La Fragua cooperative in Guatemala.

The government involvement in this export project was greater than that in any of the other projects studied. There was heavy financial, technical, and organizational assistance by various government agencies. An Israeli technical mission working with the agrarian reform program was also involved.

Nicaragua. In contrast to the other export operations, this project was shipping frozen rather than fresh produce. One large farm was the sole producer, processor, and exporter of okra in Nicaragua. The farm originally exported fresh okra but shifted to frozen to avoid the risks associated with the perishability characteristic of the crop. In 1972, it planted 196 hectares and had exported, by midyear, 400 tons of produce to its U. S. broker. The broker purchased the produce f.o.b. Nicaragua and provided technical assistance for processing and quality-control operations. The farm has also begun to cultivate peas for freezing and export.

The government provided fiscal incentives to the project through duty-free equipment imports and income- and property-tax exemptions. The Central American Bank for Economic Integration loaned the funds for the freezing plant.

Table 4–5 summarizes the organizational arrangements and manpower resources of the projects analyzed, and Table 4–6 compares four of the projects analyzed. The data include production and export volume, costs per box by expense item, profit-and-loss performance, and marketing and transport arrangements.

Overview of Common Problems

The overview that one is left with after examining the export projects in the four countries is one of a struggling new agroindustry undergoing the pains of birth. Frustrations, errors, and losses have plagued the operations, but that should not be surprising. The crops are relatively new, and time is required for farmers to work out the cultivation procedures required for successful adaptation and exploitation of the crops. The export market demands top quality, which is generally not the case in the local market; quality consciousness among producers and laborers is not easily obtained in the short run. Another problem is that the market is distant and the product very perishable; therefore, the export operation requires greater planning and coordination than are generally needed in the local market. Lastly, the newness of the industry means that volumes are relatively low, and, therefore, obtaining economies of scale or good transport or marketing services is hindered.

All of these factors make the export system for nontraditional fruits and vegetables a complex and risky one. In this section, we shall highlight the key problems that confronted the various stages of the export operations in the four countries.

At the production stage there were technical problems, deficiencies of skilled labor, and inadequate planning and control. On the technical side, fungus caused damage in all projects and insects were also a problem. There was inadequate knowledge of what agrochemicals to use, the amount to employ, and the timing and method of application. Similarly, the selection of variety, seed, and soil often lacked thoroughness and gave rise to production deficiencies. These production difficulties suggest that the technical assistance given to the farmers has not been of adequate quality or quantity. The provision of technical assistance was hampered in some cases by the limited capacity of the farmers to absorb this new technical knowledge; moreover, the technical advice came from a multitude of sources and was often conflicting. Coordination among providers of technical assistance was deficient, and this lack may have contributed to the inability to resolve production difficulties.

The laborers involved in the cultivation and harvesting operations often did not use the proper techniques, especially in harvesting. This is a reflection of inadequate training and lack of experience with these crops. The workers and even the farmers have not yet developed the quality consciousness needed to ensure extra care in cutting and handling. The use of improper techniques by laborers in any one of the multitude of cultivation tasks, such as cutting or shading, can adversely affect the quality and hence the value of the fruit. This means that both close supervision and control of worker operations are crucial. The projects frequently lacked the necessary personnel at the field-foreman level to carry out this supervisory function.

Some of the difficulties at the farm level were due to deficiencies in production programming. The selection of the variety is a basic step in the production programming process, because it is a primary determinant of the length of the cultivation cycle, and also affects the perishability of the fruit once it is harvested. In one project, the variety was selected because of its dominant use by producers in the United States and therefore its acceptance in the market place. This is clearly an important consideration, but perhaps even more important for the exporter is that the fruit be able to maintain its quality during the period of transit from farm to consumer, which is much longer from Central America than from the domestic U. S. farm. The decision on variety selection must take into consideration the intervening stages in the export system, namely, packing, international transport, handling, and domestic transport. In effect, there was a lack of a total systems focus in the production planning process.

Table 4–5. Export Projects: Organizational Arrangements and Manpower Resources.

Project	Organizational arrangement	Technical assistance	Managerial resources	Foreman resources	Laborer resources
Guatemala					
CARSVO	Production cooperative	Agronomists, horticulturists systems analysts Government ICAITI ROCAP, input salesmen	1 manager, high school 56 farmers, grade 3–12	On larger farms only, grade 2–6	Farm labor, grade 1–5 (5–10 workers per manzana)
ELCO	Packer-exporter		University	2 high school	30 graders, grade 1–5
La Fragua	Production cooperative, packer-exporter	Same as CARSVO	1 manager, high school 29 farmers, grade 5–8	1 foreman per 5 manzanas, grade 2–6 — 1 packing house foreman, grade 5	Same as CARSVO — 32 graders-packers grade 1–5
El Salvador					
Senor X	Single proprieter-ship, integrated producer-packer-exporter	1 horticulturist, marketing expert, U.S. AID, 1 entomologist, 1 agronomist Input salesmen	1 manager, MBA 1 packing supervisor bachelor's degree	2 packing foremen, grade 1–6 3 field foremen, grade 1–6	30 field hands, grade 0–3 (50 percent illiterate) 15 grader-packers, grade 0–3

Senor A	Same as Sr. X	Same as Sr. X	1 manager, high school	3 field supervisors 1 packing foreman, primary	150 field hands, grade 0–3
COPEX	Production cooperative	Same as Sr. X	1 president, lawyer 1 manager, university (both part-time) 7 farmers, high school, university	1 per farm, grade 3–6	300 field hands, grade 0–3
Honduras					
Cooperative	Production cooperatives	Agronomists, input salesmen, Israeli and Mexican technicians	7 managers, primary	10 field supervisors grade 0–3	125 field hands, most illiterate
Individual farms	Sole proprietorships	Some agronomists and government technicians	4 owner-managers, agronomists	6 supervisors, primary	70 field hands, most illiterate
United Fruit Producers	Cooperative packer-exporter	Same as above	1 manager (agronomist)	2 supervisors, primary	24 grader-packers, most illiterate
Nicaragua					
Callejas Brothers	Family farm, freezer-exporter	Importer technicians, U.S. AID Israeli technicians	3 managers, university	Field supervisor, agronomist Plant engineer, agronomist Quality-control supervisor, university	420 field hands, grade 0–6 20 grader-packers

Table 4–6. Comparative Summary of Export Projects, 1971–1972.

Item	Guatemala, cucumbers[a]		El Salvador, melons		Honduras, melons		Nicaragua, okra	
Production and export								
Area planted (manzanas)[b]	257		160		330		280	
Field production	86,574 boxes[c]		102,000 boxes[d]		71,000 boxes[e]		1,960,000 lbs.	
Field yield	337 boxes		637 boxes/mz.		215 boxes		7,000 lbs.	
Delivered to packer	51,944 boxes		30,600 boxes		39,000 boxes		1,960,000 lbs.	
Rejection in field (percent)	37		70		45			
Selected for export	30,342 boxes		24,526 boxes		25,002 boxes		1,563,000 lbs.(projected)	
Rejected in packing (percent)	45		20		36		20	
Export yield	116 boxes/mz.		151 boxes/mz.		75 boxes/mz.		5,600 lbs.	
Costs and revenue								
Production	$1.29/box[f]	(16.6%)	$1.96/box	(31.8%)	$3.52/box	(41.3%)	$0.09	(75.0%)
Packing	1.41	(18.1%)	1.20	(19.5%)	1.10	(12.9%)	0.03 est.	(25.0%)
Transport	1.67	(21.5%)	1.96	(31.8%)	2.87	(33.6%)	—	
Tariffs	1.42	(18.3%)	0.45	(7.3%)	0.55	(6.5%)	—	
Handling and repacking	1.18	(15.1%)	—		0.25	(2.9%)	—	
Commissions	0.81	(10.4%)	0.59	(9.6%)	0.24	(2.8%)	—	
Total costs	$7.78	(100.0%)	$6.16	(100.0%)	$8.53[g]	(100.0%)	$0.12/lb	(100.0%)
Average export price	8.13		6.32		8.00[h]		0.13/lb	
Profit/(loss)	$0.35/box		$0.16/box		$(0.53)/box		$0.01/lb	
Marketing and transport								
Arrangement	Producer cooperative sold exclusively to exporter-packer, who has his own U.S. import brokerage firm		Single producer, integrated through packing and export, sells on exclusive consignment to import brokers (1 in U.S.; 4 in Europe)		Producer cooperative and independent producers deliver to jointly owned packing plant and export on exclusive consignment to Florida broker		Single producer, integrated through freezing plant, sells on exclusive basis to single U.S. broker, f.o.b. freezing plant	

Local sales as percent of total sales	2.5	1.4	9.4	0
Local sales—average price	$0.15/box	$0.075/melon	$0.01/melon	$0.15/melon
Means of transport	CCT refrigerated trailer, Santo Tomás to Miami	CCT refrigerated trailers via Santo Tomás to U.S.: unrefrigerated cargo ship to Europe	CCT refrigerated trailers via Puerto Cortés to Pompano Beach; Astra Line refrigerated cargo ship via Puerto Cortés. Air cargo from San Pedro to Miami	CCT refrigerated trailers via Santo Tomás to Miami; refrigerated cargo ships via Corinto to Miami
Export markets	U.S.: Pompano Beach	U.S.: New York; Europe: Hamburg, Rotterdam, Stockholm, London	U.S.: Pompano Beach	U.S.: Miami

a. CARSVO–ELCO only.
b. 1 manzana = .7 hectares = 1.73 acres
c. 52 lb.
d. 39 lb.
e. 57 lb.
f. Price paid to farmer by packer; actual production costs were higher and the farmers incurred losses.
g. Excludes marketing and transport costs incurred for sales outside of Pompano Beach.
h. Average market prices for melons; the actual price received by Honduran exporters was $4.74 per box.

Another deficiency encountered was misestimate of the output volume. Even when the planner uses a systems viewpoint and attempts to coordinate the capacities of the inputs, packing operation, transport facilities, and marketing program, his planning will go astray if the original production estimates are erroneous. Capacity balancing of the different stages within the system is crucial to efficiency, but special care must be given to making an accurate output projection because it is the starting point of the planning process.

A final deficiency in the production planning and control process was the lack, in almost all of the projects, of accurate and up-to-date data on the production and harvesting operations. Records on costs, appearance of insects or fungi, agrochemical applications, yields, and so on, if kept at all, were not kept in an orderly manner. When data were present, they were generally not used during the export operation but rather reviewed ex post facto, so there was little information about the on-going performance of the project being fed back to the decision makers to help them during the project. Current data, if properly organized, can be used to send up warning flags to the manager, and serve as a basis for preventive or corrective action whenever it is needed. Historical data provide the manager with a solid base from which to plan his future operations. But without reasonably timely and accurate data, planning and control are an exercise in futility.

As a result of the deficiencies in technical understanding, skills, planning, and control in the production and harvesting operations, yields of exportable produce were very low, especially in Honduras and Guatemala. The Honduran melon growers obtained only 75 boxes of exportable produce per manzana, while their Salvadorean counterparts achieved a yield of 102 boxes per manzana (at 57 lbs./box). Many of the Guatemalan cucumber growers produced at a loss, given the ELCO prices and their low yields. The okra project's profitability is in jeopardy owing to the erratic yield performance. None of the fresh-produce projects was able to export over 35 percent of the crop produced in the field.

Financing is generally available, but in none of the projects did the financial institution or the project manager anticipate the start-up costs and the time lags in repayment arrangements. Repayment of the loans, therefore, became a problem. The losses incurred during the 1971–72 season made loan amortization difficult in most cases and impossible in others.

At the packing stage, there were some technical problems, but they were fewer than at the production stage. Precooling and fungicide treatment were omitted in some cases, and the quality of the fruit suffered accordingly; the exporters lacked adequate advice on proper processing procedures. These deficiencies might have been remedied in part if there had been continuous feedback from the importer to the exporter about the quality of the fruit. The packing step itself did not encounter exceptional difficulties. Previous years' experiences provided the exporters with the knowledge of grades, box sizes, and packing patterns. Also, the plant supervisors generally had experience in packing operations in other countries, such as Mexico, Chile, or Cuba. They were able to train the packers, although it reportedly took about a month before the laborers became acceptably proficient. Nonetheless, control over the packers may have been lacking, as indicated by the rejections made by the importers.

In several of the projects' packing operations, there were sometimes delays in delivery of the shipping boxes, although they were not as serious as in previous years. The 1972 effort generally did not encounter the earlier difficulties in obtaining containers of the proper size, but the box costs have remained high relative to other costs in the export operations. Lack of greater volume has kept the packing operations from achieving greater economies of scale, and in one case led to a surplus of boxes.

In the three fresh-produce export operations, refrigerated storage is lacking, subjecting the output to possible heat damage if storage were to become necessary because of shipping delays. As mentioned earlier, one of the main reasons the Nicaraguan okra operation switched from a fresh to a frozen basis was to avoid the risks of perishability.

Produce transportation was less of a problem during the 1971–72 season than in previous years, largely because CCT increased the capacity and frequency of its services. Nonetheless, some of the exporters complained that CCT did not always provide the refrigerated units when needed. Such delays can severely affect the quality of the product, except in the case of okra, which can remain in frozen storage. Although CCT services have improved, transportation remains the predominant cost factor in the export operation.

The different marketing arrangements provide an ample picture of some of the possible difficulties in linking up producers and buyers. The CARSVO–ELCO agreement removed the marketing risks from the grower, but the fixed-price contract increased the risk of losses due to inadequate production yields. Because ELCO had a sister import-brokerage firm, there was no communication or contractual problem between exporter and importer. In contrast, both La Fragua and the Honduran melon producers sold on consignment to the same Florida broker. In this case, the producers carried both the agronomic and the marketing risks; however, they also would reap the gains from favorable prices. The consignment basis lends itself to mistrust and exploitation, especially in the absence of frequent and clear communications between broker and exporter. The producers do not control the final selection and sale of their product and are thus subject to the action of the broker. The broker for Guatemala (La Fragua) and Honduras was apparently late in sending payments for shipments and negligent in keeping the farmers aware of market developments. This created a credibility gap between exporter and importer that destroyed the relation. This problem is also in part due to producer ignorance of the manner in which the import market works and the existence of few alternative buyers.

Except for ELCO and the Salvadorean operation, the growers are operating in a market information vacuum. The ELCO operation has good market information because it is, in effect, integrated from the export stage through the import stage. Also, the ELCO management seems to have good rapport with the CARSVO managers and producers; this is in striking contrast to its predecessor, the Export–Import Company (EXIMCO). Different people in the same situation often produce markedly different results. The Salvadorean melon producer maintains continuous contact with his broker, and a great deal of reciprocal trust has been developed.

A. R. Van Hoven, manager of the Western Buying Office of the Grand Union super market chain, made the following comment concerning exporter–importer relations during an interview:

> The most important step is to find a market in the target country, in this case the United States. To find markets takes a broker who not only can move and sell the merchandise, but can advise on things that should be grown. On my trips through Central America I found a distrust of brokers, apparently because of past experiences. However, most brokers are legitimate people: by obtaining a Produce Blue Book or Red Book, one can be certain how they are rated. Before the first seed goes into the ground, be sure a marketing arrangement is set up in the United States (or Europe, or Japan). Mexico has representatives at the border who have refrigerated sheds and sales organizations that cover North America.

A final marketing problem confronting all of the operations is the lack of local markets for the nonexportable surplus. The effective domestic demand for these exports is insignificant compared with available supply of seconds. A few truckloads usually flood the market. Prices are only a small fraction of the export prices. Thus, local sales cannot be counted upon for significant revenue; however, the seconds do provide a new and sizable source of animal feed.

The systems approach made it possible to identify the problems that arose at the different stages in the commodity system. The interrelated nature of the problems was also revealed. However, the project analyses that follow show that the problems involved the different personnel levels (manager, technician, foreman, and laborer) and the different types of tasks (administrative, technical, and operative). Chapter 5 will explore further these different problem categories in order to determine the educational measures required to reduce or eliminate the problems.

Many of the difficulties encountered are to be expected, given the newness of operations. In a more traditional industry, such as coffee, some of these problems do not exist, although many do. The nontraditional export business is difficult and one should expect inadequacies in the short run; overnight success will be the exception rather than the rule in this field. Progress has been made on several fronts, but clearly many obstacles to success remain. The possibilities of what can be done are demonstrated by the success of Mexico described in Chapter 2. The Mexican vegetable and fruit growers are effectively organized, have achieved production efficiency, employ tight quality controls, have adequate transport services, and possess good knowledge of market conditions. These factors plus geographical proximity have made Mexico the dominant export force in the U. S. winter market. Mexico also has two decades of experience. The challenge to Central America is how to shorten its own learning period.

Although it is difficult to make accurate cost comparisons between Mexico and Central America, owing to differences in box sizes, varieties, and accounting procedures, we have attempted in Table 4–7 to construct comparable cost data. From this table we can see that Mexico's cost per box of melons exported to the United States is about three-fourths of the cost to the Central American exporters. The Mexican unit costs for production, packing, transportation, and handling are all less. The lower unit production costs in Mexico are due to higher yields rather than to lower total costs. In fact, Mexico has a high total cost relative to Central America. Total production costs per manzana in Mexico are $372, whereas in El Salvador they are about $300 and in Honduras $233. A common laborer in Mexico earns $2.44 per day, whereas in Honduras he earns $1 per day. Despite this higher cost structure, Mexican producers and workers are apparently more efficient and have better control of the agronomic variables than their Central American counterparts. The Mexican growers produce 154 boxes (57 lbs.) of exportable melon per manzana, whereas in El Salvador the yield is 108 boxes, and in Honduras 75 boxes. A similar situation exists with cucumbers. In 1970–71 Mexico was obtaining cucumber yields of 255 exportable boxes[2] per manzana, whereas the 1971–72 cucumber yield in Guatemala was 118 boxes. Clearly, much of the future success of the Central American nontraditional export operations will depend on significantly improving the exportable yields. The lower packing costs in Mexico reflect the economies of scale from the larger volumes, and the lower transport costs are the result of the relative proximity of Mexico to the United States.

The outlook for nontraditional agricultural exports from Central America is a mixture of promising opportunities and tenacious obstacles. The demand in the winter markets of the United States is strong and very large relative to the present volume of exports from Central America. Central American fruit and vegetable exports are now only a minor factor in overall U. S. produce imports. However, if the current problems can be resolved and Central America can capture 10 percent of the projected U. S. market growth, exports

Table 4–7.   Comparative Costs of Melon Exports: Mexico, El Salvador, and Honduras (per 57-lb. box equivalent).

Item	Mexico (dollars)	Mexico (percent)	El Salvador (dollars)	El Salvador (percent)	Honduras (dollars)	Honduras (percent)
Production	2.38	47.7	2.72	41.0	3.52	47.6
Packing	0.84	16.8	1.20	18.0	1.00	13.5
Transportation and handling	1.77	35.5	2.72	41.0	2.87	38.9
	4.99	100.0	6.64	100.0	7.39	100.0

could rise to 100 million pounds valued at over $10 million, as indicated in Chapter 1. Dr. Val de Beausset of the Central American Bank for Economic Integration stated that the bank has a fund of $60 million for financing non-traditional exports, and currently has under way 12 new export projects. The bank projects an export volume of 500 million pounds, a large percentage in frozen form. The total value of exports using these estimates could be around $50 million.

The Central American exporters have been able to ship produce of a quality comparable to Mexican produce, but not with the consistency and volume required for a viable export operation. There remain serious production and quality-control difficulties as well as limited and costly transport services. Clearly a gap exists between the requirements for success identified in Chapter 3, and the actual capabilities examined in this chapter. Improved linkages between exporters and importers must be developed if effective coordination is to be achieved.

Difficulties will continue to plague this new industry, but with greater experience and improved manpower the current losses should be converted into profits. Agribusiness management education plays a key role in developing the human resources needed to make Central America a competitive participant in the fruit and vegetable export commodity system.

EXPORT–PROJECT ANALYSES: CASE STUDIES

Although space limitations do not permit a full presentation of the field data collected on the export projects studied in Central America, this final section does present somewhat detailed analyses of these projects.

Although the data contained in each project analysis vary, the format is basically the same, as follows:

I. Brief History of Export Operation

II. Production
    A. Planting cycle
    B. Key problems
    C. Output
    D. Costs
    E. Investment

III. Packing
    A. Description of operations
    B. Key problems
    C. Amounts exported
    D. Costs
    E. Investment

    IV.   Transportation
        A. Description of service
        B. Key problems
        C. Costs

    V.   Marketing
        A. Type of arrangement (producer-exporter-importer)
        B. Key problems
        C. Costs
        D. Marketing results
        E. Local market

    VI.   Financing
        A. Sources
        B. Key problems
        C. Terms

    VII.   Government role

    VIII.   Economic analysis
        A. Profitability
        B. Break-even

The above ordering of the information reflects, in part, the commodity systems approach employed. Each stage in the system is examined, as are the primary inputs and coordinating mechanisms.

GUATEMALA: CUCUMBERS

Brief History

    The first serious export effort took place in 1969–70. The main groups involved in this initial attempt were a producer cooperative, Compania Agropecuaria Regional de Servicios Varios de Oriente (CARSVO), located in Teculután, Zacapa; an export brokerage firm (FYRCO) formed by three Guatemalans expressly for the purpose of exporting nontraditional crops to the U. S. winter market; a U. S. vegetable broker (Orbit Sales) operating out of Pompano Beach, Florida; AID's Regional Office for Central America and Panama (ROCAP); and the Central American Common Market's technological research institute (ICAITI).

    In late 1968, the staff of ROCAP began focusing increasing attention on the problems and possibilities of exporting nontraditional fruits and vegetables from Central America to the United States. This effort was spearheaded by Dr. Gerald Horne, formerly Regional Food and Agriculture Officer for ROCAP, who employed a "seed-to-consumer" systems approach to the export operations. ROCAP provided some support for a trial export operation in the Zacapa region in 1970.

Zacapa Valley is located northeast of Guatemala City, about half way to the Guatemalan port in the Caribbean, Santo Tomás de Castilla. It is linked to both by means of a newly constructed paved road. The valley is nearly 240 meters above sea level and encircled by high mountains. The average annual temperature is 26.8°C (79.2°F), with a minimum of 21.2°C and a maximum of 34.2°C. It rains an average of only 39 days a year, but the valley has a plentiful supply of fluvial water for irrigation. The mean relative humidity for the year is 66 percent.

Because of these favorable climatic conditions, and the rising production costs and shrinking availability of farmland in the United States, Orbit Sales had also become interested in the Zacapa Valley as a source of vegetables for the U. S. winter market. This interest coincided with ROCAP's new orientation and the formation of FYRCO. Consequently, FYRCO, in cooperation with Orbit, ROCAP, ICAITI, and CARSVO, made some trial shipments in 1969 of 516 boxes of cucumbers and 400 boxes of melons to Pompano Beach. Owing to deficiencies in production, harvesting, packing, refrigeration, and transportation, the trial exports were not profitable, resulting in a loss of about $5000.

Despite this loss, Orbit and FYRCO were convinced that the obstacles encountered could be overcome. They therefore formed a joint venture, EXIMCO, with the intention of obtaining financing from the CABEI, technical and management assistance from ROCAP/ICAITI, and the produce from the farmer cooperative, CARSVO. EXIMCO did export 31,212 boxes of cucumbers during the 1970–71 season, but the operation resulted in sizable financial losses. ICAITI already has provided a full description of this operation, and we shall only highlight here the main problems that plagued this export attempt.[3]

EXIMCO initially projected the export of nine or more different crops, but actually exported only one. There were several reasons for this, but a common problem affecting all of the operations was inadequate planning and coordination. A primary difficulty was the failure to obtain timely financing from CABEI. Although EXIMCO had applied for a loan to provide its fixed and working capital in mid–1969, the loan was not approved until late 1969. There were various causes for this delay. First, the loan application did not contain an adequate project analysis. This probably reflects the lack of management capability to carry out such an analysis, a deficiency especially prevalent throughout the agricultural sector. Second, EXIMCO did not sign a contract with CARSVO until late 1969; therefore, CABEI had no assurance that EXIMCO was going to have a supply of produce to export. EXIMCO had held off signing this contract because they were not certain that the necessary transport services would be available to carry the produce from Guatemala to Florida. The transportation problem stemmed from the newness of the export operations. No transport company had regular, dependable cargo services from Zacapa to Florida; the small, uncertain, and seasonal volume did not justify a large investment by the transport companies in ships or refrigerated trailers.

By the fall of 1970, the pressure of the onrushing export season was intensifying. An external factor provided the catalyst for the signing of a contract between EXIMCO and CARSVO. The CARSVO farmers had been primarily involved in supplying the local vegetable canneries with tomatoes. However, in late 1970 the processors announced that they were curtailing their tomato purchases because of excessive inventories of processed tomato products. These inventory surpluses were the result of declining sales due in part to tariff barriers imposed by Honduras on Guatemalan imports. These trade restrictions stemmed from the withdrawal of Honduras from the Central American Common Market free-trade agreement. With the demand for its tomatoes greatly slashed, CARSVO was even more highly motivated to seek alternative crops. Consequently, a contract was signed with EXIMCO, but only to produce cucumbers. The exporters became aware, in part, through the use of line-of-blance and PERT charts provided by ROCAP, that the short-cycle cucumbers were the only crop they could plant, harvest, and export before the U. S. winter produce market season ended. At the same time, the transport companies indicated to EXIMCO that adequate cargo facilities would be available.

With the producer contract consummated, CABEI disbursed the funds to EXIMCO. However, it was too late to obtain the complete equipment needed for the packing station and refrigerated warehouse. Although the quality of cucumbers exported was much better than the previous year, losses were incurred owing to lack of refrigerated storage and the failure of transport vehicles to arrive when needed.

EXIMCO also had difficulties in obtaining a sufficient number of boxes. According to the farmers, this problem plus the lack of refrigerated trailers caused EXIMCO to tighten its selection standards, in effect enforcing the stipulations set forth in the agreement with CARSVO. The resultant increase in rejects created discontent among the producers. Consequently, the cooperative reportedly exerted pressure on EXIMCO to sign a new contract in which the exporter agreed to accept 80 percent of the cucumbers delivered to the packing station instead of the previous standard of about 60 percent. Table 4–8 shows the results of the export operations under the two contracts.

The large losses during the second contract due to decomposition were a result of an infection provoked by the *Pythium aphanidermatum* fungus. The total losses to EXIMCO are estimated to have been between $20,000 and $40,000. The relations between CARSVO and EXIMCO deteriorated completely, and EXIMCO was disbanded. The maintenance of mutual confidence between producers and exporter–importers is clearly an essential ingredient to a successful export operation. Reciprocity and credibility are prerequisites for effective coordination.

This brief description of EXIMCO's operations highlights the inter-

Table 4-8. EXIMCO Export Results.

	First contract		Second contract	
Disposition	*Boxes*[a]	*Percent*	*Boxes*[a]	*Percent*
Delivered to packing station	71,144	100.0	10,991	100.0
Rejected	28,896	40.6	2,200	20.0
Exported	30,512	42.9	700	6.4
Sold locally	3,578	5.0	591	5.4
Loss, decomposition	8,158	11.5	7.500	68.2

a. 55 lb.

related nature of the export–import system and the crucial need for integrated planning and coordination. The EXIMCO experience also provides the background against which we shall examine the 1971–72 operations of the organizations that succeeded EXIMCO.

For the 1971–72 season, the Guatemalan government took a more active role in each of the steps involved in the production process through the various organs created to carry out the 1971–1975 five-year National Plan for Agricultural Development. The National Institute for Agricultural Commercialization (INDECA) and the General Directorship of Agricultural Services (DIGESA) made detailed plans with two producer cooperatives and several individual farmers; CARSVO was not included because it had already obtained its line of credit for the coming year from another government agency, Servicio Cooperativo Interamericano de Credito Agricola Supervisado (SCICAS), even though this agency had been merged with the National Agricultural Development Bank (BANDESA). After the required analyses were made by INDECA and DIGESA, the necessary loan applications were presented to BANDESA.

The following project analysis will examine two of these export operations: (1) CARSVO and the ELCO, S. A., which is a Guatemalan company presently operating the packing plant started by EXIMCO; (2) La Fragua cooperative, which cultivated cucumbers for the first time in 1971–72 and contracted to export directly to a U. S. broker in Florida. Both shipped to the United States during the 1971–72 season, but in late March, 1972, La Fragua stopped exporting to its broker because of payment difficulties, and shipped the remainder of its harvest via ELCO's packing plant. These two operations will now be examined in detail.

Production

Planting Cycles. For the 1971–72 season, 257 manzanas of cucumbers were planted by CARSVO members, in four cycles, with the final shipment occurring in late March. La Fragua farmers had at first signed a contract to cultivate 300 manzanas in six 15-day cycles with the first plantings taking place on November 1, 1971, and the last on January 15, 1972. Under this schedule, the exports would have started in mid—December and ended by mid—April. In fact, the planting of each cycle was delayed from three to six days and the area to be planted was increased by 62 manzanas for a total of 362 manzanas. Out of this total, 30 manzanas were completely lost because they were planted with a variety of seed, Comanche, that did not adapt to the climatic and agronomic conditions of the Zacapa region. Another 27 manzanas of the Poinsett variety dried out without bearing fruit owing to inadequate administrative control in the irrigation system. Consequently, only 305 manzanas were planted. The average planting by the CARSVO members was 2 manzanas, and by La Fragua members 11 manzanas.

Various farmers planted melons, chile, eggplant, watermelon, and bell peppers, under the supervision of DIGESA—INDECA, with cycles that cover the exportation period of December 15 through April 15. ELCO exported 17,754 35-pound boxes of chiles; the cooperatives Motagua and El Rosario exported 1,046 50-pound boxes of melons and 5,000 30-pound boxes of eggplant, respectively.[4]

Key Production Problems. The farmers experienced difficulties with pest control, fungus infestations, and plant viruses. Damage from the mosaic fungus was the main cause of rejects in 1971—72. Irrigation timing, fertilizer application, and use of appropriate agrochemical formulations are additional areas where improvement has to be made. Most varieties of cucumbers have a ratio of six to ten male flowers to each female flower, and this makes it necessary to use a strong colony of bees for each hectare of cucumbers. Nonetheless, very few hives were used in the 1971—72 season. Inadequate pollination caused misshapen fruit and made small fruits turn yellow and drop from the vine.

An individual farmer may obtain assistance from government agencies, the input suppliers, the cooperatives, and the buyers of their products. Unfortunately, these organizations did not adequately coordinate their producer-assistance efforts, with the result that there was unnecessary duplication and farmer confusion from conflicting advice. Another factor limiting the effectiveness of technical assistance is the lack of enough trained foremen to supervise the everyday routine implementation of the technical instructions.

The failure of some of the varieties planted indicates that improved seed selection and continuous experimentation are necessary to determine which varieties are best adapted to the Zacapa Valley, especially those that have higher resistance to prevalent viruses and fungi.

Analyses of CARSVO cucumbers with good and poor skin, performed in agricultural laboratories in Fort Lauderdale, demonstrated a low content of magnesium, iron, and zinc in the cucumbers with poor skin. This suggests that further soil analysis is needed to determine which farms have the most appropriate soils. Concentrating the production area is also of great importance to CARSVO, where the average area planted per farmer is relatively small and farms are widely dispersed, thus causing problems of control and efficient delivery of services.

Output. At the end of the 1971–72 season, ELCO had accepted for export from CARSVO a total of 30,342 52-pound boxes of cucumbers.[5] La Fragua's final production report, dated May 10, 1972, showed an estimated field production of 142,417 42-pound boxes, of which 109,790 boxes were delivered to their packing shed.[6] This is the equivalent of 88,678 export boxes, which should average 52-pound net. However, La Fragua's report shows 109,790 field boxes (42-pound) or 90,028 export boxes (52-pound) received at the packing shed, of which 64,812 were sent direct to their Florida broker and 2,028 were sold through ELCO. The balance, 23,188 boxes, was rejected by the La Fragua graders. The Florida broker reported 45,081 52-pound boxes sold after repacking in Pompano Beach, which means that 19,731 boxes were rejected at the broker's packing plant. Table 4–9 presents a detailed accounting of the 24 shipments made by La Fragua direct to their Pompano Beach broker.

The net receipts by La Fragua from the broker are estimated at only $6698 for 64,812 boxes of cucumbers exported. La Fragua reportedly received $8667 net in payment for the 2,028 export boxes sold at the end of the season to ELCO rather than to the Florida broker. The late-season shipments were more profitable owing to a strong rise in prices.

CARSVO and La Fragua cooperatives had an estimated field production of 228,120 42-pound boxes (9,581,040 lbs.), which represented an increase of about 140 percent over the previous year's cucumber output in the Zacapa Valley. In these estimates, we have assumed a 25 percent rejection in the pregrading done at the field; La Fragua cooperative showed close to 23 percent field rejection in its May 10 production report.

Costs. The newness of these export operations and the lack of reliable cost records make it difficult to estimate accurately production costs. However, a range of estimates is available. As of May 31, 1972, there was an outstanding balance of $95,574 in favor of La Fragua for inputs, services, and cash advances made to its members for the 362 manzanas they planted in the season, or an average of $264 per manzana. The costs of production per manzana, as estimated by the CARSVO Cooperative and based on the previous year's experience, appear in Table 4–10, and total $500 ($715 per ha.). The cost for La Fragua, approved by BANDESA, as per estimates made by the DIGESA–INDECA experts, amounted to $571 per manzana. Both differ substantially from ICAITI's estimate of $401, that was mainly derived from costs obtained in the field by ROCAP's horticulturist in the Teculután area. The head of the

Table 4–9.   La Fragua Cucumber Exports, 1971–1972.

Shipment number	Exports (boxes)	Rejects in Pompano Beach (boxes)	Reported sales in Pompano Beach (boxes)	Reported average price (dollars per box)	Balance due La Fragua (dollars)
1	2,200	306	1,894	0.31	584.20
2	3,575	709	2,866	(0.98)	(2,809.46)
3	9,845	3,312	6,533	(0.29)	(1,897.68)
4[a]	450	—	450	1.50	675.00
5[a]	569	—	569	1.50	853.50
6	3,540	1,364	2,176	0.91	1,977.85
7	4,000	734	3,266	2.00	6,543.88
8	2,580	366	2,214	1.20	2,660.80
9	4,948	757	4,191	0.36	1,517.91
10	2,745	988	1,757	0.55	960.94
11	5,465	1,885	3,580	(0.54)	(1,948.82)
12	2,770	898	1,872	0.07	134.86
13	3,600	2,240	1,360	0.17	227.35
14	2,061	585	1,476	0.19	279.36
15	2,373	900	1,473	0.49	728.89
16	720	204	516	(0.52)	(266.15)
17	2,160	848	1,312	(2.19)	(2,875.16)
18	2,118	726	1,392	2.65	(3,684.48)
19[b]	1,645	493	1,152	2.00	2,304.00
20[b]	720	720	0	0	0
21	2,120	565	1,555	(3.94)	(6,134.25)
22	1,188	378	810	(2.24)	(1,814.10)
23	2,059	448	1,611	3.67	5,905.05
24	1,361	305	1,056	2.63	2,774.51
Season totals	64,812	19,731	45,081		6,698.00

Source: INDECA; information obtained through La Fragua Cooperative.
a. Air shipment.
b. Estimated.

Vegetables Project of the Ministry of Agriculture of Guatemala prepared a small booklet, "Commercial Cultivation of Cucumbers." On the basis of a 12-acre experimental plantation of the Poinsett variety at La Fragua, where a yield of 256 hundredweight/acre (448 cwt/manzana) was obtained, he estimated a cost per manzana of $617.

Investment. The members of both cooperatives, CARSVO and La Fragua, use the services provided by each cooperative for the preparation of land, cultivation, fertilization, fumigation, and transportation. To make these services available to its more than 200 members, the CARSVO cooperative owns the following equipment: tractors, mechanical plow; leveling equipment, rakes, fertilizers, etc.; high-pressure water and fumigating pumps; trucks; veterinarian tools; vehicles; wooden boxes to transport vegetables.

CARSVO acquired new equipment and machinery during the 1970–71 season for about $100,000 in order to give better service to its members. CARSVO's total assets as of June 30, 1971, amounted to $300,756, and liabilities were $208,407.

Individual farms have hand tools, such as machetes and rakes, and in some cases back-packed motor pumps to spray pesticides.

Since the members are charged a set fee per hectare for each service rendered by the cooperatives, many farmers try to do as much as possible on their own. The smaller the area planted, the more the farmer will try to do by himself.

La Fragua cooperative has yet to purchase a truck or other vehicle. It depends on independent truckers to haul its inputs and its produce. In general, the 26 members of this cooperative have individually more equipment than CARSVO's, which may be accounted for by the fact that they own bigger farms. About 25 percent have tractors and 30 percent drive their own vehicles.

Packing

Description of Operation. The CARSVO members deliver their cucumbers to the ELCO packing plant located a few hundred feet from CARSVO's headquarters. The packing equipment consists of two conveyor-belt machines with rotating-brush cleaners and waxers. The belts are 14 yards long and 24 inches wide, with eight compartments on each belt where the graders place the cucumbers as they are sorted. This equipment is installed in a concrete building 200 feet long and 100 feet wide, with a tin roof and cement floor.

The cucumbers are brought to the plant in wooden containers 24 inches long, 15 inches wide, and 7 inches deep. Each end of the box is raised 1 inch by means of a 15 by 2 by 1 inch piece of wood nailed so that the boxes can be stacked without damaging the contents. These boxes, which are owned by CARSVO, hold an average of 42 pounds of cucumbers. From the field the

Table 4-10. Production Costs of Cucumbers for Export, 1971–1972 (dollars per manzana).[a]

Direct expenses		
Land preparation (mechanized)		
Clean-up	7.00	
Plowing and harrowing	12.50	
Furrowing	10.00	29.50
Seed and chemical products		
Seed: 2 lbs. at $5	10.00	
Fertilizers, complete formula: 900 lbs. at $5.10	45.90	
Urea: 200 lbs. at $5.80	11.60	
Insecticide applications (10)	41.27	
Soil insecticides (2 liters)	5.40	
Fungicides	18.00	132.17
Labor at $1.00 per work day		
First fertilization	3.00	
Planting	5.00	
Irrigation	9.00	
Clearing and cultivation	24.00	
Thinning	2.00	
Second fertilization	2.00	
Fumigation	15.00	
Harvest	72.00	
Preselection and packing	18.00	
Transportation to plant (Loading and unloading included):		
400 boxes at $0.10	40.00	190.00
Subtotal		351.67
Indirect expenses		
Rent of land	20.00	
Maintenance of fences and irrigation channels	4.00	
Packing: replacement of boxes damaged	4.00	

Equipment depreciation: fumigating pumps and high-pressure pumps,		
10 percent in 2.5 months; 8 boxes at $0.35	23.60	
Management: 5 percent over direct expenses	17.58	
Social security: 3 percent over salaries	4.62	
Unforeseen: 10 percent over direct expenses	35.17	108.97
Marketing charge collected by CARSVO:		
$0.10 per box		40.00
Subtotal		148.97
Total		$500.64

Source: CARSVO (Cooperativa Agropecuaria Regional de Servicios Varios de Oriente R.L.).

a. Estimated by CARSVO, excluding interest charges.

boxes are transported aboard trucks that may be owned by the farmer, the cooperative, another farmer, or an independent trucker. Five cents per box is the standard freight charge.

The process from the field to the packing house is as follows. Approximately 60 days from the planting date, the first picking takes place. Pickers are instructed to pick only the cucumbers that are mature but not vine-ripened, of uniform size and color, without discoloration, sunburns, scars, or other undesirable traits. The workers generally were not told how these standards related to the requirements of the U. S. market. From seven to nine pickings are made during the harvesting of each cycle.

The picked cucumbers are taken to a central point in the field (if possible, under a tree or in some other shady spot) where they are pregraded and placed in boxes. Young men, under the supervision of an older man, do the pregrading. It was estimated by CARSVO's manager that in the Zacapa Valley, approximately 70 percent of the pickers are children under 15 years, half of whom are boys, half girls; another 20 percent are women, and the remaining 10 percent men.

After the preliminary grading, the boxes are left in the field to await the trucker, if, of course, the farmer does not have his own means of transportation. The rejects, which may range between 10 percent and 40 percent of the cucumbers harvested, are used mostly for animal feed. The boxes are taken to the packing plant late in the afternoon or early in the evening, where they are received to be graded.

La Fragua's packing plant, which is located very close to the cooperative's office, is an open-air shed about 90 feet long and 36 feet wide with a tin roof and a dirt floor. There is an old conveyor belt 13 yards long and 24 inches wide, with rotating cleaning brushes. The sorting and grading for export was done by 27 women, who were paid $0.80 per day and worked under the supervision of one foreman, assisted by five men who dumped the boxes onto the conveyor equipment and subsequently closed the wirebound boxes and loaded them aboard refrigerated trailers of the CCT (Coordinated Caribbean Transport). The boxes measure 18−7/8 by 12 by 11−3/4 inches on the outside. When La Fragua began to ship via the ELCO packing plant instead of to its Florida broker, several CCT trailer loads that were supposed to be ready for export were taken to ELCO to be regraded; these boxes were found to be not fully loaded and the cucumbers very poorly graded.

Key Problems. The children used as pickers normally did not do as good a job as older persons. By picking immature cucumbers, they ruined the produce, thereby causing loss of the investment made to bring that produce almost to maturity.

Another problem was that the pregrading in the field was often not done in the shade, and the cucumbers were sometimes dumped on the ground;

both of these actions damaged the fruit. It may be better to pick all of the cucumbers, not leaving the misshapen, ripe, colorless, damaged, or otherwise unsuitable ones in the field, where they may incubate fungus, virus, and pests that in turn could infect otherwise healthy cucumbers.

The pickers and graders often did not have adequate training to appreciate the fragile nature of the cucumber. Consequently, the fruit was subjected to excessively rough handling, and damaged cucumbers were occasionally shipped to the U. S. broker, who then rejected them. This meant that the exporter incurred transport, handling, and tariff costs that could have been avoided through improved handling and selection. The preselection should have been of special importance for La Fragua, since they were shipping to their broker only after a preliminary grading.

La Fragua pooled the production of all of its members. The cooperative kept track of the total number of boxes received from each member with the purpose of subsequently making payment in direct proportion to the number of boxes sold in the United States by the broker. In effect, this penalized farmers with quality output by having them subsidize the producers of poorer quality, whose crop went into the common pool. This is in part a management-control problem and in part a result of the type of marketing arrangement with the broker. This arrangement will be discussed in a subsequent section.

Both La Fragua and ELCO had a packing problem. In La Fragua the boxes were not packed full enough, with the result that the cucumbers got shifted and jostled and thus damaged during transport. The ELCO boxes, in contrast, were sometimes packed too full; consequently, some cucumbers were damaged by compression when the boxes were stacked. The availability of boxes was not a problem this year, in contrast to EXIMCO's experience, although the boxes sometimes were delivered late. The cooperatives bought their boxes from a local box manufacturer on 30-day credit. There was no formal purchase contract with the box-maker.

A final packing problem was that both ELCO and La Fragua lacked refrigeration facilities, and this led to some quality deterioration. However, ELCO will have by next season a refrigeration unit with a 400-ton capacity, the equivalent of 20 refrigerated trailers.

Amount Exported. Table 4–11 shows the amount of cucumbers received by ELCO from CARSVO during the season and the amounts classified for export, as well as their value (price to producer). As may be observed, the percentage of rejects increased sharply as the season progressed.

The rejects were largely used for animal feed, although a small amount (5 percent) was sold locally as will be described subsequently. Most (74 percent) of the CARSVO farmers had between 61 and 80 percent of the cucumbers they delivered to the packing plant accepted for export in liquidation

Table 4–11. ELCO Cucumber Receipts, Classification, and Value, 1971–1972.

Liquidation number	Quantity delivered (lb.)	Total classified (lb.)	Rejects (percent)	Classification					
				Super Select		Select		Large	
				Quantity (lb.)	Value[a]	Quantity (lb.)	Value[a]	Quantity (lb.)	Value[a]
1	658,896	440,076	33.2	380,536	$11,708.80	44,200	$ 935.00	15,340	$ 177.00
2	715,722	444,288	37.9	222,820	6,856.00	158,028	3,342.90	63,440	732.00
3[b]	—	—	—	—	—	—	—	—	—
4	414,918	226,148	45.5	87,724	2,699.00	67,548	1,428.90	70,876	823.00
5	521,220	273,052	47.6	86,008	2,446.40	138,632	2,932.60	48,412	558.60
6	390,432	194,220	50.3	74,204	2,283.20	96,096	2,032.80	23,920	276.00
7[b]	—	—	—	—	—	—	—	—	—
Total	2,701,118	1,577,784[c]		851,292	$25,993.40	504,504	$10,672.20	221,988	$2,566.60
Percent	100.0	58.4		31.5		18.7		8.2	

a. Gross price to farmer paid by ELCO to the Cooperative, which includes transportation costs to the packing plant and commission per box exported.

b. Rejects sold locally; No. 3 grossed $255.40 and No. 7, $1,262.70.

c. 1,577,784 lbs., divided by 52 lbs./box (average net weight) gives a total of 30,342 boxes exported. Since the total paid to the farmers is $39,232.20, the average price is $1.20 per box.

number 2, the modal classification percentage range being 61 to 70 percent. This suggests that most of the growers of the first cycles produced fruit of very similar quality. In the late-season shipments, rejects in the packing plant rose markedly, reportedly because of increased wilting and sun damage caused by the hotter and drier temperatures during those months.

La Fragua shipped 64,812 boxes to its broker in Pompano Beach, and exported 2,028 through ELCO. This represents about 72 percent of the total number of export boxes (90,028) the farmers delivered to the packing station. This 28 percent rejection rate is markedly lower than that of ELCO, because La Fragua was only doing a pregrading rather than a final selection. The cucumbers were sent to the broker without waxing and polishing in wirebound wooden crates (12 by 12 by 18 in.).

Of the 64,812 boxes received on consignment from La Fragua by the Florida broker, 45,081 were sold through his distribution channels, after regrading and repacking in Pompano Beach. The broker reportedly rejected at his packing plant the equivalent of 19,731 boxes, or nearly 30 percent of total deliveries. Because of the limited selection process at the producing zone, substantial costs were incurred in transportation, tariffs, regrading, and repacking of many cucumbers that were hardly even salable. This emphasizes again the importance of strict selection and classification at the shipping point. A clear understanding of quality—in terms of size, color, shape, and condition of fruits and vegetables for export—is a prerequisite to success.

Costs. The costs incurred by the ELCO packing operation are shown in Table 4–12. Most of the exporters' statistics and government analyses report $1.60 per box as the price paid by the packing house to the farmers. However, in actuality this is the price paid for Super Select cucumbers, and the packing plants also purchase and export Select ($1.10) and Large ($0.60). On the basis of the mix of grades purchased by ELCO, the weighted average price paid to CARSVO was $1.29 per box.

Table 4–12. Packing-plant Costs 1971–1972
(dollars per box).

Item	Cost
Average price paid to CARSVO	1.29
Labor for classification and handling in plant	0.20
Wax	.02
Wirebound wooden box	.40
Administration	.41
Electricity expenses	.18
Plant lease	.20
Total	2.70

Investment. ELCO had no investment in fixed assets because it leased the packing plant from CABEI at a rate of $0.20 per box exported. ELCO has an option to buy the plant from CABEI.

La Fragua owns a 90 by 36-foot packing shed and second-hand pregrading equipment valued at $3000. This equipment was provided by the broker and the cooperative agreed to pay for it over a two-year period at the rate of $0.05 per box exported.

Transportation

Description of Services. As was described in Chapter 3, export transport service is provided by Coordinated Caribbean Transport, Inc. (CCT), which is a division of the U. S. Freight Company.

After grading and packing, the cucumbers are loaded on refrigerated trailers, of dimensions 37 by 6½ by 7 feet. The trailers that the packers estimate are going to be needed are requested one week in advance from CCT's Guatemala City office. During 1972, reportedly, the service had been very good; CCT had sent directly to each packing plant as many trailers as had been required. In a letter dated January 17, 1972, sent by CCT to INDECA's general manager, the schedule was set as follows:

Ship	*Arrival*	*Departure*
Mar Caribe	Every Friday at 6 a.m.	Every Friday at 5 p.m.
Caribbean Enterprise	Every Monday at 6 a.m.	Every Monday at 5 p.m.

The attainment of this twice-weekly schedule was in part the result of negotiations with CCT by INDECA.

Near the end of the season, CCT cancelled its twice-weekly schedule and returned, without prior notice, to one weekly departure using a larger ship with 90-trailer capacity. This created a great deal of ill feeling among growers, and requests were made to the Guatemalan government by farmers, cooperatives, and shippers to grant a charter to Sea-Land Shipping Company, or to equip adequately the National Shipping Company FLOMERCA so that a reliable service might be available for the next season.

Problems. Difficulties were experienced at the beginning of the season by La Fragua with trailers that they claim had uneven refrigeration.

It is generally felt among the farmers that the lack of competition gives CCT unfair bargaining power over the cooperatives. As of 1972, only CCT was chartered to service Guatemalan ports with roll-on roll-off equipment.

Costs. The CCT charge per trailer was supposed to be based on one of three conditions: (1) one call per week, placing at the disposal of the vegetable shippers four or five trailers, at $950 per trailer; (2) a 90-trailer ship, one call per week, and making available from 25 to 30 trailers, at $1150 per trailer; and (3) two ships, two departures per week, at $1250 per trailer.

The 720-box capacity per trailer would have meant a unit cost of $1.32, $1.59, and $1.73 per box respectively for these three conditions, which makes this one of the largest cost categories in the export operation. In actual practice, CCT charged as much as $1558 per trailer, as they increased the amount collected when there were more than 720 boxes on a trailer. Most of the invoices to La Fragua were for $1409 per trailer, which included $1282 for the trailer plus wharfage, handling, inspection, and hauling to Pompano Beach from Miami. This means that the average cost per box for ocean and land transportation to the broker's place of business was $1.96. Clearly, reducing transport costs deserves the attention of exporters, importers, and the government.

Marketing

Type of Arrangement. As mentioned earlier, CARSVO contracted to sell its members' cucumbers to ELCO, S. A., a Guatemalan corporation. The manager of ELCO works in Guatemala managing the purchasing, packing, and exporting operations. Reportedly, the remaining shareholders are based in Florida and take charge of the products upon their arrival at Miami, handling the importation end of the transaction as well as the sales to wholesalers and other U. S. buyers of cucumbers. In effect, ELCO emerged as the result of the backward vertical integration by a Florida-based broker, although separate corporate entities exist. The ELCO managers spend a majority of their time in the Zacapa Valley, having established close relations with the directors and the individual members of the CARSVO cooperative. They provide technical assistance, and they also give free advice to the farmers on matters not necessarily related to cucumber cultivation. The key ELCO manager previously had extensive experience exporting fresh produce from Cuba to Florida.

The cucumbers are received from each farmer f.o.b. packing plant. Individual records are kept, but payment is made in a lump sum direct to the cooperative every 15 days. In turn, the cooperative makes a liquidation to its members, indicating the total number of boxes delivered to the packing plant, grades, value per grade, transportation expenses, cooperative's commission ($0.10 per box exported), funds credited to outstanding loans, and net payment to each farmer. The liquidations are based on the contractual prices for the three different grades as agreed upon by ELCO and CARSVO. The producers' return does not depend on the prices finally received for the exported crop. The exporter bears the risk of price fluctuations, in-transit damage, and the like; accordingly, he also obtains the benefits from favorable prices.

The marketing arrangement between La Fragua and its Florida broker contrasts with the CARSVO–ELCO agreement. La Fragua (under the supervision of INDECA) signed a contract with the broker agreeing to plant 300 manzanas with cucumbers and deliver the production exclusively to the broker, who, in turn, agreed to receive, grade, repack, and distribute the cooperative's exports. For these services the broker charged a $1 fee per box repacked in Florida, plus a 10 percent commission on the sales price of the cucumbers finally sold. Some of the cucumbers were marketed in smaller carton containers rather than in boxes. In such cases, the repacking charge was $0.60 per carton. Since there are supposed to be three cartons (of 24 cucumbers each) to a box, the charge per box packed in cartons turned out to be $1.80. This was a consignment arrangement, with the producers bearing the transport and price risks.

The broker agreed to supply the cooperative with seed (about 1800 lbs.) at cost, to send at his expense an American cucumber expert to supervise the plantations and give technical assistance, and to provide the pregrading equipment on easy sales terms.

Problems. One of the difficulties in marketing fresh produce from Central America is that the exporter is largely restricted to a single point of entry to the United States: Pompano Beach. This is mainly due to the limited transportation services and the risks. The exporter may fail to realize attractive prices because shipments from other exporting countries (within and outside Central America) arrive the same day and flood the market. Climatic conditions in Florida might reduce the Florida production and thus the supply, thereby reducing the number of buyers present in Pompano Beach. This situation occurred because of frost in a recent winter season. These market imperfections weigh heavily on the exporter who is unable to tap other markets because of transport inadequacies.

The competitive dominance of Mexico, furthermore, especially in the western states, also looms large on the market horizon. According to information published by the Mexican Unión Nacional de Productores de Hortalizas, Mexico increased its cucumber exports from 45,318 tons in 1969–70 to 67,263 tons in 1970–71, a jump of 48 percent. This compares with the 1,850 tons shipped from Guatemala in 1971–72. Although Central America is the number two supplier to the U. S. winter market, it is still a distant second.

As regards the marketing agreements, the CARSVO–ELCO arrangement represents a low-risk approach for the producers and a high-risk, high-gain strategy for the exporter. Some farmers expressed concern that they were unable to protect themselves against the possibility of the exporters paying them on the basis of prices for one grade and then exporting these same cucumbers as a higher grade. This is a control problem and also reflects the need for honesty and mutual trust between farmer and exporter.

The arrangement between La Fragua and its broker had several potential disadvantages for the cooperative. First, the producers bore the burden of risk for damages incurred during transport and handling from Guatemala to Florida. Second, the limited pregrading operation meant that the cooperative paid transport, handling, and tariff expenses for large amounts of produce that were rejected in the United States and therefore produced no revenue. Third, the cooperative paid for the grading and repacking operations in the United States, where labor costs are much higher than in Guatemala. Finally, the producers had a difficult task in attempting to control the accuracy of the broker's grading operations. Without having a direct observer in Florida, the farmers must accept the broker's report on how much of the produce delivered to Florida was non-salable. This type of arrangement makes open and frequent communication between broker and producer very important if suspicions and accusations are to be avoided. In the case of La Fragua, such information interchange apparently was not present.

In February, 1972, the broker sent to La Fragua an invoice in which the total sales were reported as $14,885 and the transport, duty, handling, and commission costs as $12,907, leaving a net for the cooperative of $1,977. In April, the broker sent another invoice to the cooperative with adjustments in the sales figure to reflect prices lower than those originally reported in the February invoice. The result was a decrease in the net proceeds to the cooperative from $1,977 to $823. This was not well received by the farmers.

Reportedly, the broker also was slow in sending the liquidations. Under the contract, the broker had agreed to pay 21 days after the arrival of the cucumbers in Pompano Beach, but apparently this agreement was not kept. After a very heated session held on the evening of March 16 by a majority of the members of the cooperative, it was decided to stop shipments to the Florida broker. All of the cucumbers that had been processed during the last few days and were supposedly ready for export were moved to ELCO's plant to be graded and packed again. An agreement was reached with ELCO that all of the crop remaining to be harvested was to be handled and exported by ELCO at La Fragua's own risk insofar as the selling price at Pompano Beach was concerned. As a result, La Fragua closed down its packing plant and no more shipments were made to the Florida broker, even though he had cabled to offer $2.00 per box of cucumbers f.o.b. packing shed. La Fragua shipped 2028 boxes through ELCO and promptly received a net payment of $8667, or an average of $4.27 per box exported. This advantageous price was largely due to a decreased supply of Mexican and U. S. cucumbers because of unfavorable weather conditions.

A final problem concerns the local markets. The Guatemalan market for cucumbers is very small relative to the disposable (nonexportable) supply. Domestic prices are only a fraction of the export prices. A subsequent section will describe the local marketing situation more fully, but it seems clear that domestic fresh sales will not be a significant outlet (perhaps less than 5 percent for seconds. Consequently, attention and resources might better be directed toward improving the exportable portion of the farmer's harvest, or exploring the alternative of pickle and relish processing.

Costs. The marketing costs for ELCO are estimated in Table 4–13. The $1 per box repacking charge reportedly incurred by both ELCO and La Fragua is a potential area for savings. If the packing operations and transport services can be improved in the future, this cost might be avoided, or at least reduced. Another major cost is the U. S. tariff, a heavy and uncertain burden, subject to political whim and largely outside the exporter's control.

Table 4–13. ELCO Marketing Costs 1971–1972
(dollars per box).

Item	Cost
Guatemalan export duty	0.10
U.S. tariff	1.32
Handling	.18
Repacking	1.00
Broker's commission[a]	.81
Total	3.41

a. At 10 percent, assuming an average weighted price of $8.13, calculated from INDECA's weekly reports of broker's prices prevailing in Pompano Beach.

Marketing Results. According to available data, La Fragua suffered great losses. ELCO indicated that they "did not become millionaires" this season, but they did make profits. The CARSVO grower incurred losses due to low exportable yields.

Local Market. The prices in the local markets have ranged from as low as $0.15 per box to as high as $1.20, depending on the quantity and timing of the produce influx. One truckload (five to six tons) is usually enough to cause prices to plummet. Many farmers do not bother to sell locally and simply feed the rejects from the packing plant to their livestock, although cucumbers are not a particularly nutritious feed. In a survey of the local market on March 17, 18, and 19, 1972, the prices were as follows:

At the packing plants, per box (approximately 72 cucumbers)	$0.15 (bulk)
Zacapa market, per box	.25
Retail marketplace, each cucumber	.01
Farmers' market, Guatemala City, one box	.50
Two or more boxes, per box	.45
More than 20 boxes, per box	.40
"Corner" grocery stores, each cucumber	.02
Super markets, each cucumber	.03

Approximately every 10 days a couple of trucks from El Salvador bought cucumbers at either CARSVO or La Fragua. The prices in San Salvador, the capital city, in mid–March were as follows:

San Salvador terminal market, per box	$2.00–2.25
"Corner" grocery stores, each cucumber	0.04
Small store, each cucumber	.05
Big super market, "special sale," three cucumbers	.04

CARSVO and ELCO sold 6491 boxes to the local markets at an average price of 0.23 per box.

Financing

The catalytic agent in the Guatemalan cooperative movement appears to have been the Servicio Cooperativo Interamericano de Credito Agricola Supervisado (SCICAS), which provided financing and some technical assistance to cooperatives. SCICAS was backed by AID and it operated in Guatemala until 1971, when its functions as well as those of the National Agrarian Bank were merged into the National Development Bank (BANDESA), where agricultural financing had been centralized. BANDESA, as its predecessor SCICAS did, extends credit directly to the cooperatives. Each individual cooperative outlines in its application the plan for the forthcoming season, and in the preparation of the application the cooperative is assisted and guided by DIGESA and INDECA to make sure that the plan proposed by the cooperative conforms to the Five-Year National Plan for Agricultural Development. No cooperative may be granted more than $200,000 in loans, and each farmer member is limited to a maximum of $10,000. The member is not provided with cash but rather with all of the necessary inputs, except for a small amount of cash to pay farm laborers. If the farmer owns a tractor and does his own cultivation jobs, he receives cash as each piece of work is completed. Otherwise, the cooperative provides the services and materials. In the case of cucumbers, the associate member is entitled to receive a total of about $57 per hectare in cash for labor.

The members receive loans through the cooperative and pledge to sell the vegetables, grains, or fruits through it. Separate loans are arranged for each crop, and it may well happen that a farmer cultivates one or two crops with funds borrowed from the cooperative and another crop with his own funds. For the crops financed by the cooperative with BANDESA funds, the farmer must use the cooperative as his exclusive supplier of inputs (seed, fertilizers, pesticides, transportation). The cooperative, through volume buying and bid solicitations, obtains lower prices for farm supplies and is able to pass on to its members part of the saving. The cooperative earns a margin on these sales that covers its operating costs. An agronomist from the cooperative gives technical assistance and simultaneously makes inspections to ensure that the farmers comply with the terms of the loan. The BANDESA loans carry an 8 percent interest rate.

Although the cooperatives are able to obtain the $200,000 loans permitted, they are apparently handicapped by the rigidity of the regulations covering the amount of the loans. The stipulation that a single cooperative cannot receive more than $200,000 represents a bias against larger cooperatives. In an environment such as Guatemala, in which the difficulties and the resources needed to create any viable rural organization are immense, it does not seem advisable to have a policy that encourages the formation of many small cooperatives rather than a few larger ones. With size comes power, and effective rural development requires that farmers have a solid power base upon which to deal with other organizations, be they suppliers, buyers, or government agencies. There are significant economies of scale to be realized in rural organizing, and these should not be lost by imposing organizational size limitations via financing policies. Similarly, the stipulation that no individual farmer within the cooperative can receive a loan greater than $10,000 does not take into account that not all farms are of equal size or have identical soil suitability.

The Role of the Government

In the Zacapa Valley, the Guatemalan government provided a vital infrastructure input by constructing irrigation canals from which the farmers may take the water they need free of charge. The government also built and maintained a paved road to the well-equipped Caribbean port of Santo Tomás de Castilla, which is the closest Central American port to the U. S. market.

Following the outlines of the 1971–1975 Five-Year Plan, the Guatemalan government decentralized the "Agricultural Public Sector" and created or consolidated several of its institutions:

1. INDECA, which began to operate in 1971 in place of the former Agricultural Marketing Division of the Ministry of Agriculture, is taking a very active role in all aspects of domestic and international marketing. Through its technical department, it has been publishing a series of promotional studies and market analyses, by product, to guide farmers and other interested persons. INDECA is also the price regulatory agency for the local basic grains.

2. DIGESA is charged with the responsibility of providing technical assistance and other related services aimed at helping the farmers to increase their productivity and raise the quality of their products. In close association with INDECA, DIGESA reviews all credit applications to BANDESA; after the loans have been granted, its extension workers act as BANDESA's inspectors to ensure that the farmers appropriately use the funds loaned and the inputs provided. As the various crops grow, DIGESA's field workers submit periodic estimates of production output to INDECA so that commercialization plans may be adjusted in accordance with the anticipated supply.

3. BANDESA had the following objectives: to achieve adequate coordination among the organizations that provide financing to the agricultural sector; to integrate into a single investment portfolio the loans that were in the hands of the other government institutions; and to create a lending institution that could serve as the financing agent for the development programs framed in the National Plan for Rural Development, with special orientation toward the small and medium-sized farmers.

4. INTA (National Institute of Agrarian Reform) was created to contribute to the agricultural development of the country by improving the land-tenure situation. To accomplish this, the Institute is obligated and empowered to obtain farm lands for redistribution in family-sized plots to landless farmers.

5. ITCA (Institute of Science and Agricultural Technology) is an agricultural investigation center dedicated to the study and the solution of agricultural production problems. Its main emphasis is on improving farming techniques for the cultivation of basic staples. It is also concerned with offsetting the unbalanced regional development and introducing new seeds and new methods through intensive and extensive experimentation, especially with beans, corn, rice, sorghum, and wheat.

6. GUATEXPRO is a joint venture in which public and private sectors have united, as equal partners, for the purpose of promoting nontraditional exports in processed or semiprocessed form. Only a few months after it began to operate, it was able to sell 400 wooden coffins per week in California.

In general, the government is placing at the disposal of the cooperatives and independent farmers technical assistance, training, and financing. Big changes were made in 1971, some of which have yet to bear fruit.

Economic Analysis

Investment. There is no generally accepted going price per manzana of land in Zacapa. The farmers say that the value varies greatly, depending on the location, and that very little land is available for sale.

Profitability. La Fragua has made it clear that under the direct advice and supervision of the various Guatemalan government agencies involved in each individual step of the entire process, they "prepared the land, selected the seed, planted, produced, and exported." They did as they were told and reportedly they even selected the Florida broker with the consent of INDECA. Yet, though they shipped practically all of their cucumbers to this broker, at the end of the season they wound up with an adverse balance, in favor of the broker, of approximately $12,000. La Fragua has received liquidations for each of the shipments made, but they are continuing to receive addendums making adjustments to the previous liquidations on the grounds that the broker not only received the cucumbers on consignment, but also shipped to his own customers in the United States on a consignment basis. This meant that the farmers' risk was carried forward all the way to the retail outlet. La Fragua's executives have reached one conclusion: the Cooperative will not be able to pay off the $177,240 agricultural loans extended to them by BANDESA for the season 1971–72.

On the basis of total deliveries to the packing plant and various rough estimates given by farmers and other members of the cooperative who were interviewed, we have made a profitability analysis of the CARSVO cucumber-farming operation as a whole, using an average yield of 118 52-pound boxes of exportable cucumbers per manzana. There was a total of 30,342 boxes classified for export by ELCO, which is 35 percent of the 86,574 boxes of estimated field yield (337 boxes per manzana), and 58.4 percent of the total estimated weight delivered to the packing plant, which is the equivalent of 51,944 boxes (60 percent of estimated field yield, or 202 boxes per manzana). In accordance with CARSVO farmers' estimates, this would indicate that the equivalent of 34,630 52-pound boxes (40 percent) was discarded during preselection in the field and used mostly for animal feed. From these estimates, it can be seen that only 35 percent of the total field yield was considered to comply with the strict standards that must be met for export to the U. S. market. It may be implied, consequently, that the main problem in the field was one of producing high-quality cucumbers. With a field yield of 337 52-pound boxes (net weight) per manzana, only 202 boxes per manzana were delivered to the packing plant, and of these only 118 were classified by ELCO graders as exportable. With this performance, the farmers on the average are estimated to have suffered considerable losses on the cucumber production during the season, as may be seen from Table 4–14.

These losses indicate that the production difficulties have not been solved and perhaps represent the most pressing problem threatening the cucumber export operation. Even if exportable quality could be improved, total yields are low. At current prices and costs, to break even the farmer would have to produce 440 exportable boxes per manzana, which is higher than current estimated field yields of 337 boxes per manzana at CARSVO. The Guatemalan Ministry of Agriculture reported total yields of 804 boxes (56 lbs. gross, 52 lbs. net) per manzana, based on seven manzanas that they had planted in the Zacapa area.[7] The Ministry report emphasized that the greater the planting density, the greater the yield. The Ministry's experiment used rows two meters apart and plants 30 centimeters apart. This system obtained a plant population of 11,700 per manzana.

If production costs remain unchanged, cucumber production can become economically viable only if yields or prices improve. Table 4–15 shows different break-even yield levels that would have to be obtained given different prices, and vice versa. For example, if prices paid to farmers were to rise from the current average of $1.29 to $2 per box, yields would have to be 253 exportable boxes per manzana to break even. Some farmers did achieve high enough yields to make a profit, but many did not. The less efficient producers or those with less suitable soils may have been eliminated from the cucumber business.

Table 4–14. Cucumber Production Profit Statement, CARSVO Farmers 1971–1972 *(dollars per manzana).*

Revenue: 118 boxes at $1.29	152.22	
Less–		
Field–packing plant transportation:		
250 42-lb. boxes at $0.085	21.25	
Cooperative commission:		
$0.10 per box	11.80	
Net revenue		119.17
Costs (Table 4–10)	500.64	
Less adjustments–		
For transportation to plant:		
40.00 − 21.25	18.75	
For cooperative commission:		
40.00 − 11.80	28.20	
For loading and unloading:		
250 instead of 400 boxes,		
at $0.10	25.00	
Net costs		428.69
Loss		(309.52)
Total loss, 257 manzanas		79,546.64
Actual cost to farmer per box exported		3.63

Table 4–15. Break-even Price and Yield Combinations.

Sales price given		*Yield given*	
Sales price per box	*No. of exportable boxes per manzana to break even*	*No. of exportable boxes per manzana*	*Sales price per box to break even*
$1.29	392	118	$4.29
1.50	337	150	3.37
2.00	253	200	2.53
2.50	202	250	2.02
3.01	168	301	1.68

Moving from the farmer level to the packer-exporter stage, we lack export price data with which to make a precise profitability analysis. We cannot estimate profits using the Florida market prices as reported by INDECA (Table 4–16) and the costs presented earlier in the packing, transportation, and marketing sections, since we do not know the grade mix used by ELCO in their sales. Combined average prices are plotted in Figure 4–3. From Table 4–17 we can see that the packer-exporter made, on the average, $0.35 per box shipped. However, if the exporter does not have to repack every box that he ships, he will save $1 in repacking costs and thereby make a profit of $1.35 per box. These are, of course, very rough estimates based on assumptions rather than on actual liquidation data, which were not available. It could well have happened that cucumbers bought by ELCO as Super Select might have been sold as much lower grades, and vice versa.

It is important for the exporter to examine the profitability of the different grades of cucumbers he is selling because his purchase and sales prices vary by grade. The exporter makes $0.63 per box of Super Select quality, loses $0.82 per box of Select, and makes $0.33 per box on Large (Table 4–18). Clearly, the quality mix of the exported produce is a critical determinant of profitability. From this analysis it is clear that the narrow profit margins mean that downward price fluctuations in the Florida market would splatter the exporter's profit statement with red ink.

A final step of the economic analysis is to examine the relative importance of the various cost categories involved in the total export operation. Table 4–19 presents a percentage analysis of these principal costs. The largest single cost is transportation and the next is tariffs. These two costs, especially the latter, are to a great extent outside the control of the manager. The transport costs perhaps can be lowered by better contract negotiations, but probably government pressure will be needed. The government could play an important role in the tariffs by eliminating the export tax and negotiating a preferential rate on the important duties charged by the United States. Before Castro, Cuba reportedly was required to pay only 50 percent of the tariffs on fruits and vegetables. The packing costs also loom large. Within the packing category, the largest cost items are the box and administration. With increased volume and centralized purchasing, the box costs could perhaps be lowered. The larger volume would also lower the unit cost of the largely fixed administrative charges.

EL SALVADOR: HONEYDEW MELONS

Brief History

The project analysis will examine the production and export operations of one of several melon producers in El Salvador. This particular producer-exporter (Señor X) of honeydew melons in El Salvador comes from a farming

Table 4–16. Cucumber Prices in Pompano Beach *(dollars per box)*.

Date	Super Select	Select	Small	Large
December 30, 1971	5.56	3.50	4.50	6.75
January 3, 1972	5.50	4.00	5.00	6.30
10	7.00	5.00	6.50	7.50
13	7.50	5.50– 6.00	7.00	7.80
17	7.50	6.00	7.00	7.80
24	7.50– 8.00	6.00– 6.50	7.50	8.25
27	8.00	6.50	7.00	8.25
31	7.50– 8.50	6.00– 7.00	8.00	8.25– 9.30
February 3, 1972	9.50	8.00	9.00	10.20–10.50
10	11.00	8.00– 9.00	9.00–10.00	11.35
16	8.00– 9.00	6.00– 7.00	7.00– 8.00	9.75
22	8.00	6.00	7.00	8.25
28	7.50– 8.00	6.00	7.00	8.25
March 2, 1972	7.50– 8.00		6.50– 7.00	7.50– 8.25
9	7.00– 8.00	5.00– 5.50	6.00– 6.50	7.50– 8.25
16	9.50–10.00	7.50– 8.00	8.50– 9.00	9.75–10.50
23	9.50–10.00	7.50– 8.00	9.00	10.20
30	11.00–12.00	7.00– 8.00	11.00	11.25–12.30
April 7, 1972	13.00–15.00	10.00–11.00	11.00–12.00	15.30
10	12.00–14.00	9.00–10.00	10.00–11.00	14.25
Average	8.74	6.64	7.81	9.34

Source: INDECA, which had two representatives in Pompano Beach at La Fragua's broker's repacking plant with direct telex communications service.

Table 4–17.   Profit Statement: Packing Export Operation 1971–1972 *(dollars per box).*

Revenue: average price per box exported[a]	8.13
Costs–	
Average price paid to farmer	1.29
Packing-plant operations[b]	1.41
Transportation[c]	1.67
Marketing[d]	3.41
Total	7.78
Profit	0.35

a. Based on the cucumber price from INDECA's reports to La Fragua (Table 4–16) and their combined average price (Figure 4–3).
b. See Table 4–12.
c. See the transportation section.
d. See Table 4–13.

Table 4–18.   Profit Analysis for Different Cucumber Grades 1971–1972 *(dollars per box).*

	Super Select	*Select*	*Large*	*Small*
Average season price (Florida)	$8.74	$6.64	$9.34	$7.81
Price paid farmers	1.60	1.10	0.60	(1)
Packing	1.41	1.41	1.41	
Transportation	1.67	1.67	1.67	
Marketing (excl. com.)	2.60	2.60	2.60	
Commission (10%)	0.83	0.68	0.93	
Sub-total costs	8.11	7.46	6.58	
Sub-total			2.76	
Less:				
Carton packing[a] (in Florida)			1.80	
Profit/Loss	$0.63	($0.82)	$0.33	

a. Packed in cartons in Florida; three cartons are the equivalent of one 52-lb. box.
(1) This grade does not appear in CARSVO's liquidations to its members. Apparently, no small cucumbers were bought by ELCO, as such, any way.

family and had considerable farming experience before he began planting melons. In the early 1960s, Sr. X started to grow cotton and ever since then he has dedicated himself full time to farming. He has also grown corn, rice, beans, and watermelons (1964–1970). He started planting honeydew melons in 1969 and is now experimenting with tomatoes and cantaloupes, with a view to exports in the near future. He hopes eventually to diversify into other nontraditional export crops.

Table 4—19.   Percentage Cost Analysis: Cucumber Exports
1971—1972.

	Cost	
Item	*Dollars per box*	*Percent of total*
Raw material[a]	1.29	16.6
Packing	1.41	18.1
Transportation[b]	1.67	21.5
Tariffs	1.42	18.2
Handling and repacking	1.18	15.2
Broker's commission[c]	0.81	10.4
	7.78	100.0

a. Average price paid to the cooperative.
b. Taken from the nominal fees reported by CCT per trailer load. The actual amount charged by CCT to La Fragua averaged $1.96 per box, and negotiations are being made for a rebate.
c. Estimated, Table 4—13.

An important stimulus to Sr. X's entering the melon export business was a seminar on the export by air of nontraditional crops to the United States during the winter season. The seminar, sponsored by Pan American Airlines, the Ministry of Economy, the Ministry of Agriculture and Livestock, AID, Banco Hipotecario, and the Compania Salvadorena de Cafe, was intended to stimulate the growth and export of nontraditional crops in El Salvador and to increase the use of air-cargo services. At about the same time, AID made a study of the possibilities and potential of exporting nontraditional crops to the United States during the winter season. As a result of this study and the seminar, Sr. X started growing honeydew melons in 1969 for the 1970 winter season in the United States.

Sr. X has an integrated production, packing, and export operation for honeydew melons. He plants the melons on two different pieces of rented land, processes and packs them on plantations themselves, and ships them to the United States and Europe on consignment to brokers.

In 1969, he planted 60 manzanas (42 ha.) of honeydew melons and exported 10,200 boxes to the United States and 1600 boxes to Europe. Although his exportable production was greater than this, the boxes did not arrive on time, so he was unable to export part of his harvest. In 1970 he planted 160 manzanas and exported 29,000 boxes to the United States and 5,000 boxes to Europe. Prices in the United States fell to a low of $3.50 per box, so that during the latter part of the season he stopped exporting melons to the United States. In 1971 he again planted 160 manzanas, from which he expected to export a total of 40,000 boxes of melons. Fungus, however, attacked the plants and he was unable to control it fully. This weakened the growth of the plants considerably and, hence, the quantity and quality of the melons. Consequently,

Figure 4–3. Combined Average Price of Cucumbers in Pompano Beach (*Super Select, Select, Small, and Carton;* season average, $8.13 per box).

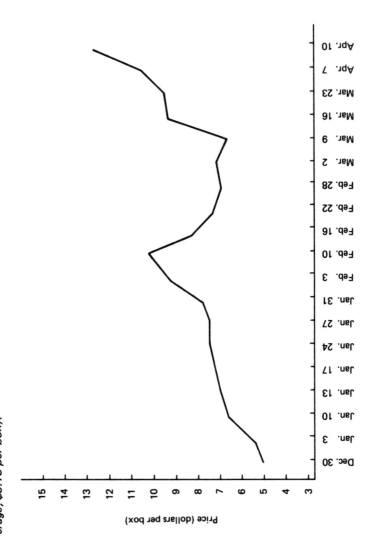

Source: INDECA—Orozco, Lionel.

he was only able to export a total of 25,000 boxes in the 1971–72 season; 17,000 went to the United States and 8000 to Europe.

Production

Planting Cycles. Sr. X plants honeydew melons on two pieces of land near the Salvadorean-Guatemalan border, 40 manzanas in Sonsonate and 120 manzanas in Ahuachapán. The lands in Sonsonate are irrigated by gravity feed; he uses the humidity system for cultivating the melons in the property at Ahuachapán. With the humidity system, the seeds are planted just after the last rains are over and the soil is still humid. While the upper layers of soil start losing their humidity, the roots of the plants grow. Since the lower layers lose their humidity later, they aid the growth of the plant.

It takes about 75 days from planting to the first harvest, after which the same field is harvested about four times more. Thus it takes approximately 100 days from planting to the end of the harvest season for a particular field. It is estimated that between 60 and 70 percent of the total melon crop is collected in the first two harvests and the remainder in the last three.

Sr. X does not plant all his lands at the same time, but rather staggers his plantings over a five-week period so as to have more even distribution in the harvest. He starts planting in October in order to start harvesting and exporting by late December. This allows him to enter the U. S. winter market before Mexico starts sending in its melons, thereby obtaining the higher early-season prices for his melons. He finishes harvesting the last melons in late February; he then plants other crops, such as rice and corn, until the next planting season of melons in October. For the crop year 1971–72, he started planting on October 10 and began harvesting in the week of December 20, with the last harvest in the week of February 16.

The lands he uses are rented on a yearly basis. Although this gives him mobility and flexibility, it also leaves him less leeway for planning his production. If he owned the lands where he plants the melons, he could get to know them better and plant more productively year after year. With rented lands, he cannot be sure that the owner will rent him the same lands the next year. Although Sr. X is very interested in buying land for his melon cultivation, he is hesitant because of the investment required ($600 per mz.) and the possible risks of expropriation stemming from the new agrarian reform law.

Whereas in the United States the land planted with melons must be rotated every year, Sr. X does not believe this to be true in El Salvador, where the same land is planted with rice or corn during the same year. This crop rotation within a year achieves the purpose of crop rotation every year in the United States. Sr. X suspects that because of this, the same land in El Salvador can be planted to melons for about four or five years.

Key Production Problems. A very important aspect of the cultivation of melons is the pollination of the female flower by the pollen from the male flower. The greater the number of female flowers that are pollinated, the greater the yield of the melon plant. When Sr. X first planted melons he had some problems with this, but AID technicians taught him about the use of bees for pollination. He now has his own bees and beehives to take care of the pollination process.

The main problems Sr. X has encountered in the cultivation of melons are fungus and insect control. Fungus is increased by excessive humidity in the soil, and for the 1971–72 crop year the fungus problem was aggravated by unexpected rains that came after the normal rainy season was over.

During the first 25 days of the melon crop, there is little fungus infection. The 25th to the 50th day is the period when the plant is most susceptible to fungus. It is also the time when the plant is being pollinated, and for this reason it is more difficult to control the fungus since the bees are in the field and one has to be careful in applying fungicide that might kill the bees. The U. S. Department of Agriculture does not allow fruit that has been treated with certain insecticides during this period to be sold in the United States. Sr. X had the crop sprayed with fungicide, using motor pumps and a tractor mounted with spray equipment. He has had difficulty in obtaining the appropriate sprayer calibration for his fungicide application. Although he applied fungicide, he was not able to control the fungus satisfactorily, and much of his crop was damaged and rendered nonexportable.

Sr. X considers the high costs of farm inputs to be another key production problem. He believes that these costs are higher in El Salvador than in the United States. Machinery and many of the agrochemicals have to be imported. It costs him less to import the seeds directly from the United States than to buy them in El Salvador from seed importers. Import suppliers in El Salvador, the majority of which are subsidiaries of U. S. firms, normally sell on credit ranging from 30 to 90 days.

Although the labor wage rate in El Salvador is much lower than that in the United States, so is worker productivity. This makes the effective labor cost much higher than the nominal wage rate. The laborers need much greater supervision; they lack the initiative to do things on their own, which may be a result of living and working under a patronal social system for centuries. According to Sr. X, one constantly has to be watching over them and teaching them. He visits the properties as often as he can to make sure that everything is working well. When one considers the distance between the properties and the office in San Salvador (120 km. from San Salvador to Ahuachapán and 70 km. from Ahuachapán to Sonsonate), the other properties and business Sr. X has to attend to, and the number of hours in a day, it is physically impossible to do this every day. Sr. X has a Chilean experienced in melon marketing and packing, helping him with the field supervision. This man visits the plantations daily during the melon season and oversees the crop, but he has had no farming experience himself.

Sr. X pointed out the following example of inefficiency stemming from lack of worker initiative. A shipment to Hamburg was leaving the next day from Guatemala, and Sr. X had reserved space for three truckloads of melons. It is a 12-hour drive to the Guatemalan port and the ship was to leave at 9 a.m. Instructions were given the foreman at Sonsonate to have the truck leave there for Ahuachapán, where it was to pick up more crates of melons at 3 p.m. This would give them time to load at Ahuachapán and arrive at the Guatemalan port with a margin of a few hours in case of a flat tire or other emergency. At 5 p.m., the truck had not arrived in Ahuachapán; it was discovered that it had been waiting for two hours in Sonsonate for the workers to finish packing the last few boxes of melons to complete the load. For a few boxes the truck was delayed so much that the entire shipment was jeopardized.

Output. Table 4–20 shows the area planted during the last three years, the field yield per manzana, the quantity sent to the packing shed, and the amount exported. Exports started at 11,854 boxes in 1969–70, peaked at 34,013 boxes in 1970–71, and then dropped to 24,526 boxes in 1971–72, reflecting the aforementioned disease problems.

Costs. The production costs are considered fixed since they have to be spent regardless of the quantity of melons produced and exported. Table 4–21 presents Sr. X's estimate of production costs per manzana.

Investment. Sr. X uses the following equipment in the production and cultivation of melons: tractors and trailers; trailers pulled by oxen; equipment to plow, rake, cultivate, plant, and fertilize the land; equipment to spray insecticide and fungicide (made up of two drums and the necessary installa-

Table 4–20.   Area Planted, Yield, and Quantity Exported: Melons, 1969–1972.

Year	Area planted (manzanas)	Field yield		Sent to packing shed		Exports	
		Boxes[a]	Boxes per mz.	Boxes[b]	Boxes per mz.	Boxes	Boxes per mz.
1969–70	60	30,000	500	14,800	240	11,854	200
1970–71	160	85,000	531	42,500	260	34,013	210
1971–72	160	67,000	381	30,600	190	24,526	150

a. Boxes containing approximately 35 lbs. of fruit (9–12 melons).

b. These are estimates. Since Sr. X does not sell locally and is interested only in the amount exported, he does not keep track of the quantity of melons produced in the field or of the quantity sent to the packing shed. He estimated that 40 percent of production is exportable and that 80 percent of the melons sent to the packing shed are actually exported.

Table 4–21. Estimated Costs of Planting Honeydew Melons 1971–1972 *(dollars per manzana).*

Rent and land preparation		60.00
Planting, including seed:		
3 lb of seed per manzana		20.00
Fertilizer: 900 lbs. per manzana		40.00
Insecticide: 25 lbs. per manzana	40	
Fungicide	24	
Labor to apply insecticide and		
fungicide	16	80.00
Labor and administration:		
40 man-days per manzana[a]		100.00
Total		$300.00

a. 6400 man-days for all operations; all workers are men.

tions); motor pumps for spraying; bees and beehives; truck. Except for the bees and beehives, he used the same equipment for his other crops and his other lands. He thus was not able to specify the amount of his fixed investment employed for melon cultivation. He has taken into account these costs, however, in his production costs by considering what he would have to pay if he had to rent the equipment.

Harvesting and Packing

Description of Operation. The harvesting-packing operations are relatively simple and are done at the production sites. There is a packing station for every 10 manzanas of melons. The stations are 20 by 25 feet in area; the earth floor is covered with straw to protect the melons from dust. Each station has a roof made out of jute sacks, that protects the melons from the sun and also provides shade for the workers. There are 34 workers to each station, or a maximum of 340 workers assigned to packing operations at any one time; sometimes there are fewer (34 is the minimum), depending on how many manzanas are left to be picked.

     Each station of 34 workers has cutters, pickers, cleaners, selector-packers, and nailers. The foreman of the station assigns a number of workers to each job, depending on the bottlenecks, so that the number of people in each job varies. Men usually do the cutting, packing, and nailing of the crates, while women do the picking and cleaning. About half of the workers are men and half women. The children of some workers also help.

     Once the melons reach the appropriate stage of ripeness, harvesting starts. The cutters have to have good eyes and are taught the color, appearance, and other characteristics of a melon that is ready to be harvested. The ripeness of the melon when it is harvested depends on whether it is to be sent to the United States (riper) or to Europe (less ripe), which require different transport times. Training is done by Sr. X, his packing manager, his farm administrator, and the foreman of each station. Training is not formal; the cutters are taken to the field, shown the melons that are ready to be harvested, and allowed to practice. The cutter has to leave a small part of the stem on the melon so it will have a good appearance.

The cutters leave the melons they cut in the rows between the plants. The pickers put them in sack-lined baskets, take these baskets to the station, and place them on tables in front of the women who clean the melons. The next group of women selects the melons that have the appearance (no blemished, no cuts) for exportation, cleans them with a flannel cloth dampened with water containing fungicide solution, and places them in the next row. The women drop the melons that are not fit for export in a section in front of them.

The men take these clean melons and make another selection of those that are of export quality. They start packing the exportable melons in cardboard-lined boxes. The melons packed in the same box have to be of uniform size. They first stick the label of Sr. X on each melon and then fit them into the box, arranging them in a pattern that depends on the number of melons to the box. The boxes are packed with seven to 18 melons, depending on the size of the melons; they do not pack 10 melons to a box because it is a trade rule in the United States that boxes of 10 are not sold. The melons are then covered with the cardboard and sent to the next row. Covers made of the same wood as the boxes are nailed on and the boxes are stacked in the station. When there are enough boxes, they are loaded on trailers pulled by a tractor or by two oxen and hauled between one and two miles to the truck-loading point. A label is then placed on each crate before being loaded onto the truck.

The boxes are assembled in the plantations by Sr. X's own workers. Wood is bought from a lumberyard with an agreement that any damaged wood may be returned. Sr. X decides on the box sizes based on the sizes his brokers handle.

Key Problems. Each station is supervised by one foreman, who is supposed to make sure that the station has all the materials needed for the packing process, that the process flows smoothly, and that the work is done correctly. Although a farm helper is in charge of sending the materials to each station, the foreman checks and informs him of how much material his station still has. The job of a foreman requires initiative, creativity, and good common sense. He moves people around in the various tasks when work does not flow smoothly because of some bottleneck; for example, if packing is going slowly because there are not enough melons in the station, he adds to the number of packers by taking some workers off another task. He makes sure the workers understand the task they are supposed to do and he thinks of ways to make the people do the work quickly and well. Although Sr. X has some exceptional foremen, he feels that the majority still lack initiative and motivation.

In order to motivate his workers in the packing stations, Sr. X has ranked them according to three categories, with different pay scales. A worker can be moved up or down at any time, depending on his work and the judgment of Sr. X.

Training of the workers in each packing station is done by the same people who train the cutters. They try to hire the same workers every year to avoid training new ones each time, but labor turnover, especially with the cutters, packers, and nailers, is high. Furthermore, after a year, the workers forget much of what they have been taught so that retraining is necessary. Some of these workers work in Sr. X's various plantations in other crops during the rest of the year.

Costs. Packing, including wood for the boxes, assembly, and other materials, costs $0.80 per box; labor, from harvesting through packing (28 man days/mz. for a total of 4480 man days), costs $0.40 per box.

Investments. Packinghouse investment is minimal: 20 by 25 foot stations with straw-covered floors and jute-sack roofs.

Transportation

Description of Service. The boxes are shipped from the farms to Miami by refrigerated trailers of CCT. The trailers go to the Guatemalan port of Santo Tomás de Castilla (a 12 hr. trip) where they are loaded onto the cargo ship for Miami (a 48 hr. trip). In Miami, they are unloaded, and the melons are transferred to other refrigerated trailers that take them to markets in Florida, New York, or elsewhere in the United States.

The melons can also be shipped to the United States by ordinary ships either from the port of Santo Tomás de Castilla or the Salvadorean port of Acajutla, but this is a much longer trip and is used only when the melons have to be shipped and CCT has no trailers available.

The boxes that are to be shipped to Europe are taken by rented truck (unrefrigerated) to Santo Tomás de Castilla or Acajutla, where they are loaded aboard ship. Ships leave Central America for Europe two or three times a month and the trip to Hamburg takes 15 to 17 days.

Problems. Transportation ranks among the most difficult problems of Central American exporters in general, but especially for those dealing with highly perishable products. Transportation from Central America to the United States as of 1972 was practically monopolized by CCT. Although there are other ships that travel from Central America to the United States, CCT was the only company that transported merchandise to the United States in refrigerated trailers without transfer.

The twice-weekly shipments of CCT would be acceptable to Sr. X, but CCT has not supplied trailers when he needs them. Although he informed CCT of the number of trailers he required during given weeks, CCT sometimes was not able to meet his demand. The company has a limited number of trailers, the use of which has to be coordinated among the different Central American countries that need them, whether to bring merchandise to or from Miami. When something goes awry in this coordination, both CCT and the exporter suffer. CCT's two most important clients are the shrimp and meat plants in Central America. It gives priority to shipments from these two industries because they use CCT all year round. The melon growers, on the other hand, need the trailers only during the melon season, or about four months of the year. CCT cannot have a set of trailers for use by the melon growers during the melon season only, for these trailers would lie idle the rest of the year. Another point is the return trip. For CCT to be able to charge low rates, there must be some cargo coming back from Miami to Central America.

Sr. X also complains about the poor service of CCT in handling the shipments. Many times CCT has failed to follow his instructions and, as a result, melons that left El Salvador in good condition have reached the United States in poor condition, and either could not be sold or had to be sold at reduced prices. CCT does not guarantee its shipments and even wants to collect for freight when the shipment arrives in poor condition owing to in-transit difficulties.

Sr. X estimates that for the crop year 1971–72, he lost $15,000 through in-transit damage. This loss includes the lower price received for the melons because of the damage, repacking, and other incidental costs. He is presently studying whether he should make a claim against CCT for this. He has also lost a total of 1000 boxes by breakage and already has an outstanding claim of $7000 against CCT.

Service to the United States could be further improved by having direct shipments to New York instead of having to unload in Miami and ship the boxes to New York in another trailer. This would not only lower the cost but reduce handling damage.

Transportation to Europe is an even greater problem for Salvadorean exporters of perishable products. As was mentioned previously, shipping service from Central America is limited and the trip is long. Moreover, the ships usually do not have refrigeration, and there has to be a constant flow of air in the hold to remove the ethylene given off by the fruit and thus avoid more rapid ripening.

Since the tip to Europe takes longer and the melons go unrefrigerated, they are harvested when they are less ripe so as to permit ripening in transit.

Costs. The cost of transporting melons via CCT from El Salvador to Miami is $1200 per truckload of about 40,000 pounds, or 1025 boxes. This comes to about $1.25 per box if the trailer is sent full. The freight from Miami to New York, where Sr. X sells his melons, comes to about $0.90 per box. Thus, it costs a total of $2.15 per box to transport melons from El Salvador to New York.

Transport cost to Europe (Hamburg) from port to port comes to $1.35 per box plus $0.20 for transport from the plantation to port; this makes total transport costs to Europe $1.55, including loading onto the ship and wharfage fees. Thus it costs considerably less to ship to Europe than to New York.

Marketing

Type of Arrangement. Sr. X sells his melons on consignment. He works through one broker in the United States and four in Europe, at Hamburg, Rotterdam, Stockholm, and London. His packing manager, a Chilean, has had experience in the packing and marketing of melons in Chile, which put him in contact with the broker in the United States.

Sr. X stresses the importance of good relations between the broker and the exporter. The business of exporting perishable goods requires close coordination. Without good relations between broker and exporter, efficient coordination is difficult at best. The broker must supply the exporter with information to enable him to send melons of the right type, quality, and size at the right time. The exporter has limited control over the size of the melons produced in the field, and over the quality, appearance, and flavor once the plants bear fruit. But he does have control over the selection process. If the market is heavy and quality requirements are stringent, he tightens his standards; otherwise, he relaxes them. He also has control over packing. In order to be able to send melons of the size that is selling best, he instructs his packers to pack the melons in boxes of the size that is most in demand. He makes sure, however, that the difference in the sizes of melons in each box is not great, since this could be detrimental to future sales. Sr. X and his broker keep in constant communication during the season by telephone, cable, or mail.

Sr. X has dealt with the same broker since he entered the melon exporting business. They have established considerable mutual confidence, thus bringing about greater rapport and coordination. Whereas in the first year payment was made by means of a letter of credit through a bank, now the broker sends Sr. X a check to pay for the melons. The broker also sends him advances at times, deducting them from future payments. This shows the confidence that has developed between them and at the same time saves them the bank commission they would have to pay for a letter of credit.

Of the melons he produces, Sr. X ships the larger ones to the United States and the smaller ones to Europe to meet the demands of the two markets. In 1971–72, he was able to sell size 13 melons in the United States and up to size 18 melons in Europe.

Problems. In his first year of exporting to the United States, Sr. X had some problems with off-sizing; the workers made the mistake of putting melons of different sizes in the same box. Furthermore, he believes the supply was great at that time so that buyers were more choosy in their purchases. The rigidity of importers' standards appears to be a direct function of supply.

Sr. X tries to get better prices by shipping his melons to the United States before the Chilean or Mexican melons start entering the U. S. market. When the other countries' melons, especially Mexican ones, start entering the United States, prices start declining slowly. This means, however, that he has to program his planting so that he can start harvesting and exporting his melons in late December and continue through late February. He thus has to start planting by October, which is just after the rainy season is over. When sporadic rains fall during October, as happened in 1971, the problem of fungus control arises.

His sales to Europe did not go well in his first year of operations. He was able to recover only his transport and marketing costs without any contribution to his packing costs, much less his fixed production costs. His second and third years were much better. In fact, he got a higher net contribution (sales price less marketing and transportation costs) to fixed costs and profits in Europe than in the United States. In 1970–71 his net contribution from Europe was $2.80 per box, whereas from the United States it was $2.05; in 1971–72 the figures were $3.40 and $3.25, respectively.

Market Outlook. As was indicated in Chapter 1, the U. S. consumer demands both attractive appearance and tastiness in fresh fruit. Accordingly, Sr. X has strict quality control, although he will relax his standards if supplies are scarce. He also sticks a label to each melon since he believes this gives the melon a better presentation and therefore a better potential in the U. S. market.

He believes there is a great future in Europe. Hamburg is a higher priced market than the United States, but it is smaller—about 3,000 boxes a month. Rotterdam can probably handle twice this, and Sweden even more. The British market alone can probably handle a total of 150,000 boxes during the entire season.

Costs. In the United States, duty is $0.25 per box, handling is $0.15, and other costs amount to $0.10, for a total of $0.50 per box. For Europe the total is $0.35 per box. Commission in the United States is 10 percent; in Europe it is 8 percent.

Marketing Results. Tables 4–22, 4–23 and 4–24 present the melon shipment statistics to the United States and Europe for the years 1969–70, 1970–71, and 1971–72. The prices received during each shipping season are plotted in Figure 4–4, which reveals the sharp decline that sets in as the season

Table 4–22. Export and Price Data, Honeydew Melons, 1969–1970.

	U.S. (New York)		Europe	
Shipment number	Quantity (cases)	Price/box	Quantity (cases)	Port
1	1,900	$6.62		
2	200[a]			
3	1,283	6.80		
4	1,000	5.46		
5	3,000	5.37		
6			500	Rotterdam
7			500	Hamburg
8			655	Goteborg
9	2,816	5.00		
	10,199		1655	
Average price		$5.85		
Gross sales	$55,000		$3000[b]	

a. Miami.
b. Estimate.

Table 4–23. Export and Price Data, Honeydew Melons, 1970–1971.

		U.S. (New York)		Europe	
Shipment number	Departure date	Quantity (cases)	Price/box	Quantity (cases)	Port
1	Jan. 14	1,000	$6.39		
2	19			350	Hamburg
3	19			426	Rotterdam
4	21	1,000	6.11		
5	21			1126	Hamburg
6	27	2,541	6.51		
7	28	1,957	4.60[a]		
8	28	2,040	5.80		
9	Feb. 5	8,070	5.52		
10	9	4,509	4.64		
11	10			300	Hamburg
12	12			425	Rotterdam
13	12			400	London
14	12	5,093	3.51		
15	16			413	Hamburg
16	19	3,090	3.60		
17	23			1273	London
		29,300		4713	
Average price			$5.19		
Gross sales		$144,000		$24,000	
Net return per case		$ 2.05		$ 2.80	

a. This shipment was not sent by CCT and arrived in New York three weeks late.

Table 4-24.   Export and Price Data, Honeydew Melons, 1971–1972.

Shipment number	Departure date	U.S. (New York) Quantity (cases)	Price/box	Europe: quantity (cases)
1	Dec. 24	181	$8.50	
2	31	223	8.50	
3				2548
4	Jan. 14	1,025	9.00	
5	21	2,058	7.00	
6	24	3,007	7.00	
7				3241
8	28	1,025	6.00	
9	31	2,164	6.00	
10	Feb. 4	2,058	5.75	
11	7	3,079	5.50	
12	11	1,050	5.00	
13				1616
14	14	885	5.00	
15				366
		16,755		7771
Average price			$6.60	
Gross sales	$110,000			$45,000
Net return per case	$ 3.25			$ 3.40

progresses. Average prices in 1971–72 were better than in any previous year, and the net contribution per box was higher accordingly.

Local Market. The local market for honeydew melons in El Salvador is very small; consumers are not familiar with these melons. In 1972, Sr. X sold about 4000 melons in the local market, for a total revenue of $300, equivalent to $0.075 per melon.

The Role of the Government

Two agronomists from the Ministry of Agriculture visit Sr. X's plantations weekly and give him advice and technical assistance on the products he cultivates. He has also received some help from AID technicians. Aside from this, however, he has received no government assistance. He does not complain about this and says that he is perfectly happy so long as the government allows him to continue working in the form of a private enterprise with no government interference.

Although the government has encouraged people to enter the melon export business, it has not played an aggressive role in promotion of exports. A law has been passed to promote exports, including nontraditional agricultural products, but it is somewhat ambiguous. It lists three types of export industries,

Figure 4–4. Prices Received for Honeydew Melons, United States, 1969–1972.

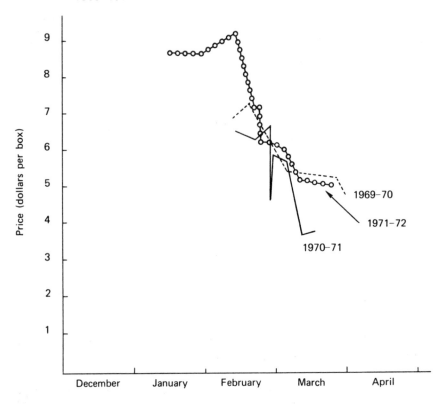

each of which has its own separate fiscal incentives: (1) industries that export all their production outside the Central American Common Market; (2) industries that export some of their production outside the Common Market and sell the rest to members of the Common Market; and (3) enterprises that export, without themselves being the producers, manufactured articles, handicrafts, and nontraditional agricultural products to countries outside the Common Market.

Industries falling under the first category are exempted from import duties for machinery, parts, and raw materials and from income and property taxes. Those in the second category are exempted from import duties on raw materials for the exported products. Those classified within the third category are exempted from income taxes.

In the export of nontraditional agricultural products, there always exists a part of the produce that cannot be exported (owing to poor quality, overripeness, or some other reason), but may very well be sold in the local market to bring in more revenue for the exporter-producer. Such a business could only fall under the second category, which has only one tax exemption.

Economic Analysis

Investment. As mentioned previously, Sr. X uses mechanical equipment in the cultivation of his melons. However, he uses this same equipment on his other lands and for other crops, and thus has been unable to separate out the portion of investment assignable to melon cultivation.

Profit and Loss. Tables 4–25 and 4–26 present Sr. X's profit and loss experience during the 1969–1971 period. Table 4–27 provides a break-even matrix given different price and yield combinations.

If the number of exportable boxes per manzana can be increased, and if they can be sold at $4.50, a price greater than the variable costs, profitability will be increased since the fixed production costs will remain the same.

Packing is a crucial point because it is the quality-control check to ensure produce acceptability in the market. It is also essential that the melons be selected well so as to avoid incurring the large transport costs for unsalable melons.

EL SALVADOR: CANTALOUPES

Brief History

The melon export cooperative COPEX was organized by 18 Salvadoreans interested in producing and exporting nontraditional agricultural crops, mainly cantaloupes.[8] Cantaloupes had been produced and exported previously by individual growers, but this was the first group production and marketing effort. The previously mentioned air-marketing seminar was a key factor in interesting the members in exporting.[9]

The crop year 1969–70 was the first in which COPEX members exported melons as a cooperative. (Melons in this case study refer, unless otherwise indicated, to cantaloupes.) The members planted 400 manzanas of melons and during January–April, 1970, they exported 10,000 boxes of cantaloupes to Miami and 1,700 boxes to New York. They lost considerable money that year and some members dropped out of the cooperative. In 1970–71, the remaining members planted about 400 manzanas and exported approximately 6,000 boxes of melons. The 1970–71 season was even worse for the cooperative and they lost considerably more money than in the previous year. All but one member, Sr. A, decided to stop planting melons, and so the cooperative disbanded.

Before the cooperative was formed, Sr. A had been cultivating melons and exporting them to the United States as an individual. He still owns the packing plant that the cooperative members used when COPEX was exporting melons to the United States. He has been in agriculture for the past 27 years, having cultivated cotton, rice, corn, and beans for the past 15 years, all on rented lands just outside Usulután.

Table 4-25.   Estimated Profit and Loss, 1969–1971.

Item	1969			1970			1971		
	U.S.	*Europe*	*Total*	*U.S.*	*Europe*	*Total*	*U.S.*	*Europe*	*Total*
Revenueᵃ	$55,000	$3,400	$58,400	$144,000	$24,000	$168,000	$110,000	$45,000[a]	$155,000[a]
Costs[b]									
Transport	21,900	2,500	24,400	63,000	7,300	70,300	36,000	12,000	48,000
Tariffs, etc.	5,100	600	5,700	14,600	1,600	16,200	8,400	2,700	11,100
Commissions	5,500	300	5,800	14,400	1,900	16,300	11,000	3,600	14,600
	32,500	3,400	35,900	92,000	10,800	102,800	55,400	18,300	73,700
Net revenue	22,500			52,000	13,200	65,200	54,600	26,700	81,300
Production costs			18,000			48,000			48,000
Packing costs			14,200			40,800			29,400
			32,200			88,800			77,400
Profit/Loss			(9,700)			(23,600)			3,900

a. Based on estimates of average price as given by owner.
b. Estimated from unit costs given by owner.

Table 4–26. Analysis of Costs, 1971.[a]

Item	Unit cost (dollars) Per manzana	Per box	Total cost Dollars	Percent
Production[b]	300	1.96	48,000	31.8
Packing[c]	183	1.20	29,400	19.5
Transport[c]	300	1.96	48,000	31.8
Tariffs[c]	68	0.45	11,100	7.3
Commissions[c]	90	0.59	14,600	9.6
	941	6.16	151,100	100.0
Revenue	966	6.32	155,000	
Profit	25	0.16	3,900	

a. On 160 manzanas the yield of exportable melons was 24,526 boxes, or 153 boxes per manzana.
b. Fixed.
c. Variable.

Table 4–27. Break-even Price and Yield Matrix, Honeydew Melons.

Given sales price Sales price (dollars/box)	No. of exportable boxes per manzana to break even	Given yield No. of exportable boxes per manzana	Sales price to break even (dollars/box)
		United States	
4	Always a loss	50	11.00
5	460	100	7.00
6	195	200	5.90
7	120	300	5.40
8	90	400	5.10
9	70	500	4.90
		Europe	
4	520	50	9.90
5	200	100	6.60
6	120	200	5.00
7	90	300	4.50
8	70	400	4.20
9	60	500	4.00

For the crop year 1971–72, Sr. A planted 200 manzanas, from which he sent his first shipment to the United States in the week of January 16, 1972.

Production

Planting Cycle. Sr. A starts planting melons in mid–November when the rainy season ends. Depending on the variety of the cantaloupe, it takes between 70 and 80 days from planting to harvest time. Sr. A plants a few different varieties of cantaloupe to see which is best suited for his rented lands. He also staggers the planting over a two-week period.

Key Problems. The producers of COPEX had problems initially in achieving adequate pollination of their melon plants, but AID technicians taught them the use of bees for pollination.

Production in the 1970–71 crop year was poor; the rains did not stop until late October and delayed or damaged the plantings. As a result of these rains and strong winds in November, production fell much lower than expected. Many members of the cooperative thus were not able to send to the cooperative's packing plant the melons they had promised.

Sr. A, the only COPEX producer in 1971–72, had no major production problems.

Output and Costs. Table 4–28 gives yields and costs for the three crop years 1969–1972.

Packing

Description of Operations. The melons are cut by workers who are trained to be able to tell by color and appearance when a melon is ready to be cut. Pickers put the melons in sacks and bring them to certain stations where they are preselected for export. The melons for export are put in special sacks while those for local sales are put in ordinary sacks. A truck collects the melons and takes them to the main station in the field. The melons for local sales are classified according to size and placed by lots for the trucks that will come and fetch them. The melons for export are selected once more and placed in boxes to be sent by truck to the packing plant, where they are dropped on top of a large platform. Here they are mechanically cleaned. They then pass to a conveyor belt to be waxed and treated with fungicide.

The melons again are carried by a conveyor belt past men who sort through them once more; those melons that are not of export quality are placed in one section, and those for export are classified by size. The melons roll down to where women pack them in boxes for export. Melons of the same size are

Table 4–28. Yields and Costs, Cantaloupes, 1969–1972.

Exporter	Crop year	Area planted (manzanas)	Quantity exported
COPEX	1969–70	400	11,700 boxes
COPEX	1970–71	400	6,000 boxes
Sr. A	1971–72	200	9,000 boxes

Costs (dollars per manzana)[a]	
Land rental	50
Labor: preharvest	55
harvest	60[b]
Rental of machinery and equipment	40
Seeds	8
Fertilizer	60
Insecticide	60
Fungicide	45[c]
Total	378

a. Based on estimates of Sr. A.
b. This could vary from $50 to $70, depending on production.
c. This could vary from $30 to $60, depending on the intensity of the attack by fungus.

packed in each box. Thus, there can be 15, 18, 24, 30, or 42 melons in a box, and the boxes are then called 15's, 18's, and so on. At this point, covers are nailed over the boxes, and the COPEX label is attached. The boxes are then sent to the refrigerated trailers, where they are kept until they are shipped.

Sr. A owns the packing plant that he rented to COPEX when it was operating. The workers are trained by Sr. A himself and a supervisor who has been working in the plant for years both for Sr. A and before that for the previous owner. There are 14 persons who work in the plant during the season.

The building that houses the packing plant has two large storage rooms that could be refrigerated if they were properly equipped. In the meantime, Sr. A uses the three refrigerated trailers that the cooperative bought the preceding year as his cold-storage room. Since the cooperative is no longer functioning and he alone exported this year, he has not yet finished the proposed cold-storage rooms. He believes, however, that for this business it would be ideal to have the cold-storage rooms functioning. He has applied for a loan from the Central American Bank for Economic Integration to complete construction of the cold-storage rooms.

Problems. An important problem in the packing operations of COPEX was the lack of a cold-storage room. The refrigerated trailers now being used by Sr. A for cold storage arrived after the 1971–72 operations. COPEX melons remained without refrigeration until the arrival of the CCT refrigerated trailers in which they were to be shipped. For this reason, many boxes of melons arrived in Miami in poor condition.

Another problem was that the number of melons delivered to the processing plant was too small. Because of this, the plant did not run smoothly and efficiently and thus the packing cost per box of melons was increased. This difficulty is now easier to resolve since Sr. A alone is producing, but he would have to increase production in order to fill up the processing plant and he does not feel he can do this unless he can be sure of a stable market in the United States.

When the demands of the market in the United States change, a minor problem occurs in that the workers in the packing plant have to be told to tighten or relax the selection standards. It is easy for the workers to be confused if this occurs too frequently.

The cooperative did not have a full-time administrator. Several of the members devoted some of their time to the supervision and administration of the cooperative, but they had other businesses to attend to. Consequently, inefficiencies occurred.

Costs. Table 4–29 lists fixed and variable costs for a year's operation, and Table 4–30 is a break-even matrix.

Transportation

Description of Service. COPEX cantaloupes were shipped to Miami aboard CCT refrigerated trailers from the packing plant in Usulután. COPEX also shipped some by air, by Pan American or Taca, but this turned out to be too expensive ($0.07/lb.). Sr. A uses CCT to ship his cantaloupes.

Problems. COPEX members had several complaints about CCT and regarded transportation as a great problem. They said that until something was done to remedy the transportation difficulties, they would not produce and export melons. CCT could not give COPEX the number of trailers they wanted

Table 4–29. Costs (dollars), Cantaloupe Processing.

Fixed costs (for the 90 days of operation)	
Rental of packing plant	3,500
Labor and supervision	4,500
Electricity and miscellaneous	3,000
Total	$11,000
Variable costs (per box)	
Boxes	0.70
Materials, wax, fungicide	.10
Labels	.03
Refrigeration	.20
Total	1.03

Table 4–30. Break-even Prices and Yield Matrix, Cantaloupes.

		Sales price given	
(1)	*(2)*	*(3)* *No. of exportable*	*(4)* *Yield required*
Sales price *(dollars/box)*	*No. of exportable* *boxes to break even*	*boxes per manzana* *to break even*[a]	*to break even* *(melons/mz.)*[b]
3	Always a loss	–	–
4	Always a loss	–	–
5	Always a loss	–	–
6	433,000	2,165	37,454
7	94,000	470	8,145
8	48,000	240	4,160
9	32,000	160	2,773
10	24,000	120	2,080
11	19,000	95	1,646

		Yield given	
(1)	*(2)*	*(3)*	*(4)* *Sales price to*
Yield *(melons/mz.)*	*No. of exportable* *boxes per manzana*[c]	*Total no. of* *exportable boxes*[d]	*break even* *(dollars/box)*
400	80	16,000	12.00
800	160	32,000	9.00
1200	240	48,000	8.00
2000	400	80,000	7.20
3000	600	120,000	6.80
4000	800	160,000	6.60
5000	1000	200,000	6.45

a. Column (2) times 0.005.
b. Column (3) times 17.33.
c. Column (1) times 0.2.
d. Column (2) times 200.

per week and there were only once-a-week shipments from Central America. COPEX wanted to use CCT's refrigerated trailers as cold-storage rooms and CCT would not allow this for more than 24 hours—which is understandable. CCT would not guarantee that the melons would arrive in Miami in good condition, and there was no way by which COPEX could insure the cargo. Once, a truckload overturned and the majority of the melons were too damaged to be exportable. CCT did not charge freight for the broken crates, but it did charge the full rate for all the rest of the truckload that was brought to Miami. This constituted a big loss since the melons could not be sold, and yet COPEX had to pay the freight. They also believed the freight rates were too high.

Sr. A feels that the service of CCT continues to be deficient. Several of his cantaloupe shipments reportedly suffered freezing damage owing to improper temperature control in the trucks. Although he felt that his melons were of better quality than those sent by Mexico, the damage in transit resulted in their arriving in Miami in poor condition. He also believes that unloading service at Miami is unreliable, thus causing further damage to the fruit.

Cost. The trip to Miami by CCT costs $1270. Although, theoretically, 40,000 pounds, or 769 boxes, of melons can be carried in one trailer, at a cost of $1.65 per box, Sr. A believes that the ideal load is 648 boxes of his cantaloupes, or about 33,700 pounds. This brings the effective transportation cost to Miami to approximately $2 per box; transport from Miami to Pompano Beach costs $0.10, and loading and unloading add $0.35, making the total cost $2.45 per box.

Marketing

Type of Arrangement. COPEX sold its cantaloupes on consignment to a broker in the United States. U. S. importers did not buy fresh fruits from Central America f.o.b. Central America. Consignment was therefore the only way of selling their melons.

In 1971–72, Sr. A arranged with a U. S. broker to sell his melons f.o.b. El Salvador. But when time for payment came, the broker said this was not the arrangement, and Sr. A suffered huge losses on these sales. Because of this, he transferred to another broker who sold the rest of the melons on consignment.

Problems. Marketing was an even greater problem for COPEX than transportation. After their two export attempts, COPEX members greatly distrust U. S. brokers. The growers believe that when the market is soft, the brokers simply tell them that the melons they sent were of poor quality and either could not be sold or were sold at reduced prices. In one instance, a member accompanied the shipment of melons and they were paid $10 a box for them. No one accompanied the melons in the next shipment and although they believed these melons were of at least as good quality as the previous shipment, they were paid only $4 a box. They have lost all confidence in the U. S. brokers.

Another problem in 1970–71 was that very few buyers went to Pompano Beach, since a frost in Florida had diminished local production and supply. There was lack of movement in Pompano Beach and the cooperative was not able to get a good price for its melons. It would have been costly to transport the melons to another market and probably not worth the effort. They only shipped 6,000 of the expected 40,000 boxes, and this may have caused some loss of leverage with their broker to sell the melons at a better price.

They also feel that selling on consignment is a great risk for the Central American exporter. They have to pay transportation costs for the melons and yet are not assured that the melons will be accepted and sold at a good price.

As mentioned above, Sr. A came to an agreement to sell his melons f.o.b. El Salvador, but it turned out that this broker was even worse than the previous ones. Out of eight shipments Sr. A sent through this broker, he was able to collect for only the first two, and then only at low liquidation prices rather than the price agreed upon. Sr. A says that he was defrauded by this broker, and although he is filing a claim against him, he does not feel he will be able to collect.

He sent his last six orders through another broker on consignment. This broker duly paid him but the prices were so low they only covered the cost of the wooden boxes and contributed nothing to the other costs, let alone profits. Thus, 1971–72 was again a bad year for Sr. A, who believes that there exists a conspiracy in the market for fruits and vegetables in the United States and that the Central American exporter is at the mercy of these people. Clearly, there is a critical information bottleneck and credibility gap between exporters and importers.

Costs. Customs duties and brokerage fees came to $1.80 per box, and handling and other costs were $0.10. Commissions were 10 percent of the sales price.

Local Market. About 75 percent of the cantaloupe production is nonexportable and is sold locally. This saturates the local market during this season and the price of melons drops considerably. Sometimes the producers are just not able to sell the melons since the supply is too great. They also send some of the melons to Guatemala, but the prices there are also low at that time, about $0.05 to $0.10 per melon.

Financing

Source. For crop year 1970–71, seven members of COPEX applied for and received a loan from the Administración de Bienestar Campesino (ABC), an autonomous government financial institution. This loan was for cultivation and preexport expenses, and covered 60 percent of their financing needs. Interest was 6 percent. Only Sr. A used his own funds and a line of credit from his bank. Sr. A does not obtain any credit from his suppliers; all purchases are on a cash basis.

Problems. COPEX did not receive the loan until December 1970. Some of the members therefore had to postpone their planting. The cooperative was not able to buy the refrigerated trailers and ice machine until after the planting season and these arrived after most of the melons had been exported.

Loans for exports are granted in El Salvador, but only on the basis of contracts; there must be a guarantee of a minimum price for the products to be exported. If one sells on consignment, one cannot obtain these export loans.

Thus, Sr. A is blocked from this source of capital and must make use of personal credit to finance his business.

The Role of the Government

COPEX was organized because of the fiscal incentives offered cooperatives by the government. Furthermore, this allowed members to receive the loan from ABC. Because of their failure and resultant losses, they were not able to avail themselves of the fiscal incentives offered. Furthermore, the law regarding the incentives to cooperatives remains ambiguous, and they do not know exactly what incentives are available.

Technicians from the Ministry of Agriculture gave them technical assistance on cultivation. The government has also done some experiments for them on the different varieties of cantaloupes.

Sr. A feels that the government could help the exporters by having someone in the consular office in the United States who is an expert in the handling and marketing of these products, and could possibly even supervise their handling when they reach the United States. A small producer-exporter cannot afford to do this himself.

Economic Analysis

Sr. A plants 200 manzanas of melons, for which his production cost is $378 per manzana; his total production cost is therefore $75,600. Packing costs for the 90 days of operation are $11,000. Total fixed costs are therefore $86,600.

Variable costs are $1.03 per box for packing, $2.45 for transportation, and $1.90 for tariffs, making a total variable cost of $5.38 per box. To this is added commissions of 10 percent of the sales price.

HONDURAS: CANTALOUPES

Brief History

The first melon exports from Honduras were made in 1965–66 by four farmers from the departments of Valle and Choluteca in southern Honduras. These farmers planted approximately 350 manzanas of cantaloupes, which yielded an estimated 11,200 pounds per manzana, of which 7,500 pounds (67 percent) were exported. This operation was a financial failure owing to planting and transport problems, and it was not until 1970–71 that cantaloupes were once again exported from Honduras.

In 1970 the National Agrarian Reform Institute (INA) became interested in promoting melon exports as one means of offsetting the adverse economic effects of a continuing decline in cotton production that had left 10,000 workers in the Choluteca area unemployed. The area planted to cotton fell from 14,500 manzanas in 1968–69 to 4,665 manzanas in 1970–71. The large drop in production in the year 1969–70 was largely the result of an exodus of Salvadorean cotton farmers from Honduras after the armed border conflict between Honduras and El Salvador.

The first step INA took to promote melon production was to bring in an Israeli Agricultural Mission to carry out agronomic experiments in the zone. (Melons in this case study, unless otherwise indicated, refer to cantaloupe melons.) The tests of the Israeli Mission determined that the area was suited for export melon cultivation. These technicians estimated that yields of 140 hundredweight of fruit per manzana could be obtained, of which 100 hundredweight would be of the quality required for export. In the opinion of the Mission the southern zone possessed two notable advantages for melon production: (1) the climatic conditions would permit the production and export of melons to the United States during January, February, and March when U. S. prices are higher; and (2) the soil in this area had high natural humidity retention, which would permit planting without irrigation, thereby resulting in investment and cost savings. A final favorable factor was that many of the farmers already had experience in cultivating melons even though the earlier crops had been destined for the domestic market rather than for export.

On the basis of the experiment and recommendations of the Israeli Mission, INA decided to promote the cultivation of melons for the 1970–71 season. Previously, as part of the Agrarian Reform, INA had organized 577 farmers into 18 rural cooperatives controlling 5569 hectares (7970 manzanas) of land. These cooperatives receive technical direction from INA and also are backed by INA's guarantee on loans from financial institutions.

Although INA wanted to have 1000 manzanas of melons planted for the 1970–72 season, the cooperatives planted only 358 manzanas. Independent farmers planted another 70 manzanas. The export operations for the 1970–71 winter season encountered many problems, which resulted in an estimated loss by INA of about $70,000. It is not certain how much money the producers lost.

In spite of these losses, many farmers as well as public institutions considered that the melon business could be attractive if they could overcome the weaknesses of the 1970–71 campaign. Consequently, four public institutions—the National Development Bank (BNF), the Superior Planning Board (CSP), the Ministry of Natural Resources (MRN), and INA—with several independent farmers and CABEI agreed to execute a joint plan for melon exports. To achieve this objective they named the National Development Bank as the coordinating organization for the second export attempt.

BNF, INA, the Agrarian Reform Cooperatives, and several independent farmers created the Unión de Productores de Frutas del Sur (United Southern Fruit Producers, UPFS), which was to be the packing and marketing organization for the area. According to original plans, it was expected that $220,000 would be invested in an automatic selector and packing plant, that 1000 manzanas would be planted (400 by the cooperatives and 600 by the independents), and that they would produce 180,000 boxes of Jumbo-type melons (18 to 42 melons per box). In actuality the investments in the packing plant were not made because they were considered by the farmers to be too large. Only 412 manzanas were planted, of which 82 were lost because of planting mistakes. Of the remaining 330 manzanas, 205 belonged to the cooperatives and 125 to independent farmers. The output totaled 25,002 boxes instead of the projected 180,000 boxes. Despite the tremendous effort by the public and private institutions, serious problems continued to hamper these pioneering export operations, and it is estimated that over $100,000 was lost on the 1971–72 export attempt.

Production

Planting Cycle. The cantaloupes were planted under nonirrigated conditions, using the natural humidity contained in the soil. The favorable ecological conditions permitting this technique are especially important in the Choluteca area because here, in contrast to the Zacapa Valley in Guatemala, the irrigation infrastructure is very limited. Not all of the lands have the characteristics that are required if this method is to be employed, but those that do are generally near the coast. Toward the end of the rainy season (September), the farmers plow the fields so that the clay soils can more readily absorb and retain the preplanting rains. Although these plowing dates were followed for the 1970–71 crop, delays in the operations in 1971–72 resulted in the plowing being postponed until November.

In both years the majority of the farmers planted between November 25 and December 20. The timing of the planting is critical because it is important to get the product on the market in the early months of the following year when prices are more favorable. However, the farmer must not plant too early because his crop might be subjected to late-season rains, which would create conditions conducive to fungus infections.

Fertilizer was generally applied every four days after germination, which occurs 15 days after planting. Weeding begins at about 20 days; seven men can weed one manzana in four days.

The fruit is generally pollinated by insects, which abound in the Choluteca area, so it is unnecessary to purchase bees and beehives.

For the 1970–71 season, the farmers' harvesting operations began 65 days after planting, in accordance with the orders sent by the import broker. Under this system, if the broker was going to sell to New York it was necessary to cut the fruit two days earlier than it would if the sale were to be to the Miami market. Moreover, in the 1970–71 campaign they used a single standard cut, which was after 70 days. A single worker can harvest approximately 25 to 35 boxes per day; 90 percent of the crop is harvested, the remainder left in the field. Before sending the fruit to the packing plant, however, the farmer usually selects 35 percent of the crop that is considered nonexportable, and sells it locally for human or animal consumption. The melons are generally transported to the packing plant in bulk in large trailers pulled by tractors or in trucks or pickups.

Key Problem Areas. One of the most critical problems was an inadequate examination of the characteristics of the particular cantaloupe variety selected for planting, given the constraints of transportation availability. As will be indicated in subsequent pages, one of the main causes of the financial losses during 1971–72 was the rapid perishability (15–17 days) of this variety once harvested.

A second problem was inadequate land preparation. Eighty-two manzanas had been planted in late November after the rains had stopped. Consequently, the soil had not obtained adequate humidity and the plants did not germinate. The loss due to this error was estimated at about $35 per manzana, resulting in a total loss of $2870.

A third problem stemmed from the lack of knowledge on how best to apply fertilizers and pesticides. As can be seen from Table 4–31 this was one of the main causes of nonexportability.

One of the factors leading to inappropriate agrochemical application was the delay in financing. The BNF had estimated that the farmers would need $139.50 per manzana; however, this turned out to be inadequate. The BNF encountered delays in obtaining the necessary authorizations for disbursement of the extra amounts of money needed to cover the production expenses. As a result, several farmers either skimped on their chemical applications or delayed harvesting because they lacked cash with which to pay their workers.

Technical assistance for the independent farmers was scarce, since only one fully qualified technician was available for full-time supervision of all of the melon plantings in the Choluteca zone. The cooperatives were in a better situation because they had the help of the INA agronomist; nonetheless, many of these farmers indicated that they still needed more technical assistance.

Table 4–31. Causes of Nonexportability, Cantaloupes.

Nonexportable fruit		Defects	Causes
Boxes	Percent		
115	15	Cracks	Excess of nitrogen in fertilizer
153	20	Worms	Low quantity of pesticides
346	45	Ripeness, sun stains, sunburns	Bad harvest and bad care of fruit
153	20	Abnormalities	Several

Although the laborers seem to adapt readily to the handling and preselection tasks, there were some difficulties owing to the rigidity of work habits. Instead of cutting three times a day during each day of the week, the majority of the farmers cut twice a day Monday through Friday, once on Saturday, and not at all on Sunday. In part this was due to the workers' custom of not working on Sundays and in part to the managers' lack of appreciation for the need of a continuous, tightly programmed harvest schedule. According to the Mexican technician, if the farmers had adhered to the original harvesting schedule, they would have been able to export 50 percent of their field production instead of the 36 percent that was actually shipped.

Both the workers and the farmers in the cooperatives generally have very low levels of education. This complicates the task of carrying out technical procedures and orders, and also, according to some government officials, leads to misunderstanding and friction. Reportedly, when the BNF additional financing was delayed, one of the cooperatives called a strike and did not cut fruit for three days. It is estimated that over 1000 boxes were lost during this period.

Output. The absence of farm production records made it impossible to determine exactly the field yield of the melon plantings. According to the Mexican technician the average field yield was 215 boxes per manzana, with the range between 200 and 250. However, quality deficiencies resulted in an exportable yield of only 75 boxes per manzana. The production and exportation of the cooperatives and the independent farmers for the 1970–71 and 1971–72 seasons are shown in Table 4–32.

Costs. Most farmers in the southern zone of Honduras do not keep accurate cost records, but on the basis of interviews with producers and estimates by the technician, production costs have been approximated in Table 4–33.

Packing

Description of the Operations. Dring the 1970–71 season the INA cooperatives and the independent farmers had separate packing stations, but employed the same basic system. This system, which was recommended by the Israeli Technical Mission, consisted of five main steps: after a preliminary selection in the field, the fruit was delivered to the packing shed; the melons were graded according to size and appearance; they were passed through tanks of water for cleaning and precooling, using ice-cooled water; the fruit was packed in wooden crates; and finally, the packed crates were loaded onto the refrigerated trailers.

This system was changed for the 1971–72 season. First, the INA cooperatives and the independent farmers joined together to form the previously

Table 4–32. Honduran Melon Exports, 1970–1972.

			Exportation	
Year	Exporter	Area planted (manzanas)	Boxes	Boxes per manzana
1970–71	Cooperatives	358	13,500	38
	Independent farmers	70	2,400	34
	Total	428	15,900	37
1971–72	Cooperatives			
	San Jerónimo	25	3,290	131.6
	Ojochal	25	2,908	116.5
	San Bernardo	30	3,414	113.8
	Nueva Concepción	20	1,972	98.6
	Asacualpa	ʼ 60	5,693	94.7
	Palenque	30	1,372	45.7
	Ojo de Agua	15	666	44.4
		205	19,315	94.2
	Independent farmers			
	Sr. Andrés Lardizabal	10	803	80.3
	Sr. Saúl Pizarro	61	3,624	59.6
	Sr. José Morán	14	335	23.8
	Sr. Ricardo Olivas	40	925	23.0
		125	5,687	45.5
	Total	330	25,002	75.8

mentioned United Southern Fruit Producers. UPFS set up a single packing station to service all of the melon growers in the south. The plant is located alongside the Pan American highway on land provided by BNF.

The second major change was that the washing and precooling steps were eliminated, reportedly on the advice of the Mexican technician. The pre-graded melons were delivered to the packing shed and underwent a selection and grading process that categorized the exportable melons into five different standard sizes. The rejects were returned to the farmer. The graded melons were then packed into 2/3–Jumbo boxes weighing about 57 pounds packed. These boxes contained from 18 to 42 melons, depending on their size. The boxes were priced by the number of melons they contained rather than their weight.

The inside measurements of the wirebound wooden boxes are 22–3/8 by 13 by 9–1/2 inches. The boxes were supplied under contract by a local manufacturer at a unit price of $0.45; BNF guaranteed payment for them. The packed boxes are loaded directly into the refrigerated trailers, since there is no refrigerated storage facility at the packing shed.

The packing shed operated for 45 days, from February 7 to

Table 4–33.   Honduran Melon Production Costs 1972 *(dollars per manzana).*

Operation	Cost
Mechanization	14
Materials	
Seed (1½ lb.)	5
Pesticides	33
Fertilizers	32
Labor	
Preparation of land	5
Planting and thinning	33
Insecticide and fertilizer application	9
Harvesting (215 boxes average)	17
Transportation (average)	35
Total direct expenses	183
Rent of land	30
Administration	20
Total	233

March 23. The personnel for the operation consisted of the general manager of UPFS, one secretary, 10 graders, 10 packers, and four loaders. All except three of the workers were men. In the harvest, in contrast, the whole family helps. The Mexican technician provided direct assistance to the packing operation and was primarily responsible for training the workers. Also, BNF assigned one of its officers to provide management advice to the export organization. BNF was instrumental in the organization of UPFS.

In 1970–71 the cooperatives' packing operation was financed by INA, whereas the independent farmers used their own funds. For 1971–72 BNF financed the entire packing operation with a 9 percent five-month loan. In addition, BNF provided the plant site and office facilities gratis.

Key Problem Areas.   During the 1970–71 season one of the main problems was the lack of locally manufactured boxes. INA was forced to import boxes from the United States, and 70 percent of these eventually had to be discarded because they were secondhand and did not comply with U. S. requirements. For the 1971–72 season the problem was not too few boxes but too many. BNF had refused to sign a contract in 1970–71 and, accordingly, the manufacturer refused to run the risk of producing without a guaranteed outlet. In 1971–72, 60,000 boxes were produced, of which 40,000 had been delivered and 20,000 were in process. However, only 25,002 boxes were used. The final clause in the contract stated that if for any reason the contract terms could not be fulfilled, there would be an amicable, extrajudicial settlement. This clause was invoked to deal with excess inventory. The 40,000 finished boxes were paid for in full and for the 20,000 boxes in process a payment of $0.10 per box was made. Thus UPFS has $8750 worth of inventory of boxes for future export.

The excess inventory is a result of deficient production programming. BNF made its packing and transport arrangements on the basis of a volume of 100,000 boxes as estimated by the Mexican technician. When this output failed to materialize, problems of excess capacity arose in all the post-production stages. The need for accurate harvest projections is clear. Control over the packing or transport stages is superfluous if output is not also controlled.

A second problem area was the lack of grading and packing skills by the workers. Reportedly, it took about a month to train the employees, but thereafter they performed very well. The problem now becomes how to ensure that these workers return next year so as to minimize future training needs.

Another packing problem was the failure to wash the fruit with small doses of fungicide at specific temperatures. The absence of such treatment resulted in the loss of 500 to 1000 boxes due to fungus damage.

A final problem is the susceptibility of the producers to outside, "expert" advice. The Israeli Mission recommended one packing system and the Mexican technician another. Conflicting advice can erode the farmer's confidence and desire to pursue cultivation of nontraditional crops.

Amount Exported. Between February 10 and April 5, 1971, the INA cooperatives exported 24 trailers containing 13,504 boxes. In addition, the independent farmers shipped out 2400 boxes. During the 1971–72 season the growers exported 24,665 boxes, which represented 56 percent of the produce delivered to the plant. The Mexican technician indicated that 95 percent of the boxes shipped were 27's, 36's, and 45's, which supposedly are the favored sizes in the U. S. market. The shipments for the 1971–72 season, which were 50 percent above the previous year's, are shown in Table 4–34.

Costs. The costs for the packing operations in 1970–71 and 1971–72 are shown in Table 4–35. The 1972 costs are lower than those of the previous year because of a less expensive packing system.

Transportation

Description of Service. During the 1970–71 season, INA shipped its melons to Miami in two steps: from Choluteca to San Pedro Sula by refrigerated trailer; and from San Pedro Sula to Miami by air cargo. The independent farmers availed themselves of the services provided by CCT, using the roll-on roll-off system.

The trucking firm that transported the INA cooperatives' melons from Choluteca to San Pedro Sula contracted with INA to provide all of the

Table 4–34. Honduran Melon Shipments, 1972.

Date	Trailers	Boxes	Transport
February 10	1	178	CCT roll-on roll-off refrigerated trailer
17	4	2,769	CCT
21	1	722	Air
22	2	1,440	Air (2 shipments)
23	1	322	Air
24	6	3,851	CCT
28	4	2,888	Astra Line conventional ship
March 2	4	2,874	CCT
6	3	2,161	Astra Line
9	3	2,085	CCT
12	3	1,305	Astra Line
16	2	1,340	CCT
23	3	2,051	CCT
27	1	679	CCT
	38	24,665	
Preshipment losses		337	
Total		25,002	

Table 4–35. Honduran Melon Packing Costs 1972
(dollars per box).[a]

Item	1970–71	1971–72
Classification, packing, and handling	0.27	0.22
Boxes and materials	.69	.46
Administration	.19	.28
	1.15	0.96

a. For a volume of 25,000 boxes.

trailers needed, charging $550 per trip. The loading capacity of each trailer is 40,000 pounds (700 boxes) and the trip took 15 to 16 hours.

The air portion of the trip was handled by an American company that placed the planes at the disposal of the exporters whenever they were needed. INA tried to coordinate the arrival of a trailer with the arrival of the plane in San Pedro Sula. The cost of each planeload (700 boxes) was $2400. The flight to Miami took two hours.

CCT has been operating in Honduras for the last three years and has a monthly movement of 20 trailers. When shipped by CCT the fruit is loaded onto a refrigerated trailer at the packing house and stays in the trailer until it is unloaded at its destination. There are no delays in the port as the trailer is moved directly aboard ship; it is possible to load a vessel in six hours. The CCT truck-ship combination makes the trip from Choluteca to Miami in 72 hours, leaving Puerto Cortés for Miami every Thursday. CCT charges $1520 per trailer for its services.

During 1971–72 three different systems of transportation were used: (1) Choluteca–Pompano Beach by refrigerated trailers provided by CCT; (2) Choluteca–Puerto Cortés by refrigerated trailers, Puerto Cortés–Miami by conventional ship with refrigerated storage rooms, and Miami–Pompano Beach by refrigerated trailer; and (3) Choluteca–San Pedro Sula by refrigerated trailer and San Pedro Sula–Pompano Beach by air freight.

For the first system the contract with CCT had the following clauses: a fee of $1250 per refrigerated trailer with a capacity of 40,000 pounds from Choluteca to Miami; a trailer temperature of 35°F; an additional charge of $150 if it became necessary to unload at a different port (in case of strike); CCT obligation to provide 10 refrigerated trailers each week; CCT provision of five additional refrigerated trailers if notified eight days in advance; no CCT responsibility for damages caused by *force majeure*.

The second system consisted of three parts. The first part from Choluteca to Puerto Cortés was in trailers belonging to BNF, which rented the truck tractor (at $350 per trip) to haul the trailer. The trip from plant to port of embarkation took 16 hours. The second part was carried out by Astra Line ships having two refrigerated storage rooms with capacities of 400,000 pounds each, or the equivalent of 7,000 boxes. A freight fee of $66 per ton was arranged and INA committed to fill any storage rooms that were not filled to capacity. It took 24 hours to load the ship and 90 hours to reach Miami from Puerto Cortés.

The third system (air cargo) was used because of an emergency resulting from lack of capacity in the Astra Line ships. BNF's trailers and rented tractors hauled the fruit to San Pedro at $350 per trip. The planes then transported the melons to Miami at a cost of $2200 per trip with a capacity of 40,000 pounds or 700 boxes.

Key Problem Areas. The main problem in 1970–71 was insufficient transport services. INA tried to obtain reliable sea transportation with two or three departures per week, but the only available transportation company was CCT with its a once-a-week departure. Because of the urgent need for transportation, INA contracted for the services of an airline to make 60 flights during February and March 1971. This latter arrangement cost $4.20 per box as compared with $2.17 for CCT.

For the 1971–72 season it was possible to obtain sea transportation with two departures per week: CCT on Thursdays and Astra Line on Sundays. The Astra Line, however, would not guarantee shipment unless the ships had a full cargo. Plans were made to utilize Astra service for six weeks (42,000 boxes, approximately), but the limited production was only sufficient to use Astra Line for three weeks at a cost of $2.10 per box. This created a problem for BNF inasmuch as it had 2,000 boxes left to transport. It was necessary to use air flights, at a cost of $3.43 per box.

The manager of CCT in Honduras stated that the company was very much interested in transporting melons from Honduras. The company mainly carries meat from Honduras and Nicaragua to the United States and during the months of February and March there is a contraction in the production of meat; consequently, cargo space is available for the melon business. The company owns a ferryboat that can transport 98 trailers, and it covers the ports of Limón in Costa Rica, Puerto Cortés in Honduras, and Santo Tomás de Castilla in Guatemala.

For the 1971–72 season, BNF assured the company of the use of 10 trailers a week during six weeks. However, the final results were discouraging because only 24 trailers were used. As a result, CCT is somewhat distrustful of any future plans.

Another problem was the failure to fill each trailer to capacity, thus increasing unit transportation costs. In contrast, sometimes they were filled too full, which risked a U. S. fine of $0.05 per pound.

Both the underloading and overloading indicate deficiencies in production and shipment programming. Less production than projected may be available for shipment at a given time from uncontrollable causes, such as unfavorable weather. In this case, the exporters should decide whether or not the amount available is sufficient to justify the higher unit freight costs. CCT charges are entirely fixed, whereas with Astra Line and air cargo there are fixed and variable charges in transportation and handling. In general, it is less expensive to ship large amounts by CCT and small amounts by Astra Line. However, if the amount available is less than planned, the following equation can be used to determine whether one will break even on the transport and related costs using a particular transport system:

$$bxy - ax - c - dx - e = 0.$$

Where
y = expected sales price in the United States;
x = number of boxes to be shipped;
a = variable handling and tariff costs;
b = 100 − commission (percent);
c = fixed cost charge via CCT;
d = variable cost charge via Astra Line; and
e = fixed cost charge via air.

When only one transport method is examined, the variables corresponding to the other methods become zero. If the equation yields an amount greater than zero, then transport and related costs are covered and a contribution has been made to the already sunk costs of production and packing.

Costs. During 1971 INA incurred the following transportation costs: for 25 trailers at $550 each. $13,750, and for 19 flights at $2,400 each, $45,600, for a total of $59,350. Since 12,500 boxes were exported, the cost per box was $4.75.

During the 1972 season the costs dropped considerably, to $2.87 per box (Table 4–36), reflecting better transport capacity utilization.

Marketing

Type of Arrangement. For the 1970–71 season, officials from INA tried to make contacts with brokers in the United States. After several trips, and conversation with brokers and super markets, some letters of intent to purchase were obtained for shipments c.i.f. Miami. No price was set and the purchase was subject to the quantity and quality of the product. The independent farmers were able to get some brokers under the same conditions as INA.

For the 1971–72 season, a contract was signed between UPFS and a Florida broker, under which UPFS agreed to give the broker exclusive distribution for two consecutive years and to pay him a 10 percent commission plus reimbursement for transportation, customs, and port charges. The broker agreed to pay all the transportation, handling, and duty expenses, to make the maximum effort to sell the product at the best prices, to maintain the product under

Table 4–36. Honduran Melon Transport Costs, 1972.

		Cost (dollars)	
Transport	Trip	Per shipment	Total
24 CCT trailers	Choluteca–Pompano Beach	1520	36,000[a]
4 tractors	Choluteca–San Pedro Sula	350	1,400[b]
4 air freight	Choluteca–Pompano Beach	2200	8,800[a]
10 tractors	Choluteca–Puerto Cortés	350	3,500[b]
6354 boxes	Puerto–Cortés–Pompano Beach	66[c]	10,500[a]
14 trailers	Miami–Pompano Beach	150[d]	2,100[a]
14 BNF trailers		20[e]	280[b]
Total			62,580
Exported boxes sold	21,826		
Cost per box	$2.87		

a. Paid by broker, chargeable to exporter.
b. Paid by exporter.
c. Per ton by Astra Line.
d. Estimated by BNF personnel.
e. Approximate costs of refrigeration and maintenance.

adequate conditions, to make payment 21 days after each shipment was received, and to keep his account books open for inspection by UPFS at the time of liquidation. There was no obligation as to quantities of melons to be shipped or handled. The melons were to carry the label "Oro"; since this is not a registered trademark in the United States, UPFS would not be responsible for any court trial. Rejects were to be officially certified.

Reportedly, BNF had reviewed three other possible marketing arrangements before making the final selection. One possibility was a joint venture with a New Orleans–based group that had considerable experience in marketing bananas. The Honduran consulate in New Orleans had provided the initial contact. This group was going to advance 50 percent of the cost of the melons f.o.b. Puerto Cortés, cover the cost from Honduras to New Orleans, and then split 50–50 the profits resulting from the sale of the produce in the United States. The group planned to charter a ship to transport the melons, but in January they reviewed the planting situation and decided that the volume would be insufficient to justify a charter. This means that shipments would have to be made aboard banana boats going to New Orleans. Availability of space was not certain and therefore this alternative was discarded.

Another possibility was an arrangement with a New York investor who was developing businesses in Honduras, but the ship he was going to employ sank in Miami and with it this alternative. The third alternative was through a fruit and vegetable broker who had previously been in contact with INA during a visit to Central America. His terms were identical to those of the Miami broker but his operations were based in New York rather than in Florida. Consequently, the Miami broker was chosen by a process of elimination.

Key Problem Areas. The first problem the farmers have is ignorance of the American market as regards possible channels of distribution, contacts with brokers, quality requirements, and the like. It is commonly believed among farmers that the American brokers are not trustworthy.

The second problem is the lack of information received by the farmer on several points. One is the price behavior in the U. S. market; this information is very important in deciding on dates and quantities of shipments. Another is the percentage of rejects in the United States and the reasons for them. UPFS was not informed that the fruit was arriving overripe. Had this information been available the farmers might have been able to make changes in their harvesting schedule or even to cancel shipments in order to cut losses. Actually, the revenue in 1972 did not even cover the transportation and marketing costs (Table 4–37). A third point on which information is lacking is the time required by the broker to market the produce within the United States. The farmer tends to believe that his melons should be ready for consumption upon arrival in Pompano Beach. However, this is a case of marketing myopia because it makes no allowance for the time needed to get the fruit from the importer to the wholesaler, the retailer, and the consumer. Table 4–38 shows that the time

Table 4–37.   Revenue and Marketing Costs of Honduran Melon Exports, 1972 (dollars).

Shipment No.	Number of boxes		Average price per box	Total revenue	Transport cost	Taxes and inspection	Commission and handling	Other	Total costs	Gross profit (loss)
	Exported	Sold								
1	178	178	11.80	2,100	1,675	275	250	—	2,200	(100)
2	2,769	1,879	2.57	4,825	10,175	4,275	1,375	—	15,825	(11,000)
3–6	2,484	2,410	4.27	10,300	11,800	2,350	2,250	300	16,700	(6,400)
7	3,851	2,890	4.39	12,700	13,400	830	3,400	20	17,650	(4,950)
8	2,288	2,826	2.71	7,650	8,000	1,100	2,100	—	11,200	(3,550)
9	2,874	2,872	4.70	13,500	10,600	800	3,350	150	14,900	(1,400)
10	2,161	2,042	2.84	5,800	5,900	800	1,500	—	8,200	(2,400)
11	2,085	2,097	3.95	8,300	7,800	900	2,000	—	10,700	(2,400)
12	1,305	1,297	4.74	6,150	3,700	400	1,300	150	5,550	600
13	1,340	1,335	6.22	8,300	5,000	450	1,800	—	7,250	1,050
14	2,051	1,326	6.67	8,850	5,000	400	1,950	50	7,400	1,450
15	679	674	7.72	5,200	1,700	225	675	—	2,600	2,600
Total	24,665	21,826	4.29	93,675	84,750	12,805	21,950	670	120,175	(26,500)

Table 4—38. Time Required to Market Honduran Melons.

Operation	Time (days)	
	Minimum	Maximum
Harvesting and packing	1	6
Transport to Pompano Beach	4	6
Distribution by broker	1	3
Transport within United States	1	3
Retailer	1	5
Consumer	1	4
Total	9	27

required to market the Honduran melons is between 9 and 27 days. The Honduran variety reportedly can last only 15 days after harvest, and then only with the proper precooling and fungicide application, which was missing in 1972. Consequently, the producers were faced with time-consuming transportation and U. S. marketing arrangements.

The third problem is lack of experience in making contacts with importers. It was believed by UPFS that the broker would assume the risks and the costs of any sales he made outside of Pompano Beach. This was not stipulated in the contract and consequently all the costs of the non-Pompano sales were charged to the exporters. UPFS entered negotiations with the broker concerning these charges and potential adjustments were identified.

Communications between exporter and importer were defective and mutual confidence was lacking. These same problems plagued the La Fragua— broker relation in the Guatemalan cucumber export operation. It is interesting to note that La Fragua and UPFS were exporting to the same Miami broker. One Honduran official involved in the export operation commented, "Definitely it will be necessary to change brokers, but he was not the main cause of the project's problems, even though there is a tendency to blame him for all difficulties. The real problem was that our fruit just did not reach the consumer in good condition."

Costs. For the 1972 shipments the broker incurred on behalf of the Hondurans the costs shown in Table 4—39.

Marketing Results. During the 1970—71 season, INA transported 13,500 boxes from Choluteca to San Pedro and approximately 12,550 boxes (7—8 percent rejects due to internal transport damage) from San Pedro Sula to Miami. Approximately 11,880 boxes were sold in Miami. The remaining 1,620 boxes were rejected as unsalable because of poor quality. The prices received for the 1971 shipments ranged between $3 and $8 per box, with the average estimated to have been $5.50.

Table 4–39. Honduran Melon Marketing Costs Incurred by Broker, 1972 *(dollars).*

Cost	*Honduras to Pompano Beach*	*Pompano Beach to U.S. markets*
Tariff	9,800	
Transportation[a]	58,000	26,750
Inspection	2,200	800
Handling	5,400	2,100
Brokerage (commission)	5,350	9,100
Other	670	–
Total	81,420	38,750

a. Does not include costs paid directly by exporter.

During the 1971–72 season UPFS exported 24,665 boxes, of which 2870 were unsalable owing to damage caused by rotting, fungus infection, and freezing. The majority of the 21,795 sold were classified as overripe and therefore had to be sold at low prices. Approximately 74 percent of the Honduran melons were sold outside of Florida, with 47 percent going to the New York market. These reshipments incurred additional transport, handling, and brokerage costs as well as increased ripeness. In most cases the fruit arrived in poor condition and had to be sold at liquidation prices.

Over half of the melons marketed outside of Florida were sold for less than $4 per box, the average price being $4.21. The Florida market was more favorable; there the average price was $5.53 per box. The lower prices outside of Florida may have been the result of increased deterioration of the fruit caused by the additional transport time and handling.

Local Market. During February and March 1972, 68 percent of the production (51,000 boxes) was reportedly sold in bulk in the local market for human or animal consumption. Prices ranged from $0.005 to $0.025 per melon. The estimated revenue per manzana from local sales ranges from $25 to $40 and may be considered a constant contribution to the fixed production costs.

The Role of the Government
During 1970–71, the Agrarian National Institute was in charge of the entire Honduran cantaloupe business. INA has a team of economists, lawyers, engineers, and agronomists; it also has agricultural equipment, a packing house, and a warehouse. Its specific objective in Choluteca during the 1970–71 season was to be responsible for the packing, grading, transporting, and marketing operations of the production turned out by the cooperatives. In order to guarantee some income to the cooperative, the Institute paid $1.50 per box exported, f.o.b. the packing plant.

INA has built some of the infrastructure in the region, the most important of which is a 21-kilometer highway, which cost $73,500 and has benefited a cultivation area of 4000 hectares. INA was able to withstand the losses incurred in the melon operation during the 1970–71 season.

Another INA objective was to lower the input prices to all the farmers. To accomplish this, they imported agrochemicals directly from the United States, which entered the country duty free and through a port where the unloading and handling charges are lower. Unfortunately, lack of adequate services and port installations caused a high percentage of loss in transit. INA had to absorb the losses of these inputs.

In 1971, the National Development Bank took the initiative to carry forward the country's pioneering melon export efforts. BNF is divided into two departments: loans and operations, and development. Through the development department BNF has assisted the melon export project by making feasibility studies, giving direct counsel on the foundation of UPFS, and providing advice on administrative questions. It also contracted with the Mexican technician to advise on matters pertaining to grading and packing. In late 1971 BNF invested $60,000 to purchase nine refrigerated trailers to facilitate the internal transport of the melons. They may possibly be used during the nonexport months of April through December to transport fresh milk from San Pedro Sula to Tegucigalpa.

For the 1971–72 season, BNF extended a $500,000 line of credit, of which only $60,000 was utilized. The interest charged by the bank is 9 percent on the unpaid balances. The bank opened an account with the Bank of America, Miami, for deposit of liquidations by the broker. BNF uses the money to pay the outstanding loans, and if there is a favorable balance it proceeds to distribute it to the cooperative members. The balance in 1972 was in favor of the broker.

CABEI offers the largest financial resources available to the agribusiness managers in Central America. Its main objective there is to pursue the creation of the most adequate conditions for the integral development of the area. The technical department of CABEI has studied and promoted the melon operation. It has, at present, funds available for the creation of marketing enterprises that involve the operations of grading, packing, and transportation. According to conversations with high officials of CABEI, they would be willing to back technically and financially the establishment of a brokerage office in the United States to handle the Central American products.

Direction of Cooperative Development (DIFOCOOP) provides technical advice on legal and administrative matters to the cooperatives in the process of being organized as well as those already organized. There are at present 216 cooperatives, of which 56 are agriculturally based.

Economic Analysis

Profitability. The financial results for the 1971–72 season, based on price and cost data available at the time of this writing, are shown in

Table 4–40, from which we see that the farmers once again lost money on their melon operations. In total the losses are estimated at $121,000. These results could change, depending on adjustments being made by the broker.

Table 4–41 shows the break-even prices per box for different yield levels and areas planted. From this matrix we infer that yields are critical and must be improved to attain profitability. If the farmers planted 1000 manzanas, obtained a yield of 150 boxes per manzana (more than double current yields), and received a price of $8 per box,[10] the profit picture would improve markedly, as shown in Table 4–42. The break-even price would drop from the 1972 figure of $8.83 per box to $6.83, and the operation would produce a profit of $1.17 per box or $175.50 per manzana. This would mean exports valued at $1.2 million for Honduras.

Table 4–40. Profit and Loss Statement, Honduran Melon Exports, 1972 *(dollars).*

		Per manzana	Per box
Sales			
United States[a]	93,675	284.00	4.29
Local	9,900	30.00	0.45
Total	103,575	314.00	4.74
Costs to Pompano Beach			
Production	76,890	233.00	3.52
Packing	24,000	73.00	1.10
Transport	62,580	190.00	2.87
Tariffs	12,000	36.00	0.55
Handling	5,400	16.00	0.25
Commission	5,350	16.00	0.24
	186,220	564.00	8.53
Deficit	(82,645)	(250.00)	(3.79)
Costs post Pompano Beach			
Transport	26,750	81.00	1.23
Inspection	800	2.40	0.04
Handling	2,700	6.00	0.10
Commission	9,100	27.60	0.42
	38,750	117.00	1.79
Total loss	(121,395)	(367.00)	(5.58)

a. 21,826 boxes.

Table 4—41. Break-Even Prices *(dollars per box)* Given Plantings and Yields, Honduran Melon Exports.

Total area planted (manzanas)	Exportable boxes per manzana		
	75	150	200
330	8.73	6.93	6.58
500	8.60	6.88	6.54
1000	8.48	6.83	6.51

Table 4—42. Profit Projection *(dollars)* Given Yield, Price, and Area Planted, Honduran Melon Exports 1971—1972.

Item	Per box	Per manzana[a]	For 1000 manzanas
Revenue	8.00	1200.00	1,200,000
Break-even price	6.83	1024.50	1,024,500
Profit	1.17	175.50	175,500

a. With yield of 150 boxes/manzana and 1000 manzanas.

NICARAGUA: OKRA

Brief History

Before entering the okra business, the Callejas brothers of Chinandega, Nicaragua, had invested heavily in the production of "gros michel" bananas. When, for competitive reasons, they decided to abandon the banana business, they did not want to discharge all the workers who had been employed in their banana operation, and so they started to look for some other crop to cultivate.

Francisco Callejas remembered seeing the high prices of okra in the winter market in the United States and discussed this crop with his brothers. While in Miami on family business, he talked with a horticulturist who suggested that they plant "clemson spineless" okra. Sr. Callejas returned from Florida with the okra seeds in late 1969. His brother Eduardo then took charge, planting 10 manzanas of okra in exactly the same way he planted cotton, and obtained excellent results. Since then the results have gone from very good to very bad.

The first year they exported 160 20-pound boxes of fresh okra to the United States, and the second year 5000 boxes. They suffered losses both times—about $3,000 the first year and $20,000 the second year. In 1971 they bought and installed a processing and freezing plant and are now exporting frozen okra to the United States. They are starting to plant peas, which they intend to freeze and export to the United States.

The Callejas brothers have been in agriculture for a long time and own 12,000 manzanas of agricultural land (not all under cultivation). In addition to okra and peas they grow cotton, sesame, bananas, and plantains.

Production

Planting Cycle. The first two years (1969 and 1970), the brothers planted okra only for the fresh-produce winter season in the United States. Okra starts to bloom 55 days after planting. Since they are now exporting only frozen okra, they can cultivate and export it throughout the year.

Problems. Their main problem is that they do not know how to cultivate okra and have not found anybody to explain the proper techniques. They feel that nobody really knows how to grow okra under Nicaraguan conditions. Although they have been looking for books on okra, they have found very few that even mention it, and none that can give them the information they need.

The brothers are now experimenting with 219 different varieties of okra, which come from Turkey, Egypt, the United States, India, and China. They hope to be able to find the variety that is most suitable to their soil and that will give them high yields and good quality.

Although their first crop produced 10,000 pounds/manzana, they have never attained such a high yield since. In fact, yields have been going down, leading to disastrously low results in their mid–1972 crop. Fungus disease and nematodes destroyed most of that crop, and they stopped operating the freezing plant. Another problem is that no one in Nicaragua knows how to fertilize okra properly. Despite their experience, the Callejas brothers have not found the best technique, and are having problems with nitrogen and minor elements. They are now making some analyses to see if they can determine the fertilization requirements of their okra crop.

They are also having water-management problems, and have hired an American technician. He did not want to irrigate because in the United States he did not irrigate the crop at that early stage of the plant's development. The brothers did irrigate some areas, however, and those produced better than the technician's. They still do not have any definite conclusion as to the water needs of the crop, and they would like to grow okra during the rainy season to avoid irrigation cost.

During harvesting some improper-sized okra was picked, until the workers were trained on the site and shown the proper size. They were also taken to the packing shed so that they could see the huge amount of culled oversize okra that must be thrown away.

Rubber gloves have to be worn by workers who pick okra. According to Sr. Callejas, the Guatemalan supplier of these gloves is unreliable and they sometimes have not arrived on time. The brothers keep an inventory of the gloves, but rely on the workers to notify them when the supply is running out. Often the workers fail to do so.

Balancing production and processing capacity has been a key problem. Planting is programmed so as to stagger the harvest, but this has not always worked out well, owing to erratic yields. Consequently, the processing plant has sometimes been flooded and at other times been idle.

Inputs. The seed variety the brothers use is "clemson spineless," which is treated with fungicide and insecticides to prevent diseases. They purchase the seed from a United States seed company and pay for it in cash. Despite the fact that the seed is treated, they also apply insecticide and fungicide to the plants because fungus diseases have attacked them. These agrochemicals, as well as fertilizer, are purchased locally for cash. When the okra is picked, it is put in wooden boxes holding 20 pounds, to be taken to the processing plant. The brothers use wood from their own mahogany trees to make these boxes, which are assembled by their own carpenters in their sawmill at a cost of $0.50 per box. They own the equipment they use for the cultivation of okra, and use it also on their other crops.

Three workers harvest two manzanas of okra; they are paid $0.21 for every 20-pound box of okra they pick. Of these workers, 80 percent are male and 20 percent are female. With the 280 manzanas of okra they planted in 1971—72, the brothers employed a total of 420 workers to harvest the crop.

Output. During 1969—70 they planted 10 manzanas of okra and exported 3,200 pounds. In 1970—71 they increased plantings to 140 manzanas and exported 100,000 pounds. Because of the problems they are having with fungus diseases and nematodes, accurate estimates of yields are not possible. For 1971—72, they planted 280 manzanas and had exported to their U. S. broker about 800,000 pounds of frozen okra as of mid—1972.

Costs. According to Sr. Francisco Callejas, their cultivation costs do not differ much from those compiled and reported by "Proyecto Adelante," a nearby irrigated experimental farm (Table 4—43). Sr. Callejas takes $250 per manzana for cultivation cost. Assuming a yield of 7000 pounds/manzana labor for harvesting, at $0.21 per 20-pound box, costs $75 per manzana; 350 baskets per manzana at $0.50 per basket, usable for three years, cost $55; depreciation in irrigation and other equipment is estimated at $40, and miscellaneous costs at $60. Thus the total cost per manzana comes to $480.

Administration and Supervision. At first, the Callejas brothers made all decisions, from long-range planning to daily operations. They now have two engineers working for them—one in the field and one in the processing plant—who are in charge of making most of the daily operating decisions; this

Table 4–43. Proyecto Adelante, Nicaraguan Okra Cultivation Costs *(cordobas per manzana).* [a]

Operation	Hours per manzana	Labor	Fuel and repairs	Material Kind and quantity	Material Cost	Total	Dollars
Chop previous crop	1.5	3.40	21.00			24.40	3.50
Plow: 2 men	2.0	8.30	40.40			48.70	6.90
Furrow: 2 men	1.2	5.00	28.00			33.00	4.70
Preirrigate: 2 men	1.1	4.20	12.40	Water: 7.5 in. at 7.50	56.25	72.85	10.40
Disk twice: 2 men	2.0	8.30	37.60			45.90	6.50
Disk with drag: 2 men	1.0	4.15	19.00			23.15	3.30
Plant and fertilize: 5 men	.7	6.90	15.60	Seed: 15 lbs. at 10 30–90–0	150.00 80.00	252.50	36.10
Thin and weed	50.0	95.00				95.00	13.60
Weed	30.0	57.00				57.00	8.10
Cultivate 3 times: 2 men	3.5	14.50	66.00			80.50	11.50
Cultivate and fertilize: 4 men	1.5	11.90	21.40	100–0–0	90.00	123.30	17.60
Irrigate 16 times: 2 men	17.6	67.00	95.00	Water: 59 in. at 7.50	442.50	604.50	86.30
Spray 3 times				Application Material	30.00 120.00	150.00	21.40
Miscellaneous		29.40	36.80		58.40	124.60	17.80
Total		315.05			1027.15	1735.40	247.70

a. Proyecto Adelante is an experimental irrigation project which has grown many different crops under irrigated conditions. Labor is calculated at $2.25 and $1.90 per hour, including wages, food, and housing.

has removed some of the burden from the brothers. They also have a purchasing department that takes care of all supply acquisitions.

The brothers discuss major plans among themselves, but each has charge of one area of operations. Alfonso handles sales, Eduardo runs the farm, and Francisco manages the processing plant.

Processing

Description of Operations. The freezing and packing plant is about 15 minutes away from the okra fields. The plant houses the processing equipment and the freezing system. When the okra is harvested in the field, it is brought to the plant and placed on a receiving platform, from which it passes to a grading belt where it is selected. Next it is carried by a dumbwaiter to the women who pass it through an instrument like a pencil sharpener to cut the tips off; it then undergoes inspection, If the okra is to be cut, it moves through a line where cutting is done mechanically (optional). It is then blanched to a certain degree in a blanching machine, passes through water to cool it, and is again inspected; any damaged pieces are removed. It next moves along the freezing conveyor belt. The frozen okra is placed in plastic bags which are put inside cardboard boxes; each box contains 40 pounds. The boxes and plastic bags are purchased locally for cash. The brothers have no fixed contract with the container manufacturers.

The brothers have invested over $200,000 in the processing plant. They bought the blancher and conveyor belt from their broker for $10,000, payable in produce, and have fully paid for it. They imported the rest of the equipment from the United States.

The number of people working in the processing plant depends on the quality and quantity of okra brought from the field. About 90 percent of the workers in the plant are women. These workers are trained on the job by the quality-control supervisor and her assistant, who have been sent to Nicaragua at the expense of the U. S. broker.

Problems. When they were exporting fresh okra, the brothers had problems with the mahogany boxes used as export containers. Mahogany is brittle and the boxes often split or broke so that the okra spilled out. They used these boxes for shipping because they knew of no reliable box manufacturer in Central America and the other timber on their farm was also unsuitable for shipping fresh okra.

They have had several problems in the processing of frozen okra. This was their first experience in freezing and they did not know how to use the equipment in the freezing plant and the different lines for processing okra. Part of the equipment was secondhand and therefore not 100 percent efficient. They have had to redesign some of the equipment to adapt it to their operation.

Another problem was the lack of produce. Because of the problems in the field, they have not been able to run the plant efficiently. Although they have also started to process frozen peas in the plant, they still do not have adequate volume. In mid–1972, the plant was not in operation; there was no produce coming from the field because fungus diseases and nematodes had just about wiped out the crop. The plant cannot be run smoothly and efficiently unless there is a continuous flow of produce from the field. The interdependence of the production and processing stages in this commodity system is clear.

Materials and parts in the plant also gave rise to some problems. The cardboard boxes in which the frozen okra was packed were not always delivered on time. Once they had 30,000 pounds of frozen okra in plastic bags but no cardboard boxes, so they had to use burlap sacks until the boxes arrived; this added the cost of the sacks to that of the boxes. There are no local suppliers of parts for the processing equipment, which represents a potential problem if the unit breaks down and a part has to be replaced.

Amount Exported. Of the okra brought to the plant from the field, an average of 20 percent is discarded. The brothers have thus far exported about 800,000 pounds of frozen okra to their U. S. buyer.

Costs. The processing plant has been operating for less than a year. It has not been operating smoothly and efficiently because of start-up problems and because of the previously mentioned production problems in the field, which prevented the plant from operating at economic levels. Hence it is difficult to estimate standard costs of processing the frozen okra. The costs that have been incurred in the operations of the plant are erratic, and a cost analysis based on the present situation could not be considered typical for an ongoing mature operation.

Transportation

Description of Service. The okra harvested is brought to the edge of the field by trailers pulled by a farm tractor. There it is unloaded from the trailers onto a truck, or the same trailers are pulled by the truck, and the okra is brought to the processing plant.

The frozen okra is transported to the United States in refrigerated CCT trailers when they are available. These trailers go to the Guatemalan port of Santo Tomás, where they are loaded aboard the ship bound for Miami on Tuesdays and Fridays. When CCT trailers are not available, the frozen okra is taken by nonrefrigerated trucks to the port of Corinto, which is 20 minutes from Santo Thomás; thence it goes to Miami in refrigerated cargo vessels. The ability to store the frozen produce makes this project less vulnerable to losses due to transport delays than the fresh-produce export projects.

When there is a supply of frozen okra ready to be shipped, the U. S. buyer is informed by telephone. The buyer pays for the frozen okra f.o.b. the processing plant. When the brothers were exporting fresh okra, all of it was flown to their U. S. buyer.

Problems. The brothers have the same transportation problem as other Central American exporters—the shortage of CCT trailers or space aboard cargo ships. Since they export frozen rather than fresh okra, this problem is not so serious for them. Furthermore, they have increased the capacity of their frozen storage room to 500,000 pounds. Their frozen okra can thus be warehoused in their storage room until transportation is available.

Shipping the fresh okra was a very serious problem. Fresh okra can last for only 7 to 10 days before spoiling, and cargo space was limited and unreliable. Most of the air cargo space is taken up by meat. In passenger planes there was often little room for the fresh okra that might have been waiting in the airport. Therefore, spoilage was frequent.

Costs. The U. S. buyer of their frozen okra pays for the transportation cost to the United States.

Marketing

Type of Arrangement. The brothers have a three-year exclusive contract to supply their U. S. buyer with frozen okra because he is the only one they know. They also have a contract with him to sell their frozen peas. He pays them $0.13 per pound for okra and $0.12 per pound for peas, f.o.b. their plant. This buyer pays the Callejas brothers on the 20th of the month for all shipments made from the 1st to the 15th, and on the 5th of the next month for all shipments made from the 16th to the 30th. The fresh okra exports have been on consignment to two different U. S. brokers.

Problems. The consignment sales of fresh okra proved to be a disaster. The brokers were not okra specialists and their sales effort was not effective. The Callejas' losses on the export of fresh okra were large and caused them to lose interest in fresh okra exports.

They had no information on other U. S. importers interested in okra and therefore were forced to use the broker.

Costs. Since they have a contract with their U. S. purchaser who pays for the frozen okra f.o.b. their processing plant, they incur no marketing costs.

Local Market. There is no local market for okra. Nicaraguans do not know or consume okra.

Financing

The brothers finance their frozen-okra business and other businesses from family funds and personal bank accounts. They reinvest their profit from all operations. They have a $100,000 line of credit with the Managua branch of the First National City Bank of New York.

The used equipment that they bought from their U. S. supplier was purchased on credit payable in produce. They have since paid fully for this equipment. The Central American Bank for Economic Integration (CABEI) gave them a loan to build the processing-freezing plant. They applied for this loan in December 1970 and received the money in November 1971, after the plant was built with other funds. They bought the rest of the equipment with a loan from the Bank of London and Montreal, which they have since paid back.

The Role of the Government

Government assistance has been in the form of fiscal incentives. They have been allowed to import equipment for the processing-freezing plant without payment of duty, and they have received income-tax exemption for 10 years and property-tax exemption on the processing plant.

Economic Analysis

Investment. The brothers have the following investment in farm equipment: four tractors, $60,000; four plows, $3,000; four seeders, $4,000; five fertilizer applicators, $3,000; four cultivators, $2,000; one fumigator spray pump, $4,000; two trailers, $2,000; the total is $78,000. They also have six irrigation pumps. They use this farm equipment, however, on all the lands they have under cultivation, and have never broken down the investment among their various crops.

They have an investment of slightly over $200,000 in the processing plant.

Profit and Loss. Because of their short experience in processing frozen okra, their problems in cultivation, and the lack of any relevant cost analysis for their processing plant, it would be misleading to make any profit-and-loss analysis of thier operations.

Assuming a yield of 7000 pounds of okra per manzana and a 20 percent loss in the processing plant, the yield per manzana of exportable frozen okra is 5600 pounds. Assuming the production cost of $480 per manzana to be a fairly accurate estimate, the production cost per pound of exportable frozen okra would be $0.085. Since the U. S. purchaser pays them $0.13 per pound (f.o.b. the processing plant), the processing costs per pound of frozen okra would have to be less than $0.045 in order to make a profit.

NOTES TO CHAPTER FOUR

1. 1 manzana = 0.7 ha. = 1.73 acres.
2. Derived from data presented in *Analisis de la Situación Agricola de Sinaloa* (CAADES, Boletín Bimensual No. 73, September–October 1971).
3. ICAITI, *La Producción y Exportación de Productos Agricolas No Tradicionales en Centroamerica* (Guatemala, August 1971; second edition, August 1972).
4. INDECA, "Programa General de Exportación de Hortalizes de Clima Calida y Platano" (Guatemala, October 1972).
5. ICAITI estimated that ELCO exported 32,925 52-pound boxes.
6. ICAITI estimated that field production was 219,103 43-pound boxes and 65,925 52-pound boxes were exported to the Florida broker.
7. Marco T. Guillen, *Cultivo Commercial de Pepino* (Ministry of Agriculture, Guatemala, 1970).
8. We do not have complete information on COPEX because records have not been kept. The cooperative was disbanded in 1971; for the crop year 1971–72, one former member of COPEX, Sr. A, exported cantaloupes to the United States. Despite these limitations, we have included this brief project analysis to provide a more complete picture of the problems of melon exports from El Salvador.
9. Another two-day seminar on exporting fruits and vegetables was held in April 1970, sponsored by the Ministry of Agriculture, AID–El Salvador, and ROCAP.
10. An average price for Mexican melons of good quality.

Chapter Five

Agribusiness Education:
The Research Perspectives

In the previous chapters we have described and analyzed selected commodities of the fruit and vegetable export-import system as a means of developing the commodity systems approach as the foundation for agribusiness education in Central America. We recognized that there are many problems facing Central American agribusiness. Among these problems are the dependence of the agricultural sector on a limited number of crops and the corresponding need to develop physical and human resources able to diversify the agricultural nature of the region and to meet new foreign and domestic food needs. Underlying the necessity of agricultural diversification are the needs to generate new sources of export earnings, to improve the rural economy, and to make effective use of the abundant labor supply.

In developing a commodity systems approach we have been guided by the needs of the general economy and of the specific commodity system, balanced against the current and potential educational resources of the area. In order for these physical and human resources to be developed effectively, some understanding of the dynamics of integrated commodity systems is needed. Viewing the purposes and priorities of each commodity complex from the perspective of both public and private policy enables public and private policy makers to have a framework against which various types of educational operations can be organized and utilized.

Needs of the Economy

Education is the basic vehicle for developing the human resources of a country so as to make its people and its organizations more capable of fulfilling the social and economic needs of the nation. Needs generally outrun resources and it is therefore necessary to attach priorities to the needs. The country's educational efforts should reflect those priorities and be directed toward the critical needs of the economy.

We mentioned at the start of this study that one of the main reasons for selecting for investigation the nontraditional fruit and vegetable export industry was its perceived potential importance to the economies of Central America. All of the Central American governments have emphasized the need and desirability of diversifying their agricultural production to include nontraditional crops. Crops are being sought that are labor-intensive and thus offer hope of alleviating the pressing problem of rural unemployment and subemployment. It is hoped that the greater employment will raise rural incomes and living standards, which in turn could reduce the rural migration that is increasingly straining the already overburdened cities. Similarly, all of the nations are making attempts to promote exports of nontraditional products so as to generate badly needed foreign exchange and to reduce the overdependence on a few unstable primary export commodities, mainly coffee, bananas, sugar, and cotton.

Thus, the export of nontraditional fruits and vegetables fits well into the priority needs and goals of Central America. Clearly, these new exports today are insignificant compared with those of traditional crops; the fruit and vegetable export industry is still in its infancy. Nonetheless, the experience of Mexico, which exports annually over $200 million worth of fruits and vegetables to the United States, is indicative of the potential for Central America.

So this study deals with a new, high-potential export industry; accordingly, the educational recommendations in the initial portion of this chapter are aimed at an agribusiness subsector that is perceived as being potentially important to the economies of Central America. The final section of the chapter discusses some of the implications of the study for agribusiness education in general in Central America. That section will also touch on the limitations of generalizing from the analysis of this relatively new commodity system.

Needs of the System

The second concept in our framework is that the content and form of the educational efforts should be tailored to the needs of the public and private organizations operating in the commodity system. In short, the education should be recipient-oriented in order to ensure relevancy. This means that the educational effort must emerge first from an understanding of the problems and needs of the participants in the commodity system.

On the basis of this concept, we undertook in the current research first to analyze, by means of a commodity systems approach, the fruit and vegetable export-import system in order to identify the actual problems facing the industry. This problem-identification phase of the study examined the gap between the requirements for successful entrance into the U. S. fruit and vegetable import system and the capabilities of the Central American export projects. This created the basis for delineating the industry's agribusiness education needs, which will be presented subsequently in this chapter.

Scope of Agribusiness Management Education

Management is the art and science of organizing and operating a series of activities as a coordinated, productive whole; therefore, the agribusiness manager must be concerned not only with his own training needs, but also with those at all the different levels in his organization. Although the main focus of our educational recommendations will be on the administrative dimensions, we shall also discuss the needs of technicians, foremen, and workers, without whom the system could not function.

The study's examination of the export-import operations revealed the interrelated nature of the various components of the fruit and vegetable system. This characteristic is common to all agribusiness commodity systems and means that an educational effort must be concerned not only with the training needs at the different personnel levels within an organization, but also with the needs of the different organizations at the various stages in the system. Consequently, the study examines the training needs at each of the main stages in the export system: input supplies, production, harvesting, packing, transportation, and marketing. The educational needs are viewed from the perspective of the Central American farm suppliers, producers, packers, and exporters, and the technicians assisting them.

In effect, we are taking a systems view of the educational services to be delivered to the various participants in the commodity system. The educational delivery system must aim its services at the total training needs of the industry if it is to avoid creating manpower bottlenecks at particular levels in the system or fragmented training in the face of a highly interrelated system. Despite this ideal, the educational system is operating with limited resources and capabilities, and therefore it is necessary to balance the needs of the fruit and vegetable system with the capacity of the actual and potential educational system.

Figure 5–1 presents an overview of the research approach used in the study; this chapter wil focus on steps III, IV, and V. The recommendations on education emerging from this study are aimed specifically at the Central American nontraditional fruit and vegetable export industry. Not all of these particular recommendations will be totally applicable to the Central American agribusiness sector as a whole. Nonetheless, we do believe that many are applicable and that the conceptual framework and research approach that we employed to study the fruit and vegetable industry could be used to design educational programs for other parts of Central American agribusiness. These implications will be discussed in the last section of the chapter.

Figure 5–1. Agribusiness Education Research Approach: Component Steps

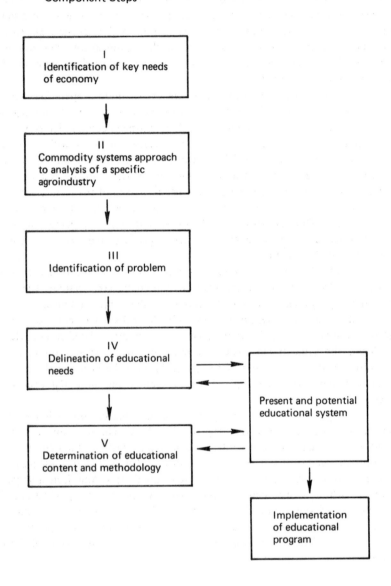

NONTRADITIONAL FRUIT AND VEGETABLE
COMMODITY SYSTEM: PROBLEMS AND
EDUCATIONAL NEEDS

The previous chapters of this study employed a commodity systems approach to analyze nontraditional export operations in four production countries, and their relation to the U. S. fruit and vegetable system. This approach enabled us to identify the problems present at each of the four main stages in the export-import system. Table 5–1 summarizes these problems by country and by stage.

This summary presentation does not list all the problems identified by the commodity systems analysis as presented in the previous chapters, but rather only sets forth those believed to have had a clearly significant impact on the projects' performance. Despite this paring down, the problem inventory is still large, reflecting the expected abundance of difficulties in the early stages of development of an industry that requires close coordination, timeliness, and high quality. As can be seen in Table 5–1, the different projects had many problems in common at each stage in the system. For example, at the production level insufficient soil analysis was a key problem in both Guatemala and Nicaragua, inadequate selection of seed and variety was a problem in both of these countries and in Honduras, and insect control caused difficulties in all four of the countries studied. Similarly, common problem areas exist in harvesting and packing, transportation, and marketing.

The relative criticality of the problems identified in Table 5–1 is difficult to assess precisely. In one sense, all are critical because weakness in one part of the system will debilitate the functioning of the total system. However, what is a weakness in one project might not be a problem in another, given the diversity of the projects studied. Nevertheless, it is possible to provide some rough quantitative measures of the impact of the major problems: (1) The series of problems in the production stage combined to adversely affect field and exportable yields of the crops. In the projects studied, 37 to 70 percent of the produce was rejected even before reaching the packing house. Both total production and the exportable percentage must be increased to make these operations economically feasible, as was indicated in the previous chapter. (2) Harvesting and handling operations were also deficient, as revealed by the rejection during the packing operation of between 20 and 45 percent of the produce delivered to the plant. (3) The packing and selection operation itself was inadequate, as shown by a high rejection rate, the necessity for repacking the exported fruit upon arrival in the United States, and the lower prices frequently paid for Central American exports. Rejects ran between 10 and 60 percent of exports, repacking costs per box were as high as 20 percent of the sales, and prices at times were only half those paid for exports from Mexico and Belize (British Honduras). (4) Transportation costs per box were generally the largest single cost item in the export operation, and this put a severe constraint on profita-

Table 5–1.   Major Problems Encountered in Central American Nontraditional Fruit and Vegetable Export Operations.

Problem	Guatemala	El Salvador	Honduras	Nicaragua
Production				
Insufficient soil analysis	x			x
Inadequate variety and seed selection	x			x
Erroneous timing for land preparation			x	
Inadequate fungus control	x	x	x	
Inadequate insect control	x	x	x	x
Improper fertilizer application	x		x	x
Erroneous timing of irrigation	x		x	x
Delayed financing	x	x	x	
Insufficient capacity of farming personnel to absorb technical assistance	x		x	
High cost of agrochemicals	x	x	x	
Inadequate initiative among workers and foremen		x		
Excessive need for close supervision of workers		x		
Harvesting and packing problems				
Improper harvesting and field selection techniques	x		x	x
Inadequate adherence to harvesting schedules			x	
Incorrect box specifications	x		x	x
Erroneous estimates of boxes needed	x		x	
Late delivery of boxes	x	x	x	x
Improper processing techniques	x			
Deficient packing procedures	x		x	
Lack of refrigeration	x	x	x	
Lack of local equipment supplier			x	x
High labor turnover		x	x	
Conflicting technical advice			x	
Transportation problems				
High cost	x	x	x	
Inadequate availability and frequency		x	x	
Under-utilization of trailer capacity			x	
In-transit damage to product	x	x	x	
Regular services only to Miami	x	x	x	

Marketing problems				
High tariffs	x	x	x	
Small local market	x	x	x	
No local market				x
Ignorance of U.S. markets, tariffs, brokers and prices	x	x	x	x
Poor communication between exporter and importer	x	x	x	
Inadequate control of product once exported	x	x	x	x

bility. (5) Misunderstandings or inadequate analysis of contract terms led to extra costs, which in one case were estimated to be as much as $65,000, or approximately the equivalent of the revenue generated from the sale of 10,000 boxes of produce. (6) Defective planning and coordination, stemming to a great extent from the lack of a commodity-systems perspective, were major factors contributing to costly delays throughout the system, supply inventory excesses or shortages, difficulties in maintenance of quality, and expensive imbalances in utilization of transport. Much of the losses incurred in the Central American export operations can be traced to these weaknesses in planning and coordination.

The purpose of the problem-identification phase is to provide a reality-based foundation from which one can delineate the educational needs of the industry. Consequently, we have constructed in Table 5–2 a matrix consisting of (1) a summary of the problems identified by the commodity-systems analysis of the various projects in the four countries, which can be remedied partly or wholly by educational means (this summary is, in effect, a consolidation of the problems presented in Table 5–1); (2) a categorization of the problems in the four main stages of the exports system as in Table 5–1; and (3) a delineation of the educational needs of top managers, technicians, foremen, and laborers corresponding to each of the problems identified; top managers are public as well as private administrators and technicians are nonadministrative operational specialists such as agronomists or packing experts.

This matrix, like most such summary presentations, is a simplification of reality; for example, different export projects have different organizational structures and different educational levels of personnel. The previous chapter described these differences in each of the export operations studied. For example, in some projects the manager is a single entrepreneur running his own farming operation and in others he is the manager of a cooperative through which many farmers channel their produce. Similarly, in some organizations the foremen are university-trained agronomists and in other projects they have not even completed a primary education.

Despite the variability among the different projects, the matrix in Table 5–2 does help us to pinpoint educational needs confronting the industry at its different stages for each of the four personnel categories. From the commodity-system analysis it became clear that the success of the activities at each stage depended on the effective, coordinated operation of the total system. Therefore, it was important to identify the problems at each stage in the system, as well as their interrelatedness. However, since the system is fundamentally based on the effective functioning of people, it was necessary to translate the problems into the training needs of the different types of personnel operating within the system. Just as one cannot be concerned with only one stage in the system, one cannot focus on just one personnel level, such as management. It is necessary to look at the other levels of personnel because without adequately prepared human resources at all levels the operations will suffer. Figure 5—2 presents diagrammatically the steps through which we moved from the commodity-systems analysis of the fruit and vegetable import-export system to the construction of the educational-need matrix.

In Table 5—2, the column for top managers lists special managerial training needs that correspond to the particular problems identified at each stage of the system—production, harvesting and packing, transportation, and marketing. By using the commodity system approach, we were able more systematically to determine what the training needs were by relating them to specific, actual operating problems. In so doing, our specification of educational requirements is based on reality rather than on theoretical suppositions as to what those needs might be. Table 5—2 presents a similar inventory of needs for technicians, foremen, and laborers. It should be mentioned that the focus of the study is primarily on the manager group, and therefore it is given relatively more attention. Other educators, professionals, and managers more familiar and skilled than the authors with the nonmanagement operational aspects should be able to elaborate more fully the training needs of the nonmanager categories on the basis of the problems identified in the commodity analysis.

The utility of the educational-need matrix is that it helps us to pinpoint those who need to be trained and to delineate what they need training in on the basis of actual problems they confront in their operations. For example, from Table 5—2 we see that top managers in the production area need to understand the importance of soil analyses, how they can be obtained, and how to employ the results to program production more systematically. These requirements arose because managers, especially in Nicaragua and Guatemala, encountered production difficulties and unsatisfactory yields that were the result, in part, of not having undertaken the appropriate preplanting soil analysis. We see further that the manager must have a fuller understanding of the factors to be considered in selecting the appropriate seed variety. Problems occurred in three of the countries studied because the manager failed to determine the appropriateness of the seed to either the agronomic conditions in the planting area, the durability requirements during the farm-to-consumer transit period, and the appearance requirements of the end consumer. The excessive disease and insect damage found in all the projects revealed the necessity for managers to know the appropriate agrochemicals. An information and control system that would make possible early detection of the plant damage is required to facilitate preventive or corrective action. By continuing down the list in Table 5—2 the reader can find the training needs for top managers arising out of the actual problems encountered in Central American export operations at each successive stage in the commodity system. This gives a fairly complete view of the management education needs for the industry. Training needs for the other personnel can be determined in the same way.

Table 5—2 demonstrates that a single problem can simultaneously

Table 5-2. Central American Educational Needs for Fruit and Vegetable Industry.

	Personnel	
Problem	*Top manager*	*Technician*
1. Production		
(a) Insufficient soil analysis	Same as foreman, plus greater systematization of production procedures and knowledge of where soil analysis services are available	Knowledge of soil-analysis techniques and availability of necessary testing equipment
(b) Inadequate variety and seed selection	Fuller understanding of requirements imposed by each stage in total system on variety characteristics: agronomic, perishability, fragility, taste, appearance; fuller information about location and reliability of suppliers	Greater knowledge of varieties and procedures for adapting them to local agronomic conditions and to export marketing constraints
(c) Excessive disease and insect damage	Information on availability, costs, and effectiveness of various agrochemicals and other disease- and insect-control procedures; data collection and analysis system to facilitate preventive and corrective action	Increased skills in entomology and botany and ongoing research on actual insect and plant disease problems; skills in agrochemical application techniques
(d) Improper fertilizer application	Same as 1 (c), with special emphasis on effect of fertilizer on maturity rate and appearance of fruit	Same as 1 (a), plus procedures for on-going testing of soil and plant responsiveness to fertilizer applications
(e) Erroneous timing of land preparation	Need to program with anticipated production schedule so as to match market and agronomic conditions optimally	Greater awareness of implications of seasonal export market conditions for timing of planting
(f) Improper irrigation application	Same as foreman plus information on costs, yields, and quality impact of irrigation	Training in irrigation techniques and experimentation with actual and potential export crops
(g) High cost of agrochemicals	Input control system plus budgeting and cost-effectiveness analysis techniques	Greater understanding of economic implications of input use

Table 5-2. (cont.)

Personnel	
Foreman	*Laborer*
Greater understanding of why preplanting soil analyses are made and how to use results	—
Better control procedures for using and retaining quality seeds while selecting out weaker varieties	—
Knowledge of what, when, and how to apply agrochemicals; need for periodic warning and control procedures	Skills in agrochemical application techniques
Same as 1 *(c)*	Same as 1 *(c)*
Need for production plan consistent with agronomic conditions	—
Knowledge of irrigation techniques and crop requirements; programming of irrigation operation	Skills in irrigation procedures
Same as laborers plus control procedures for agrochemical usage	Create cost consciousness to avoid wastage

Table 5-2. (cont.)

Problem		Personnel	
		Top manager	*Technician*
(h)	Delayed financing	Production programming consistent with financing availability; sensitization of bankers to importance of timely funding	Greater awareness of coordinating production schedule with financing availability
(i)	Excessive need for close supervision of workers	Development of worker and foreman training programs and motivation systems; detailed work procedure plan	
(j)	Insufficient capability of farm personnel to absorb technical assistance	Greater knowledge of training and communication techniques: simplification of tasks and procedures; greater understanding of potential utility of modern technology and professionally trained personnel	Skills in adapting communication to language of recipient and in effecting demonstrations of practical utility
2.	Harvesting and packing		
(a)	Improper harvesting and field selection	Coordination of overall production, harvesting, and packing schedule with market conditions; knowledge of broker standards and mechanisms for continual quality-control checks and feedback	Knowledge of export market quality standards and harvesting and handling techniques
(b)	Deficient selection and processing	Same as 2 *(a)*, plus knowledge of proper treatment requirements and techniques	Same as manager but with greater detailed knowledge
(c)	Defective packing	Knowledge of market packing requirements and alternative packing techniques	Same as manager plus skills in packing techniques
(d)	Incorrect box specifications	Knowledge of market requirements and standards for boxes; knowledge of alternative packing materials	Same as manager plus knowledge of how to construct and seal
(e)	Late delivery of boxes	Input programming coordinated with production and packing schedule; contractual arrangements with box suppliers to ensure timely delivery; knowledge of alternative box suppliers	Awareness of need to coordinate input delivery with production schedule

Table 5–2. (cont.)

Personnel	
Foreman	*Laborer*
–	–
Skills in training laborer and better indirect control procedures	Better understanding of task techniques and incentive system
Training in technical terms and basic concepts	Training in fundamental education: reading, writing, arithmetic
Same as laborer plus coordinating procedures to balance flow between field and packing plant; field quality control checks	Knowledge of maturity and quality standards and techniques for cutting and handling
Same as laborer plus sampling procedures to verify quality control	Knowledge of quality standards and treatment techniques
Same as laborer plus control procedures to check on packing performance	Knowledge of packing procedures and standards
Knowledge of correct box size, shape, and construction	–
Box inventory control and re-corder system	–

Table 5—2. (cont.)

Problem	Personnel	
	Top manager	*Technician*
(f) Surpluses and shortages of boxes	Need for accurate production estimating procedures, and contractual or other arrangements to ensure realization of production requirements	Techniques for estimating output
(g) Damage from inadequate refrigeration	Same as foreman plus coordination with transport services; investment analysis techniques to verify economic merits of investment; information on refrigeration-equipment suppliers and alternative refrigeration techniques	Knowledge of refrigeration requirements of fruits and skills in temperature control and storage techniques; equipment-maintenance skills
3. Transportation		
(a) Damage in farm-to-plant transport	Scheduling and conditioning of transport vehicles	Same as laborer
(b) Inadequacy of availability and frequency	Same as foremen plus improved negotiating abilities to obtain contractual or other arrangements which will ensure adequate and timely transport services	Same as foreman
(c) Underutilization of trailer capacity	Same as foremen plus economic analysis techniques to help select appropriate transport vehicle given volume fluctuations	Same as foreman
(d) In-transit damage to produce	Better negotiating ability to ensure compensation for damage	Same as foreman
(e) High cost	Better negotiating ability to lower costs; better production-transport programming to ensure capacity utilization	Knowledge of alternative transport services and economic analysis techniques for weighing alternatives
4. Marketing		
(a) Difficulties in locating brokers	Information on location, credit worthiness, and product line and interests	—
(b) Ignorance of market structure and functioning	Information on structure and dynamics of import marketing system	Same as manager

Table 5–2. (cont.)

Personnel	
Foreman	*Laborer*
Same as 2 *(c)*	—
Knowledge of refrigeration requirements and procedures; skills in refrigerated-equipment maintenance	Storage and handling techniques under refrigerated conditions
Same as laborer	Storing procedures in transport vehicles
Production-transportation coordinated scheduling techniques	—
Same as 3 *(b)*	—
Greater knowledge of proper trailer-loading procedures	Knowledge of proper handling and storage techniques
—	—
—	—
—	—

Table 5-2. (cont.)

	Personnel	
Problem	*Top Manager*	*Technician*
(c) Disadvantageous contracts with broker	Same as 4 *(a, b)* plus greater knowledge of alternative contractual arrangements and better negotiating skills	–
(d) Absence of data on market conditions	Information system to provide market and price data	–
(e) Misunderstandings between exporters and brokers	Clearer contractual arrangements and better communication system and knowledge of each others' needs, problems, and operating procedures	–
(f) Small local market	Analysis of local consumer habits and demand and opportunities for processing	–

carry educational implications for the various personnel levels in an organization. Here the reader must look at the rows rather than the columns in the table. For example, in the production stage excessive disease and insect damage was a problem common to all the export projects studied. At the top-manager level this problem indicated, as previously discussed, the need for an information and control system that would program preventive applications of fungicide or insecticide and detect early signs of damage, thus permitting corrective action; such systematic programming and control procedures were largely absent in the projects studied. The top manager or his own financial analyst, depending on the size of the organization, also would need information on the availability, costs, and effectiveness of different agrochemicals; this would stem from greater availability of information and the programming and control system that the manager would develop. The technicians would need knowledge of the application techniques and also greater skills in entomology and botany as applied to the nontraditional fruits and vegetables. At the worker level the need is for specific skills in applying the agrochemicals.

A close examination of the educational-need matrix will also reveal that for a single personnel category many of the training needs delineated in the different stages have common characteristics. These commonalities allow us to regroup the needs and view them not by stages in the system, but rather from three new perspectives that will facilitate the next task of specifying the content and form of the educational effort required to meet the training needs. These

Table 5–2. (cont.)

Personnel	
Foreman	*Laborer*
–	–
–	–
–	–
–	–

three perspectives are: (1) commodity systems approach to agribusiness management; (2) design of management systems; and (3) operating techniques.

These perspectives for viewing training needs are from the vantage point of the educator as well as the operating manager in the commodity system. This shared perspective is integral to our approach to agribusiness education because it is critical that the educational programs be tailored to the actual and future needs of the commodity system, within the constraints of limits on resources. Such a tailoring requires the close cooperation and interaction of the educators and the managers. Each of the three perspectives will now be described more fully.

Commodity Systems Approach

Many of the educational needs of the top managers (including public officials providing planning and policy assistance) are related to the necessity of comprehending the totality and the interrelatedness of the export–import system; in other words, the need to employ a commodity systems perspective. For example, in the production stage there was the problem of inadequate variety selection. In choosing the melon variety the farm managers and their advisors selected one that was consumed in the United States and was also grown in the exporting area; in effect, the variety had known consumer acceptability and production feasibility, which are two key criteria. However, what was not fully considered was the perishability of the fruit in relation to the transport

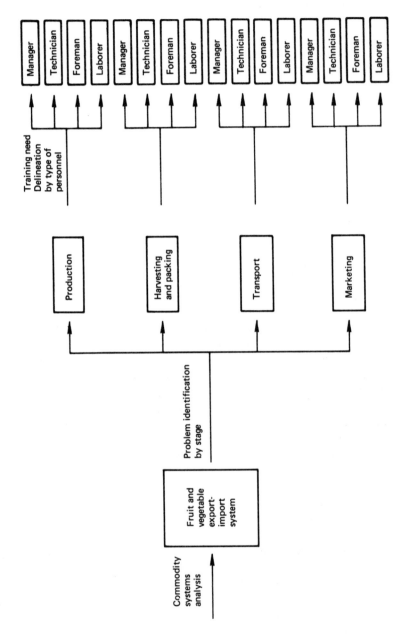

Figure 5–2.   Derivative Steps for Construction of Educational-Need Matrix

time required to get the fruit from the field to the U. S. broker, then to the retailer, and finally to the end consumer. This failure to consider fully the transport and redistribution dimensions of the system resulted in large spoilage losses. Other manifestations of the lack of a thorough appreciation of the system linkages were problems in coordinating and synchronizing the inputs to the operations and different stages in the system. Boxes were delivered late, financing was delayed, transportation was not available when needed. Production and packing operations were carried out without fully recognizing the quality requirements and standards of the marketplace. Plantings were made without adequate consideration of the optimum time for marketing the produce, given the seasonality of the export market. Examples of fragmented planning in dealing with parts of the system without fully considering the implications of the decisions for the rest of the system were common.

The absence of systematic planning was notorious in most of the export projects and is the root cause of many of the problems and training needs listed in Table 5–2. Given the characteristics of the emerging fruit and vegetable export industry—high product perishability, seasonal markets, variable weather conditions, high quality requirements, long farm-to-consumer distances, and very limited transportation services—the need for planning and coordination of all of the components of the commodity system is critical. The commodity systems approach as employed in this study to analyze the fruit and vegetable industry provides the private and public manager with an analytical framework that will help him avoid the costly pitfalls of piecemeal planning.

Technicians and foreman also need to use a commodity systems approach so that they may be aware of the implications of their individual advice and decisions for the rest of the system and may take into account the requirements and characteristics of the total system in formulating their decisions. For example, inadequate understanding by technicians of the market requirements in terms of appearance partially led to inadequate concern about and control of fertilizer and other agrochemical applications, with the result that surface defects occurred that greatly reduced the market value of the product. The individual laborer could not be expected to have the same in-depth grasp of the commodity systems approach as the manager, nor is such a grasp essential to the performance of his tasks. However, he must understand how his particular job fits into the total operation and why it is important. Such awareness can be a powerful motivating device for worker performance. For example, if a picker sees his job only as getting the fruit from the field to the processing plant, he may be less careful in handling it than he would be if he knew that bruises or sunspots caused by his poor handling would make that fruit nonexportable. In effect, even a minimal understanding of the demanding nature of the export market could lead to greater quality consciousness and reduced produce losses.

Design of Management Systems

From a second perspective, many of the needs listed in Table 5–2 are related to the necessity to develop management systems for planning, coordination, and control. Underlying these three systems there must be a management information system designed to generate and handle the data needed by the other systems. These systems are tools to help accomplish the basic management task of organizing and operating a series of activities as a coordinated, productive whole. These tools attempt to systematize procedures and information so as to facilitate and enhance the decision making of the manager and his subordinates. The need exists for training top managers or administration consultants in how to design such management systems. If the export operations were sufficiently large, the organization might employ specialists within the firm to design the system and help the top manager operate it.

Table 5–2 shows that there are examples of insufficient or inadequate planning and coordination in each of the four states (1a, e, h: 2a, b, c; 3e; 4d, e). Planting has to be programmed, within the constraint of climatic conditions, so that harvesting and exportation place the produce on the market during the optimum demand period. Inputs such as agrochemicals, boxes, and labor have to be scheduled with anticipation so that the right quantities are available at the right time. The growing process is continuous and, unlike a manufacturing process, cannot be stopped when critical inputs do not arrive on time. The perishability of the fruit allows for little slippage in the coordination of the different stages of the produce flow. Consequently, there is an urgent need for planning systems and coordinating procedures to avoid unnecessary and costly spoilage. (It should also be recognized that inherent agronomic risks in this type of business, such as inclement weather, drought, or unforeseeable disease, can cause sizable losses even in the face of thorough, systematic planning.)

The educational-need matrix also shows a similar need for control systems at each of the different stages in the system (1c, g; 2a, b; 3b; 4d, e). The management control needs fall into two general subcategories: operating and financial. The former concerns operating activities, and the latter data on cost, revenue, and fund flow. For example, at the production level the problem of insect and disease damage indicated the need for an operating control system that would delineate procedures for anticipating and avoiding crop damage. This could involve, for example, scheduling periodic insect counts and fruit inspection, which could be compared with predetermined acceptable levels; if the inspection revealed amounts in excess of the standards, agrochemicals would be applied. A quality-control system is another example of operating controls. Such a system could involve, first, the setting of standards based on market requirements and, second, sampling procedures on rejects and selected fruit to check whether standards were being enforced and to find the causes of the rejects. This latter use represents a feedback mechanism to trace the problem to its roots, for example, improper handling or shading or agrochemical application. The manager could then take remedial action. Such a quality-control system must also be linked to market conditions in the United States; if standards change, the quality-control procedures must be adjusted accordingly. Quality control must occur at each stage in the system because exposure to damage exists throughout the entire farm-to-consumer chain and quality is one of the key determinants of price. Also, pesticide control becomes critical for limiting the health hazard both for workers in the field and for consumers of the end product.

Financial controls are also needed at all stages in the export system because all the main operating activities carry financial implications in terms of costs, prices, or required funds. This control system could be used to provide cost data on agrochemical application to permit an analysis of the cost implications of the disease- and insect-control procedures. More generally, budgets could be employed to plan expenditures and to compare data on actual costs with those budgeted. Deviations of actual from budget costs would serve as warning flags to the manager against overspending. In the projects analyzed, financial controls and records were almost nonexistent. Where cost information did exist, it was largely not used until after the export operation had ended for the season. Consequently, the managers were often operating with no information about either the economic implications of their operating decisions or the overall profitability of their operations.

This points up the essential nature of a management information system. Most management decisions are taken under conditions of uncertainty, but availability of information helps the manager deal more analytically and systematically with that uncertainty. The agronomic and marketing characteristics of the fruit and vegetable export operations make this a high-risk industry and, therefore, information relevant to operating decisions becomes exceptionally important.

Many of the problems shown in Table 5-2 could be resolved in whole or part if the individual concerned had relevant information at his disposal. Part of these data are of an operating nature, such as U. S. market prices, broker standards, box specifications, transport availability, broker's location and credit-worthiness, job descriptions, and so forth. Such information, if made available, could help solve certain problems, but to do so it must be timely and the recipient must have the skill to use such data correctly.

One Central American cooperative exporting produce to the United States had posted on its office wall the weekly market prices of the fruit in Pompano Beach. When they discussed their operations prospects they optimistically referred only to the highest price during the season. When the sales results of their exports arrived they were surprised and very disappointed to find that the actual prices they received were much below their expectations. The cooperative had only a rudimentary information system, and they did not know how to interpret the minimal data it did generate. The more successful export operations in Central America had relatively better information systems than the less successful operations.

In addition to the operating type of data provided by a management information system, other types of information can supply the manager with useful educational resource support. For example, a description or analysis of the operations of a broker or the structure and dynamics of the import market can serve to enhance the producer's or exporter's understanding of the agribusiness system he is participating in. Multiple-country project analyses such as are included in this study can serve to amplify the public or private manager's or technician's perspective of the export business. Also, manuals of operating techniques or agronomic concepts or procedures could serve as permanent reference sources from which the technicians or foremen could carry on a continual self-education process.

We have described these needs as requiring increased ability to design the management planning, coordination, information, and control systems. The situation may well be that the system is designed by a public or private management consultant rather than by the operating manager himself. Accordingly, the educator must identify the specific target recipient of his training services before designing or implementing his program.

It is important to note that this section on management system design has focused only on the individual firm. However, mechanisms that will assist in the planning, control, and coordination of the entire industry commodity system are also essential. Industry participants and public policy-makers should explore means of cooperation and interinstitutional linkages, which enhance the system's total efficiency and effectiveness and thereby benefit the individual firms. The experience of the Mexican grower-exporters described in Chapter 3 is highly relevant in this regard. They joined together to create industry quality standards, set production levels, carry out market research, and obtain financing. In effect, they were planning, coordinating, and controlling much of their entire commodity system. They were acting as what Dr. Harry Strachan, academic dean of the Central American Graduate School of Business Administration (INCAE), has termed the "functioning brain of the system."

We have assumed that the design also involves the manager's knowing how to use the system. One of the key purposes of the system is to simplify the tasks of the nonmanagerial employees in the organization. Consequently, another system need is one for training and motivating these personnel to use the systems in the desired manner. Using a systems procedure begins to involve specific operating techniques, and this moves us into the next perspective for viewing the educational needs.

Operating Techniques

Besides the commodity systems approach and the management systems design, the manager and the educator are concerned about the specific operating techniques needed to implement the tasks to be performed. These particular skill requirements and training needs exist for all four personnel levels.

The top manager must understand how to employ cost-effectiveness techniques for the evaluation of agrochemical application procedures or a quality-control program. Other management operating techniques needed are cash-flow analysis, budgeting, investment-return analysis, and communication procedures. The top manager must also be skilled in contract negotiation, since contractual arrangements are basic coordinating mechanisms that link the different components of the system—producer with packer, packer with transporter, exporter with importer, input supplier with producer or packer. Difficulties have frequently arisen over contract terms, many of which might have been avoided had the parties had a better grasp of contract design and negotiation.

At the technician level the specific operating techniques needed include soil analysis, variety adaptation, disease and insect detection, agrochemical application, irrigation procedures, economic cost-effectiveness analysis so that technicians can better understand the economic implications of their technical advice, packing procedures, production estimating, refrigeration scheduling, and loading.

The foreman has to know how to use the portion of the management system corresponding to his job—seed selection, agrochemical application, irrigation techniques, training and supervision skills, cutting, handling, transportation, and packing procedures, sampling techniques, refrigeration operation and maintenance, scheduling, and trailer loading.

Many of the skills that the worker must have are similar to those of the foreman, because the foreman has to know the tasks being performed by his subordinates in order to carry out properly his supervisory function. The laborer's needs include agrochemical application techniques, irrigation procedures, cutting, handling, transportation, and packing skills, and storage and loading procedures.

By grouping the training needs shown in the educational-need matrix under the three perspectives discussed above, we were able to consolidate according to their common characteristics the variety of needs found at the various stages in the commodity system and at the different levels. Understanding the factors that are common to the industry's training needs as well as the differences among them is important to educators in designing effective training programs.

THE EDUCATIONAL DELIVERY SYSTEM

Up to this point we have used a commodity systems approach to identify the opportunities and problems facing the Central American fruit and vegetable export industry and the training needs stemming from those problems. In this section we discuss what kinds of educational approaches and programs can best meet those needs.

Concept

Our starting point is the same commodity systems approach that we have used in prior sections, but now we look at the training problem from the vantage point of the educator. If the commodity systems approach is important and relevant to the manager's task, as was indicated in the previous section, then it is a vital perspective for the educator as well. If the educational system is to meet effectively the training needs of the fruit and vegetable industry as well as those of other commodity systems in Central America, then educators must be concerned about the training needs at all stages and personnel levels in the system as identified by the commodity systems approach. The approach stresses the necessity of educational efforts being coordinated so that training given at one level—say for the farm manager—does not disregard the rest of the system, but includes an examination of the other components as they relate to the farmer's tasks. Too often farmers have been trained to use new production methods to achieve higher yields, only to find that the sought-for bumper crop rots in the field for lack of adequate storage or transport facilities or appropriate market conditions.

Several Central American agribusiness leaders have expressed the desirability of employing this commodity systems approach to agribusiness education. Dr. Ernesto Cruz, dean of INCAE, stated at a recent conference that "we need to employ a systems approach to agricultural education aimed at strengthening the entire system through all components and at all levels." Guillermo Medina Santos, president of the National Development Bank of Honduras, which has been a key promoter of melon exports, commented, "Our experience in this institution shows that the majority of the problems at the different levels of operating activities are closely interrelated. It appears to me that the commodity systems approach deserves high priority and that education and training should be built on such an approach." Ing. Juan Restrepo, head of the newly formed Agro-Administration Department of the Escuela Agricola Panamericana, said: "A survey of our graduates revealed that they encountered in their work administrative, financial, and marketing problems for which they lacked sufficient training. We had been training primarily for production skills and doing a good job at this, but it is not only a problem of production. We have to get the food from the farm to the consumer and this requires additional skills which we are now trying to provide with our new program." Ing. Noel Somarriba Barreto, director of Nicaragua's National School of Agriculture and Livestock, wrote, "As regards the commodity systems approach, it appears appropriate to us and we believe that in our environment much educational work is needed among agribusiness managers to raise the consciousness of the interdependence of all the aspects of the agribusiness system." Dr. Emilio Araujo, director of the Organization of American States Interamerican Institute of Agricultural Sciences, wrote, "This approach can give us a useful vehicle in determining training needs and educational programs, in the light of the total marketing system."

Just as the manager should not take a piecemeal approach to planning, the educator should not provide fragmented, isolated training programs. This is not to say that schools should avoid specializing in certain areas, such as agroproduction or marketing. Rather, it means that even though one stage or aspect is emphasized in the training, the other stages must also be dealt with in the training program because they are an essential complement to the area of specialization. In agribusiness education no individual stage can be ignored without running the risk of producing graduates who have a myopic perspective inconsistent with the demands and realities of the commodity systems in which they will be working.

The systems perspective for the educator also means that coordination among different educational institutions must receive explicit attention. Effective agribusiness development requires adequately trained personnel at all levels—manager, technician, foreman, laborer—but a single educational institution probably directs its programs at only one or two of these levels. Consequently, the different organizations should work together to ensure that all levels of personnel in the commodity system are receiving the appropriate training. Just as the stages in a commodity system have to be coordinated to achieve success, so must the different components and programs in the educational system be coordinated. Failure of the educators to pay adequate attention to the different training levels can create imbalances and manpower bottlenecks. Professor Joseph Ganitsky B. of the Universidad de Los Andes in Bogotá, Colombia, remarked on this problem, "In Colombia we were training a good number of managers, but we discovered that there was not an adequate supply of foremen and supervisors. Therefore, the effectiveness of the top managers was severely limited by not having done a good enough job of training of lower level personnel."

A final value of the commodity systems approach for educators is that by delineating a multiplicity of needs for different types of personnel it can also serve as a stimulant and guide for pinpointing a multitude of educational approaches to meet these needs rather than relying exclusively on traditional formal training methods.

Structure

Given the systems perspective as the basic conceptual framework through which the educators should view their task, we must now examine exactly what the Central American fruit and vegetable educational delivery system is composed of. There are basically three components: (1) the educational producers; (2) the training vehicles; and (3) the recipients (Figure 5–3).

The Educational Producers. These are the training organizations and the supportive institutions behind these organizations. The Central American governments are key components of the delivery system through the operations of the ministries of agriculture and education, as well as other public

Figure 5-3. Fruit and Vegetable Educational Delivery System

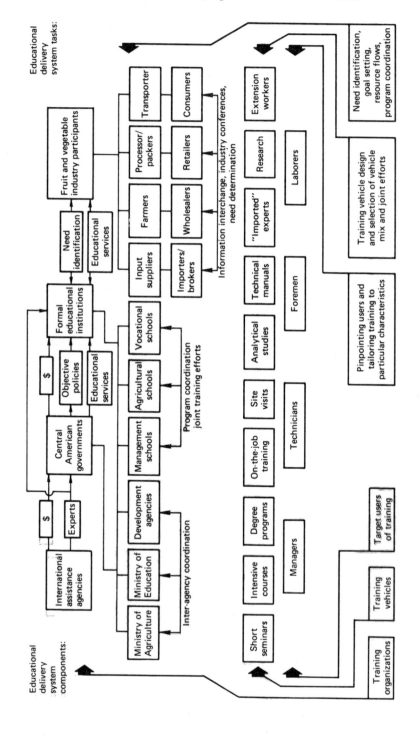

agencies, such as development banks and export centers involved in strengthening the agribusiness sector. These government agencies set policies and priorities for the agribusiness sector and it is critical that the educational programs be designed to meet the manpower requirements implicit in the agricultural and developmental objectives. In other words, interagency coordination of educational programs is essential to avoid gaps in the delivery system. Many of the government agencies provide direct assistance through their extension service which could be a contributing force for effective on-the-job training. Government agencies also engage in agronomic research.

The central government is also a supportive agent in the system because it is the major provider of financial resources to the country's educational institutions as well as the guiding force in setting forth educational objectives. However, these objectives and policies should be set mutually by the training institutions and the government so that objectives may be consistent with resources. Thus, governments have the dual role of being a provider of both direct training services and key supportive inputs. At the same time the government itself is a recipient of training services from other educational institutions.

Another set of supporting institutions are the various international assistance organizations that have, or could provide, useful input to the fruit and vegetable export industry. These inputs might be in the form of financial aid or technical assistance to the central governments or directly to educational institutions. Among the international agencies important to the industry are the following: PROMECA, the Central American Common Market Export Promotion Agency; the Central American Bank for Economic Integration (CABEI); the U. S. Agency for International Development, through both the local AID offices in each country and the Regional Office for Central America and Panama (ROCAP); the OAS–sponsored Inter-American Institute for Agricultural Sciences (IICA); ICAITI, the common market's Technical Research Institute; the World Bank; the Inter-American Development Bank; and the FAO. A coordinated and forceful effort by these institutions could provide the critical resources and impetus needed to strengthen the human resources of this industry.

The formal educational system is composed of schools of many different types, but for the fruit and vegetable industry the three primary types are management, agricultural, and vocational schools. These organizations have the capabilities, or can develop them, to provide much of the training needed by the industry. There are 15 public and private universities, of which two have graduate schools. In addition there are 10 postsecondary agricultural schools equivalent to junior colleges, 21 agricultural or vocational high schools, and 15 nondegree training centers. These 61 Central American institutions are listed in Appendix L, together with 11 in Panama. However, as was mentioned above, to be most effective these formal educational institutions will have to coordinate their training efforts to avoid gaps and take fuller advantage of their comparative advantages. Such system coordination could determine which institution should undertake what type of training and when joint efforts would be advisable.

For the schools to develop relevant programs they must be attuned, as we have stressed earlier, to the needs of the participants in the commodity system being served. Therefore, the fruit and vegetable industry members also play the critical role of providing feedback to the educational institutions as to their training needs and the relevance of current training efforts. Government agencies, banks, and other institutions that help integrate the system are also key participants in it, and therefore must also provide such feedback so that the system can best meet their needs. The industry participants can also serve as trainers, because they have the expertise of experience that when shared with other participants can help to strengthen the total system, which, in turn, will benefit the individual participants. The health of the industry is the responsibility of its members; the commodity system participants are both contributors to and recipients of the training services in the agribusiness educational delivery system.

Training Vehicles. The second basic component of the delivery system is the training vehicle that the educational institutions can employ to provide their training input. These include short seminars, intensive courses, degree programs, on-the-job training, site visits, analytical studies, and technical manuals. These vehicles are listed in Table 5–3 and will be discussed more extensively following this overview description of the educational delivery system. The task of the training institutions, both individually and by mutual consultation, is to determine which mix of vehicles should be used. In selecting this mix the costs and benefits of each vehicle should be examined individually in the light of the particular capacities of the training organizations and the characteristics of the end recipients of the training. This leads us to the final component in the delivery system.

Target Users. As we have mentioned, the four categories of recipients of the educational services that we have used in this study—managers, technicians, foremen, and laborers—do not reflect the diversity that exists among the levels of preparation and organizational structures of the various fruit and vegetable export projects. Consequently, it is critical that the design of each training service be tailored to the preparation and experience level of the recipients. In effect, the educational delivery system, like the commodity system, must be market oriented. Moreover, this delivery system is to a great extent self-regenerating, that is, many of the initial recipients of training services in turn become trainers as well as operators. A trained foreman, for example, can teach other foremen or the laborers; similarly, technicians, such as government extension workers, can teach foremen and laborers. Thus, as the industry grows, the internal capacity to develop its manpower resources will also increase.

Table 5–3. Educational Vehicles for Fruit and Vegetable Export Industry.

Vehicle	Personnel			
	Manager	*Technician*	*Foreman*	*Laborer*
Short seminars	Commodity systems approach Management systems design Operating techniques	Commodity systems approach Management systems design Operating techniques	Commodity systems approach Operating techniques	
Intensive courses	Management systems design Operating techniques	Operating techniques	Operating techniques	
Degree programs	Commodity systems approach Management systems design Operating techniques	Operating techniques	Operating techniques	
On-the-job-training		Operating techniques	Operating techniques	Operating techniques
Site visits	Commodity systems approach Management systems design Operating techniques	Commodity systems approach Management systems design Operating techniques		
Descriptive or analytical studies	Commodity systems approach	Commodity systems approach		
Technical manuals	Management systems design Operating techniques	Management systems design Operating techniques	Operating techniques	

Recommendations

The magnitude of the training task is large. In order to reach the export volume of 100 million pounds described in Chapter 2, based on the man-to-land ratios and improved man-to-yield ratios in the projects studied in this research, the fruit and vegetable export industry will need approximately 270 new farm managers, 390 new foremen, 200 new technicians, and 15,300 laborers. If the volume reaches the 500 million pounds estimated by the Central American Bank for Economic Integration, these manpower need estimates would probably triple. Given this need and the overview of the educational delivery system, we shall now set forth recommendations concerning which methods could be effective in providing a certain type of training to particular kinds of end users in the commodity system.

There are various types of training vehicles that could productively be employed; they are listed in Table 5–3, together with the four types of personnel toward which we would be directing our training effort. In each cell we have indicated which training needs could best be transmitted by that specific training vehicle to that particular personnel type.

Table 5–3 does not put a priority ranking on the relative appropriateness of the different types of vehicles, because we believe that effectiveness will often depend on the particular situation. Consequently, the individual educators and commodity-system participants can better select which vehicle would be best in their case. Similarly, we again remind the reader that our primary attention has been on the managers, and others more familiar with training at other levels may well be able to amplify and enrich our listings of training vehicles.

Skills in understanding and using the commodity systems approach are primarily needed at the top public and private managerial level, and these can be developed to some extent in short three to five-day seminars (Appendices O and P are included as examples of what issues such seminars might expect to address). These seminars can also be used to strengthen the abilities of managers to design management systems and understand their use; similarly, specific operating techniques can also be taught in such a short course. The seminars could employ case studies of fruit and vegetable export operations that would serve as a basis for meeting all three need categories. INCAE has developed several case studies that are concerned with the problem of the early efforts to export melons and cucumbers from Guatemala. These cases have been tested in a management seminar situation and have proved to be effective in achieving the goal of increasing the manager's skills in conceptualization, system design and use, and operating techniques. In addition to the cases, the seminars could employ a simulation model, computer based or not, of the fruit and vegetable system. Such a model could be developed with the data contained in the study and the students could be given exercises in planning and making operating decisions based on the manipulation of key variables. By altering the number of variables or changing external factors (such as damage by weather or disease or drops in market price), the exercises could be made to vary from relatively simple to highly complex.

One of the reasons for recommending short management seminars is that a prohibitively large investment of funds is not required to develop, organize, and implement them. The infant stage of development of the industry means that the actual numbers of managers in the fruit and vegetable export business and of those that have high potential interest in the industry are small. Consequently, a major outlay of funds would not be consistent with the size of the industry. The short duration of the seminar is important because prior research showed that most of the actual or potential industry managers can spare only small amounts of time from their other current businesses. The newness and the relatively small size of the fruit and vegetable export industry mean that most managers are not dedicated full time to those operations. We recommend that such a seminar be offered in each of the five Central American countries and that a sixth seminar be held to which would be invited educators, actual and prospective growers, exporters, suppliers, and importers from all the countries for the purpose of discussing common problems facing the industry and exploring means of collaboration. The experience of the Mexican fruit and vegetable grower organizations serves as a model or point of reference. Richardo Alfaro, melon exporter from El Salvador, stressed this need for cooperation in a recent conference: "We all must collaborate . . . government, educators, private industry. If we do so intelligently, we can have a major impact on the utilization of this industry."

Intensive courses of from two to six weeks could serve the same purpose as the short seminars and would allow a more thorough training than the seminars, especially for systems design and operating techniques. Nonetheless, the major limitations are the time required and the investment necessary to develop such a program. Whereas it would not be difficult to recruit 25 people in each country to attend a short seminar on fruit and vegetable export management, it might not be feasible to obtain 25 to 50 people to participate in a month-long course, given the industry's size and stage of development.

Another way to meet the managers' educational needs is to provide them with studies on the various aspects of the industry. For example, a draft of the present study was shown to several top managers. One, a high-level public-sector manager involved in fruit exports from Guatemala, commented, "After having read the analysis of the fruit and vegetable exports, we understood that what we had to do was to rid ourselves of the notion that we were supermen and that we knew it all." Similarly, a Honduran manager said, "The study revealed to us that 80 percent of our exports were sold for between $1 and $5 per box and this is hardly enough to cover shipping and marketing costs." In effect, the study demonstrated to him the need for an improved information and control system as well as providing useful operating information. Guillermo Medina Santos, president of the National Development Bank of Honduras, remarked about the draft of this study, "Already in their present shape and form the documents represent most valuable educational material for planners as well as top managers and technicians in charge of or associated with education and training programs in the field of agribusiness."

Another vehicle, which would be relatively inexpensive and of short duration but would have potentially high utility for the manager, is visits to the operations of on-going export projects. Such visits could be to farms, packing plants, transport facilities, customs offices, importer operations, and wholesale-retail outlets. These visits could help the manager get an overview of the actual system, see examples of management systems, and learn about specific operating techniques. Such visits could also increase the flow of information among the different participants in the system, thereby helping to diminish misunderstandings and to build the confidence essential to effective and efficient system coordination.

J. J. Liotta, manager of national produce buying for the Grand Union super market chain, made the following comment: "In the educational needs of the top managers, I would feel that if they had a fuller understanding of U. S. inspection grades and standards, as well as what the chain store expects of the given commodity, it would possibly save them needless financial loss in their picking, packing, and shipping operation." Currently, there is only informal and sporadic interchange of information between importers and exporters. We recommend that at least an annual visit be made by each side to the operating sites of the other. Much of the success of the Mexican exporters can be traced to the close links between the growers and their U. S. distributors. They exchange information frequently; in addition, the brokers often provide credit and technical assistance in packing and growing.

The seminars, courses, and visits are oriented toward meeting the short-run needs of industry. Yet the educational approach for the industry should look to the longer-run evolution of fruit and vegetable exports. This newly emerging industry will grow, and therefore it is important to prepare for its managerial needs in the future. This can be done by incorporating degree programs in administration and agriculture into existing undergraduate and graduate instruction. These programs will help provide the instruction in conceptual systems design, operating technique, and information analysis areas needed by future managers. This probably implies that the first step will be retraining through seminars, documents, or courses by visiting professors. One seminar was held in early 1973 for professors of the Central American agricultural schools to familiarize them with the systems approach to nontraditional fruit and vegetable exports. This seminar was organized, in great part, through the efforts of Ing. Edgar Leonel Ibarra, dean of the School of Agriculture of the University of Guatemala and key collaborator in the research presented herein. In these institutions the training process is slower and, of course, not exclusively for fruit and vegetable exports. The schools must put the requirements of this particular industry within the context of the needs of other areas, such as traditional crops. Priorities must be established when resources are scarce. In the case of fruits and vegetables such priorities should be assigned on the basis of relative potential importance, not just actual size; a $1 million export industry now could rise to $500 million by 1980.

The foregoing was dealt only with the vehicles to be employed to meet the manager's needs. For the technician some needs could also be met with short-term seminars or courses. The content of these seminars would be focused on operating techniques. The previous observations concerning magnitude, duration, time perspective, and priorities apply also to the technician-level seminar. In many cases the seminar will concentrate on reorienting the technician's existing skills to the peculiarities of fruit and vegetable production, packing, and export. Technical and procedural manuals would be another useful input. Site visits to those parts of the system in which the technician would be involved could also be very useful.

The future needs can also be addressed by integrating courses into the existing degree programs of agricultural and vocational schools that are oriented specifically to fruit and vegetable exports. The heavy orientation toward specific skills also means that on-the-job training should be employed, or at least field training should be a complement to the classroom sessions.

At the foreman level seminars and courses could be useful, but on-the-job training seems to be advisable because of the specific operating nature of the skills, including the use of management system procedures.

Similarly, the worker training should be almost exclusively at the work site, on the job. Learning by doing is the most efficient path to meeting the laborers' educational needs, except for those that refer to basic reading and writing skills which require more of a classroom environment. Training workers in these latter skills should also be of concern to the manager, both to upgrade the capability of his employees and to provide additional motivation and opportunity for their self-development.

Having delineated the types of educational instrument needed to meet most effectively the industry's needs, we now discuss which of the educational producers in the delivery system could act as the implementers of these educational activities. The choice depends on the content being taught, the recipients of the training, and the capabilities of the implementing institution or individual. In effect, the task now is to design an educational delivery system that balances the training needs of the fruit and vegetable industry with the capabilities of the different organizations that can provide training services to the industry. The essence of a systems approach to education is that the participants in that system be involved in the program design. Consequently, the suggestions in this section are put forth as a starting point for discussion among the several organizations that might form part of the educational delivery system.

For managers, a strong institution in Central America that could carry out the management seminar programs suggested could be INCAE (see Appendix L). This graduate business school already has a program of short seminars and intensive six-week courses. Managers from all of the Central American countries have participated in this program. Thus, a delivery system already exists, and it should probably be used to avoid the costly set-up effort for a similar program exclusively for the fruit and vegetables industry. Course development would still be necessary for INCAE, but, given the institute's capacities and its involvement in this research study, the task would be less for it than for another organization.

The participants in these seminars should include, if possible, managers from each of the stages in the system, that is, farmers, packer-exporters, transporters, brokers, and government policy-makers. This would provide a greater opportunity for understanding the different perspectives, needs, and problems of the system's participants and thus facilitate coordination, conceptualization, and management system design. Local chambers of commerce and universities also provide management training, and they might be used effectively to meet the managerial training needs of the fruit and vegetable industry.

Visits of producers and packers to the operations of the importers and vice versa would be another advisable vehicle for achieving this comprehensive overview and for removing some of the existing information bottlenecks that have created barriers and mistrust between exporters and importers. Such visits perhaps could be arranged by PROMECA, ROCAP, the importers or exporters themselves, or other involved institutions.

When we consider training managers to meet the medium-run needs of the industry, the spectrum of participating institutions should be broadened to include the degree-granting Central American agricultural schools from which will come many of the managers and technicians for the industry. This would probably require a change in program content and emphasis for most of the agricultural schools. Most of the curriculums place relatively little, if any, emphasis on administrative concepts or skills. The stress is on agronomic technical know-how, primarily at the production level rather than at the processing or commercialization stages. Generally, some courses do deal with certain management aspects. Appendix M presents the curriculum of the Escuela Agricola Panamericana, which is located in Zamorano, Honduras, and is one of the leading agricultural schools in Latin America. As can be seen, only about 10 percent of the curriculum is allocated to administrative training. However, the school has recently set up a special department for agricultural economics and administration, thus indicating a growing concern about management training.

When we move to the technician level, the seminars take on more of a technical than a managerial flavor, although the latter is still present. Probably the best implementing institutions would be the agricultural schools and productivity centers, although INCAE or other business administration schools should consider participating in such seminars in order to provide a mix of technical and administrative training. Agrochemical companies, packaging suppliers, and transport companies should also be approached to sponsor seminars on their services and products. In fact, in the past some of these organizations have sponsored conferences on air transportation, agrochemical application, and packaging techniques. These seminars could be sponsored by ICAITI, PROMECA, national export centers, international assistance agencies, or local development institutions. Importers could also play a major role here by providing instruction and training as to the quality requirements and packing techniques needed to compete effectively in the U. S. market.

In the existing degree programs at schools of agriculture, horticulture is studied but the emphasis is primarily on production, and the nontraditional export crops are not always dealt with. Appendix N presents a description of the horticulture course taught in Nicaragua's National Agricultural School. Greater stress on nontraditional crops would be helpful to budding technicians.

We have already stressed that for technicians and foremen, in addition to formal institutional training, on-the-job, field-oriented training is critical. To carry out such training we recommend that each country's government, in cooperation with the growers and exporters, bring in outside experts with practical fruit and vegetable export experience to serve as trainers of the foremen and technicians. Such talent should be available in Mexico and Belize, or from Cuban immigrants. Currently there is a scarcity of qualified, knowledgeable experts in Central America. A primary task of the imported experts should be to train locals in the requisite production, harvesting, handling, selection, and packing skills. These newly trained technicians and foremen would in turn train the workers in an on-the-job situation. Caution must be used to ensure that the techniques being taught by the imported experts are adapted to the environment and peculiarities of the producing zone.

The foregoing recommendations can serve, we believe, as a tentative blueprint for designing a detailed educational program that would help the budding Central American fruit and vegetable industry to develop the manpower capability needed to survive the difficulties of its infancy as well as to meet the requirements of rapid expansion. Nonetheless, in order to realize the possible benefits accruing from this research, it is vital that the potential participating training institutions, including the commodity system participants, be involved in the elaboration and refinement of an educational program for the industry. To this end we recommend an extensive dissemination of this study to these groups and a subsequent international conference in Central America to study the possible forms the educational effort could take to lay out a specific course of action for program implementation.

IMPLICATIONS FOR CENTRAL AMERICAN
AGRIBUSINESS EDUCATION

The recommendations in this chapter have primarily focused on agribusiness education for the Central American fruit and vegetable export industry. A basic principle in our systems approach to agribusiness education was that the form and content of the educational delivery system should be tailored to the needs of the particular commodity system being serviced. Accordingly, not all the analyses and recommendations for the fruit and vegetable industry are appropriate for the other commodity systems in the Central American agribusiness sector. Other commodities, for example, are more traditional, are in a more mature stage of development, are grown on a much larger scale, operate in government-regulated markets, are less perishable and fragile, and have year-round rather than seasonal markets. These differences and others mean that the problems and training needs of the agroindustries may be somewhat different from those of the fruit and vegetable system.

Nonetheless, many of the problems we identified in our commodity analysis of fruit and vegetable exports are also found in other commodity systems that we surveyed briefly during our research. The major problem areas that are shared by most of the commodity systems are: lack of trained agribusiness managers in the public and private sectors; absence of a commodity systems perspective in planning and managing agribusiness; inadequacy of management systems; information bottlenecks and faulty coordination among system participants; and ignorance of proper operating techniques. These deficiencies in part reflect the current state of agribusiness education in Central America, and point out the need for a broader educational effort to strengthen the human resources in the Central American agribusiness sector.

Given these common factors, we do have a basis for believing that many of the findings in the fruit and vegetable study are applicable at a more general level. However, in order to pinpoint more precisely the training needs of the rest of the agribusiness sector, it would be necessary to analyze the other major or high-potential commodity systems. We believe that the commodity systems research approach employed in this study is completely transferable to the task of identifying the problems and training needs of the rest of the commodity systems and to the job of designing the educational delivery system needed by the total agribusiness sector in Central America. We hope that the methodology of the study will provide a research framework for on-going efforts to maintain a feasible and relevant agribusiness educational system.

There are several recommendations for agribusiness education in Central America that stem from our previous analysis of the fruit and vegetable industry. These are put forth as suggestions to be discussed by the participants in the Central American agribusiness educational delivery system:

1. The organizations involved in agribusiness education and operations in the Central American countries should establish a coordinating committee for agribusiness education. The purpose of this committee would be to create a vehicle for promoting interinstitutional cooperation and coordination. The interaction among Central American institutions involved directly or indirectly in agribusiness education is currently sporadic and unsystematic. However, an underlying spirit of cooperation definitely exists. What is lacking is the organizational conduit to take advantage of this willingness to work together.[1] During recent conferences at Harvard to discuss this research project, the Central American educators also recommended that such a coordinating committee be established.

2. The specific composition and operating norms of this committee would depend on the desires of and constraints on the participating members. To organize such a committee we recommend the holding of a conference to be attended by educators, managers, and public officials of the leading agribusiness institutions in Central America as well as by representatives of international development agencies. The purpose would be to assess the current state of agribusiness education in Central America, to organize a coordinating committee, and to develop a course of action for inter-institutional cooperation. The idea is not to add another bureaucratic organization to the educational system but rather to find a means of using more efficiently and effectively the existing and potential agribusiness institutions. The additional recommendations that follow concern avenues of joint action that could occur via the committee.

3. Information and teaching materials could be exchanged. Much can be learned from studying the educational efforts of other training organizations. Economies can perhaps be achieved by making available existing teaching materials. Gaps in meeting the educational needs of the agribusiness sector can be better identified if we have a complete picture of the existing educational services being offered. INCAE is currently organizing a case clearing house for the interchange of case studies; the school has indicated that this vehicle could be expanded to include other types of information relevant to those groups interested in agribusiness education.

4. Programs should be coordinated so that the gaps identified above can be filled. The recently begun coordinated specialization of the countries' agricultural schools is a start in this direction.

5. Joint training programs could be established between universities or between departments within the same university. This is especially important in order to fuse administrative agronomic training so as to create efficient and effective agribusinesses. This need suggests the importance of closer cooperation between schools of agriculture and of business. In Mexico the employers of the graduates of the Instituto Technologico de Monterrey observed that the

business school graduates knew administrative techniques well but had difficulty applying them in the agribusiness context, and the agricultural school graduates had excellent technical agronomic training but were very weak in administration. Consequently, the school has set up a joint agribusiness program between the undergraduate business and agricultural schools. In a broader sense, we urge that the schools employ a commodity systems approach to agribusiness education.

6. Joint research projects are another area for fruitful collaboration. In fact, recommend that the management and agricultural schools jointly undertaken a series of studies applying the commodity systems approach to analyze the remaining major and high-potential commodity systems in Central America. Such studies could help strengthen systematically the total agribusiness education system and provide direct training assistance to the specific agroindustries. INCAE has already begun, in part, to pursue this recommendation by undertaking a study of the banana industry in Costa Rica. The Inter-Bank Coordinating Committee of Costa Rica has recommended that INCAE undertake such a study and then administer a training seminar to which participants from all levels of the system would be invited. Another high-priority commodity system in Central America that could be the focus of a joint research effort is the beef industry.

7. The underlying motives for the above-mentioned industry seminar reflect another need, namely, consulting services. The agribusiness sector in Central America is in need of assistance on both management and technical problems. This presents an excellent opportunity for the management and agricultural institutions to combine their expertise to provide necessary problem-solving consulting services to agribusiness organizations. It is quite probable that the human resources exist to implement such an inter-institutional consulting effort, but the vehicle for coordinating it is lacking.

8. The individual educational institutions should form agribusiness advisory committees composed of agribusiness managers from both public and private sectors. This committee can help ensure that the schools' educational programs are tied into the realities of the problems and needs of the agribusiness organizations. Committee members can help in student job placement and provide leads for research and consulting opportunities. This committee should also make periodic surveys of the school's graduates to determine the type of employment they are obtaining and the adequacy of the training they have received for the work they are doing. This can serve as a critical feedback from the marketplace to the educator so that training content can remain attuned to the realities of the problems and needs of the agribusiness sector. Such a survey should attempt to determine the quantitative as well as the qualitative demand for the school's graduates. The Escuela Agricola Panamericana has used this type of survey very effectively. INCAE has also

begun to implement this recommendation by forming an International Advisory Committee for Agribusiness Education.

9. Central American agribusiness institutions should attempt to establish linkages with other educational institutions outside of Central America both in developing countries and in the larger, more developed nations. These linkages can serve to enrich both the Central American agribusiness-education programs and those in other countries via a flow of teaching and research information and perhaps personnel. Opportunities for joint training, research, and consultation should also be explored via these linkages.

NOTES TO CHAPTER FIVE

1. The agricultural schools within the public universities in each of the Central American countries have agreed to specialize in certain areas and have formed a committee to coordinate their programs.

Chapter Six

Conclusions

As indicated at the beginning of this study, the purpose of this project is to provide a systems perspective as one useful approach to developing and making more relevant the formal and informal agribusiness educational teaching and research activities of Central American institutions. There were many reasons why we chose the fruit and vegetable sector as an example of an agribusiness commodity systems approach. These include its export potentials to the United States and its relation to a kind of agriculture that could make use of both small holdings of producers and large-scale operations. Even though it is a highly fragmented sector in both Central America and the United States, it demonstrates the interrelated and interdependent nature of all the functions that have to be performed in the system from input supplies and farming to processing and distribution. It also is illustrative of the need to develop, understand, and then utilize effectively all of the coordinating institutions and arrangements that hold the system together, including markets, contractual integration, vertical integration, cooperatives, government programs, special trade associations, unique financial and transportation arrangements, and so on. In essence, this interrelated and interdependent commodity sector is but one example of how decision-makers, labor, government policy-makers, and educators must take an interdisciplinary approach to agribusiness problems and opportunities.

To understand and make use of a systems approach one must: (1) systematically describe the agribusiness of the country and region, including its general environment and public policy priorities; (2) describe and analyze each dynamic sector of the agribusiness economy commodity by commodity; and (3) analyze specific case examples of problems of firms within the commodity system at an organizational level and relate these problems to the system of which each firm is a part. This threefold approach has been the organizational structure of this study. Obviously, owing to limitations of time and resources, each of these levels of description and analysis is only illustrative of the work yet to be done by other researchers in Central America and the United States. At the same time, this study indicates how necessary is cooperation among the educational, business, governmental, farming, and labor communities in order to do the research for this approach as well as to utilize it.

We recognized the need for the support of this project by government policy-makers, private decision-makers, and educators, both in Central America and the United States. Through interviews and meetings in both prior to undertaking the project and in the course of the project, we were encouraged to pursue it by participants in the system and by the managers of private and public institutions that help coordinate this system. In addition, many firms and private financial agencies have supplied us with confidential data that not only added to the description and analysis of the study, but also renewed interest on the part of the cooperators in the potential of the fruit and vegetable sector and in ways to improve the training of the men and women needed by this sector.

Participation in this project by those attending the meetings, and the written comments of those who could not attend, indicate that this approach seems to be accepted by all the groups involved in the study, and their very participation has begun to provide the interchange and change in perspective that were the original purposes of this study.

The present and future utility of this project would appear to be multifaceted. First, it provides a new perspective for the agribusiness educational institutions of Central America, both formal and informal, on-the-job training, industry seminars, and so forth. Second, it has produced a by-product in the creation of descriptions and analyses of fruit and vegetable commodity systems that, to our knowledge, have not existed before in Central America or the United States. Third, it has created a greater interchange than had existed before between a good many of the private and public agribusiness policy-makers in Central America, so that they are beginning to understand each other's needs and are finding specific ways to cooperate with one another. An agribusiness systems perspective and the specific information on the fruit and vegetable system of Central America and the United States appear to have already influenced the policies, operations, and investment decisions of a number of firms and institutions. Indicative of these new attitudes and new perspectives are statements received from a number of participants in conferences held at the Harvard Business School in 1972 and 1973. In each case, changes in operational, organizational, and firm and institutional perspectives have been influenced by this study. The help and cooperation of these types of agribusiness leaders in agribusiness education and research is most appreciated, but even more encouraging is their responsiveness to the use of the systems approach in meeting the changing needs of their domestic and international agribusiness economies. Similarly, educational leaders in Central America have already begun to develop various types of agribusiness courses and programs in their institutions and are having specialized short seminars on specific agribusiness problems and opportunities in horticulture and other areas.

In addition to these specific responses to the agribusiness commodity systems approach are the welcome exchanges from institutions that are already utilizing this market-oriented approach. One very important institution is the Latin American Agribusiness Development Corporation headed by Robert Ross. Mr. Ross has concentrated on the growth agribusiness industries in Latin America, such as beef, floriculture, aquaculture, and fruits and vegetables. In addition to financial aid, his organization has provided a means of linking producers in Central and Latin America to the United States. He has developed joint venture marketing agencies, owned 40 percent by the producers, 40 percent by the distributors, and 20 percent by LAAD. Through this ownership position LAAD has provided market information, market orientation, quality control, and a fair transfer price mechanism, as well as financial help. In many ways it also acts as an informal educational institution, training producers to be responsive to market needs and training distributors to provide feedback and incentives to producers as well as to understand the unique agronomic pressures that are faced by the producers. Similarly, transportation executives, in evaluating the needs of the agribusiness economy in Central America and the United States, have developed materials useful to the industry and to education, which they have made available. Also, in their investment proposals they have included a budget item not only for training their own and related personnel in Central America but also for holding seminars for potential users of their services.

In summary, as noted in Figure 1–8, there is a common perspective useful both to educators and to public and private managers in viewing the needs and opportunities available in a rapidly changing Central American and world agribusiness. This common perspective calls for an interdisciplinary approach that blends the business policy and functional educational approach of business and general educational colleges with agricultural economics and the technical, mechanical, agricultural, nutritional, and logistical disciplines of the agricultural and technical schools. This interdisciplinary approach must also take into consideration the importance of governmental activities. These activities not only include the setting of priorities, export and import policies, price policies, and nutritional policies, but also the governmental involvement in specific operational activities, from transportation and communication entities to marketing boards. These activities also include the important supportive roles of quality and grading rules and regulations, health standards, market news and information, and techniques, research, and education in production and marketing. With the changing nature of the world food situation, from one of market surpluses to one of very short supplies, governmental activities became even more important.

This interdisciplinary educational approach will call not only for changes in perspective in designing and teaching educational materials but also imaginative cross-fertilization of teaching programs and research by Central American educational institutions and entities.

A method for implementing this cooperation has already begun with the formation of an informal advisory group to utilize the agribusiness commodity systems approach in Central American agribusiness education. The group discussed and plans to implement the following topics:

1. The establishment of an agribusiness information center in Central America. This will collect case studies and cross-files of all published and unpublished information on Central American agribusiness. The cases developed in this project, together with the background material on Central America, are typical of the information to be gathered, together with the back-up sources for this study.
2. The development of an agribusiness survey of Central America. This survey will provide a descriptive and analytical base on which other research and teaching material may be developed. It will also provide a bench mark for measuring changes in the structure, organization, and operation of Central American agribusiness.
3. The development of commodity groups and associations to carry out more specific agribusiness commodity studies as suggested by this research project.
4. The development of liaisons with other agribusiness educational groups to eventually form a global agribusiness educational network.
5. The development of an advisory group to this agribusiness educational group that would represent business, governmental, and other academic entities that are involved in agribusiness in Central America.

The broadening of the perspective of private and public managers, educators, and workers in Central American agribusiness will also develop a different kind of human relation. It will be necessary not only to provide technical and perspective training but also some retraining in norms and values in order to effectively utilize the agribusiness commodity systems approach. Given training, workers will expect, and should receive, higher wages. It might be useful to consider programs in which managers, technicians, and foremen are trained together to allow them to learn not only the requirements of their own positions but also the patterns of relations necessary for the system to work well. Similarly, laborers and foremen might train together, especially as we are asking workers to assume more initiative and responsibility than they have in the past. Private and public managers, together with transportation people, brokers, and credit suppliers, should also have common educational experiences in order that the system may work as smoothly as possible. In addition, commercial training schools, national apprentice programs, and agricultural schools should develop joint programs to provide a truly agribusiness systems approach to education in Central America. Similarly, firms and institutions in the United States should work more closely with these institutions in supplying people, information, and training manuals to the academic institutions in Central America.

Finally, education and training programs, to be relevant for the participants in the new kinds of agribusinesses emerging in Central America, must be based on the best traditions of the past while utilizing the perspective of a commodity systems approach. This will enable educators to provide the participants not only with skills to carry out their responsibilities more effectively, but also with a vision of the new society into which they have been recruited.

Appendix A

Winter and Early Spring Fresh Produce, U.S. Grown and Imports 1960–1970

Table A-1. Tomatoes (10^5 lb.).[a]

Area and season	1960	1961	1962	1963	1964	1965	1966	1967	1968	1969	1970
Florida											
Winter	1,552	3,230	3,280	3,222	3,360	3,247	2,934	2,831	2,340	2,248	1,368
Early spring	2,195	2,360	2,294	2,440	2,520	2,691	3,125	3,218	2,840	2,606	2,178
California											
Early spring	710	718	525	504	400	429	232	273	320	444	434
Texas											
Early spring	580	897	1,026	452	307	368	108	128	80	150	195
Total U.S. winter and early spring	5,037	7,205	7,125	6,618	6,587	6,735	6,399	6,450	5,580	5,448	4,175
Mexican imports	2,518	1,561	2,332	2,400	2,461	2,655	3,587	3,624	3,874	4,462	6,410
Other imports	609	201	30	20	31	35	19	35	29	34	57

Sources: U. S. data compiled from *Vegetables for Fresh Market*, Statistical Bulletins 300 and 412, and *Vegetables—Fresh Markets*, Vg. 2–2 (70), (Statistical Reporting Service, U. S. Department of Agriculture). Mexican data from *Fruits and Vegetables, U. S. Imports from Mexico* (Foreign Agricultural Service, USDA, March 1971). Other data compiled from reports of the Bureau of the Census, U. S. Department of Commerce.

a. Production not marketed because economic abandonment has been excluded in the U. S. data.

Table A–2. Cucumbers (10^5 lb.).[a]

Area and season	1960	1961	1962	1963	1964	1965	1966	1967	1968	1969	1970
Florida											
Early spring	686	968	792	1,147	1,189	1,025	1,107	872	914	1,080	950
Texas											
Early spring	94	105	110	96	104	104	95	144	108	112	147
Total U.S. spring	780	1,073	902	1,243	1,293	1,129	1,202	1,016	1,022	1,192	1,097
Mexican imports	87	104	158	214	172	394	481	584	599	1,100	1,222
Other imports	574	339	432	398	342	364	233	281	175	248	211

Sources: U. S. data compiled from *Vegetables for Fresh Market*, Statistical Bulletins 300 and 412, and *Vegetables–Fresh Markets*, Vg. 2–2 (70), (Statistical Reporting Service, U. S. Department of Agriculture). Mexican data from *Fruits and Vegetables, U. S. Imports from Mexico* (Foreign Agricultural Service, USDA, March 1971). Other data compiled from reports of the Bureau of the Census, U. S. Department of Commerce.

a. Production not marketed because economic abandonment has been excluded in the U. S. data.

Table A–3. Peppers (10⁵ lb.).ᵃ

Table A–3. Peppers (10^5 lb.).[a]

Area and season	1960	1961	1962	1963	1964	1965	1966	1967	1968	1969	1970
Florida											
Winter	451	653	662	564	644	682	582	746	828	618	224
Spring	643	586	475	704	640	558	812	700	724	780	416
Texas											
Spring	84	105	68	108	120	120	63	150	77	126	126
Total U.S. winter and early spring	1,178	1,344	1,205	1,376	1,404	1,360	1,457	1,596	1,629	1,524	766
Mexican imports	222	129	173	162	131	177	246	278	244	407	639
Other imports	6	4	2	—	10	9	2	2	26	47	60

Sources: U. S. data compiled from *Vegetables for Fresh Market*, Statistical Bulletins 300 and 412, and *Vegetables—Fresh Markets*, Vg. 2–2 (70), (Statistical Reporting Service, U. S. Department of Agriculture). Mexican data from *Fruits and Vegetables*, *U. S. Imports from Mexico* (Foreign Agricultural Service, USDA, March 1971). Other data compiled from reports of the Bureau of the Census, U. S. Department of Commerce.

a. Production not marketed because economic abandonment has been excluded in the U. S. data.

Table A–4. Eggplant (10^5 lb.).[a]

Area and season	1960	1961	1962	1963	1964	1965	1966	1967	1968	1969	1970
Florida											
Winter	54	98	129	116	104	139	110	129	92	98	47
Spring	150	154	126	135	140	136	150	144	108	135	116
Total U.S. winter and spring	204	252	255	251	244	275	260	273	200	233	163
Mexican imports	18	19	21	27	34	44	57	72	104	178	216
Other imports	27	4	5	20	18	9	16	9	0	0	1

Sources: U. S. data compiled from *Vegetables for Fresh Market*, Statistical Bulletins 300 and 412, and *Vegetables—Fresh Markets*, Vg. 2–2 (70), (Statistical Reporting Service, U. S. Department of Agriculture). Mexican data from *Fruits and Vegetables, U. S. Imports from Mexico* (Foreign Agricultural Service, USDA, March 1971). Other data compiled from reports of the Bureau of the Census, U. S. Department of Commerce.

a. Production not marketed because economic abandonment has been excluded in the U. S. data.

Table A–5. Cantaloupes (10⁵ lb.).ᵃ

Area and season	1960	1961	1962	1963	1964	1965	1966	1967	1968	1969	1970
Florida Spring	72	75	68	77	88	120	90	90	70	72	84
Texas Spring	399	518	759	910	840	1,062	428	1,312	938	1,260	1,246
Arizona Spring	2,010	1,668	2,062	2,249	1,970	1,690	1,800	1,308	1,392	1,664	1,276
California Spring	1,188	988	1,068	942	550	611	912	1,175	1,441	1,852	1,120
Total U.S. spring	3,669	3,249	3,957	4,178	3,448	3,483	3,230	3,885	3,841	4,848	3,726
Mexican imports	793	796	978	1,104	1,301	1,465	1,365	1,172	721	1,183	1,478
Other imports	1	0	2	7	16	22	13	61	7	3	10

Sources: U. S. data compiled from *Vegetables for Fresh Market*, Statistical Bulletins 300 and 412, and *Vegetables—Fresh Markets*, Vg. 2–2 (70), (Statistical Reporting Service, U. S. Department of Agriculture). Mexican data from *Fruits and Vegetables, U. S. Imports from Mexico* (Foreign Agricultural Service, USDA, March 1971). Other data compiled from reports of the Bureau of the Census, U. S. Department of Commerce.

a. Production not marketed because economic abandonment has been excluded in the U. S. data.

Table A–6. Strawberries (10^5 lb.).[a]

Area and season	1960	1961	1962	1963	1964	1965	1966	1967	1968	1969	1970
Florida Winter	65	78	135	166	238	256	209	176	152	160	144
California Spring	858	1,325	1,435	1,540	1,411	1,047	1,173	1,481	2,132	2,024	2,154
Louisiana Early spring	138	128	146	78	154	143	145	116	109	78	84
Texas Early spring	24	33	31	24	24	20	20	15	13	12	10
Total U.S. winter and early spring	1,085	1,564	7	1,808	1,827	1,466	1,547	1,788	2,406	2,274	2,392
Mexican imports	6	6	9	34	41	58	117	205	263	442	490
Other imports	1	1	1	2	11	6	14	12	27	30	24

Sources: U. S. data compiled from *Vegetables for Fresh Market*, Statistical Bulletins 300 and 412, and *Vegetables–Fresh Markets*, Vg. 2–2 (70), (Statistical Reporting Service, U. S. Department of Agriculture). Mexican data from *Fruits and Vegetables, U. S. Imports from Mexico* (Foreign Agricultural Service, USDA, March 1971). Other data compiled from reports of the Bureau of the Census, U. S. Department of Commerce.

a. Production not marketed because economic abandonment has been excluded in the U. S. data.

Appendix B

Provisions of Federal and California Marketing Orders, Fruits and Vegetables, 1971–1972

Table B–1.   Provisions of Federal and California Marketing Orders, Fruits and Vegetables, 1971–1972.

Commodity	Grade, size, maturity, quality	Quantity marketed	Pack, container	Promotion, market research	Inspection
			Federal orders		
Florida oranges	x				
Florida grapefruit	x				
Florida tangerines	x				
Florida tangelos	x				
Texas oranges	x		x		
Texas grapefruit	x		x		
California–Arizona navel oranges	x	x			
California–Arizona valencia oranges	x	x			
California–Arizona desert grapefruit	x				
California–Arizona lemons	x	x			
Florida limes	x	x	x		
Indian River (Fla.) grapefruit		x			
Interior (Fla.) grapefruit		x			
Interior (Fla.) oranges		x			
Florida avocados	x		x		
California nectarines	x		x		
California tree fruits	x				
(Freestone peaches, plums, bartlett pears)					
Georgia peaches	x				
Colorado peaches	x				
Washington peaches	x		x		
Washington apricots	x		x		
Washington sweet cherries	x		x		
Washington–Oregon fresh prunes	x				
California tokay grapes	x		x		
Pacific Coast winter pears	x				
Papayas	x				
Cranberries		x			

Commodity	1	2	3	4	5	6
Red tart cherries					x	
Washington–Oregon bartlett pears	x	x	x			
California olives	x	x				x
Idaho–E. Oregon potatoes	x	x				
Washington potatoes	x	x				x
Oregon–California potatoes	x	x				
Colorado potatoes (San Luis Valley)	x	x				
Colorado potatoes (Area No. 3)	x	x				
Southeastern States potatoes	x	x				
Idaho–E. Oregon onions	x	x				
South Texas onions	x	x	x			
Florida tomatoes	x	x	x			
Florida celery	x	x	x		x	
South Texas lettuce	x	x			x	
California–Oregon walnuts	x	x			x	
California dried prunes	x	x		x	x	
Peanuts	x	x				
California raisins	x	x			x	
California almonds	x	x			x	
Washington–Oregon filberts	x	x			x	
California dates	x	x			x	

(Table B–1 cont'd next page)

Table B-1. (cont.)

Commodity	Grade, size, maturity, quality	Quantity marketed	Pack, container	Promotion, market research	Inspection
			California orders[a]		
California apples	x			x	
California early apples		x	x	x	x
California apricots				x	
California globe artichokes				x	
California avocados				x	
California dry beans	x			x	x
California lima beans	x	x		x	x
California bush berries for processing				x	
California brandy				x	
California dried figs	x	x		x	x
California desert grapefruit	x		x	x	x
California desert grapes	x	x	x		x
California extracted honey	x			x	
California dry-pack lettuce	x	x		x	
California cling peaches for processing	x			x	x
California clingstone peaches	x			x	
California fresh peaches	x		x	x	x
California fresh bartlett pears	x			x	x
California fresh fall and winter pears	x	x	x	x	x
California hardy pears for canning	x			x	
California dried prunes				x	
California raisins				x	
California brussels sprouts for freezing	x				x
California strawberries				x	
California strawberries for processing	x			x	x
California wine				x	

a. California Marketing Act of 1937.

Appendix C

**Tariff Schedules
of the United States**

TARIFF SCHEDULES OF THE UNITED STATES ANNOTATED (1972)

SCHEDULE 1. - ANIMAL AND VEGETABLE PRODUCTS
Part 8. - Vegetables

Item	Stat. Suf- fix	Articles	Units of Quantity	Rates of Duty	
				1	2
		PART 8. - VEGETABLES			
		Subpart A. - Vegetables, Fresh, Chilled, or Frozen			
		Subpart A headnotes:			
		1. In the assessment of duty on any kind of vegetables, any foreign matter or impurities mixed therewith shall not be segregated nor shall any allowance therefor be made.			
		2. For the purposes of item 137.25 in this part, if for any calendar year the production of white or Irish potatoes, including seed potatoes, in the United States, according to the estimate of the Department of Agriculture made as of September 1, is less than 21,000,000,000 pounds, an additional quantity of potatoes equal to the amount by which such estimated production is less than the said 21,000,000,000 pounds shall be added to the 45,000,000 pounds provided for in the said item 137.25 for the year beginning the following September 15. Potatoes, the product of Cuba, covered by item 137.25 or 137.26 shall not be charged against the quota quantity provided for in item 137.25.			

Item		Articles	Units	Rates of Duty 1	Rates of Duty 2
		Vegetables, fresh, chilled, or frozen (but not reduced in size nor otherwise prepared or preserved):			
		Beans:			
		Lima beans:			
135.10	00	If entered during the period from June 1 to October 31, inclusive, in any year	Lb	3.5¢ per lb.	3.5¢ per lb.
135.11	00	If products of Cuba		2.8¢ per lb. (s)	
135.12	00	If entered during November in any year	Lb	2.1¢ per lb.	3.5¢ per lb.
135.13	00	If products of Cuba		1.4¢ per lb. (s)	
135.14	00	If entered during the period from December 1 in any year to the following May 31, inclusive	Lb	2.34¢ per lb. (s)	3.5¢ per lb.
135.15	00	If products of Cuba		1.4¢ per lb.	
135.16	00	Other than lima beans	Lb	3.5¢ per lb.	3.5¢ per lb.
135.17	00	If products of Cuba		3.1¢ per lb. (s)	
135.20	00	Beets (not including sugar beets)	Lb	Free	17% ad val.
135.30	00	Cabbage	Lb	0.55¢ per lb.	2¢ per lb.
135.40	00	Carrots	Lb	6% ad val.	50% ad val.
		Cauliflower:			
135.50	00	If entered during the period from June 5 to October 15, inclusive, in any year	Lb	5.5% ad val.	50% ad val.
135.51	00	Other	Lb	12.5% ad val.	50% ad val.
		Celery:			
135.60	00	If imported and entered during the period from April 15 to July 31, inclusive, in any year	Lb	0.25¢ per lb.	2¢ per lb.
135.61	00	Other	Lb	1¢ per lb.	2¢ per lb.
135.70	00	Chickpeas or garbanzos	Lb	1¢ per lb.	2¢ per lb.
135.75	00	Corn-on-the-cob	Lb	25% ad val.	50% ad val.

(s) = Suspended.   See general headnote 3(b).

TARIFF SCHEDULES OF THE UNITED STATES ANNOTATED (1972)

SCHEDULE 1. - ANIMAL AND VEGETABLE PRODUCTS
Part 8. - Vegetables

Item	Stat. Suf-fix	Articles	Units of Quantity	Rates of Duty	
				1	2
		Vegetables, fresh, chilled, or frozen, etc. (con.):			
		Cowpeas:			
135.80	00	Black-eye....................	Lb......	3.5¢ per lb.	3.5¢ per lb.
135.81	00	Other.......................	Lb......	Free	Free
		Cucumbers:			
135.90	00	If entered during the period from December 1 in any year to the last day of the following February, inclusive...........	Lb......	2.2¢ per lb.	3¢ per lb.
135.91		If products of Cuba.........		1¢ per lb. (s)	
135.92	00	If entered during the period from March 1 to June 30, inclusive, or the period from September 1 to November 30, inclusive, in any year...	Lb......	3¢ per lb.	3¢ per lb.
135.93		If products of Cuba.........		2.4¢ per lb. (s)	
135.94	00	If entered during the period from July 1 to August 31, inclusive, in any year.........	Lb......	1.5¢ per lb.	3¢ per lb.
136.00	00	Dasheens.........................	Lb......	12.5% ad val.	50% ad val.
136.10	00	Endive, including Witloof chicory....	Lb......	0.15¢ per lb.	2¢ per lb.
		Eggplant:			
136.20	00	If entered during the period from April 1 to November 30, inclusive, in any year.....	Lb......	1.5¢ per lb.	1.5¢ per lb.
136.21		If products of Cuba.........		1.2¢ per lb. (s)	
136.22	00	Other.......................	Lb......	1.1¢ per lb.	1.5¢ per lb.
136.23		If product of Cuba.........		0.5¢ per lb. (s)	
136.30	00	Garlic...........................	Lb......	0.75¢ per lb.	1.5¢ per lb.
136.40	00	Horseradish......................	Lb......	1.1¢ per lb.	3¢ per lb.
136.50	00	Lentils..........................	Lb......	0.1¢ per lb.	0.5¢ per lb.
		Lettuce:			
136.60	00	If entered during the period from June 1 to October 31, inclusive, in any year.....	Lb......	0.4¢ per lb.	per lb.
136.61	00	Other.......................	Lb......	2¢ per lb.	2¢ per lb.

Item		Description	Unit	Rate (col. 2)	Rate (col. 1)
136.70	00	Lupines..	Lb......	0.25¢ per lb.	0.5¢ per lb.
136.80	00	Okra..	Lb......	25% ad val.	50% ad val.
136.81		If product of Cuba and entered during the period from December 1 in any year to the following May 31, inclusive...........	....	15% ad val. (s)	
		Onions:			
136.90	00	Onion sets..................................	Lb......	0.6¢ per lb.	2.5¢ per lb.
136.91	00	Other......................................	Lb......	1.75¢ per lb.	2.5¢ per lb.
		Peas:			
		If entered during the period from July 1 to September 30, inclusive, in any year:			
136.98	00	Fresh or chilled......................	Lb......	0.5¢ per lb.	3.9¢ per lb.
136.99	00	Frozen................................	Lb......	1¢ per lb.	3.9¢ per lb.
137.01	00	Other.................................	Lb......	2¢ per lb.	3.9¢ per lb.
137.10	00	Peppers:	Lb......	2.5¢ per lb.	2.5¢ per lb.
137.11	00	If products of Cuba..........................	....	2.2¢ per lb. (s)	
		Potatoes, white or Irish:			
		Seed, certified by a responsible officer or agency of a foreign government in accordance with official rules and regulations to have been grown and approved especially for use as seed, in containers marked with the foreign government's official certified seed potato tags:			
137.20	00	For not over 114,000,000 pounds entered during the 12-month period beginning September 15 in any year...............	Cwt......	37.5¢ per 100 lbs.	75¢ per 100 lbs.
137.21	00	Other.................................	Cwt......	75¢ per 100 lbs.	75¢ per 100 lbs.

(s) = Suspended. See general headnote 3(b).

TARIFF SCHEDULES OF THE UNITED STATES ANNOTATED (1972)

SCHEDULE 1. - ANIMAL AND VEGETABLE PRODUCTS
Part 8. - Vegetables

Item	Stat. Suffix	Articles	Units of Quantity	Rates of Duty	
				1	2
137.25	00	Vegetables, fresh, chilled, or frozen, etc. (con.): Potatoes, white or Irish (con.): Other than such certified seed: For not over 45,000,000 pounds and such additional quantity as may be allowed pursuant to headnote 2 of this part, entered during the 12-month period beginning September 15 in any year....	Cwt......	37.5¢ per 100 lbs.	75¢ per 100 lbs.
137.26	00	If products of Cuba and entered during the period from December 1 in any year to the last day of the following February, both dates inclusive.	....	30¢ per 100 lbs. (s)	
137.28 137.29	00	Other........ If products of Cuba and entered during the period from December 1 in any year to the last day of the following February, both dates inclusive.	Cwt......	30¢ per 100 lbs. (s) 75¢ per 100 lbs.	75¢ per 100 lbs.
137.40 137.50 137.51	00 00	Radishes........ Squash........ If product of Cuba........	Lb..... Lb.....	30¢ per 100 lbs. (s) 6% ad val. 1.1¢ per lb. 0.8¢ per lb. (s)	50% ad val. 2¢ per lb.
137.60	00	Tomatoes: If entered during the period from March 1 to July 14, inclusive, or the period from September 1 to November 14, inclusive, in any year........	Lb.....	2.1¢ per lb. 1.8¢ per lb. (s)	3¢ per lb.
137.61 137.62	00	If products of Cuba........ If entered during the period from July 15 to August 31, inclusive, in any year........	.... Lb.....	1.5¢ per lb.	3¢ per lb.

Item		Description	Unit		
137.63	00	If entered during the period from November 15, in any year, to the last day of the following February, inclusive............	Lb......	1.5¢ per lb.	3¢ per lb.
137.64	00	If products of Cuba........		1.2¢ per lb. (s)	
137.66	00	Turnips or rutabagas........................	Cwt.....	Free	25¢ per 100 lbs.
		Other:			
137.75	00	Chayote (Sechium edule)................	Lb......	12.5% ad val.	50% ad val.
137.80	00	Parsnips............................	Lb......	12.5% ad val.	50% ad val.
137.85	00	Other.............................	Lb......	25% ad val.	50% ad val.
138.00	00	Vegetables, fresh, chilled, or frozen, and cut, sliced, or otherwise reduced in size (but not otherwise prepared or preserved)............	Lb......	17.5% ad val.	35% ad val.

(s) = Suspended. See general headnote 3(b).

TARIFF SCHEDULES OF THE UNITED STATES ANNOTATED (1972)

SCHEDULE 1. - ANIMAL AND VEGETABLE PRODUCTS
Part 8. - Vegetables

Item	Stat. Suf- fix	Articles	Units of Quantity	Rates of Duty	
				1	2
		Subpart B. - Vegetables, Dried, Desiccated, or Dehydrated			
		Vegetables, dried, desiccated, or dehydrated, whether or not reduced in size or reduced to flour (but not otherwise prepared or preserved):			
		Dried, desiccated, or dehydrated:			
		Beans:			
		If entered for consumption during the period from May 1 to August 31, inclusive, in any year:			
140.09	00	Mung..................	Lb........	0.6¢ per lb.	3¢ per lb.
140.10	00	Red kidney............	Lb........	1¢ per lb.	3¢ per lb.
140.11	00	Other.................	Lb........	0.75¢ per lb.	3¢ per lb.
		If entered for consumption outside the above-stated period, or if withdrawn for consumption at any time:			
140.14	00	Mung..................	Lb........	1.2¢ per lb.	3¢ per lb.
140.16	00	Other.................	Lb........	1.5¢ per lb.	3¢ per lb.
		Chickpeas or garbanzos:			
140.20	00	Split.................	Lb........	1.2¢ per lb.	2.5¢ per lb.
140.21	00	Other.................	Lb........	1.4¢ per lb.	1.75¢ per lb.
		Cowpeas:			
140.25	00	Black-eye.............	Lb........	0.37¢ per lb.	3¢ per lb.
140.26	00	Other.................	Lb........	Free	Free
140.30	00	Garlic................	Lb........	35% ad val.	35% ad val.
140.35	00	Lentils...............	Lb........	0.15¢ per lb.	0.5¢ per lb.

140.38	00	Lupines	Lb.	0.15¢ per lb.	0.5¢ per lb.
140.40	00	Onions	Lb.	35% ad val.	35% ad val.
		Peas:			
140.45	00	Split	Lb.	0.4¢ per lb.	2.5¢ per lb.
140.46	00	Other	Lb.	0.4¢ per lb.	1.75¢ per lb.
140.50	00	Potatoes	Lb.	1.3¢ per lb.	2.75¢ per lb.
140.55	00	Other	Lb.	13% ad val.	35% ad val.
		Reduced to flour:			
140.60	00	Garlic	Lb.	35% ad val.	35% ad val.
140.65	00	Onions	Lb.	35% ad val.	35% ad val.
140.70	00	Potatoes	Lb.	1.2¢ per lb.	2.5¢ per lb.
140.75	00	Other	Lb.	13% ad val.	35% ad val.

TARIFF SCHEDULES OF THE UNITED STATES ANNOTATED (1972)

SCHEDULE 1. - ANIMAL AND VEGETABLE PRODUCTS
Part 8. - Vegetables

Item	Stat. Suf- fix	Articles	Units of Quantity	Rates of Duty	
				1	2
		Subpart C. - Vegetables, Packed in Salt, in Brine, Pickled, or Otherwise Prepared or Preserved			
		Subpart C headnotes:			
		1. For the purposes of this subpart -- (a) the term "in brine" means provisionally preserved by packing in a preservative liquid solution such as water impregnated with salt or sulphur dioxide, but not specially prepared for immediate consumption; and (b) the term "pickled" means prepared or preserved in vinegar or acetic acid whether or not packed in oil or containing sugar, salt, or spices.			
		2. Candied, crystallized, or glacé vegetables are covered in part 9 of schedule 1.			
		Vegetables (whether or not reduced in size), packed in salt, in brine, pickled, or otherwise prepared or preserved (except vegetables in subpart B of this part): Beans:			

Item		Description	Unit		
141.05	00	Soybeans	Lb.	8.5% ad val.	35% ad val.
		Other:			
141.10	00	In brine or packed in salt	Lb.	0.7¢ per lb.	3¢ per lb.
141.15	00	Pickled	Lb.	9% ad val.	35% ad val.
141.20	00	Other	Lb.	3¢ per lb. on entire contents of container	3¢ per lb. on entire contents of container
141.21		If products of Cuba	....	2.4¢ per lb. on entire contents of container (s)	
		Cabbage:			
141.25	00	Sauerkraut	Lb.	7.5% ad val.	50% ad val.
141.30	00	Other	Lb.	8.5% ad val.	35% ad val.
141.35	00	Chickpeas or garbanzos	Lb.	0.75¢ per lb. on entire contents of container	2¢ per lb. on entire contents of container
141.40	00	Black-eye cowpeas	Lb.	1.5¢ per lb. on entire contents of container	3¢ per lb. on entire contents of container
		Onions:			
141.45	00	Packed in salt, in brine, or pickled	Lb.	8% ad val.	35% ad val.
141.50	00	Other	Lb.	17.5% ad val.	35% ad val.
141.55	00	Peas	Lb.	1¢ per lb. on entire contents of container	2¢ per lb. on entire contents of container
141.60	20	Pimientos	lb.	4.8¢ per lb.	6¢ per lb.
		In containers holding 8 oz. or less	*lb.*		
	40	*Other*	*lb.*		
141.61		If products of Cuba	....	3.6¢ per lb. (s)	
		Tomatoes:			
141.65	00	Paste and sauce	Lb.	13.6% ad val.	50% ad val.
141.66	00	Other	Lb.	14.7% ad val.	50% ad val.
141.70	00	Waterchestnuts	Lb.	17.5% ad val.	35% ad val.
		Other:			
141.75		Packed in salt, in brine, or pickled	Lb.	12% ad val.	35% ad val.
	20	*Artichokes*	*lb.*		
	40	*Other*	*lb.*		
		Other:			
141.79	00	Palm hearts	Lb.	8.5% ad val.	35% ad val.
141.81		Other	....	17.5% ad val.	35% ad val.
	20	*Artichokes*	*lb.*		
	40	*Asparagus*	*lb.*		
	60	*Other*	*lb.*		

(s) = Suspended. See general headnote 3(b).

TARIFF SCHEDULES OF THE UNITED STATES ANNOTATED (1972)

SCHEDULE 1. - ANIMAL AND VEGETABLE PRODUCTS
Part 8. - Vegetables

Item	Stat. Suf-fix	Articles	Units of Quantity	Rates of Duty 1	Rates of Duty 2
		Subpart D. - Mushrooms and Truffles			
		Mushrooms, fresh, or dried, or otherwise prepared or preserved:			
144.10	00	Fresh...	Lb......	5¢ per lb. + 25% ad val.	10¢ per lb. + 45% ad val.
144.12	00	Dried..	Lb......	3.2¢ per lb. + 10% ad val.	10¢ per lb. + 45% ad val.
144.20		Otherwise prepared or preserved......................	....	3.2¢ per lb. on drained weight + 10% ad val.	10¢ per lb. on drained weight + 45% ad val.
		In containers each holding not more than 9 ounces:			
	10	Whole (including buttons).........................	Lb.		
	20	Sliced...	Lb.		
	30	Other..	Lb.		
		In containers each holding more than 9 ounces:			
	40	Whole (including buttons).........................	Lb.		
	50	Sliced...	Lb.		
	60	Other..	Lb.		
144.30	00	Truffles, fresh, or dried, or otherwise prepared or preserved..	Lb......	Free	Free

TARIFF SCHEDULES OF THE UNITED STATES ANNOTATED (1972)

SCHEDULE 1. - ANIMAL AND VEGETABLE PRODUCTS
Part 9. - Edible Nuts and Fruits

Item	Stat. Suf- fix	Articles	Units of Quantity	Rates of Duty 1	Rates of Duty 2
		PART 9. - EDIBLE NUTS AND FRUITS			
		Part 9 headnote:			
		1. This part covers only edible products.			
		Subpart A. - Edible Nuts			
		Subpart A headnotes:			
		1. No allowance shall be made for dirt or other impurities in nuts of any kind, shelled or not shelled.			
		2. The provisions for prepared or preserved nuts include nut pastes and nut butters but do not include candied, crystallized, or glacé nuts (see subpart D of this part).			
		Chestnuts, including marrons, crude, or prepared or preserved:			
145.01	00	Crude, or peeled, dried, or baked..........	Lb......	Free	Free
145.02	00	Otherwise prepared or preserved..........	Lb......	3.5¢ per lb.	25¢ per lb.

145.04	00	Coconuts..	No......	Free	0.5¢ each
145.07	00	Coconut meat (except copra), fresh, desiccated, or otherwise prepared or preserved: Fresh or frozen, whether or not shredded, grated, or similarly prepared, and whether or not sweetened with not over 10 percent by weight of sugar, but not otherwise prepared or preserved.......	Lb......	Free	2.2¢ per lb.
145.08	00	Shredded and desiccated, or similarly prepared.....	Lb......	1¢ per lb.	3.5¢ per lb.
145.09	00	Otherwise prepared or preserved........	Lb......	10% ad val.	20% ad val.

TARIFF SCHEDULES OF THE UNITED STATES ANNOTATED (1972)

SCHEDULE 1. - ANIMAL AND VEGETABLE PRODUCTS
Part 9. - Edible Nuts and Fruits

Item	Stat. Suf-fix	Articles	Units of Quantity	Rates of Duty 1	Rates of Duty 2
		Other edible nuts, shelled or not shelled, blanched, or otherwise prepared or preserved:			
		Not shelled:			
145.12	00	Almonds..................	Lb......	5.5¢ per lb.	5.5¢ per lb.
145.14	00	Brazil nuts..............	Lb......	Free	1.5¢ per lb.
145.16	00	Cashews..................	Lb......	Free	2¢ per lb.
145.18	00	Filberts.................	Lb......	5¢ per lb.	5¢ per lb.
145.20	00	Peanuts 1/...............	Lb......	5¢ per lb.	4.25¢ per lb.
		If products of Cuba 1/		3.4¢ per lb. (s)	4.25¢ per lb. (s)
145.21	00	Pecans...................	Lb......	5¢ per lb.	5¢ per lb.
145.22	00	Pignolia.................	Lb......	0.7¢ per lb.	2.5¢ per lb.
145.24	00	Pistache.................	Lb......	0.45¢ per lb.	2.5¢ per lb.
145.26	00	Walnuts..................	Lb......	5¢ per lb.	5¢ per lb.
145.28	00	Other....................	Lb......	2.5¢ per lb.	2.5¢ per lb.
145.30	00				
		Shelled, blanched, or otherwise prepared or preserved:			
		Almonds:			
145.40	00	Shelled..............	Lb......	16.5¢ per lb.	16.5¢ per lb.
145.41	00	Other................	Lb......	18.5¢ per lb.	18.5¢ per lb.
145.42	00	Brazil nuts..............	Lb......	Free	4.5¢ per lb.
145.44	00	Cashews..................	Lb......	Free	2¢ per lb.
145.46	00	Filberts.................	Lb......	8¢ per lb.	10¢ per lb.
145.48	00	Peanuts 1/...............	Lb......	7¢ per lb.	7¢ per lb.
	40	*Peanut butter.*	*Lb.*		
	70	*Other.*	*Lb.*		
		If peanut butter the product of Cuba....		5.6¢ per lb. (s)	
145.49	00	Pecans...................	Lb......	10¢ per lb.	10¢ per lb.
145.50	00	Pignolia.................	Lb......	1¢ per lb.	5¢ per lb.
145.52	00	Pistache.................	Lb......	1¢ per lb.	5¢ per lb.
145.53	00				

Item		Description	Unit	Rate 1	Rate 2
145.54	00	Walnuts: Pickled, immature walnuts..............	Lb.......	5¢ per lb.	15¢ per lb.
145.55	00	Other..........................	Lb.......	15¢ per lb.	15¢ per lb.
		Other edible nuts:			
145.58	00	Shelled or blanched..............	Lb.......	5¢ per lb.	5¢ per lb.
145.60	00	Other........................	Lb.......	28% ad val.	35% ad val.
145.90	00	Mixtures of two or more kinds of edible nuts.............	Lb.......	The highest rate applicable to any of the component nuts	The highest rate applicable to any of the component nuts

(s) = Suspended. See general headnote 3(b).

1/ Imports of peanuts (except peanut butter) are subject to additional import restrictions. See item 951.00 in part 3, Appendix to Tariff Schedules.

TARIFF SCHEDULES OF THE UNITED STATES ANNOTATED (1972)

SCHEDULE 1. - ANIMAL AND VEGETABLE PRODUCTS
Part 9. - Edible Nuts and Fruits

Item	Stat. Suf- fix	Articles	Units of Quantity	Rates of Duty	
				1	2
		Subpart B. - Edible Fruits			
		Subpart B headnote			
		1. For the purposes of this part -- (a) the term "fresh" covers fruit crude or in its natural state, whether green (immature) or ripe, and whether or not chilled (but not frozen), and includes fruit notwithstanding the use of nonpreservative coloring or other matter to maintain or improve its appearance; (b) the term "dried" means dried, desiccated, or evaporated; (c) the term "in brine" means provisionally preserved by packing in a preservative liquid solution such as water impregnated with salt or sulphur dioxide, but not specially prepared for immediate consumption; (d) the term "pickled" means prepared or pre- served in vinegar or acetic acid whether or not packed in oil or containing sugar, salt, or spices; and (e) the term "prepared or preserved" covers fruit which is dried, in brine, pickled, frozen, or otherwise prepared or preserved, but does not cover fruit juices (see part 12A of this schedule), or fruit flours, peels, pastes, pulps, jellies, jams, marmalades, or butters (see subpart C of this part), or candied, crystallized, or glacé fruits (see subpart D of this part).			

146.10	00	Apples, fresh, or prepared or preserved: Fresh..........................	Lb.......	Free	0.5¢ per lb.
146.12	00	Dried..............................	Lb.......	0.75¢ per lb.	2¢ per lb.
146.14	00	Otherwise prepared or preserved........	Lb.......	0.5¢ per lb.	2.5¢ per lb.
146.20	00	Apricots, fresh, or prepared or preserved: Fresh or in brine................	Lb.......	0.2¢ per lb.	0.5¢ per lb.
146.22	00	Dried..............................	Lb.......	1¢ per lb.	2¢ per lb.
146.24	00	Otherwise prepared or preserved........	Lb.......	35% ad val.	35% ad val.
146.30	00	Avocados (alligator pears), fresh, or prepared or preserved........................	Lb.......	7.5¢ per lb.	15¢ per lb.
146.31		If products of Cuba...........	....	Free (s)	
146.40	00	Bananas, fresh, or prepared or preserved: Fresh..............................	Lb.......	Free	Free
146.42	00	Dried..............................	Lb.......	3.5% ad val.	35% ad val.
146.44	00	Otherwise prepared or preserved........	Lb.......	7.5% ad val.	35% ad val.

(s) = Suspended. See general headnote 3(b).

TARIFF SCHEDULES OF THE UNITED STATES ANNOTATED (1972)

SCHEDULE 1. - ANIMAL AND VEGETABLE PRODUCTS
Part 9. - Edible Nuts and Fruits

Item	Stat. Suf- fix	Articles	Units of Quantity	Rates of Duty 1	Rates of Duty 2
		Berries, fresh, or prepared or preserved:			
		Fresh or in brine:			
146.50	00	Blueberries................	Lb......	0.3¢ per lb.	1.25¢ per lb.
146.52	00	Lingon or partridge berries........	Lb......	Free	1.25¢ per lb.
		Loganberries and raspberries:			
		If entered during the period from July 1 to August 31, inclusive,			
146.54	00	in any year........	Lb......	Free	1.25¢ per lb.
146.56	00	If entered at any other time......	Lb......	0.3¢ per lb.	1.25¢ per lb.
		Strawberries:			
		If entered during the period from June 15 to September 15,			
146.58	00	inclusive, in any year........	Lb......	0.2¢ per lb.	1.25¢ per lb.
146.60	00	If entered at any other time......	Lb......	0.75¢ per lb.	1.25¢ per lb.
146.62	00	Other berries........	Lb......	Free	1.25¢ per lb.
		Dried:			
146.64	00	Barberries........	Lb......	2.5¢ per lb.	2.5¢ per lb.
146.66	00	Other........	Lb......	1¢ per lb.	2.5¢ per lb.
		Otherwise prepared or preserved:			
		Blueberries:			
146.68	00	Frozen........	Lb......	3% ad val.	35% ad val.
146.70	00	Other........	Lb......	3.5% ad val.	35% ad val.
146.73	00	Black currants, gooseberries, lingon or partridge berries, and loganberries........	Lb......	7% ad val.	35% ad val.
146.75		Other berries........	......	14% ad val.	35% ad val.
	20	*Strawberries, frozen*........	*Lb.*		
	40	*Other*........	*Lb.*		
146.80	00	Cashew apples, mameyes colorados, sapodillas, sour-sops, and sweetsops, fresh, or prepared or pre-served........	Lb......	7% ad val.	35% ad val.

Item		Description	Unit		
146.90	00	Cherries, fresh, or prepared or preserved: Fresh: Not in airtight or watertight containers...	Lb.......	0.2¢ per lb.	2¢ per lb.
146.91	00	In airtight or watertight containers...	Lb.......	1¢ per lb.	2¢ per lb.
146.93	00	Dried...	Lb.......	6¢ per lb.	6¢ per lb.
146.95	00	In brine: With pits...	Lb.......	5.5¢ per lb.	5.5¢ per lb.
146.96	00	With pits removed...	Lb.......	9.5¢ per lb.	9.5¢ per lb.
146.97	00	Frozen...	Lb.......	3.5¢ per lb. + 5% ad val.	9.5¢ per lb. + 40% ad val.
146.99	00	Otherwise prepared or preserved...	Lb.......	7¢ per lb. + 10% ad val.	9.5¢ per lb. + 40% ad val.
		Citrus fruits, fresh, or prepared or preserved: Citrons:			
147.00	00	Fresh, dried, or in brine...	Lb.......	Free	Free
147.02	00	Otherwise prepared or preserved...	Lb.......	1.7¢ per lb.	6¢ per lb.
147.10	00	Grapefruit: If entered during the period from August 1 to September 30, inclusive, in any year...	Lb.......	1¢ per lb.	1.5¢ per lb.
147.11		If product of Cuba...	Lb.......	0.3¢ per lb. (s)	
147.13	00	If entered during the month of October...	Lb.......	0.8¢ per lb.	1.5¢ per lb.
147.14		If product of Cuba...	....	0.6¢ per lb. (s)	
147.16		If entered during the period from November 1, in any year, to the following July 31, inclusive...	Lb.......	1.3¢ per lb.	1.5¢ per lb.
147.17	00	If product of Cuba...	....	1.2¢ per lb. (s)	
147.19	00	Lemons: Fresh...	Lb.......	1.25¢ per lb.	2.5¢ per lb.
147.21	00	Prepared or preserved...	Lb.......	0.6¢ per lb.	2.5¢ per lb.
147.22	00	Limes: Fresh or in brine...	Lb.......	1¢ per lb.	2¢ per lb.
147.23		If products of Cuba...	.;	0.8¢ per lb. (s)	
147.26	00	Otherwise prepared or preserved...	Lb.......	17.5% ad val.	35% ad val.
147.27		If products of Cuba...	....	14% ad val. (s)	

(s) = Suspended. See general headnote 3(b).

TARIFF SCHEDULES OF THE UNITED STATES ANNOTATED (1972)

SCHEDULE 1. - ANIMAL AND VEGETABLE PRODUCTS

Part 9. - Edible Nuts and Fruits

Item	Stat. Suf-fix	Articles	Units of Quantity	Rates of Duty 1	Rates of Duty 2
		Citrus fruits, fresh, or prepared or preserved (con.):			
		Oranges:			
147.29	00	Mandarin, packed in airtight containers	Lb	0.2¢ per lb.	1¢ per lb.
147.30	00	Kumquats, packed in airtight containers	Lb	0.5¢ per lb.	1¢ per lb.
147.31	00	Other	Lb	1¢ per lb.	1¢ per lb.
147.32		If products of Cuba		0.8¢ per lb. (s)	
		Other citrus fruits:			
147.33	00	Fresh	Lb	8.5¢ ad val.	35% ad val.
147.36	00	Prepared or preserved	Lb	35% ad val.	35% ad val.
147.37		If products of Cuba		14% ad val. (s)	
		Dates, fresh, or prepared or preserved:			
		Fresh or dried:			
		With pits:			
		Packed in units weighing (with the immediate container, if any) not more than 10 pounds each			
147.40	00		Lb	7.5¢ per lb.	7.5¢ per lb.
147.42	00	Other	Lb	1¢ per lb.	1¢ per lb.
		With pits removed:			
		Packed in units weighing (with the immediate container, if any) not more than 10 pounds each			
147.44	00		Lb	7.5¢ per lb.	7.5¢ per lb.
147.46	00	Other	Lb	2¢ per lb.	2¢ per lb.
147.48	00	Otherwise prepared or preserved	Lb	35% ad val.	35% ad val.
		Figs, fresh, or prepared or preserved:			
147.50	00	Fresh or in brine	Lb	1.5¢ per lb.	5¢ per lb.
		Dried:			
147.51	00	In immediate containers weighing with their contents over 1 pound each	Lb	4.5¢ per lb.	5¢ per lb.
147.53	00	Other	Lb	3.5¢ per lb.	5¢ per lb.
147.54	00	Otherwise prepared or preserved	Lb	12% ad val.	40% ad val.

		Grapes, fresh, or prepared or preserved: Fresh (in bulk, or in crates, barrels or other packages):			
147.60	00	Hothouse............................	Cu. ft.v Lb.	6¢ per cu. ft. of such bulk or the ca- pacity of the package	25¢ per cu. ft. of such bulk or the ca- pacity of the package
		Other than hothouse: If entered during the period from February 15 to March 31, inclusive,			
147.61	00	in any year........................	Cu. ft.v Lb.	5.25¢ per cu. ft. of such bulk or the ca- pacity of the package	25¢ per cu. ft. of such bulk or the ca- pacity of the package
		If entered during the period from April 1 to June 30, inclusive,			
147.63	00	in any year........................	Cu. ft.v Lb.	Free	25¢ per cu. ft. of such bulk or the ca- pacity of the package
147.64	00	If entered at any other time........	Cu. ft.v Lb.	6¢ per cu. ft. of such bulk or the ca- pacity of the package	25¢ per cu. ft. of such bulk or the ca- pacity of the package
		Dried: Raisins: Made from seedless grapes:			
147.66	00	Currants........................	Lb......	1¢ per lb.	2¢ per lb.
147.68	00	Sultana.........................	Lb......	1¢ per lb.	2¢ per lb.
147.70	00	Other...........................	Lb......	1¢ per lb.	2¢ per lb.
147.72	00	Other raisins.......................	Lb......	2¢ per lb.	2¢ per lb.
147.75	00	Other dried grapes..................	Lb......	2.5¢ per lb.	2.5¢ per lb.
147.77	00	Otherwise prepared or preserved.....	Lb......	17.5% ad val.	35% ad val.
147.78	00	If products of Cuba.................	....	14% ad val. (s)	

(s) = Suspended. See general headnote 3(b).

TARIFF SCHEDULES OF THE UNITED STATES ANNOTATED (1972)

SCHEDULE 1. - ANIMAL AND VEGETABLE PRODUCTS
Part 9. - Edible Nuts and Fruits

Item	Stat. Suf- fix	Articles	Units of Quantity	Rates of Duty 1	Rates of Duty 2
		Guavas, fresh, or prepared or preserved:			
147.80	00	Fresh, dried, in brine, or pickled............	Lb......	7% ad val.	35% ad val.
147.85	00	Otherwise prepared or preserved............	Lb......	4% ad val.	35% ad val.
147.90	00	Mangoes, fresh, or prepared or preserved............	Lb......	3.75¢ per lb.	15¢ per lb.
147.91		If products of Cuba............	......	3¢ per lb. (s)	
		Melons, fresh, or prepared or preserved:			
		Fresh:			
		Cantaloupes:			
148.10	00	If entered during the period from August 1 to September 15, inclusive, in any year............	Lb......	20% ad val.	35% ad val.
148.11		If products of Cuba............	......	14% ad val. (s)	
148.15	00	If entered at any other time............	Lb......	35% ad val.	35% ad val.
148.16		If products of Cuba............	......	14% ad val. (s)	
148.20	00	Watermelons............	Lb......	20% ad val.	35% ad val.
148.21		If products of Cuba............	......	Free (s)	
		Other melons:			
148.25	00	If entered during the period from December 1, in any year, to the following May 31, inclusive............	Lb......	8.5% ad val.	35% ad val.
148.30	00	If entered at any other time............	Lb......	35% ad val.	35% ad val.
148.31		If products of Cuba............	......	14% ad val. (s)	
148.35	00	Prepared or preserved............	Lb......	35% ad val.	35% ad val.
148.36		If products of Cuba............	......	14% ad val. (s)	
		Olives, fresh, or prepared or preserved:			
		Fresh............			
		In brine, whether or not pitted or stuffed:			
148.40	00	Not ripe and not pitted or stuffed:	Lb......	5¢ per lb.	5¢ per lb.

Item	Stat. Suffix	Articles	Unit of Quantity	Rate 1	Rate 2
148.42	00	Not green in color and not packed in airtight containers of glass, metal, or glass and metal......	Gal......	15¢ per gal.	20¢ per gal.
148.44		Other:......		20¢ per gal.	20¢ per gal.
	20	*In containers each holding not more than 0.3 gallon*......	*Gal.*		
	40	*In containers each holding more than 0.3 gallon*......	*Gal.*		
		Ripe, but not pitted or stuffed:			
148.46	00	Not green in color and not packed in airtight containers of glass, metal, or glass and metal......	Gal......	15¢ per gal.	30¢ per gal.
148.48	00	Other......	Gal......	30¢ per gal.	30¢ per gal.
148.50	00	*Pitted or stuffed:*	*Gal.*	30¢ per gal.	30¢ per gal.
		Pitted:			
	20	*In containers each holding not more than 0.3 gallon*......	*Gal.*		
	40	*In containers each holding more than 0.3 gallon*......	*Gal.*		
		Stuffed:			
		In containers each holding not more than 0.3 gallon:			
	65	*Placed packed*......	*Gal.*		
	70	*Other*......	*Gal.*		
	80	*In containers each holding more than 0.3 gallon*......	*Gal.*		
		Dried:			
148.52	00	Not ripe......	Lb......	5¢ per lb.	5¢ per lb.
148.54	00	Ripe......	Lb......	2.5¢ per lb.	5¢ per lb.
148.56	00	Otherwise prepared or preserved......	Lb......	5¢ per lb.	5¢ per lb.
		Papayas, fresh, or prepared or preserved:			
148.60	00	Fresh......	Lb......	8.5% ad val.	35% ad val.
148.61	00	If products of Cuba......	......	Free (s)	
148.65	00	Prepared or preserved......	Lb......	7% ad val.	35% ad val.

(s) = Suspended. See general headnote 3(b).

TARIFF SCHEDULES OF THE UNITED STATES ANNOTATED (1972)

SCHEDULE 1. - ANIMAL AND VEGETABLE PRODUCTS
Part 9. - Edible Nuts and Fruits

Item	Stat. Suf-fix	Articles	Units of Quantity	Rates of Duty 1	Rates of Duty 2
		Peaches, fresh, or prepared or preserved:			
		Fresh or in brine:			
148.70	00	If entered during the period from June 1 to November 30, inclusive, in any year	Lb......	0.2¢ per lb.	0.5¢ per lb.
148.72	00	If entered at any other time	Lb......	0.1¢ per lb.	0.5¢ per lb.
148.74	00	Dried	Lb......	1¢ per lb.	2¢ per lb.
		Otherwise prepared or preserved:			
148.77	00	White fleshed	Lb......	10% ad val.	35% ad val.
148.78	00	Other	Lb......	20% ad val.	35% ad val.
		Pears, fresh, or prepared or preserved:			
		Fresh or in brine:			
148.81	00	If entered during the period from April 1 to June 30, inclusive, in any year	Lb......	0.25¢ per lb.	0.5¢ per lb.
148.82	00	If entered at any other time	Lb......	0.5¢ per lb.	0.5¢ per lb.
148.83	00	Dried	Lb......	1.5¢ per lb.	2¢ per lb.
148.86	00	Otherwise prepared or preserved	Lb......	18% ad val.	35% ad val.
		Pineapples, fresh, or prepared or preserved:			
		Fresh:			
148.90	00	In bulk	No......	1-1/6¢ each	1-1/6¢ each
148.91	00	If products of Cuba		0.84-2/3¢ each (s)	
148.93	00	In crates	Crate of 2.45 cu. ft.	35¢ per crate of 2.45 cu. ft.	50¢ per crate of 2.45 cu. ft.
148.94	00	If products of Cuba		20¢ per crate of 2.45 cu. ft. (s)	
148.96	00	In packages other than crates	Crate equiv. of 2.45 cu. ft.	27¢ per 2.45 cu. ft.	50¢ per 2.45 cu. ft.

Item no.	Stat. suf.	Description	Unit of quantity	Rate (1)	Rate (2)
148.97		If products of Cuba..........	....	20¢ per 2.45 cu. ft. (s)	2¢ per lb.
148.98	00	Prepared or preserved........		0.75¢ per lb.	
	20	*In airtight containers....*	*Lb.*		
	40	*Not in airtight containers.*	*Lb.*		
148.99		If products of Cuba..........	....	0.55¢ per lb. (s)	
		Plantains, fresh, or prepared or preserved:			
149.10	00	Fresh........................	Lb.	Free	Free
149.15	00	Prepared or preserved........	Lb.	7.5% ad val.	35% ad val.
		Plums, prunes, and prunelles, fresh, or prepared or preserved:			
		Fresh:			
149.19	00	If entered during the month of January in any year.............	Lb.	0.1¢ per lb.	0.5¢ per lb.
149.20	00	If entered during the period from February 1 to May 31, inclusive, in any year......	Lb.	0.1¢ per lb.	0.5¢ per lb.
149.21	00	If entered during the period from June 1 to December 31, inclusive, in any year.	Lb.	0.5¢ per lb.	0.5¢ per lb.
149.24	00	In brine.....................	Lb.	0.1¢ per lb.	0.5¢ per lb.
149.26	00	Dried........................	Lb.	2¢ per lb.	2¢ per lb.
149.28	00	Otherwise prepared or preserved.	Lb.	17.5% ad val.	35% ad val.
149.40	00	Tamarinds, fresh, or prepared or preserved..................	Lb.	Free	Free
		Other fruits, fresh, or prepared or preserved:			
149.48	00	Chinese gooseberries (Actinidia Chinensis Planch.), fresh......	Lb.	Free	1.25¢ per lb.
149.50	00	Other fruits, fresh..........	Lb.	8.5% ad val.	35% ad val.
149.60	00	Prepared or preserved........	Lb.	17.5% ad val.	35% ad val.
149.61		If products of Cuba..........	....	14% ad val. (s)	
150.00	00	Mixtures of two or more fruits, prepared or preserved........	Lb.	17.5% ad val.	35% ad val.
150.01		If products of Cuba..........	....	14% ad val. (s)	

(s) = Suspended. See general headnote 3(b).

TARIFF SCHEDULES OF THE UNITED STATES ANNOTATED (1972)

SCHEDULE 1. - ANIMAL AND VEGETABLE PRODUCTS
Part 9. - Edible Nuts and Fruits

Item	Stat Suf-fix	Articles	Units of Quantity	Rates of Duty 1	Rates of Duty 2
150.50	00	Any of the prepared or preserved products covered by this subpart containing 0.5 percent or more ethyl alcohol by volume........	Pf. gal.	An additional duty of $2.50 per proof gal. on such alcohol content	An additional duty of $5 per proof gal. on such alcohol content
		Subpart C. - Fruit Flours, Peels, Pastes, Pulps, Jellies, Jams, Marmalades, and Butters			
		Fruit flours:			
152.00	00	Banana and plantain............	Lb........	7% ad val.	20% ad val.
152.05	00	Other....................	Lb........	15% ad val.	20% ad val.
		Fruit peel, crude, dried, or otherwise prepared or preserved:			
		Crude, dried, or in brine:			
152.10	00	Citron....................	Lb........	Free	Free
152.14	00	Orange....................	Lb........	0.6¢ per lb.	2¢ per lb.
152.18	00	Lemon....................	Lb........	0.9¢ per lb.	2¢ per lb.
152.22	00	Other....................	Lb........	1¢ per lb.	2¢ per lb.
		Otherwise prepared or preserved:			
152.26	00	Citron....................	Lb........	1.7¢ per lb.	6¢ per lb.
152.30	00	Orange....................	Lb........	3.4¢ per lb.	8¢ per lb.
152.34	00	Lemon....................	Lb........	3¢ per lb.	8¢ per lb.
152.38	00	Other....................	Lb........	8¢ per lb.	8¢ per lb.
152.39		If products of Cuba and grapefruit, or pomelo or shaddock, peel........	....	6.4¢ per lb. (s)	

		Fruit pastes and fruit pulps:			
152.42	00	Apricot	Lb......	17.5% ad val.	35% ad val.
152.46	00	Cashew apple, mamey colorado, papaya, sapodilla, soursop, and sweetsop.	Lb......	17.5% ad val.	35% ad val.
152.47		If product of Cuba.	....	10% ad val. (s)	
152.50	00	Fig.	Lb......	5¢ per lb.	5¢ per lb.
152.54	00	Guava.	Lb......	7% ad val.	35% ad val.
152.58	00	Mango.	Lb......	7% ad val.	35% ad val.
152.62	00	Orange.	Lb......	17.5% ad val.	35% ad val.
152.63		If product of Cuba.	Lb......	14% ad val. (s)	
152.72	00	Banana and plantain.	Lb......	7.5% ad val.	35% ad val.
152.74		Other.	Lb.	15% ad val.	35% ad val.
	20	*Strawberry*	*Lb.*		
	40	*Other.*	*Lb.*		
152.75		If product of Cuba.	....	14% ad val. (s)	
		All jellies, jams, marmalades, and fruit butters:			
153.00	00	Cashew apple, mango, mamey colorado, papaya, sapodilla, soursop, and sweetsop.	Lb......	5% ad val.	35% ad val.
153.04	00	Currant and other berry.	Lb......	3% ad val.	35% ad val.
153.08	00	Guava.	Lb......	5% ad val.	35% ad val.
153.16	00	Orange marmalade.	Lb......	5.5% ad val.	35% ad val.
153.24	00	Pineapple.	Lb......	5% ad val.	35% ad val.
153.28	00	Quince.	Lb......	8.5% ad val.	35% ad val.
153.32	00	Other.	Lb......	7% ad val.	35% ad val.

(s) = Suspended. See general headnote 3(b).

Appendix D

Sample Grower–Processor Contract

1970 Pea Acreage Contract

Contractor's No. ....   Date ...., 19............

IT IS AGREED BETWEEN THE UNDERSIGNED "CONTRACTOR" AND The Processor Co. (HEREIN CALLED "COMPANY") AS FOLLOWS:

1   During the 1970 season the Contractor will, at such times as directed and on such land as is approved by the Company, properly prepare the soil, plant, and care for the acreage and varieties of peas set forth below.

2   COMPENSATION: The Company will pay the Contractor by August 16, 1970, compensation for the production of peas computed as hereinafter provided, less authorized deductions and any other amounts owing to the Company. Payment will be made payable to tenant and owner in case of leased land, unless a release signed by owner is on file at this factory office at least 30 days before payment date. This also applies to crop lien holders properly recorded. If the completion of harvest occurs later than August 2, 1970, payment will be made within 14 days of completion of harvest of all contracted acreage for this factory.

3   PEAS FIT FOR PROCESSING AND HARVESTED: The Company will accurately weigh the peas fit for processing and harvested and take representative samples of each load of peas. The samples from each load shall be graded together in a tenderometer. The resulting grade of the combined sample from any one load shall be the grade for that particular load. A deduction from the gross weight of peas will be made to cover tare for weed seed, chaff, and foreign matter as may be determined by passing representative samples through a cleaner designed for determining such tare. After tare determination if samples contain one or more weed particles (thistle buds, parts of weed stems, nightshade berries, morningglory seed clusters) per pound, the schedule of compensation for the load tested shall be reduced 1% for each such weed particle; but such reduction shall not exceed 50%. The Contractor may have the peas regraded or reweighed if he so requests before the Company commences to process them. The Contractor shall be furnished a record of weight and grade of each load. The Contractor's compensation for the production of peas fit for processing and harvested shall be computed as follows:

4

SCHEDULE OF COMPENSATION PER 100 NET LBS. OF SHELLED GREEN PEAS

Tenderometer	Early Junes	Sweets	Tenderometer	Early Junes	Sweets
85-down	$4.45	$3.35	106-110	$2.60	$2.15
86-90	3.90	3.00	111-115	2.45	2.05
91-95	3.50	2.70	116-125	2.25	1.90
96-100	3.05	2.50	126-135	2.10	1.75
101-105	2.80	2.30	136-145	2.00	1.65
			146-up	1.85	1.55

5   LATE PLANTING PREMIUM: The Contractor's compensation, as computed under Paragraph Nos. 3 and 4 hereunder, will be increased for the production of Sweet peas planted after May 17, 1970, as follows: 2% for peas planted on May 18; 4% for peas planted on May 19; and depending upon the particular planting date, increasing at the same rate of 2% per day to a maximum of 30%, and for Early June peas planted after May 9, 1970, as follows: 1¼% for peas planted on May 10; 2½% for peas planted on May 11; and depending upon the particular planting date, increasing at the same rate of 1¼% per day to a maximum of 30%.

6   PLANTING AND PAYMENT DATA:

........................Acres of Early Junes   ....Acres of Sweets

Land Located in Section .... Township .... County ....

Location No. .... Miles from Factory .... Root Rot Index ....

Ave. Yield Rating .... Years .... Plowing .... Crop Rotation Last Year .... 2 Yrs. Ago ....

Fertilizer: Contracted Crop Variety .... Lbs. Per Acre .... Analysis ....

       Variety .... Lbs. Per Acre .... Analysis ....

Materials Applied Previous Crop:

Fertilizer Analysis .... Lbs. Per Acre ....

Insecticide Applied .... Active Material .... Rate Per Acre ....

Herbicide Applied .... Active Material .... Rate Per Acre ....

Payment To Be As Follows:

Tenant .... Phone .... Tax No. ....

Street or R. R. No. .... City .... Zip Code ....

Owner .... Phone .... Tax No. ....

Street or R. R. No. .... City .... Zip Code ....

7   SUCCESSORS: This contract shall be binding upon the heirs and representatives of the Contractor and upon the successors or assigns of the Company.

8   THE FOREGOING, TOGETHER WITH ALL THE TERMS AND CONDITIONS OF THIS AGREEMENT APPEARING ON THE REVERSE SIDE HEREOF, CONSTITUTES THE WHOLE AGREEMENT BETWEEN THE PARTIES HERETO; AND NO REPRESENTATIONS, ORAL OR WRITTEN, SHALL BE BINDING UPON EITHER OF THE PARTIES HERETO UNLESS CONTAINED HEREIN. NO FAILURE OR OMISSION BY EITHER PARTY TO INSIST UPON OR ENFORCE ANY OF THE PROVISIONS HEREUNDER BREACHED BY THE OTHER PARTY SHALL BE DEEMED A WAIVER OF SUCH PROVISION UNLESS THE SAME SHALL BE EXPRESSLY WAIVED IN WRITING.

....
Contractor

....
Contractor

(SEE TERMS AND CONDITIONS ON REVERSE SIDE HEREOF)

Form 1348-11/69

Reproduced by permission of the processor corporation who wishes to remain anonymous.

CONTINUATION OF PEA ACREAGE CONTRACT

9   **PEAS FIT FOR PROCESSING AND NOT HARVESTED:** The Contractor's compensation for the production of peas fit for processing and fit for harvesting but not harvested at the direction of the Company shall be computed as follows: If a portion of a planting has been harvested hereunder, Contractor shall be compensated for the unharvested portion on the basis of net yield and grades of the harvested portion, and the schedule of compensation stated on the reverse side hereof. If the Company, for any reason, is not able to harvest any portion of a planting, Contractor's compensation shall be computed on the basis of the estimated yield and the schedule of compensation stated on the reverse side hereof, using 108 tenderometer as the grade for Early June peas and 103 tenderometer as the grade for Sweet peas. The Company may use any of the peas not harvested at its direction for seed peas; and if not so used, the Contractor may use them only for a green manure crop.

10   **MINIMUM GUARANTEE:** The Company guarantees that the gross compensation, as computed under Paragraph Nos. 3, 4, and 5 herein, payable to the Contractor for the production of each variety of peas fit for processing will average not less than $30.00 per acre before any deduction for weed control and any other amounts owing the Company.

11   **PEAS UNFIT FOR HARVESTING:** Whenever the Company determines that a field of peas or part thereof is unfit for harvesting purposes, it shall so notify the Contractor in writing. Peas are unfit for harvesting if a field or part thereof contains peas unfit for processing, or if the field or part thereof is affected by the following causes or other causes – plant disease, worms, insects, thistles or other weeds, excessive heat or moisture, hail, wind, frost, or inaccessibility due to excessive water, or unapproved chemicals which have been applied to this pea crop or to a previous crop upon which land this pea crop is grown. Peas unfit for processing are peas affected by any or all of the above causes or other causes. The Contractor's compensation for the production of peas unfit for harvesting shall consist exclusively in his personal right to use the crop only for a green manure crop.

12   **SEED:** The Company will furnish the Contractor without charge the recommended amount and variety of seed peas to be planted hereunder and will use due care in supplying seed of suitable quality but does not warrant, expressly or impliedly, its germination, purity, or any other quality. The Company will charge the Contractor $6.00 for each bushel of seed peas planted in excess of the amount recommended by the Company. The Contractor understands that the seed to be furnished hereunder will be chemically treated, thereby rendering it dangerous to the life and health of animals, poultry, and human beings; and he agrees to hold the Company harmless from, and indemnify the Company for, any liability for injuries to persons or damages to property in any manner arising out of such treatment.

13   **TITLE TO SEED AND CROP:** The title to the seed and the crops grown therefrom shall at all times be and remain in the Company; and the entire crop, except as herein otherwise expressly provided, shall be delivered to the Company. The Contractor shall not acquire any right, title, or interest in or to the seed furnished him nor the crops grown therefrom; and his possession of the seed and crop shall be that of a bailee only.

14   **HARVESTING AND HAULING:** The Company will determine the time and manner of harvesting. The Company will endeavor but does not guarantee to procure labor and equipment to harvest and haul the peas without charge to the Contractor. Contractor shall keep the field clear from rock and other debris and maintain adequate access to the field to facilitate the operation and transportation of harvesting equipment. Where such harvesting and hauling equipment is unable to operate effectively under its own power because of field conditions, the Contractor shall provide a minimum of two appropriate tractors (4-bottom plow size) with operators and tow chains as may be required or the Company may acquire such power at Contractor's expense. Any complaint of unsatisfactory harvesting must be reported by the Contractor to the Agricultural Office immediately and, in no event, no later than 24 hours after the harvesting is completed, and the field must be left in the same condition as immediately after harvest for a period of 36 hours.

15   **INSECT AND WEED CONTROL:** The Company reserves the right to treat any field or part thereof for insects and weeds if it considers such treatments necessary. **In no event shall the Contractor apply such treatments to the crops at his own discretion.** The Company will make no charge for the treatment of insects but will charge Contractor $2.50 for each acre of peas treated for weeds before the field of peas reaches 80% bloom. The Company will endeavor to use the best equipment and material available for such treatments but does not guarantee the results. The Contractor understands that such material may be harmful to plant life, poultry, animals, and human beings; and he agrees to hold the Company harmless from, and indemnify the Company for, any liability for injuries to persons or damages to property in any manner arising out of such treatments. At the Contractor's request and with Company's consent, the Company will pay Contractor at the rate of $2.75 per acre for Treflan applied to the acreage specified in Paragraph No. 6 of this contract. The Company will determine the time and manner of application of Treflan. Unless otherwise agreed to, Treflan shall be applied by the Contractor who agrees to hold the Company harmless from, and indemnify the Company for, any liability for injuries to persons or damages to property in any manner arising out of such treatments. The provisions of this paragraph shall not render inoperative the deduction in Paragraph No. 3 on the reverse side hereof.

16   **AN INDEPENDENT CONTRACTOR:** The Contractor hereby undertakes the production hereunder as an independent contractor and not as an employee of the Company. He shall have exclusive possession of the property upon which the crop is to be grown and shall not be subject to discharge by the Company, who holds no control over him in the performance of this contract other than as to the results to be accomplished. He may use such facilities and employ such labor as he desires to carry out this contract, and all persons employed by him for that purpose shall be his employees and not those of the Company.

17   **INSPECTION:** At all reasonable times the Contractor may enter upon the Company's factory receiving platform and any representative of the Company may enter upon the land where the crop is being planted, grown, or harvested hereunder, to ascertain whether the provisions of this contract are being complied with. The Contractor must provide and maintain an adequate right-of-way into the land to facilitate the Company's harvesting operation and removal of equipment thereafter.

18   **ARBITRATION:** Any controversy or claim arising out of or relating to this contract, or the breach thereof, shall be settled by arbitration in the City of Le Sueur in accordance with the Rules of the American Arbitration Association. Upon a party's receipt of written notice of a demand to arbitrate from the initiating party, both parties shall attempt for ten calendar days to select a mutually agreeable Arbitrator. If that attempt shall fail, the initiating party shall, within two calendar days, request selection of a single Arbitrator by the American Arbitration Association and according to its Rules. It is mutually agreed that the decision of the Arbitrator shall be a condition precedent to any right of legal action that either party may have against the other and that the award of the Arbitrator shall be final and binding upon both parties. The applicable law shall be the law of the State of Minnesota. Judgment upon the award rendered by the Arbitrator may be entered in any court having jurisdiction thereof. The losing party shall pay all costs of the arbitration exclusive of individual costs such as attorney fees. A claimant shall be the losing party in claims for money in which he is awarded less than 50% of his claim.

19   **EMERGENCY:** Notwithstanding any of the other provisions of this contract, if the Contractor's production hereunder or the Company's harvesting, business or processing operations are hindered or prevented in whole or in part by field conditions, fire, wind, floods, frost, action of the elements, act of God, strikes or other labor disturbances, failure or lack of transportation facilities, shortages of labor, material, containers, or supplies, inability to obtain machinery or parts therefor, breakdown of machinery and equipment, interruption of power or water, invasion, war, civil commotion, commandeer, enactment of legislation or issuance of Governmental orders or regulations restricting Contractor's or Company's operations or affecting prices or compensation, or other casualty or cause, whether similar or dissimilar, beyond either party's control, performance by either party hereunder shall be excused. In such event, the Contractor shall be under no obligation to produce hereunder, and his compensation shall consist exclusively in his right to use such crop as is grown only for a green manure crop.

Appendix E

Hypothetical Production Data, Sales, and Operating Costs for a Typical Vegetable Packing Plant in the Culiacán Area

Table E-1.   Hypothetical Production, Data, Sales, and Operating Costs for a Typical Vegetable Packing Plant in the Culiacán Area (10³ Mexican dollars).

Item	1	2	3	4	5	6	7	8-11
Production (10³ boxes)								
Tomatoes[a]	—	300	300	300	300	300	300	300
Cucumbers[b]	—	40	40	40	40	40	40	40
Bell peppers[c]	—	15	15	15	15	15	15	15
Sales (f.o.b. border)								
Tomatoes[d]	—	16,986.0	16,986.0	16,986.0	16,986.0	16,986.0	16,986.0	16,986.0
Cucumbers[e]	—	3,557.6	3,557.6	3,557.6	3,557.6	3,557.6	3,557.6	3,557.6
Bell peppers[f]	—	842.0	842.0	842.0	842.0	842.0	842.0	842.0
Total income	—	21,385.6	21,385.6	21,385.6	21,385.6	21,385.6	21,385.6	21,385.6
Operating costs								
Purchase of vegetables[g]	—	8,016.4	8,016.4	8,016.4	8,016.4	8,016.4	8,016.4	8,016.4
Labor[h]	—	1,537.2	1,537.2	1,537.2	1,537.2	1,537.2	1,537.2	1,537.2
Electricity, fuel, and water[i]	—	175.7	175.7	175.7	175.7	175.7	175.7	175.7
Wooden boxes, labels, and other items[j]	—	1,881.5	1,881.5	1,881.5	1,881.5	1,881.5	1,881.5	1,881.5
Administrative expenses[k]	—	40.0	40.0	40.0	40.0	40.0	40.0	40.0
Maintenance and repairs[l]	—	351.9	351.9	351.9	351.9	351.9	351.9	351.9
Taxes and insurance[m]	—	5,413.6	5,437.4	5,477.6	5,551.2	5,624.9	5,624.9	5,624.9
Others[n]	—	239.1	239.1	239.1	239.1	239.1	239.1	239.1
Total operating costs	—	17,655.4	17,679.2	17,719.4	17,793.0	17,866.7	17,866.7	17,866.7
Contingencies[o]	—	882.8	884.0	886.0	889.6	893.3	893.3	893.3
Total costs	—	18,538.2	18,563.2	18,605.4	18,682.6	18,760.0	18,760.0	18,760.0

Year

	1	2	3	4	5	6	7	8–11
Cash inflow								
Annual sales	–	21,385.6	21,385.6	21,385.6	21,385.6	21,385.6	21,385.6	21,385.6
Producers' contribution[p]	2,880.0	–	–	–	–	–	–	–
Long-term loans	5,250.0	–	–	–	–	–	–	–
Working-capital resources[q]	–	–	–	–	–	–	–	–
Last year's cash balance	–	–	2,144.9	3,372.0	2,500.0	2,500.0	2,500.0	2,500.0
Short-term loans	–	2,500.0	355.1	–	–	–	–	–
Total expected cash inflow	8,130.0	23,885.6	23,885.6	24,757.6	23,885.6	23,885.6	23,885.6	23,885.6
Cash outflow								
Investments								
Producers' contribution	2,250.0	–	–	–	–	–	–	–
Long-term loan	5,250.0	–	–	–	–	–	–	–
Operating costs								
Exclusive of loan interest	–	18,538.2	18,563.2	18,605.4	18,682.6	18,760.0	18,760.0	18,760.0
Loan interest								
On short-term loans[r]	–	125.0	17.8	–	–	–	–	–
On long-term loans[s]	630.0	577.5	577.5	467.5	233.8	–	–	–
Loan repayments								
Short-term loans	–	2,500.0	355.1	–	–	–	–	–
Long-term loans[t]	–	–	1,000.0	2,125.0	2,125.0	–	–	–
Producers' cash withdrawals[u]	–	–	–	1,059.7	344.2	2,625.6	2,625.6	2,625.6
Total expected cash outflow	8,130.0	21,740.7	20,513.6	22,257.6	21,385.6	21,385.6	21,385.6	21,385.6
Expected cash balance at year's end	–	2,144.9	3,372.0	2,500.0	2,500.0	2,500.0	2,500.0	2,500.0

Table E—1. (cont.)   Financial Projection for Vegetable Packing Plant in the Culiacán Area (10^3 Mexican dollars).

a. 13.3–kg boxes, including 2–kg package.
b. 23.0–kg boxes, including 2–kg package.
c. 15.0 kg boxes including 2–kg packages.
d. At $56.62 per box.
e. At $88.94 per box.
f. At $56.13 per box.
g. At $21.60 per tomato box; $29.41 per cucumber box; $24.00 per bell pepper box.
h. Direct labor, 42 man years at $18,201.40 each; marketing, 5 man years at $52,800.00 each; and indirect labor 6 man years at $84,800.00 each.
i. At $0.495 per box.
j. At $5.300 per box.
k. Includes stationery, telephone and telegraph bills, and so forth.
l. At 2 percent of building cost, 4 percent of equipment investment, and 8 percent of vehicle cost per year.
m. Includes exportation taxes, customary expenses, federal taxes, income tax, and insurance on vehicles and freight.
n. Includes brokerage fees and promotional expenses at $0.673 per box.
o. At 5 percent of operating costs.
p. Includes producers' contribution for first long-term loan interest payment plus 1 percent for evaluation and technical-services expenses.
q. Working-capital resources are assumed to equal at least 13 percent of operating costs (exclusive of loan interest).
r. At 12.0 percent per year.
s. At 11.0 percent per year on the outstanding balance plus 1 percent in the first year for evaluation and technical expenses.
t. Total term of 5 years including 2 years of grace.
u. Represents funds available for divident payments (it is assumed that no dividend is paid until the long-term loan is repaid).

The Role of a Growers' Association (CAADES) in West Mexican Fresh Tomato Exports

Background to Tomato Production in Western Mexico

The state of Sinaloa in western Mexico supplies, through Nogales, Arizona, 20 to 25 percent of annual U. S. fresh tomato supplies and over 50 percent of U. S. consumption during the period from November to May. In 1970, the value of U. S. tomato imports from Mexico reached a peak of $95 million. The preliminary 1972 value was $88 million (Table F–1), about two-thirds of the value of all vegetable exports from Mexico to the United States.

The United States tomato hectarage in 1970 was about 170,000 ha., with some 83 percent of production used for processing into canned whole tomatoes, catsup, chili sauce, paste, juice, and so on. The U. S. grower achieved yields averaging about 16.5 tons per hectare for fresh produce and 44 for processing.

Mexico's tomato production area in 1970 was about 60,000 ha., and average yields, 9.9 t/ha., were only about one-half of U. S. standards, although on some of the better farms they approached the U. S. level. In contrast to the United States, over 90 percent of Mexican tomato production is for fresh consumption,[1] with very small amounts processed.

Worldwide, fresh tomatoes are one of the most important fresh vegetables moving in international trade, achieving a volume of nearly 1,100,000 t in 1970 with a total value of about $300 million. Mexico during the past decade has managed to significantly increase its share of the world fresh--tomato market, from 10 percent (125,400 t) in 1960 to 29 percent (320,100 t) in 1970; most of this production went to U. S. and Canadian winter-spring markets, with only small, though increasing (1100 t in 1971), amounts going to markets in northern Europe.

Among the reasons for this west Mexican success in the U. S. winter tomato market are these: (a) Mexico has invested heavily, over the past two

Table F—1.   U.S. Imports of Tomatoes From West Mexico.

Year	Weight (10^6 lb)	Value (10^3 U.S. dollars)
1958	226	18,952
1964	246	29,425
1968	387	46,973
1970	641	94,967
1971	570	84,131
1972 prel.	582	88,150

Source: USDA, *U.S. Imports of Fruits and Vegetables from Mexico* (FAS, March 1973).

decades, in new irrigation facilities, particularly on the west coast; (b) several districts have a better climate for winter production of certain crops than any area in the United States; (c) labor supplies are ample; (d) much U. S. capital and technology has gone into development of farm operations; (e) medium-term development credit for growing and packing-house investments was available through official sources;[2] (f) strong Mexican growers' associations play an active role; and (g) local markets take up to 40 percent of the lower-quality production.

However, several factors have limited Mexico's competitive capabilities, including distance from markets, high summer temperatures, and seasonal conditions of rainfall and high humidity. In addition: (a) labor costs are going up; five or six years ago the daily wage for a field hand was $1 per day, whereas today it is $3 to $6; (b) it is important to be able to rotate vegetable land to keep disease down but western Mexico, especially, does not have this advantage because its supply of good land is limited; (c) Mexican producers cannot import fertilizer and, at times, are not able to get the blend of nutrients needed for the most effective crop production; (d) there have been reports that outbreaks of disease that are difficult to control are beginning to appear in Mexico, and growers have predicted that disease control will become an increasing problem in Mexico.

Production

In Sinaloa, tomato production is concentrated on surface-irrigated lands opened up by government-sponsored dams and distribution channels built in the late 1940s and 1950s.

Tomato growers have established a tightly connected system of production and marketing. Growers own most of the packing houses. Some 30 packing houses procure from about 50 farms authorized to grow staked tomatoes.[3] Most of these are well over 40 hectares in size, and operate with advanced machinery and U. S. cultivation and pesticide practices. There is little procurement from *ejidatarios* (small farmers), though recently the government set a maximum size on *new* growers at 16 hectares, still a very large farm for staked-tomato production. Each packing house draws from a large farm or set of farms associated with it, with total supplying area averaging 500 hectares to each packer. A few large growing units reserve 1000 hectares of their farm for vegetables that they pack in their own plants.

Close ties to American technical expertise, in most cases financially related, have greatly assisted Mexican producers, who

> have developed considerable expertise in various phases of production. This expertise, coupled with the supervision and substantial capital provided by American firms in the area, enables producers to handle most production problems. For example, untimely rains and high humidity in the spring of 1968 brought on the most severe outbreak of late blight the area had ever experienced. Initially, it looked as if the tomato crop would be destroyed. However, Mexican producers, with the assistance of American backers, hurriedly rushed in sufficient fungicides and application equipment to treat this disease. As a result, the blight was retarded and production continued on new growth at the top of the diseased plants.[4]

Marketing

The Culiacán growers and packers do not appear to be as dissatisfied with the 50 or so brokers at Nogales as the strawberry processors are with their brokers. A number of the Nogales companies are shareholders in Mexican operations; one source estimated that 70 percent of the volume of Mexican exports of fresh tomatoes to the United States are handled by distributors who have a significant Mexican shareholding. In addition, these distributors provide over $25 million of seasonal production credit to their Mexican packer-grower counterparts,[5] as well as providing telecommunications for the Mexican industry. One source argues that Mexican banks are perhaps becoming increasingly wary of extending their own lines of credit to Culiacán growers because of the uncertainties of land tenure and the increasing pressure on the Mexican government by the small farmers to allocate these irrigated tomato acreages to landless *ejidatarios.*

In the face of more difficult marketing problems for fresh tomatoes, a number of packers are turning to processing (canned whole tomatoes, juice, and paste). Those in the Culiacán area appear to have done fairly well in this field. Some of the more imaginative packers have bought surplus stainless-steel milk trucks and hope to begin shipments of bulk tomato paste and juice to California processors if Food and Drug Administration (FDA), USDA, and transport problems can be resolved—likely a long process. Competition for world tomato paste and markets is keen. CAADES has completed a survey indicating that Portugal is selling paste at $270/ton, Tunisia at $300/ton, and Israel at $320/ton. CAADES believes that Mexican production costs of staked tomatoes are too high at present to compete effectively with these suppliers in the world market.

The Role of CAADES as a Grower Association

Within the state of Sinaloa, some nine farmers' associations were formed in the 1960s. These in turn formed a confederation called CAADES. This confederation performs a wide variety of functions for its members, principally designed to ensure the orderly production and marketing of fresh tomatoes to the United States and to develop new markets, for both fresh and processed tomato products. Toward this end, CAADES keeps in hourly contact with U. S. market conditions. It also has its own in-house computer to assist in matching projected monthly U. S. demand allocations of available production acreage. It also specifies sizes, color, and packaging standards.

CAADES not only has legal sanctions it can apply and dues it can exact, but it collects them through the government when the latter collects export taxes from the growers. The tomato growers, which constitute one section of CAADES, have such a close-knit organization and such resources that they financed a $115,000 promotional campaign in the United States to increase the consumption of tomatoes.[6] This was financed through a 10 cent charge for each box exported.

In addition, CAADES is actively developing a northern European market for West Mexican fresh tomatoes. Currently, it transships through Nogales to New York, where the tomatoes are air-freighted to northern Europe. This market is developing rapidly, but still is costly, with a 30-lb lug of tomatoes costing $12–13 c.i.f. at northern European airports. Sales have been: for 1969, 1,000 lugs: for 1970, 15,000 lugs; for 1971, 120,000 lugs.

CAADES has been making strenuous efforts to develop alternative transport systems, experimenting with trucks to Norfolk and containers to Europe (14 days) or possibly 25-knot container ships, each carrying 1600 40,000-lb. containers from West Mexican ports. These ships, if feasible, would make the trip in seven to eight days. Their disadvantage is that half the ship would be occupied by the power plant, requiring very high-value cargo on both legs of the trip. To assist their planning, CAADES has calculated the alternative costs in time and money for shipping by air and by land-sea combinations. Table F–2 sets forth the estimated costs, showing clearly the tradeoff between cost per pound and time consumed. A trip of 21 days in transit leaves little time left to market the product before its shelf life is exhausted. Only green tomatoes and asparagus have sufficient marketable days to withstand a 21-day trip and still be salable.

Table F–2. Alternative Transportation Costs to Europe (Netherlands) from Culiacán, Sinaloa, Mexico.

Mode		Cost (U. S. dollars/lb.)		Transit time (days)
Ship: 15 knots		0.03		21
22 knots		.03		15
Air		.64		1
Land to New York	0.06		5	
Air to Netherlands	.21	.27	1	6
Land to New York	.06		5	
Ship to Netherlands	.02	.08	7	12

Source: Union Nacional de Productores de Hortalizas, *El Problema de Transporte de Hortalizas al Mercado Europeo: Posibles Soluciones* (Annual Report, January 1972).

NOTES TO APPENDIX F

1. Organization for Economic Cooperation and Development *Tomatoes: Present Situation and 1970 Prospects* (Paris, 1968), pp. 11, 79.
2. For example, the FONDO credit system referred to earlier has made some 230 loans to agroindustry firms since 1965, of which 30 were for fruit and vegetable packing and processing companies.
3. USDA, *Supplying U. S. Markets with Fresh Winter Produce* (Agricultural Economic Report No. 154, March 1969), p. 22.
4. Ibid., p. 27.
5. Large sums of money are involved in grower-shipper agreements. For the more important shippers, the total annual outlay can amount to a half-million dollars." Ibid., p. 24.
6. The Unión Nacional de Productores de Hortalizas and their broker partners, the West Mexico Vegetable Distributors Association, commissioned a prominent Arizona advertising company to prepare an in-season "commodity promotion" for West Mexican tomatoes. This company, after analyzing USDA data, concluded that West Mexico should concentrate its advertising budget on media in cities west of Chicago, since Florida had a significant share of eastern markets and a national promotion would mainly assist Florida sales. Florida growers were not interested in a joint promotion. The promotion itself stressed building a better hygiene image for Mexican tomatoes, tying tomatoes in ads with branded salad dressings, and developing an effective representative function in Washington, D. C.

Mexican Exports of Frozen Strawberries: The Case of Fresas Congeladas

Background to Mexican Strawberry Industry

Strawberry production in Mexico is a comparatively new industry, burgeoning from modest beginnings in the early 1960s to a significant employer (40,000) and earner of foreign exchange ($19 million) by 1971. Most of the crop comes from an area of central Mexico broadly defined as the Bajio Valley, ranging in elevation from 3700 to 5000 feet above sea level. Strawberries are grown in this area almost wholly by small farmers (some 12,000) supplying 25–50 packers and freezers in the area. An additional 30,000 people are employed seasonally in the packing and freezing plants. Thus, strawberry production in Mexico supports, in part, well over 100,000 people, on balance making the industry economically more important as an employer than as a foreign exchange earner.

The Oversupply Problems of 1970 and 1971

Despite a relatively stable annual U. S. consumption of about 263 million pounds of frozen strawberries, Mexico increased its exports to the United States to 101.5 million pounds in 1970 as compared with 88.0 million in 1969. The increase in total supply resulted in severe pressure on prices at all levels of the system. As Table G–1 implies, for example, average f.o.b. value of frozen strawberries declined from 17¢/lb in 1969 to 14¢/lb in 1970.

There was both private and public reaction to this price decline. Private freezers felt that U. S. brokers were responsible by manipulating stocks of frozen Mexican berries to drive prices of the U. S. pack down, taking title to the Mexican pack at the low price, then releasing the frozen berries gradually as prices firmed. Whether this was true or not, the major Mexican processors, few of whom had cold-storage space, reacted. They got together in 1971 and

Table G–1. **Exports of Fresh and Frozen Strawberries from Mexico to the United States.**

	Fresh			Frozen	
Year	Weight $(10^3$ lb)	Value $(10^3$ U.S. dollars)		Weight $(10^3$ lb)	Value $(10^3$ U.S. dollars)
1960	562	43		25,017	3,233
1965	5,791	845		51,796	7,805
1967	20,499	3,180		72,693	9,991
1968	26,261	4,425		68,199	11,377
1969	44,218	7,083		87,962	14,713
1970	48,966	8,333		101,519	14,458
1971	49,248	8,206		83,166	10,577
1972 prel.	42,074	7,088		81,157	12,278

Source: USDA, FAS, *United States Imports from Mexico* (March 1973).

attempted to increase their price by 1¢/lb. and at the same time to sell directly to the U. S. reprocessors, thus eliminating the brokers. The result was that the U. S. frozen-strawberry brokers organized and refused, as a group, to take any Mexican berries. The Mexicans, lacking cold-storage space and U. S. industry contacts, could not move their pack without the aid of brokers, and large losses resulted in the Mexican industry. The typical Mexican firm reportedly lost $200,000 to $300,000 during this direct-sales campaign.

The public reaction by the Mexican government was to call for the organization of a National Strawberry Board (Comision Nacional de Fresas) to control shipments of frozen berries to the United States. The Board was organized in 1970 to set and allocate quotas on exports to the United States and to encourage market and product diversification. Substantial annual contributions, running to $50,000 or more, are required from each firm. The Board was also the principal negotiator of a voluntary frozen-berry export quota of 82 million pounds to the United States. At the same time, U. S. growers and freezers put considerable pressure on the U. S. government to severely restrict Mexican imports. This restriction, however, came at a time when U.S. production was considerably reduced, partly as a result of the low prices of the previous year and partly owing to a labor shortage on the West Coast at picking time. The short supply situation created a relative scarcity by 1972, resulting in the return to previously profitable prices for Mexican growers and processors.

Having overcome the earlier immediate problem of oversupply, the Strawberry Board, which has run into staffing problems, is now facing the problem of allocating increased quotas to keep up with a rapidly rising demand for frozen strawberries in Canada and Europe, as well as balancing the supply situation in the United States.

The Case of Fresas Congeladas

Against this recent history, the case of Fresas Congeladas (a pseudonym) in Mexico illustrates many of the potentials—and the problems—of the processed export strawberry business. This Mexican-owned company has operated in Central Mexico for about 10 years.

Contractual Arrangements. The company contracts 80 per cent of its strawberry production with low-income small farmers. Individual farm areas vary, but total in the aggregate 400 hectares divided among 120 growers. The company provides these small farmers with extensive technical services on strawberry production, employing a graduate specialist and two technical assistants for this purpose. It also supplies credit to its growers under contract, the amounts of which are deducted upon delivery.

Marketing Strategy. The company is one of the principal Mexican processors and exporters of frozen berries. It also exports fresh berries by air both to the United States and to Germany. Air-freight cost to Europe is about 5¢/lb. The large berries are normally sold fresh; the smaller ones are processed and frozen for later use in jams, jellies, syrups, juices, and ice cream. Although 70 percent of the product is exported, the company has contracts to supply both McCormick of Mexico and International Foods, who further process the frozen berries into jams and jellies for local Mexican consumption. These local reprocessors and distributors are important because they will often take a somewhat smaller berry. This has led Fresas Congeladas to contract for all production, regardless of size, from their small growers. Other processing firms will only take a grower's production that meets a certain size. This practice has enabled Congeladas to develop strong grower loyalties.

The Mexican jam and jelly makers pay cash on delivery for frozen berries. However, these firms are selling exported production mainly through U. S. brokers, who pay only 60–90 days after delivery. These U. S. import brokers, however, do supply a major part of the working capital needed by the Mexican processors. One major firm, receiving about $2 million at no interest each year from its broker, can secure local credit up to only $350,000 at an average cost of 12–14 percent. Even with these lines, this firm appears to be continually short of working capital.

The manager of Congeladas has undertaken several promotion trips to Europe and found a demand that could not be met on a regular shipment basis. The Germans are apparently offering $2/lb for regular deliveries, transshipped through McAllen, Texas. This diversified marketing effort was also undertaken by other processors as well.

Probably the most significant change in the Mexican strawberry picture is a new awareness of marketing strategy. Prior to the huge crop in 1965–66, the area was going through a period of seemingly endless expansion in acreage and production facilities. Although commercial production started in 1948, most of the expansion has occurred in the last decade.

Following the big crop, growers and freezers realized that emphasis on production alone was insufficient. They became aware that marketings must be geared to what could be sold to freezers at profitable prices. Currently (1968) about half of the freezers are operating only marginally or not at all. Others are expanding operations to include other commodities, and some have converted their freezing lines to processing fruit juices or nectar concentrates (pineapple, apricot, and pear).[1]

Diversification. Recognizing in the mid–1960s that as processors they were vulnerable to the price and supply vagaries of a one-crop commodity, as well as to cover overheads, strawberry processors, including Fresas Congeladas, began to extend their season by diversification.

Strawberries are and will continue to be the principal crop grown in the area, but diversification has become of major concern to most growers. Processors also are trying to diversify so as to spread their risks and extend their operation over a longer period of the year. The strawberry season lasts only about 5 months, with peak deliveries to the freezers during early March. If crops could be processed prior to and following the strawberry season. overhead on the plants could be reduced. There may be some overlap on harvesting seasons, but processors are more interested in expanding their processing seasons.

Growers are experimenting with various vegetable crops, of which asparagus is currently creating the most interest. Plantings were started about 3 years ago by direct seeding. Now entire fields are being planted using crowns from the direct-seeded beds. Most of the asparagus is being canned and frozen, but some fresh shipments have been made on an experimental basis. Other crops being tried are broccoli, brussels sprouts, and sweet peppers. The broccoli is frozen as spears are chopped, and the peppers are frozen diced. Some brussels sprouts have been shipped fresh.[2]

Summary In summary, this review indicates that Fresas Congeladas was successful in generating very substantial employment opportunities, in stimulating local production by small farmers with contracts, credit, and technical service, and in earning foreign exchange with a product containing a very high labor value-added component. Its main problems still remain: getting adequate seasonal financing, broadening and diversifying its market outlets, and establishing a more reliable and trusting relation with its U. S. broker.

NOTES TO APPENDIX G

1. Higgins, William J., *Mexico's Production of Horticultural Products for Export,* U. S. Department of Agriculture, Foreign Agricultural Service, FASM–199 (June, 1968).

2. Ibid.

Appendix H

Sources and Notes for Fruit and Vegetable Flow Chart: Figure 2-1

Value Added

1. The $25.0 billion retail value of fruit and vegetable consumption in 1971 is based on the estimate of consumer expenditures of $23.4 billion for domestically produced fruits and vegetables contained in Terry Crawford, "The Bill for Marketing Farm Food Products," *Marketing and Transportation Situation,* MTS–186 (August 1972), p. 24, plus an estimated value of $1.6 billion for 1971 imports.

2. Total retail value has been allocated 53 percent to fresh and 47 percent to processed fruit and vegetables is based on average 1971 ratios derived from "market basket" data, USDA, *Marketing and Transportation Situation,* MTS–188 (February 1973), p. 36.

3. Retail gross margins of 31 percent for fresh and 19 percent for processed produce are based on *Chain Store Age* (July 1972), p. 71. These percentages were corroborated by selective cross-check interviews with chains, independent food stores, and HRI operators. The percentage for processed produce is consistent with USDA, ERS, *Prices, Margins and Farm Value for Frozen Fruits, Vegetables and Juices,* Statistical Bulletin 477 (October 1971).

4. Gross margins of wholesalers, chain warehouse distribution centers, and terminal markets are derived from *Census of Business* data for 1967 and Statistical Bulletin 477.

5. The value added in transportation is based on study estimates of 1971 tonnages, average distances moved, and average freight rates. These estimates may be somewhat high, especially for processed produce. They represent about twice the average for all farm foods reported in Crawford, "Bill for Marketing," p. 19.

6. The estimate for value added of fresh produce by shipper-packers is a residual.

7. Processor gross margins are based on Statistical Bulletin 477, adjusted to eliminate packing, warehousing, and marketing costs.

8. The $6.0 billion estimate for total farm value of fruits and vegetables is based on $5.3 billion for domestic U. S. production from Crawford, "Bill for Marketing," p. 24, plus $0.7 billion for the estimated value of imports at U. S. ports of entry. The import figure includes customs duties, transport costs outside the United States, costs of foreign packing, shipping, processing, and so forth. Data are not available to permit an accurate estimate of foreign farmgate value.

9. The division of total farmgate value between fresh and processed fruits and vegetables is based on 1971 "market basket" data from MTS–188, p. 36, and unpublished USDA data for domestic production.

10. The division of farmgate value between labor and other inputs is based on study estimates, USDA data for farm production expenses in 1971, *Farm Income,* ERS, USDA FIS 220 (Supplement, August 1972), pp. 57–58, and the 1969 *Census of Agriculture.*

Market System Flow Chart

Estimated percentage distributions of total value flows at each stage are derived from and consistent with value added estimates detailed above. Additional detail based on the following.

1. The division of total farm shipments between U. S. and foreign growers assumes that foreign gross margins are similar to U. S. margins (see item 8 above).

2. The division of fresh produce between direct chain purchases and terminal markets is based on unpublished USDA estimates for unloads in 23 cities.

3. The division of processed produce between chains and affiliated wholesalers and independent wholesalers is estimated on the basis of the 1967 *Census of Business* and discussions with selected industry participants.

4. The division of wholesaler shipments between retail grocery stores and HRI is estimated on the basis of the 1967 *Census of Business,* updated to 1971 to reflect the growing importance of the HRI market.

5. The division of total shipments between retail grocery stores and HRI shipments and of HRI shipments between public eating places and institutions based on Terry Crawford, "The Bill for Marketing Farm Food Products," *Marketing and Transportation Situation,* MTS–186 (August 1972), p. 24.

6. The division of retail grocery store sales by type of outlet is derived from data for all food stores in Leland Southard and Terry L. Crawford, "Changes in Food Wholesaling," USDA, ERS, *Marketing and Transportation Situation,* MTS–181 (May 1971), and USDA, *Market Structure of the Food Industries,* Marketing Research Report 971 (September 1972).

Employment Contribution

1. Labor estimates in man years for both fresh and processed fruits and vegetables at the farm level are estimates based on 1971 preliminary data for number of man hours worked divided by 1800 hours per year.
2. Numbers of employees in fruit and vegetable processing are derived from the 1967 *Census of Manufacturers* and various issues of the *Annual Survey of Manufacturers*.
3. Numbers of trade employees are derived from the 1967 *Census of Business*, updated on the basis of estimates made for this study.

Appendix I

Seasonal Patterns of U.S. Winter Produce (Fresh) Shipments, October–June 1966–1967

Figure I–1. Tomatoes

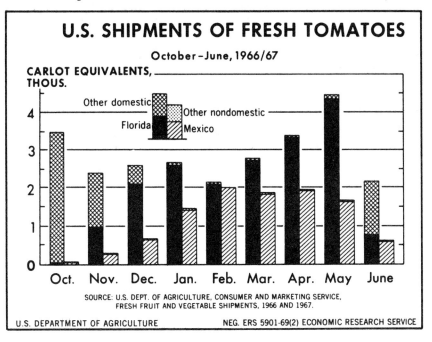

U.S. SHIPMENTS OF FRESH TOMATOES

October–June, 1966/67

SOURCE: U.S. DEPT. OF AGRICULTURE, CONSUMER AND MARKETING SERVICE, FRESH FRUIT AND VEGETABLE SHIPMENTS, 1966 AND 1967.

U.S. DEPARTMENT OF AGRICULTURE   NEG. ERS 5901-69(2) ECONOMIC RESEARCH SERVICE

Figure I–2. Cantaloups

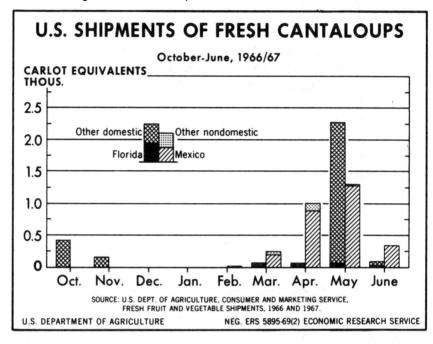

Figure I–3. Strawberries

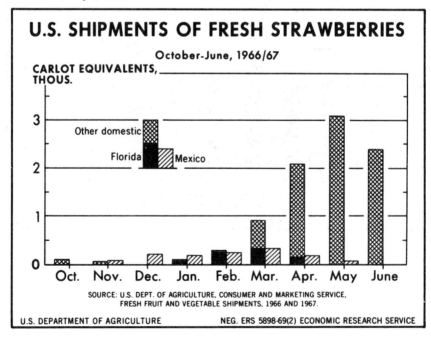

Figure I–4. Cucumbers

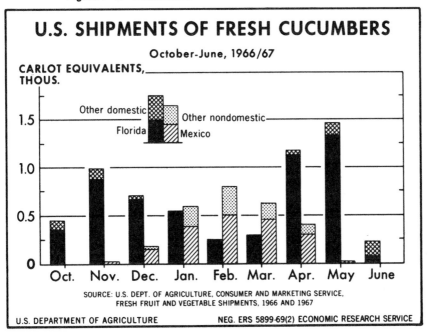

U.S. SHIPMENTS OF FRESH CUCUMBERS

October-June, 1966/67

CARLOT EQUIVALENTS, THOUS.

Other domestic
Other nondomestic
Florida
Mexico

SOURCE: U.S. DEPT. OF AGRICULTURE, CONSUMER AND MARKETING SERVICE, FRESH FRUIT AND VEGETABLE SHIPMENTS, 1966 AND 1967

U.S. DEPARTMENT OF AGRICULTURE   NEG. ERS 5899-69(2) ECONOMIC RESEARCH SERVICE

Figure I–5. Green Peppers

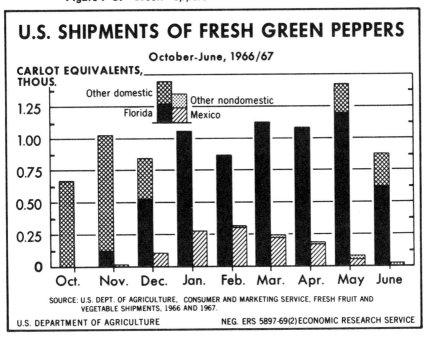

U.S. SHIPMENTS OF FRESH GREEN PEPPERS

October-June, 1966/67

CARLOT EQUIVALENTS, THOUS.

Other domestic
Other nondomestic
Florida
Mexico

SOURCE: U.S. DEPT. OF AGRICULTURE, CONSUMER AND MARKETING SERVICE, FRESH FRUIT AND VEGETABLE SHIPMENTS, 1966 AND 1967.

U.S. DEPARTMENT OF AGRICULTURE   NEG. ERS 5897-69(2) ECONOMIC RESEARCH SERVICE

Appendix J

U.S. Commercial Floriculture

Definitions of floriculture vary widely. In this study, the analysis is confined to cut flowers and potted plants, both blooming and foliage. Unfinished products, such as bulbs and seeds, and nursery products, such as bedding plants, trees, and shrubs, are exclused.

Floriculture is included in this report because of two factors: first, the demand for floriculture products in the United States is growing much faster than that for fruits and vegetables, which were examined in the preceding sections; second, the structure of the floriculture industry is changing significantly, creating new opportunities for Central American suppliers. The purpose of this section is to analyze briefly the American commercial floriculture industry and to identify changes in it that have relevance for Central American producers.

The Dynamics of the United States Market

Consumer Demand. The rate of growth of retail sales of floriculture products in the United States has accelerated since 1967, and annual sales currently exceed $2 billion. Although comprehensive data are not available, per capita retail sales (in constant dollars) apparently grew at an annual rate of less than 2 percent from 1949 to 1967. Per capita retail sales since then have been at a rate of approximately 4 percent per year. Despite this growth, expenditures per household are still under $35 per year, or about 0.003 percent of disposable income.

The increased demand for floriculture products during recent years has not been shared equally by all the principal varieties of plants and flowers. Among cut flowers, shipments of carnations and standard chrysanthemums exhibited strong growth, while pompons increased more slowly, and gladioli

359

actually declined. Shipments of roses declined until the mid–1960s, but since then demand has apparently outstripped available supply, resulting in a significant increase in prices. Data on potted plants are less complete than for cut flowers. It seems clear, however, that shipments of blooming plants and the larger-sized foliage plants have exhibited stronger growth than smaller foliage plants.

Purchases of floriculture products are closely related to specific occasions or needs, such as funerals, illness, weddings, and anniversaries. A survey of retail florists by the United States Department of Agriculture in 1964–65 reported that 75 percent of retail sales were for funerals, memorials, hospitals, and weddings.[1] Only 10 percent of the total sales were identified as being for in-home use unrelated to a specific occasion. A similar survey in 1966–67 by the Department of Agriculture of consumer floriculture purchases from all sources indicated that 23 percent of the unarranged cut flowers and 27 percent of the potted plants purchased were intended for in-home use (Table J–1).[2]

Participants at all levels in the floriculture industry believe that the growth in the demand for floriculture products will be substantial during the next two decades, though estimates of the rate of this growth vary greatly. One unpublished industry study estimates that per capita expenditures for floriculture products will grow at an annual rate of about 7.5 percent during the present decade. Other knowledgeable industry spokesmen predict that by 1980 annual retail sales of floriculture products will be over $4 billion, and by 1990 almost $8 billion.

Optimism regarding growth in the demand for floriculture products, particularly for uses not related to special occasions, is based on several factors:

Table J–1. Percentages of Cut Flowers and Potted Plants Purchased by Consumers for Special Occasions, 1966–1967.

	Cut Flowers			
Occasion	*Arranged*	*Unarranged*	*Corsages*	*Potted plants*
Garden	0.4	–	–	11.1
Funeral; memorial	64.0	17.0	2.2	10.0
Home	3.6	22.6	1.1	27.1
Special day	5.1	10.6	28.8	22.6
Illness; hospital	12.6	17.5	1.3	16.7
Anniversary	6.9	13.5	13.5	3.6
Gift	2.0	9.0	3.9	5.3
Wedding	2.4	2.3	9.9	–
Other	3.0	7.5	34.3	3.6
Total	100.0	100.0	100.0	100.0

Source: USDA, Economic Research Service, *Commercial Floriculture and Related Products,* Statistical Supplement to Marketing Research Report 955 (October 1969).

(1) a steady increase in discretionary income available to consumers, of which only a negligible fraction is now being spent on flowers and plants; (2) more aggressive consumer-oriented marketing activities, stimulated in part by recent corporate entries into commercial floriculture; (3) greater emphasis on the quality of life and increased consumer awareness of the beauty of flowers and plants in an era of concern over ecology and pollution; (4) more widespread programs of consumer education in the selection, care, and use of flowers and plants; (5) improved product quality and greater reliability of delivery to retail outlets; (6) increased interest by supermarkets and variety stores in floral products as an important new source of profits; (7) lower consumer prices charged by mass outlets, as compared with prices charged by retail florists; (8) the expanding demand for foliage plants in offices, plants, schools, and public buildings.

Supply of Floriculture Products. The production capacity of United States growers does not appear to be keeping pace with the current and potential future growth in demand. Output of cut flowers has declined since 1970, following several years of rapid expansion. Table J–2 shows the trends from 1966 to 1973 in production of the five leading varieties of cut flowers, and of potted chrysanthemums–the only potted flowering plant for which data are available–and foliage plants. In contrast to cut flowers, there has been a further marked increase in production of potted plants since 1970. These data are from the annual U. S. Department of Agriculture surveys which cover the 23 states that accounted for 95 percent of the total U. S. production in the 1959 *Census of Agriculture.*

The major centers of flower production in the United States are California, Florida, and Colorado. Cut flowers historically were produced in climate-controlled greenhouses located outside major population centers. With the advent of economical airfreight in the 1950s, farsighted growers moved to areas with better climatic conditions. The growth in California and Colorado has been exceptionally impressive.

In 1970, according to Bureau of the Census data, 39,590 acres of land–an area slightly larger than the District of Columbia–were used in floriculture. Approximately 12 percent of the producing land area was under glass; the remainder was open acreage.

The available evidence suggests that growers have experienced a significant cost-price squeeze, and that gross margins have declined since the late 1960s. Costs of labor, materials, and other inputs have risen faster than sales prices. This pressure on the margins of Florida growers has been confirmed in each of the special surveys conducted since 1968 by the Florida Cooperative Extension Service of the University of Florida. Some participants feel that by 1980 it will not be economically feasible to produce cut flowers on a year-round basis in many current production areas in the United States.

Table J-2. Number of Growers, Plants in Production, and Wholesale Value of Principal Cut Flowers and Potted Plants, 1966–1973.

Flowers	1966	1967	1968	1969	1970	1971	1972	1973[a]
				Number of growers				
Carnations	2183	2055	1988	1861	1749	1548	1384	—
Standard chrysanthemums	2984	2756	2599	2457	2243	2134	1955	—
Pompons	2988	2738	2660	2497	2349	2168	1912	—
Roses	376	376	371	384	384	338	312	—
Gladioli	581	541	492	398	366	321	271	—
Potted chrysanthemums	1545	1538	1540	1455	1543	1394	1359	—
Potted foliage plants	1039	1014	939	890	927	835	898	—
				Plants in production (10^6)				
Carnations	52.8	54.3	56.2	60.8	61.8	61.5	60.2	60.1
Standard chrysanthemums	105.3	109.8	110.3	117.7	130.2	130.4	120.8	119.5
Pompons	119.7	115.1	126.4	138.5	128.9	127.8	129.2	135.1
Roses	15.1	15.6	16.8	18.0	18.9	18.9	18.4	18.9
Gladioli[b]	13.4	12.7	12.9	13.1	11.6	11.0	10.4	10.5
Potted (10^6 pots)	11.8	13.4	14.0	15.1	17.0	18.0	19.6	20.4
Potted (10^6 ft^2)	32.4	31.6	20.0	31.5	32.6	36.5	38.8	40.5
				Wholesale value (10^6 dollars)				
Carnations	36.7	40.2	44.9	47.7	47.7	46.3	51.7	—
Standard chrysanthemums	23.3	24.4	26.4	26.8	26.9	27.5	28.8	—
Pompons	22.2	22.8	25.6	27.2	26.7	29.2	29.6	—
Roses	40.7	42.3	49.2	53.9	54.0	54.7	59.5	—
Gladioli	18.9	17.8	21.1	21.3	18.7	19.1	20.3	—
Potted	15.9	18.2	19.6	21.9	24.5	26.8	30.2	—
Potted foliage plants	24.0	26.1	25.9	29.2	27.7	37.6	48.1	—
Total	181.7	191.8	212.7	228.0	226.3	241.2	268.2	—

Source: USDA, Crop Reporting Board, Flowers and Foliage Plants: Production and Sales in Selected States (April 1969, 1970, 1971, 1972, and 1973).
a. Estimated.   b. Acres in production.

Although U. S. cut-flower production appears to have leveled off during the past two years, imports have continued to increase at a rapid rate. Although the totals are still relatively small, there is increasing concern among U. S. growers regarding the threat of foreign imports. At the same time, a substantial number of U. S. producers are participating directly or indirectly in the development of foreign production sources, particularly in Central America, Colombia, and Ecuador.

Table J–3 shows the trends in dollar value of imports into the United States of cut flowers and cut foliage between 1966 and 1972. The value of cut flowers increased by almost $4 million during this period, with about half of the total gain taking place since 1970. Colombia, Ecuador, and Canada accounted for more than 75 percent of the 6-year increase. Imports of cut foliage also increased sharply between 1966 and 1972, with a big jump since 1970. Brazil and Italy accounted for most of the increase. Although precise comparisons are not possible, particularly for foliage plants, knowledgeable industry participants estimated that, in 1970, imports supplied approximately 3 percent of the total domestic market for carnations, 6 percent of the chrysanthe-

Table J–3. Value of U.S. Imports of Cut Flowers and Cut Foliage, 1966–1972 (10^3 *dollars*).[a]

Country	1966	1967	1968	1969	1970	1971	1972
			Cut flowers				
Ecuador	78	118	217	293	505	405	442
Colombia	25	41	73	124	406	880	1764
Other Latin America	10	27	38	39	122	222	447
Netherlands	14	12	34	102	178	305	384
Other Europe	26	40	61	43	44	32	24
Australia	133	150	164	169	221	193	202
Canada	23	9	208	425	742	684	743
Rest of world	23	9	7	3	2	15	16
Total	332	406	802	1198	2220	2737	4030
			Cut foliage				
Brazil	115	242	285	315	717	715	1347
Other Latin America	3	4	15	22	67	95	102
Italy	589	484	472	677	800	997	2311
Spain	–	–	15	52	150	99	400
Other Europe	58	104	130	200	336	516	728
Japan	79	98	88	74	108	78	136
Rest of world	42	63	80	86	116	160	328
Total	886	995	1085	1426	2294	2662	5352

Source: U.S. Bureau of the Census, *U.S. Imports: General and Consumption*, FT–135.
a. Shipments valued at less than $250 are excluded.

mums, and perhaps 5 to 7 percent of the foliage. All of these market shares have increased since 1970.

Table J–4 shows recent data on the volume of imports of selected cut flowers. This information is based on reports of inspections by the Plant Protection and Quarantine Program of the Department of Agriculture. Guatemala is a major source of supply for six of the eight varieties shown. Colombia is the dominant foreign supplier of carnations, and a major competitor with Central America in chrysanthemums, pompoms, and daisies.

Table J–4. Volume of U.S. Imports of Selected Cut Flowers, 1971 and 1972 *(number of stems).*

Flower and country of origin	1971	1972
Carnations	33,244,000	56,153,000
Colombia	29,014,000	47,829,000
Ecuador	2,403,000	3,867,000
Chrysanthemums	11,398,000	15,866,000
Guatemala	4,290,000	6,716,000
Colombia	4,031,000	4,945,000
Ecuador	1,848,000	2,672,000
Pompons	12,326,000	25,241,000
Guatemala	4,454,000	8,035,000
Colombia	4,371,000	13,181,000
Ecuador	1,465,000	1,197,000
Roses	1,038,000	1,676,000
Guatemala	109,000	372,000
Brazil	107,000	114,000
Costa Rica	96,000	336,000
Netherlands	600,000	648,000
Daisies	1,700,000	3,395,000
Colombia	794,000	1,617,000
Guatemala	482,000	1,623,000
Tulips	2,288,000	1,856,000
Netherlands	2,285,000	1,854,000
Chamaedorea	283,819,000	366,038,000
Mexico	135,710,000	230,802,000
Guatemala	145,714,000	131,546,000
Statice	1,414,000	2,542,000
Guatemala	700,000	1,097,000
Mexico	650,000	959,000

Source: U.S. Department of Agriculture, Agricultural Marketing Service, *San Francisco Ornamental Crops Report* (April 21, 1972; December 29, 1972; May 4, 1973); reports of inspections by Plant Protection and Quarantine Program, U.S. Department of Agriculture.

**The Structure and Coordination
of the Industry**

The U. S. floriculture industry historically has been composed of a large number of small enterprises at each stage of the distribution chain, linked together by a complex network of middlemen (Figure J–1). In the typical case, the small local growers sell to brokers or larger grower-shippers, who then move the product to wholesalers. The wholesaler might be a large regional operator

Figure J–1. Structure of the U.S. Floriculture Industry.

Source: Interviews with industry participants.

who sells to large retailers or to other small wholesalers. Retail distribution is primarily through florists, variety stores, and food chains. There has been traditionally a 20 to 25 percent commission for the grower-shipper or broker who sells directly to a wholesaler. The wholesaler adds on another 20 percent for his services. Retail florists probably add on an additional 100 to 300 percent, variety stores 50–150 percent, and retail chain stores, approximately 50 percent. This structure is beginning to change significantly. There is increased concentration throughout the system and the distribution channel is shortening.

Approximately 65 percent of floriculture sales are made through some 22,500 retail florists' shops. Over 95 percent of these outlets are single-unit, owner-operated enterprises. The 1967 Census of Business showed that, at that time, there were no retail florist chains with more than 10 units, and only 28 with between 4 and 10 units.[3] At the time of this survey, the average annual sales of a retail florist outlet were $50,500. Today, the average annual sales of an outlet are estimated at $60,000. One percent of the firms are responsible for over 10 percent of the total volume handled by retail florists. Table J–5 shows that during the past 20 years there has been a significant increase in the percentage of retail florists with sales of over $50,000 per year, and a decline in the percentages of outlets with sales under $19,000 annually.

The retail florist depends largely on his local reputation, creativity in flower arrangements, and service in making sales. He emphasizes service and offers the customer a wide range of services. The Department of Agriculture survey[4] showed that 97 percent of retail florists offer free delivery, 95 percent offer credit, and 84 percent offer worldwide coverage in transmitting orders. The same survey revealed that 55 percent of the sales of the typical retail florist come from fresh-flower arrangements, 18 percent from flowering and foliage potted plants, and 12 percent from fresh flowers sold loose. The remaining 13 percent of the sales are from artificial flowers, giftware items, and similar products.

The typical retail florist is not located in a place to attract heavy in-store customer traffic. He receives 75 percent of his orders by telephone and knows many customers only by name and voice.

Retail florists spend less than 2 percent of gross sales on advertising. Marketing strategy is based on maintaining high prices and high margins. Demand is generated by the need for flowers or plants in connection with a specific occasion and price is a secondary factor. Sales of retail florists will continue to increase as the market expands, but probably at a slower rate than the industry as a whole.

Mass retailers, supermarkets, and variety stores are becoming important outlets for floriculture products. In fact, expansion of floriculture sales through mass outlets appears to be accelerating. An estimated one-third of all flower and plant sales were made by mass outlets in 1970, compared with 25 percent in 1960, and 20 percent in 1950.

Table J-5. Number of Retail Florist Shops for Selected Years, 1948–1967.

Sales Volume	1948		1954		1958		1963		1967	
	No.	Percent	No.	Percent	No.	Percent	No.	Percent	No.	Percent
Less than $19,000	6,976	47	7,648	47	8,315	43	6,969	35	7,405	33
$20,000–$49,000	4,008	27	5,600	34	6,652	35	6,804	34	7,295	33
$50,000–$299,000	1,845	13	2,462	15	3,246	17	4,497	23	6,741	30
$300,000 and over	31	*a	47	*a	75	*a	108	*a	224	1
Not operating entire year	1,889	13	522	3	888	5	1,423	7	786	3
Total	14,749	100	16,279	100	19,176	100	19,801	100	22,451	100

Source: U.S. Bureau of the Census data.
a. Less than 1 percent.

Supermarkets especially have begun to recognize the profit and growth potential in flowers and plants. A private unpublished study estimated that in 1968, 80 percent of all supermarkets carried some potted plants, but only 10 percent offered cut flowers for sale. Surveys by both the University of Colorado[5] and *Progressive Grocer*[6] magazine indicate that this latter percentage has increased sharply. The Colorado study, which was based on 79 retail food chains, showed that 50 percent of the chains offered cut flowers on some basis, and that 90 percent sold potted plants. The Alpha Beta chain on the West Coast, an early pioneer in floriculture marketing, estimates that cut flowers and potted plants currently represent about equal shares of their total sales.

Despite increased marketing activities by mass outlets, there are still major problems to be resolved: (1) absence of a real commitment to, and understanding of, floriculture at the central management level, owing partly to the lack of knowledge and partly to unsatisfactory past experience; (2) lack of experience in handling, at the store level, floriculture products, which require more intensive care than other perishables in the produce department; (3) a strong tendency by retail chains, especially supermarkets, to promote floriculture items on a periodic basis rather than as a consistent year-round operation, the varieties selected for promotion being chosen on the basis of price and availability, rather than market development; (4) a strong tendency to maintain higher margins on floriculture items instead of using them as a basis for building in-store turnover; (5) high loss rates for floriculture products as a result of poor quality and poor handling; (6) inability to obtain adequate varieties and volume from a single dependable source of supply.

A recent significant development in the retail marketing of floriculture products was the acquisition by the Pillsbury Company of Backman's European Flower Markets (BEFM) in 1971. BEFM has small retail units managed by its own personnel in locations with high pedestrian traffic, such as supermarkets, discount houses, department stores, and airport terminals. The host establishment receives 10 percent of the gross sales from the unit.

BEFM does not open an outlet unless it believes the location has the potential for sales of $60,000 per year. The product line reportedly comprises about 30 percent artificial flowers and gift items. Prices generally are 40 to 60 percent below those in retail floral shops for comparable products.

The BEFM retail outlets in a metropolitan area are served by a central distribution center that performs supplying, warehousing, preparation, pricing, and delivery functions. Pillsbury has indicated that it plans to expand BEFM operations by establishing distribution centers and retail outlets in major metropolitan centers. BEFM is an innovator in the floriculture industry, and its methods of operation may be heralding future activities within the industry.

Historically, the chief coordinator in the distribution system has been the floral wholesaler, located approximately in the middle of the traditional distribution system with access to both producers and retailers. Formerly, wholesalers handled flowers and plants almost exclusively on a consignment basis. Today, however, an estimated 50–60 percent of their volume is obtained by purchase.

Wholesalers have the very important function of providing credit to the system. Over 90 percent of their sales are to retail florist shops, and virtually all of these are on credit. Reportedly, credit losses are minimal because of personal knowledge of individual customers and their capacity to pay.

The growing importance of mass floriculture marketing outlets is reducing the importance of the wholesaler in the total industry structure. Not only are food and variety chains expanding their activities, but other large, well-capitalized companies are entering the retail floriculture industry. Examples include BEFM, franchised "Flowers from Sears" outlets, Green Giant garden centers, and others. The operations of these companies tend to be partially integrated to include many of the functions traditionally performed by wholesalers. Large-volume retailers want full product lines, stable prices, and dependable year-round supplies of quality products. The future growth of mass retailing will exert far-reaching influence on the vertical chain of production and distribution in commercial floriculture.

The trend toward greater concentration in the industry also is occurring at the grower level. Despite the increase in production of commercial floriculture products, the number of growers has declined significantly since 1966. Furthermore, partly because of improved transportation, production has become more concentrated geographically. California and Colorado have emerged as the primary producers of cut flowers, while Florida dominates foliage-plant production. Not only have smaller growers tended to leave the industry, but those that remain have tended to become suppliers to other large growers or grower-shippers interested in filling out their product lines, supplying seasonal requirements, or meeting the specialized needs of large retailers.

Floriculture in the United States is still, however, essentially an industry of small businesses. A Department of Agriculture survey[7] of growers in California, Florida, and Colorado indicated that only 12 percent had total sales in excess of $1 million per year. Large growers appear to play a more dominant role in foliage plants than in cut flowers. During the late 1960s, two large national corporations, United Brands and Stratford of Texas, acquired floriculture production facilities. Both of these operations are primarily in live plants rather than cut flowers.

Along with the increase in concentration has come a shortening of distribution channels throughout the vertical structure of the floriculture industry. One approach is through forward integration from growing into shipping, distribution, or both. The Department of Agriculture survey referred to above indicates that 70 percent of the floriculture shippers are also growers.[8] Traditional floriculture brokers have virtually disappeared except to the extent that large growers also act as brokers in obtaining supplies needed by regular customers that they are unable to provide themselves.

Not only has vertical integration increased, but there has been an even greater increase in the volume of direct selling from large grower-shippers to retail chains, other mass outlets, and, to a lesser degree, retail florists. Bachman's European Flower Markets, for example, procures virtually its entire supply of flowers and plants directly from growers or grower-shippers.

As the industry changes from a highly fragmented, uncoordinated network of small individual units to a more concentrated structure, there is a growing need to develop an efficient logistics systems for procuring, consolidating, and distributing floriculture products from both domestic and foreign sources to large retail buyers throughout the United States. On the one hand, the economics of large-scale production makes it attractive for growers to specialize in one or a few varieties. On the other hand, successful mass marketing will require a full product line.

Despite technological advances in airfreight and refrigerated-truck transportation, the cost and reliability of transport remains a major problem for all participants in the system. Jewell Foliage of San Antonio, Texas, has found, for example, that it can provide better service to many of its customers at cheaper costs by having its own fleet of delivery trucks. These trucks deliver 80 percent of Jewell's greenery. The remaining 20 percent is delivered by common carriers. However, the loss rate for foliage delivered by common carrier is twenty times that experienced by Jewell's own fleet of trucks.

Air shipments are increasing in importance because growing areas are becoming more concentrated in areas far removed from major markets. However, shipping by air offers no assurance that the product will arrive in good condition because most of the total transit time is spent on the ground, often in an environment lacking proper temperature control. Several years ago the Department of Agriculture conducted a series of studies that showed that it typically requires 18 hours for a shipment of cut flowers to go from the West Coast to a wholesaler on the East Coast. Only 33 percent of this time, or about 6 hours, was spent on the plane. Forty-five percent of the time was spent on the ground in the airports, and 22 percent was spent in transit to and from the airport.

The government has begun to assume a more significant role in the floriculture industry. It is the source of most of the funds used for research in floriculture. The Department of Agriculture now provides information on prices, shipments, and imports of floriculture products on a regular basis through the Agricultural Marketing Service. Increasing attention is being given to establishing government standards for grading cut flowers and potted plants. In March 1972 a draft was circulated to industry participants that focused on grades for cut carnations. If the ideas in this draft are approved, carnations will become the first cut flower or potted plant with established government grading standards.

Central America: Potential and Problems

Central America, although still accounting for only a small fraction of the total supply, has begun to develop as a significant exporter of floriculture products to the United States. According to 1972 trade statistics, the value of cut flowers and foliage imports from Central America amounted to $443,000, compared with only $27,000 six years earlier.[9] Furthermore, these figures are understated since they exclude individual shipments valued at $250 or less. Central America accounted for between 4 and 5 percent of total U. S. imports of cut flowers and foliage in 1972. Guatemala, as Table J–4 shows, was in 1972 the U. S. market's leading foreign supplier of standard chrysanthemums, daisies, and statice, and an important source of pompons, roses, and chamaedorea.

The increase in Central American floriculture exports to the United States has come about as the result of several built-in economic and climatic advantages.

1. Weather conditions favor production in Central America. Not only is there little danger of damage or loss due to frost or cold weather, but, more important, growing times of many large-volume varieties are significantly shorter than for the same product in Florida and other U. S. producing locations. Furthermore, the cool nights and the altitude produce very sturdy and durable blooms and plants with good shelf life.
2. Land suitable for floriculture is both plentiful and inexpensive. Land preparation costs in Central America have been estimated at less than 10 percent of comparable costs in Florida.
3. There is a readily available supply of relatively cheap labor. Basic daily wage rates paid to agricultural labor in Central America range from $0.80 to $1.50 per day. Even after allowing an additional 50–100 percent for social security, medical benefits, severance pay, and other costs required by government regulations, wage costs per employee are far below U. S. levels.
4. A nucleus of floricultural knowledge has been developed in each of the Central American countries during the last several years. Many projects have been undertaken primarily to serve the expanding local market, but in the process, experience applicable to producing flowers and plants for export markets has been accumulated. Also, the very fact that the floriculture industry is relatively young, with most of its accumulated experience concentrated in the last 4–5 years, suggests that it may be in a position to respond effectively to the requirements of a changing market structure in the United States.
5. Proximity to the United States gives Central American produces an important locational advantage. Many Central American producing areas are closer to major East Coast cities than is California.
6. There may be a significant long-run opportunity for Central America to produce and to develop a market for a wide variety of tropical floriculture products now sold in only very small quantities in the United States. This

could include such varieties as bird of paradise, anthurium, heliconia, and ginger.

Despite these advantages, the Central American floriculture industry faces major problems in achieving a significant share of the U. S. market for cut flowers and plants. A detailed analysis is beyond the scope of this study, but the principal problems may be summarized as follows:

1. Knowledge of the U. S. market and its import and distribution procedures is, at best, very limited among Central American producers. Few growers understand the strucutre of the U. S. floriculture industry. Growers frequently do not know how to penetrate the market nor do they have contacts to assist them in making an effective entry.
2. The problem most often mentioned by Central American producers is the high cost and unreliability of available transport facilities. Despite the advances that have been made in both air cargo and containerized roll-on roll-off shipping, efficient low-cost transportation of floriculture products from Central America to foreign markets is not available at the present time. The reasons are complex but they include the lack of physical facilities, poor handling techniques, absence of substantial back-haul volume to Central America, relatively small individual shipments, and government regulation of the operations of national airlines.
3. Other government regulations tend to be an important constraint in some countries. These include high duties on imported materials needed for production, and in some cases export taxes on flowers and plants leaving the country; in addition, industrial incentives to manufacturing businesses are lacking.
4. Central America faces formidable competition from other Latin American sources, notably Colombia and Ecuador, which are aggressively developing their floriculture export industries. In 1972, for example, Central American exports of cut flowers amounted to barely 20 percent of exports from Colombia and Ecuador combined.
5. Little coordination exists within the industry, despite the relatively small number of participants. Contact and communication among growers are infrequent. Coordinating activities and cooperation to solve joint problems, such as inadequate transportation, do not take place.
6. There are problems with production inputs. Imported supplies from the United States and Europe are subject to high duties and much delay, but local substitutes frequently are inferior in quality. A large part of the differential in wage cost between Central America and the United States is not translated into a corresponding advantage in labor cost per unit because of low productivity and high costs of training in Central America. The lack of trained personnel at both farm-supervisor and field-worker levels will be especially acute as the industry expands at a more rapid rate.

7. Most Central American floriculture growers are small by U. S. standards, and, in general, tend to be quite diversified in the number of varieties grown. This makes it impossible to achieve the potential economies of scale that are inherent in large-scale floriculture production.

Linkages tying Central American production more closely to the American floriculture market are developing. Large U. S. retailers and wholesale distributors are beginning to enter contractual arrangements with Central American producers. These contracts take many forms, but generally they state that the grower will supply the retailer or wholesaler with a specified quantity of a particular kind of flower or plant of a given quality within a certain time period.

Some U. S. companies are integrating backward into Latin American production. This appears to be occurring more in the foliage than the cut-flower industry. Both United Brands and Stratford of Texas have production operations of several hundred acres in Central America.

Transfer of production and other technical knowledge from the United States to Central America is taking place on a limited scale. Central America's production potential is beginning to attract people with training and experience in the U. S. floriculture industry. This increased use of persons with U. S. training and experience will strengthen the linkages between production locations in Central America and markets in the United States.

Two distinct market segments are emerging in the U. S. floriculture industry. One is very service-oriented, and its needs are being supplied primarily by retail florist shops. The other is more product- and price-oriented, and its needs are being met primarily by mass outlets. It appears that the greatest opportunity for Central American growers will be in serving the needs of the mass retailers.

Central American growers can produce high-quality products at reasonable costs. They have climatic advantages that enable them to be dependable, year-round sources of supply. They are not bound by a traditional system, as are many American producers, and are in a position to be more innovative in serving the mass marketer interested in shortening the distribution channel, broadening the product line, and providing quality products at reasonable costs to the consumer.

Cheaper labor costs may enable the Central American producers to perform many merchandising operations at lower costs than U. S. retailers. For example, one Central American producer now is cutting flowers to lengths specified by his buyer and ships the flowers in packages ready for immediate display in retail outlets.

The opportunities for Central America to become a significant supplier of floriculture products to the U. S. market is great. The structure of the industry is changing, and this is creating new opportunities for growth and profit for Central American producers.

NOTES TO APPENDIX J

1. U. S. Department of Agriculture, Economic Research Service, *A Graphic View of the Retail Florist Industry* (Marketing Research Report 788, April 1967).
2. U. S. Department of Agriculture, Economic Research Service, *Commercial Floriculture and Related Produces* (Statistical Supplement to Marketing Research Report 855, October 1969).
3. U. S. Department of Commerce, Bureau of the Census, *Census of Business* (Washington, D. C.: U. S. Government Printing Office, 1971).
4. U. S. Department of Agriculture, Economic Research Service, *A Graphic View of the Retail Florist Industry.*
5. Leonard E. Daykin, "Flowers Boom as New Profit Category," *Progressive Grocer* (February 1972).
6. *Ibid.*
7. U. S. Department of Agriculture, Economic Research Service, *Shipping Point Markets for Flowers: Practice and Problems of California and Florida Shippers* (Marketing Research Report 972, August 1972).
8. *Ibid.*
9. U. S. Department of Agriculture, Economic Research Service, *U. S. Foreign Agricultural Trade Statistical Report* (Supplement to Foreign Agricultural Trade of the U. S., 1966; and 1972).

Appendix K

Press Release: Chester, Blackburn & Roder, Inc.

CHESTER, BLACKBURN & RODER, INC.

1040 BISCAYNE BOULEVARD, MIAMI, FLORIDA 33132
TELEPHONE 305/377-3781, TWX 810-848 6535, CABLE CHEBLAROD

SHIP BROKERS · OPERATORS · AGENTS

OFFICES IN:
NEW YORK
ST. THOMAS
TRINIDAD
ST. CROIX

MAILING ADDRESS:
P. O. BOX 1470
MIAMI, FLORIDA
33101

P R E S S   R E L E A S E

June 6, 1974

FOR IMMEDIATE RELEASE

      CHESTER, BLACKBURN & RODER (MIAMI), INC. has announced that FLOMERCA TRAILER SERVICE will commence weekly Roll-on/Roll off service from Miami to Central America this month.

      FLOMERCA TRAILER SERVICE, the result of an agreement between Flota Mercante Gran Centro Americana, S.A. and Pan American Mail Line, Inc. has received the approval of both the Federal Maritime Commission and the Government of Guatemala.

      In Guatemala the service will be represented by Flota Mercante Gran Centro Americana, S. A. Managing Agents in the U.S.A. for FLOMERCA TRAILER SERVICE are Chester, Blackburn & Roder, Inc. of Florida.

      The trailership M/V PANATLANTIC is being designated by FLOMERCA TRAILER SERVICE. John Lynch, Vice President of Chester, Blackburn & Roder, Inc. stated that "this vessel would increase the frequency of service between Miami and Guatemala without overtonnaging the trade".

CHESTER, BLACKBURN & RODER, INC.

1040 BISCAYNE BOULEVARD, MIAMI, FLORIDA 33132
TELEPHONE 305/377-3781, TWX 810-848 6535, CABLE CHEBLAROD

SHIP BROKERS · OPERATORS · AGENTS

OFFICES IN:
NEW YORK
ST. THOMAS
TRINIDAD
ST. CROIX

MAILING ADDRESS:
P. O. BOX 1470
MIAMI, FLORIDA
33101

PRESS RELEASE
PAGE 2

      As an instrument of Flota Mercante Gran
Centro Americana, S.A., the Guatemalan National Line,
the new service is authorized to carry Guatemalan
cargo subject to the industrial promotion law and the
Central American tax incentives agreement for industrial
development. The fully trailerized service will be
from Miami's new Dodge Island Seaport to Santo Tomas de
Castilla, Guatemala and all inland points. Through
Bills of Lading will be issued. Cargo will be received
in Miami at Marine Terminals, Inc., Cargo Shed "D",
Dodge Island Seaport, Miami, Florida.

      "Over 100 refrigerated trailers have been
allocated to the service", Mr. Lynch stated. "It is
all first-class equipment capable of handling frozen
meats, shrimp, refrigerated fruits and vegetables.
Additional equipment such as flatbeds, lowboys, dry
trailers and reefers will be drawn from the Marine Terminals'
equipment pool at Miami when it is needed."

For further information on FLOMERCA TRAILER SERVICE, please
contact CHESTER, BLACKBURN & RODER, INC. in Miami.

Appendix L

Agricultural Educational Institutions in Central America by Country and Education Level

Country	Institution	Level
Costa Rica	Universidad de Costa Rica	University
	Escuela Superior de Ciencias Contables	University
	Instituto Interamericano de Ciencas Agricolas (IICA)	University
	Escuela Tecnica Agrícola de San Carlos	University–vocational
	Escuela Tecnica Agrícola de Santa Clara	University–vocational
	Escuela Tecnica Agrícola de Alajuela	University–vocational
	Instituto Profesional Agropecuario (9 branches)	University
	Instituto de Capacitación Tecnica Agropecuario (12 branches)	Secondary
	Escuela Normal Superior–Heredia	Secondary
	Centro de Desarrollo Industrial	Short course
El Salvador	Universidad El Salvador	University
	Universidad Jose Simeon Canas	University
	Escuela Nacional de Agricultura	University–vocational
	Instituto Nacional de Agricultura de Chalatenango	Secondary
	Instituto Nacional de Agricultura de Morazán	Secondary
	Servicio de Formación Profesional y Aprendizaje del Departamento National de Mano de Obra	Short course
	Centro de Productividad Industrial	Short course
	Centro de Estudios Económicos	Short course
	Institute Salvadoreno de Fomento	Short course
	Dirección Comercial de Agricultura	Short course
Guatemala	Universidad de San Carlos	University
	Universidad Rafael Candivan	University
	Universidad Francisco Marroquin	University
	Universidad de Rafael Landivar	University
	Universidad de Mariano Galvez	University

	Universidad de Guatemala	
	(Facultad de Agronomía)	University
	Universidad del Valle	University
	Instituto Tecnico de Agricultura	University–vocational
	Instituto Tecnico de Capacitación	
	y Productividad (INTECAP)	Short course
	Centro de Fomento de Productividad	Short course
Honduras	Universidad Nacional Autónomo de	
	Honduras	University
	Escuela Agrícola Panamericana	University–vocational
	Universidad Nacional de La Cieba	
	(Facultad de Agronomía)	University
	Universidad Nacional de Honduras	
	(Tegucigalpa)	University
	Universidad Nacional San Pedro de Sula	University
	Facultad de Ciencias–Forestales La Cieba	University
	Centro Universitario Regional del Norte	University
	Escuela Nacional de Ciencias Forestales	University–vocational
	Escuela Nacional de Guardabosques	Vocational
	Escuela Nacional de Agricultura de	
	Catacamas	Secondary
	Escuela Agricola de El Zamorano	Vocational
	Escuela Agricultura "John F. Kennedy"	Secondary
	Escuela Forestal de Siguatepeque	Vocational
	Centro Cooperative Tecnico Industrial	
	(CCTI)	Short course
	Servicio de Formacion Profesional y	
	Aprendizaje (INFOP)	Short course
Nicaragua	Instituto Centroamericana de Adminis-	University
	tración de Empresas (INCAE)	
	Universidad Centroamericana	University
	Universidad Nacional Autónomo de	
	Nicaragua	University
	Escuela Nacional de Agricultura	University
	Instituto Politecnico de Nicaragua	University–vocational
	Escuela International de Agricultura y	
	Ganadería	University–vocational
	Escuela de Agricultura de Esteli	University–vocational
	Centro Superior de Estudios de	
	Contadores	Vocational
	Liceo Agrícola Esteli	Vocational
	Escuela de Agricultura de Rivas	Secondary
	Liceos Agrícolas de Nicaragua (officiales)	Secondary–vocational
	Centro de Cooperación Tecnico Industrial	Short course
	Camera de Industrias	Short course
	Camera de Comercio	Short course
	Instituto Nacional de Aprendizaje (INA)	Short course
Panama	Administración de Empresas	
	(Facultad de Comercio)	University
	Administración de Empresas	
	(Facultad de Comercio)	University
	Universidad Nacional de Panama	
	(3 branches)	University

Salomon Ponce Aguilera	Secondary–vocational
Granja de Caimito	Secondary–vocational
Felix Olivares	Secondary
La Palma	Secondary
Instituto de Artes Mecanicas	Secondary
Granja de Tonosi	Secondary
Centro Vocacional de la Chorrera	Secondary
Instituto Nacional de Agricultura	Secondary

Appendix M

Escuela Agricola Panamericana Curriculum

Table M–1. Escuela Agricola Panamericana Curriculum

Quarter[a]	Course	Lecture	Laboratory	Valuation units[b]
		Hours per week		
I	English	3	2	4
	Basic mathematics (Mathematics I)	3	0	3
	Vegetable production	3	0	3
	Principles of agricultural economics	3	0	3
	Technical writing and library use	2	0	2
		14	2	15
II	Systematic botany	3	2	4
	Algebra (Mathematics II)	3	0	3
	Horticulture I	3	0	3
	English II	3	0	3
	Inorganic chemistry	3	2	4
	Introduction to statistics	3	0	3
		18	4	20
III	Zoology	3	2	4
	Plant propagation	3	0	3
	Organic chemistry and biochemistry	3	2	4
	Plane trigonometry (Mathematics III)	3	0	3
		12	4	14
IV	Farm machinery I	2	2	3
	Forestry	3	2	4
	Agronomy I	4	0	4
	English III	3	0	3
	Applied mathematics (Mathematics IV)	3	0	3
		15	4	17

Table M–1.   (cont.)

| Quarter[a] | Course | Hours per week | | Valuation units[b] |
		Lecture	Laboratory	
V	Soils	3	2	4
	Genetics	4	0	4
	Agricultural accounting	3	0	3
	Agronomy II	4	0	4
	English IV	3	0	3
		17	2	18
VI	Soil fertility	3	2	4
	Vegetable physiology	3	2	4
	Horticulture II	3	0	3
	Farm machinery II	2	2	3
		11	6	14
VII	Pig culture	3	0	3
	Topography	3	2	4
	Animal anatomy and physiology	3	0	3
	Farm management	3	0	3
		12	2	13
VIII	Entomology	3	3	4
	Agriculture	3	0	3
	Veterinary science	3	0	3
	Beef cattle	3	0	3
	Dairy cattle	3	0	3
		15	2	16
IX	Animal nutrition	3	1	3
	Agrostology	3	2	4
	Soil conservation	3	0	3
	Dairy products	3	2	4
	Agricultural extension	2	0	2
		14	5	16
	Total	128	31	143

a. 15 weeks each.
b. 1 valuation unit or credit corresponds to 1 lecture hour or 2 laboratory hours per week.

Horticultural Course Outline

**NATIONAL SCHOOL OF AGRICULTURE
AND LIVE STOCK, MANAGUA, NICARAGUA**

**Analytical Program of Cultivation II
(Horticulture)**

Prerequisite: Edaphology and plant physiology
Intensity: 3 hours of theory and 2 hours of practice per week; 4 credits

A. *Theory*
1. *Importance of horticulture*
   1.1 Economics; market; prices; present and future demand
   1.2. Diet: vitamins, protein content, etc.
   1.3. Present situation of farming

2. *Classification*
   2.1. Major and secondary fruits
   2.2. Botany
   2.3. Other

3. *Ecological factors*
   3.1. Soils: pH, depth, drainage, fertility, topography
   3.2. Climate: temperature, rainfall, light intensity and duration
   3.3. Latitude

4. *Propagation*
   4.1. Sexual (seeds)
       4.1.1. Controlled pollination, methods and advantages
       4.1.2. Seed production, handling, vitality, dormancy, germination

4.2. Asexual
    4.2.1. Parthenocarpy
    4.2.2. Apomixis and polyembryony
    4.2.3. Main factors in methods of vegetative propagation
    4.2.4. Clones or varieties
    4.2.5. Factors affecting pollination, flower fertilization, and fruit setting

5. *Genetic variability*
    5.1. Mutations and chimeras
    5.2. Natural and controlled crossing
    5.3. Selection of local individuals for outstanding production and quality

6. *Establishment of groves*
    6.1. Production of seedlings: methods, location, spacing, etc.
    6.2. Nurseries: location, preparation, seeding, season, systems, fertilization, and other cultivation practices
    6.3. Definite seeding: location and transplantation
        6.3.1. Land preparation, staking and hole digging
        6.3.2. Spacing and interplanting of crops
        6.3.3. Cultivation practices: weed control, pruning, fertilization, pest and disease control

7. *Generalities on principal diseases, pests, and nutritional problems*

8. *Factors determining quality*
    8.1. Variety
    8.2. Ecological conditions
    8.3. Cultivation practices
    8.4. Harvest

9. *Commercialization*
    9.1. Classification
    9.2. Packaging and transportation
    9.3. Transportation

10. Study of the five fruit crops that have the greatest economic importance in the country. This will be in accordance with point one (1) and (9) mentioned above, according to cultivation the five (5) fruits will be selected from the following list:

    1. Avocado
    2. Banana

  3. Prune
  4. Citrics
  5. Coconut
  6. Peach
  7. Mango
  8. Maranon
  9. Papaya
  10. Pear and apple
  11. Pineapple

11. Secondary fruits with economic potential for the area:

  1. Haw
  2. Annonaceae
  3. Starapple
  4. Caramboca
  5. Passion fruit
  6. Guava
  7. Castor
  8. Saboticaba
  9. Jocote
  10. Mamey
  11. Nispero
  12. Pejibaye
  13. Zapote
  14. Tamarind

B. *Practices*
  1. *Propagation*
     1.1. Seed germination
     1.2. Rooting of cuttings. Use of growth-stimulating substances

  2. *Nurseries: establishment and handling*

  3. *Grafting*
     3.1. Equipment, patterns, twigs, etc.
     3.2. Mechanics of the various methods

  4. *Transplantation*
     4.1. Root pruning
     4.2. Rooting out with or without soil balls
     4.3. Field sowing

5. *Fungicides, insecticides. herbicides, and fertilizers*
    5.1. Mix preparation
    5.2. Forms of application
    5.3. Precautions

6. *Pruning methods*

7. *Harvesting, classification, and packaging of fruits*

Visits to plantations in experimental fields and private farms are recommended in order to observe and comment on the ways in which the various operations are implemented. Visits to fruit-processing plants are also recommended.

Appendix O

Schedules and Lists of Participants for Meetings: 1972–1973

PROJECT 928 MEETING
May 15 & 16, 1973

List of Participants

Sr. Ricardo Alfaro–Castillo
Edificio Mercury
Calle Ruben Dario No. 100
San Salvador, El Salvador

Dr. Robert Armour, Director
Escuela Agricola Panamerican
Tegucigalpa, Honduras

Professor Henry Arthur
Emeritus
Baker 103
Harvard Business School
Soldiers Field
Boston, Massachusetts 02163

Mrs. Ernette Au
Research Assistant
Harvard Business School
Anderson 21
Soldiers Field
Boston, Massachusetts 02163

Mr. Francisco Bazzani
Calle 38 #8–56 of 201
Bogota, Colombia

Mr. Robert Brisker
Vice President of Corporate
  Procurement
The National Tea Company
8303 W. Higgins Road
Chicago, Illinois 60631

Mr. Phillip Busby
Vice President
SEA–LAND
Elizabeth, New Jersey

Mr. Hector Calderon
General Manager & Executive
  Vice President
Coordinated Caribbean Transport
1001 Port Boulevard
Miami, Florida 33132

Dr. David Cole
Department of Agricultural Economics
Michigan State University
East Lansing, Michigan

Mr. Geronimo Collado
c/o Doctoral House
Harvard Business School
Soldiers Field
Boston, Massachusetts 02163

Mr. Val deBeausset
Asesor del President
Banco Centromericano de Integracion
   Economica (BCIE)
Tegucigalpa, Honduras, C.A.

Mr. R. Alexander Detrick
General Manager of Grocery Procurement
The National Tea Company
8303 W. Higgins Road
Chicago, Illinois 60631

Mr. Thomas F. DiMare
General Manager
DiMare Brothers, Inc.
30 Water Street
Arlington, Massachusetts 02174

George Eason
Central Africa
Agricultural Officer
Room 4636
New State Department Building
Washington, D. C.

Dr. Edward Felton
Iran Center for Management Studies
P. O. Box 11–15–73
Tehran, Iran

Professor Ray A. Goldberg
Harvard Business School
Agribusiness Department
Anderson 21
Soldiers Field
Boston, Massachusetts 02163

Dr. Joseph Ganitsky
Decano
Facultad de Administracion
Universidad de los Andes
Apartado Area 51,570
Bogota, Colombia

Mr. Alan Haberman
President
First National Stores, Inc.
5 Middlesex Avenue
Somerville, Massachusetts 02143

Mr. Kenneth Hoadley
Research Assistant
INCAE
Apartado 2485
Managua, Nicaragua, C. A.

Mr. Gerry Horne
Deputy Director
Bureau of Technical Assistance
AID, State Department Building
Washington, D. C. 20523

Mrs. Diane Hunt
Research Assistant
Harvard Business School
Anderson 22
Soldiers Field
Boston, Massachusetts 02163

Ing. Edgar Leonel A. Ibarra
Decano
Facultad de Agronomia
Universidad de San Carlos de
   Guatemala
Apartado Postal No. 1545
Guatemala, C. A.

Mr. Ludwig Ingram
Chief, Industrial Service
ICAITI
Guatemala, Guatemala, C. A.

Mr. Kamran Kashani
Harvard Business School
Doctoral House
Soldiers Field
Boston, Massachusetts 02163

Mr. Jack Koteen
Director, Bureau of Technical Assistance
AID, State Department Building
Washington, D. C. 20523

Dr. David Korten
Director of Planning & Institutional
  Development
Apartado Postal 2485
Managua, Nicaragua

Mr. Robert Laubis
Rural Development
Latina American Bureau AID
State Department Building
Washington, D. C. 20523

Mr. Juan Lleras
Harvard Business School
McCulloch A–21
Soldiers Field
Boston, Massachusetts 02163

Dr. Millard Long
Development Advisory Service
1737 Cambridge Street
Cambridge, Massachusetts 02138

Mr. Richard C. McGinity
Research Assistant
Harvard Business School
Anderson 21
Soldiers Field
Boston, Massachusetts 02163

Professor Noel McGinn
Harvard Graduate School of Education
503 Larson Hall
Harvard University
Cambridge, Massachusetts 02138

Professor Robert Merry
Director Course Development and
  Educational Services
Harvard Business School
Soldiers Field
Boston, Massachusetts 02163

Ms. Christopher Mock
Mellon A–21
Harvard Business School
Soldiers Field
Boston, Massachusetts 02163

Lic. Sergio U. Molina
Assistente al Presidente
Banco Central
Managua, Nicaragua

Ing. Antonio Mora R.
Ministro de Educacion
Ministerio de Educacion
Managua, Nicaragua

Dr. Michael J. Moran
General Coordinator of Agricultural
  Marketing Program
Inter-American Institute for
  Atricultural Sciences (IICA)
Apartado Postal 10281
San Jose, Costa Rica

Mr. J. David Morrissey
Farmer Cooperative Service
United States Department of
  Agriculture
Washington, D. C. 20250

Ms. Christina W. O'Bryan
Research Assistant
Anderson 21
Harvard Business School
Soldiers Field
Boston, Massachusetts 02163

Mr. Arturo Padilla-Lira
Instituto Nacional de
  Commercialization Agricola
  (INDECA)
11 Calle 3–23, Zona 9
Guatemala, Guatemala, C. A.

Prof. Rodolfo Paiz
Faculty, INCAE
Apartado Postal 2485
Managua, Nicaragua

Sr. Eduardo Polo
President, CARRULA
Carrera 68–D #21
Bogota, Colombia

Mr. Paris Q. Reidhead
Director General
Institute for International
  Development, Inc.
1901 North Moore Street, Suite 809
Arlington, Virginia 22209

Professor Paul Roberts
Building 1–181
Massachusetts Institute of
  Technology
Cambridge, Massachusetts 02139

Mr. Robert Ross
President & Chief Executive Officer
Latin American Agribusiness
  Development Corporation
100 Biscayne Boulevard
Miami Beach, Florida 33132

Mr. Robert W. Schmeding
Acting Director of the Office of
  Education of the Technical
  Assistance Bureau of AID
State Department Building
Washington, D.C.

Professor Lee Schrader
Agribusiness Department
Harvard Business School
Soldiers Field
Boston, Massachusetts 02163

Ing. Noel Somarriba Barreto
Director, Universidad Nacional
  Autonoma de Nicaragua
Escuela Nacional de Agricultura
  y Ganaderia
Apartado Postal 453
Managua, Nicaragua

Dr. Kenneth Simmonds
INCAE
Apartado Postal 2485
Managua, Nicaragua

Dr. Harry Strachan
Dean, INCAE
Apartado Postal 2485
Managua, Nicaragua

Mr. Steve Tavilla
President, P. Tavilla Co., Inc.
78 New England Produce Center
Chelsea, Massachusetts 02150

Dr. Eric Thor
Administrator
Farmer Cooperative Service
U. S. Department of Agriculture
Washington, D. C. 20250

Mr. George A. Truitt
President
International Development
  Foundation, Inc.
Nicolas de Rivera 745
San Isidro, Lima, Peru

Mr. Thomas Wenstrand
Special Projects
Arizona—Colorado Land & Cattle Co.
201 Third Street South
Hopkins, Minnesota

Mr. Leonard Wilson
Economic Consultant to Agribusiness
36 Washington Street
Wellesley Hills, Massachusetts 02181

Ing. Noel Zuniga A.
Secretario General
P. O. Box 453
Escuela Nacional de Agricultura
  y Ganaderia
Managua, Nicaragua

PROJECT 928
Spring 1973 Meeting

DISCUSSION GROUPS AND ROOM ASSIGNMENTS

Group 1: Implementation of findings

	Room No.
Alfaro–Castillo	1
Armour	2
deBeausset	3
Busby	4
Goldberg	
Haberman	5
Hoadley	
Lleras	
McGinn	
Reidhead	6
Ross	7
Tavilla	8

Group 3: Central American fruit and vegetable system

	Room No.
Austin	
Eason	1
Koteen	2
Long	3
McGinity	
Mora	4
Morrissy	5
O'Bryan	
Paiz	
Roberts	
Strachan	6
Thor	7
deVos	8

Group 2: Central American educational system and adaptation to needs of agribusiness

	Room No.
Arthur	
Chaparro	1
Detrick	
DiMare	
Hunt	
Ibarra	2
Ingram	3
Laubis	4
Mock	
Moran	5
Padulla	6
Schrader	
Somarriba	7

Group 4: United States fruit and vegetable system

	Room No.
Au	
Brisker	
Calderon	2
Cole	3
Collado	
Felton	4
Horne	5
Korten	1
Merry	
Schmeding	6
Wenstrand	
Wilson	
Zuniga	7

PROJECT 928
AGRIBUSINESS MANAGEMENT FOR DEVELOPING COUNTRIES
MEETING

May 15 and 16, 1973

SCHEDULE

Tuesday, May 15

4:00–5:00 p.m.	Registration, McCollum 2
5:00–6:00 p.m.	Cocktails, South Terrace Dining Room Kresge Hall
6:00 p.m.	Dinner, South Terrace Dining Room Kresge Hall
7:00–8:00 p.m.	Opening Meeting, McCollum 2

Summary of the Project

8:00–10:00 p.m.   Subcommittee Discussion Groups:

1. Implementation of findings.

2. Central American educational system and adaptation to needs of agribusiness.

3. Central American fruit and vegetable system.

4. United States fruit and vegetable system.

Wednesday, May 16

7:30 a.m.	Breakfast, Faculty Club Kresge Hall
8:15–9:45 a.m.	First Session, McCollum 2

Report of first two subcommittee discussion groups.

9:45–10:15 a.m.	Coffee, McCollum East–West Lounge
10:15 a.m.–12:15 p.m.	Second Session, McCollum 2

Report of remaining subcommittee discussion groups.

12:15 p.m.	Lunch, South Terrace Dining Room Kresge Hall
1:30–3:30 p.m.	Wrap-up Session, McCollum 2

PROJECT 928 MEETING
November 28 and 29, 1972

List of Participants

From Central America

Sr. Ricardo Alfaro–Castillo
Edificio Mercury
Calle Ruben Dario No. 100
San Salvador, El Salvador

Dr. Rodolfo Quiros
Director
PROMECA
Guatemala, Guatemala

Ing. Edgar Leonel Ibara A.
Decano
Facultad de Agronomia
Cuidad Universitaria, Zona 12
Guatemala, Guatemala

Ing. Juan Esteban Restrepo
Director
Agro–Administration Department
Escuela Agricola Panamericana
Tegucigalpa, Honduras

Ing. Antonio Mora R.
Ministro de Educacion
Ministerio de Educacion
Managua, Nicaragua

Lic. Sergio U. Molina
Assistente al Presidente
Banco Central
Managua, Nicaragua

Ing. Noel Zuniga A.
Secretario General
P. O. Box 453
Escuela Nacional de Agricultura
  y Ganaderia
Managua, Nicaragua

Dr. Ernesto Cruz
Rector
INCAE
Apartado Postal 2485
Managua, Nicaragua

Dr. David C. Korten
INCAE
Apartado Postal 2485
Managua, Nicaragua

Dr. Gerrit de Vos
INCAE
Apartado Postal 2485
Managua, Nicaragua

Mr. Michael J. Moran
General Coordinator of Agricultural
  Marketing Program
Inter-American Institute for Agricultural
  Sciences (IICA)
Apartado Postal 10281
San Jose, Costa Rica

From South America

Mr. Joseph Ganitsky
Universidad los Andes
Ap. Aereo 51,570
Bogota, Colombia

From The United States

Mr. Jack Koteen
Director
Bureau of Technical Assistance
AID
State Department Building
Washington, D. C. 20523

Dr. Gerald Horne
Deputy Director
Bureau of Technical Assistance
AID
State Department Building
Washington, D. C. 20523

Mr. David Gaumer
Bureau of Technical Assistance
AID
State Department Building
Washington, D. C. 20523

Mr. Glen Coombs
ROCAP
Department of State
Agency for International Development
APO New York 90891

Mr. August Schumacher
International Bank for Reconstruction
 and Development
1818 H. Street N. W.
Washington, D. C. 20250

Mr. J. David Morrissy
Farmer Cooperative Service
U. S. Department of Agriculture
Washington, D. C. 20250

Mr. James Wayne
Louis-Dreyfus Corporation
One State Street Plaza
New York, New York 10004

Mr. Jasper Liotta
Head Buyer
The Grand Union Company
East Paterson, New Jersey

Mr. Thomas F. DiMare
General Manager
DiMare Bros. Inc.
30 Water Street
Arlington, Massachusetts 02174

Professor Paul Roberts
Massachusetts Institute of Technology
Cambridge, Massachusetts 02138

Dean George Lombard
Dean of Educational Affairs
Harvard Business School
Soldiers' Field
Boston, Massachusetts 02163

Professor Robert Merry
Director of Course Development and
 Educational Services
Harvard Business School
Soldiers Field
Boston, Massachusetts 02163

Professor James Austin
Agribusiness Department
Harvard Business School
Soldiers Field
Boston, Massachusetts 02163

Professor Lee Schrader
Agribusiness Department
Harvard Business School
Soldiers Field
Boston, Massachusetts 02163

Mr. Leonard Wilson
Economics Consultant to Agribusiness
36 Washington Street
Wellesley Hills, Massachusetts 02181

Mr. Geronimo Collado
c/o Doctoral House
Harvard Business School
Soldiers Field
Boston, Massachusetts 02163

Mr. Thomas Wenstrand
Agribusiness Department
Harvard Business School
Soldiers Field
Boston, Massachusetts 02163

Mrs. Diane Hunt
Agribusiness Department
Harvard Business School
Soldiers Field
Boston, Massachusetts 02163

Professor Ray Goldberg
Moffett Professor of Agriculture
  and Business
Harvard Business School
Soldiers Field
Boston, Massachusetts 02163

PROJECT 928 MEETING
November 28 and 29, 1972

Group Assignments

Group I: Role of agribusiness management education at the graduate level.

Group II: Role of agribusiness education within business firms.

Group III: Role of agribusiness education in college, technical and short course programs.

Group IV: What are the key management problem areas impeding the development of agribusiness firms?

Group V: What are the research priorities in Central American agribusiness:

Group I Morris N)

Dr. Ernesto Cruz
Mr. Joseph Ganitsky
Professor Ray Goldberg
Ing. Edgar Ibara A.
Professor Robert Merry
Dr. Michael Moran
Dr. Gerrit de Vos

Group II (Morris O)

Sr. Ricardo Alfaro C.
Mrs. Diane Hunt
Mr. Jack Koteen
Mr. Jasper Liotta
Lic. Jose Salazar Navarrete
Professor Paul Roberts
Mr. Jim Wayne
Mr. Tom Wenstrand

Group III (Morris P)

Professor Jim Austin
Ing. Alvaro Cordero R.
Mr. Tom DiMare
Dr. Gerry Horne
Dr. David Korten
Mr. David Morrissy
Ing. Edwin Navarro B.

Group IV (Morris Q)

Mr. Alan Haberman
Lic. Sergio U. Molina
Ing. Antonio Mora R.
Professor Lee Schrader
Mr. August Schumacher
Mr. Steve Tavilla

Group V (Morris S)

Mr. Gerry Collado
Dr. Glen Coombs
Dr. Rudolfo Quiros
Ing. Juan Esteban Resprepo
Mr. Leonard Wilson
Ing. Noel Zuniga A.

PROJECT 928 MEETING
November 28 and 29, 1972

Schedule

Tuesday, November 28

5:00 p.m.—6.00 p.m.	Cocktails, South Terrace Dining Room, Kresge Hall
6:00 p.m.—7:00 p.m.	Dinner, South Terrace Dining Room Kresge Hall
7:00 p.m.	Cordials and coffee, Kresge Hall
	Welcoming remarks Purpose and scope of meeting Discussion of meeting logistics

Wednesday, November 29

7:15 a.m.—8:00 a.m.	Breakfast, Faculty Club, Kresge Hall
8:15 a.m.—9:30 a.m.	First Session, Cotting House Library
9:30 a.m.—10:00 a.m.	Coffee, Cotting House Lounge
10:00 a.m.—11:00 a.m.	Group meetings: Group I — Morris N Group II — Morris O Group III — Morris P Group IV — Morris Q Group V — Morris S
11:00 a.m.—12:00 Noon	Second Session, Cotting House Library
12:15 p.m.—1:15 p.m.	Lunch, South Terrace Dining Room, Kresge Hall
1:30 p.m.—2:30 p.m.	Group Meetings: Group I — Morris N Group II — Morris O Group III — Morris P Group IV — Morris Q Group V — Morris S
2:30 p.m.—3:00 p.m.	Coffee, Cotting House Lounge
3:00 p.m.—4:00 p.m.	Final Session, Cotting House Library Summary and conclusions

PROJECT 928 MEETING
April 5 and 6, 1972

List of Participants

From Harvard

Dean George Lombard
Professor Robert Merry
Professor Paul Roberts
Dr. Edward Felton
Mr. August Schumacher
Mr. David Morrissy
Mr. Leonard Wilson
Mr. Geronimo Collado
Mr. Joseph Ganitsky
Mr. James Wayne
Mr. John Edmunds
Mr. James Wayne
Miss Joan Lanigan
Professor Ray Goldberg

From AID

Mr. Jack Koteen
Deputy Director
Bureau of Technical Assistance

Dr. Gerald Horne
Agricultural Director of ROCAP

From Central America

Mr. Dan Finberg
ROCAP

Mr. Ricardo Alvaro Castillo
El Salvador

Mr. Rudolfo Quiros
Director, PROMECA

Mr. Ludwig Ingram
Chief, Industrial Service, ICAITI

Dean Harry Strachan
INCAE

Professor James Austin
INCAE

Mr. Jaime Roman
INCAE

Brokers

Mr. Steve Tavilla
New England Produce Center

Retailers

Mr. Robert Brisker, Vice President
First National Stores

Mr. Jasper Liotta, Head Buyer
The Grand Union Company

World Bank

Mr. Elkyn Chaparro

PROJECT 928 MEETING
April 5 and 6, 1972

Agenda

Wednesday, April 5

7:00 p.m.—8:00 p.m.	Cocktails, Oriental Room, Kresge Hall
8:00 p.m.—9:00 p.m.	Buffet Dinner, Kresge
9:00 p.m.—9:30 p.m.	Cordials, Kresge

	Welcoming remarks
	Purpose and Scope of Meeting
	Preliminary Implications of Retailer's
	  Processor's, and Broker's
	  Questionaires
	Ray A. Goldberg

Thursday, April 6

7:45 a.m.	Breakfast, Kresge
8:30 a.m.—10:00 a.m.	Session #1—Cotting A

	8:30—9:30 Fruit and Vegetable System:
	  Trends, Marketing Orientation,
	  Critical Factors, and Alternative
	  Strategies August Schumacher and
	    David Morrissy
	9:30—10:00 Paul Roberts:
	  Transportation and Logistics

10:00 a.m.—10:30 a.m.	Coffee, Cotting Lounge
10:30 a.m.—12:00 Noon	Session #2—Anderson Lounge

	10:30—11:15 James Austin:
	  Central American Response to
	  Marketing Opportunities in the U.S.

	11:15—12:00 Len Wilson: The Floriculture Industry
12:00 Noon	Lunch, Kresge
1:00 p.m.—2:30 p.m.	Session #3—Anderson Lounge
	1:00—1:45 Ed Felton: Educational Programs

1:45–2:30 Len Wilson: Integration of Systems Applications and Managerial Needs

2:30 p.m.–3:00 p.m.　　　Coffee, Morris Lounge

3:00 p.m.–4:00 p.m.　　　Summary Session—Ray A. Goldberg

1) Business Managers' Opportunities
2) Education's Response to Managerial Requirements
3) Governmental Support of Activities

Anderson Lounge

Seminario Regional Sobre Horticultura con Enfasis en Olericultura

Guatemala, 8–17 de abril de 1973

PROGRAMA

Domingo 8   Arribo de participantes

Lunes 9

 8:30–10:00   Inauguración (programa aparte)

10:00–12:00   Importancia de los cultivos horticolas en el desarrollo
                     economico nacional y regional
                               Dr. Philip Church
                               ROCAP–AID

15:00–17:30   Panel sobre las hortalizas en la dieta humana
                               Moderator: Lic. Lucia Ramazzini
                               Tecnicos de INCAP

Martes 10

 8:30–10:00   Factores ecologicos en la producción de hortalizas
                               Dr. Jose Mondonedo
                               Professor Visitante UPR

10:00–12:00   Fisiología de hortalizas: propagación y control del
                     desarrollo
                               Ing. Romeo Martinez
                               Universidad de San Carlos

15:00–18:00   Demostraciones de fenómenos fisiologicos en hortilizas

> Ing. Jorge Benitez, Carlos
> Aguirre y Romeo Martinez
> Facultad de Agronomía, USAC

Miercoles 11

8:30–10:00   Fitomejoramiento en hortalizas

> Dr. Francisco Jordan
> Professor Visitante UPR

10:00–12:00   Plagas mas importantes en las hortalizas

> Dr. Jose de J. Castro
> Universidad de San Carlos

15:00–16:30   Enfermedades mas importantes en las hortalizas

> Ing. Nery Sosa

16:30–18:00   Manejo de hortalizas durante y despues de la cosecha

> Ing. Leonel Orozco
> INDECA

Jueves 12

7:00–18:00   Gira de estudios a Teculutan para ver las cucurbitaceas y solanaceas.

Viernes 13

8:30–10:30   Mesa redonda sobre problemas en la comercialización de hortalizas

> Moderator: Ing. Leonel Orozco
> INDECA

10:30–12:00   Plan de inversión para una empresa horticola

> Ing. Neptali Monterroso
> Facultad de Agronomía, USAC

15:00–18:00   Groupos de trabajos: formulación de planes de inversión

> Coordinadores de Grupo:
> Ing. Neptali Monterroso
> Ing. Felipe Garcia Solos
> Lic. Romeo Martinez
> Ing. Sergio Morales

Sabado 14

    7:00   Gira de estudios a Almolonga, Zunil, Labor Ovalle y La Cienega. Pernoctar en Motel El Campo, Quezaltenago

Domingo 15

   18:00   Regreso a Guatemala

Lunes 16

8:30–10:00   Mesa redonda sobre las tecnicas de ensenanza
                       Ing. Marco Tulio Urizar M.
                       IICA–Zona Norte

10:00–12:00   Métodos de extensión
                       Ing. Hernan Frias
                       IICA–Zona Norte

15:00–18:00   Trabajo de grupos: sobre asignaturas o cursos que debe ofrecer una facultad con orientación regional en horticultura
                       Coordinadores de Grupo:
                       Dr. Francisco Jordan
                       Ing. Romeo Martinez
                       Dr. Jose Mondonedo

Martes 17

8:30–12:00   Presentación, discusión y aprobación de trabajos, recomendaciones y acuerdos
                       Moderador:
                       Ing. Marco Tulio Urizar M.
                       IICA–Zona Norte

   12:00   Clausura (programa aparte)

Appendix Q

Acronyms and the Proper Names They Represent[a]

ABC*	— Administration of Small Farmer Well Being	
ADELA	— Atlantic Community Development Group for Latin America	(144)
AID	— Agency for International Development	(xviii)
ARS	— Agricultural Research Service	(61)
BANDESA*	— National Agricultural Development Bank	(171)
BNF*	— National Development Bank	(219)
CAADES*	— Confederation of Agricultural Associations of the State of Sinaloa	(84)
CAB	— Civil Aeronautics Board	(125)
CABEI*	— Central American Bank for Economic Integration	(124)
CARSVO*	— Eastern Regional Agricultural Cooperative of Various Services	(155)
CCT	— Coordinated Caribbean Transport	(117)
COPEX*	— El Salvador Cooperative	(155)
CSP*	— Superior Planning Board	(219)
DIFOCOOP*	— Direction of Cooperative Development	(234)
DIGESA*	— General Directorship of Agricultural Services	(171)
ELCO*	— Guatemalan packer-shipper	(155)
EXIMCO	— Export–Import Company	(164)
FAO	— Food and Agriculture Organization of the United Nations	(88)
FDA	— Food and Drug Administration	(343)
FLOMERCA*	— Central American Merchant Marine	(117)
FONDO*	— Guarantee Fund for Agriculture, Livestock, and Poultry	(83)

*Asterisked items have been translated from Spanish.
a. Numbers in parenthesis indicate location of first appearance in the text.

FTC	— Federal Trade Commission	(56)
FYRCO*	— Guatemalan export—brokerage firm	(168)
GUATEXPRO*	— Guatemalan Export Promotion Agency	(189)
HRI	— Hotel, Restaurant, and Institutional	(21)
IABD	— Inter-American Development Bank	(144)
IBEC	— International Basic Economy Corporation	(144)
ICAITI*	— Central American Institute for Technological Investigation	(155)
ITCA*	— Institute of Science and Agricultural Technology	(189)
IICA*	— Inter-American Institute for Agricultural Sciences	(271)
INA*	— National Agrarian Reform Institute	(218)
INCAE*	— Central American Graduate School of Business Administration	(266)
INDECA*	— National Institute for Agricultural Commercialization	(171)
INTA*	— National Institute of Agrarian Reform	(189)
LAAD	— Latin American Agribusiness Development Corporation	(4)
MRN*	— Ministry of Natural Resources	(219)
OAS	— Organization of American States	(268)
PERT	— Program Evaluation Review Technique	(170)
PROMECA*	— The Central American Common Market Export Promotion Agency	(144)
ROCAP	— Regional Office for Central America and Panama	(155)
SCICAS*	— Inter-American Cooperative Service of Supervised Agricultural Credit	(171)
TOPCO	— Legal Cooperative	(57)
UPFS*	— United Southern Fruit Producers	(219)
USDA	— United States Department of Agriculture	(27)

Appendix R

Tables of Weights and Measures

Linear Measure

1 inch	=	2.54 centimeters
12 inches = 1 foot	=	0.3048 meter
3 feet = 1 yard	=	0.9144 meter
5½ yards or 16½ feet = 1 rod (or pole or perch)	=	5.029 meters
40 rods = 1 furlong	=	201.17 meters
8 furlongs or 1,760 yards or 5,280 feet = 1 (statute) mile	= 1,609.3	meters
3 miles = 1 (land) league	=	4.83 kilometers

Square Measure

1 square inch	=	6.452 square centimeters
144 square inches = 1 square foot	= 929	square centimeters
9 square feet = 1 square yard	=	0.8361 square meter
30¼ square yards = 1 square rod (or square pole or square perch)	=	25.29 square meters
160 square rods or 4.840 square yards or 43,560 square feet = 1 acre	=	0.4047 hectare
640 acres = 1 square mile	= 259	hectares or 2.59 square kilometers
1 acre	=	.578 manzanas

Cubic Measure

1 cubic inch	= 16.387 cubic centimeters
1,728 cubic inches = 1 cubic foot	= 0.0283 cubic meter
27 cubic feet = 1 cubic yard	= 0.7646 cubic meter

(in units for cordwood, etc.)

16 cubic feet = 1 cord foot	
8 cord feet = 1 cord	= 3.625 cubic meters

Avoirdupois Weight

(The grain, equal to 0.0648 gram, is the same in all three tables of weight)

1 dram or 27.34 grains		=	1.772 grams
16 drams or 437.5 grains	= 1 ounce	=	28.3495 grams
16 ounces or 7,000 grains	= 1 pound	= 453.59	grams
100 pounds	= 1 hundredweight	= 45.36	kilograms
2,000 pounds	= 1 ton	= 907.18	kilograms

In Great Britain,
14 pounds (6.35 kilograms) = 1 stone, 112 pounds (50.80 kilograms) = 1 hundredweight, and 2,240 pounds (1,016.05 kilograms) = 1 long ton.

THE METRIC SYSTEM

Linear Measure

10 millimeters	= 1 centimeter	=	0.3937 inch
10 centimeters	= 1 decimeter	=	3.937 inches
10 decimeters	= 1 meter	=	39.37 inches or 3.28 feet
10 meters	= 1 decameter	=	393.7 inches
10 decameters	= 1 hectometer	=	328 feet 1 inch
10 hectometers	= 1 kilometer	=	0.621 mile
10 kilometers	= 1 myriameter	=	6.21 miles

Square Measure

100 square millimeters	= 1 square centimeter	=	0.15499 square inch
100 square centimeters	= 1 square decimeter	=	15.499 square inches
100 square decimeters	= 1 square meter	= 1,549.9	square inches or 1.196 square yards
100 square meters	= 1 square decameter	= 119.6	square yards
100 square decameters	= 1 square hectometer	= 2.471	acres
100 square hectometers	= 1 square kilometer	= 0.386	square mile

Land Measure

1 square meter	= 1 centiare	= 1,549.9	square inches
100 centiares	= 1 are	= 119.6	square yards
100 ares	= 1 hectare	= 2.471	acres
100 hectares	= 1 square kilometer	= 0.386	square mile
1 hectare	= 1.43 manzanas		

Volume Measure

1,000 cubic millimeters	= 1 cubic centimeter	=	.06102 cubic inch
1,000 cubic centimeters	= 1 cubic decimeter	= 61.02	cubic inches
1,000 cubic decimeters	= 1 cubic meter	= 35.314	cubic feet

(the unit is called a *stere* in measuring firewood)

Capacity Measure

10 milliliters	= 1 centiliter	=	.338 fluid ounce
10 centiliters	= 1 deciliter	=	3.38 fluid ounces
10 deciliters	= 1 liter	=	1.0567 liquid quarts or 0.9081 dry quart
10 liters	= 1 decaliter	=	2.64 gallons or 0.284 bushel
10 decaliters	= 1 hectoliter	=	26.418 gallons or 2.838 bushels
10 hectoliters	= 1 kiloliter	=	264.18 gallons or 35.315 cubic feet

Weights

10 milligrams	= 1 centigram	= 0.1543 grain
10 centigrams	= 1 decigram	= 1.5432 grains
10 decigrams	= 1 gram	= 15,432 grains
10 grams	= 1 decagram	= 0.3527 ounce
10 decagrams	= 1 hectogram	= 3.5274 ounces
10 hectograms	= 1 kilogram	= 2.2046 pounds
10 kilograms	= 1 myriagram	= 22.046 pounds
10 myriagrams	= 1 quintal	= 220.46 pounds
10 quintals	= 1 metric ton	= 2,204.6 pounds